Business Writing

3rd Edition

by Natalie Canavor

A Wiley Brand

Business Writing For Dummies®, 3rd Edition

Published by: **John Wiley & Sons, Inc.**, 111 River Street, Hoboken, NJ 07030-5774, www.wiley.com

Copyright © 2021 by John Wiley & Sons, Inc., Hoboken, New Jersey

Published simultaneously in Canada

For general information on our other products and services, please contact our Customer Care Department within the U.S. at 877-762-2974, outside the U.S. at 317-572-3993, or fax 317-572-4002. For technical support, please visit https://hub.wiley.com/community/support/dummies.

Wiley publishes in a variety of print and electronic formats and by print-on-demand. Some material included with standard print versions of this book may not be included in e-books or in print-on-demand. If this book refers to media such as a CD or DVD that is not included in the version you purchased, you may download this material at http://booksupport.wiley.com. For more information about Wiley products, visit www.wiley.com.

Library of Congress Control Number: 2020952452

ISBN 978-1-119-69669-8 (pbk); ISBN 978-1-119-69670-4 (ebk); ISBN 978-1-119-69671-1 (ebk)

Manufactured in the United States of America

SKY10024077_011821

Table of Contents

Introduction

Delivering your message well and being heard. What could be more important in today's world, which demands that we connect and compete for what we want? When the second edition of this book was published just a few years ago, it didn't seem necessary to talk about who needs to practice business writing. *Business writing* was assumed to mean writing for work purposes, typically in an office setting, but also encompassing independent contractors and professional specialists.

Today, who needs to write? Who doesn't? We all stand on our own for everyday messaging to get the job done, build relationships and prevent and solve problems. We may need to create traditional materials like reports, proposals and marketing copy. And we typically aim to play a role in the online world and use websites, blogs, networking sites and/or social media to our advantage.

But we also need to write well for personal purposes. Do you want to be a good advocate for a cause you believe in — or yourself? Have you needed to write an effective letter of complaint when you were dissatisfied with a purchase, or write a good message when you needed a favor from a friend or relative or stranger? Have you ever competed for something important — like buying a home that other people wanted — by writing a good letter that explained why you were a perfect match? Did you know you could do that?

We're all making our way today through a rapidly changing culture. This affects the role of writing, who uses it and how we apply those skills. For example, the line between "work" and "life" grows blurrier every year. Our friends become our business network; we look for work schedules that accommodate our personal lives; we like recreational opportunities at the office; we bring work home if it engages us.

Let's put that in a fuller perspective of what is changing, how that affects communication and how you can use what this book teaches for your own success.

Change #1 is how fluid our lives are becoming. Today's executive is tomorrow's consultant, a scientist builds a business based on his discovery, a lawyer becomes a stay-at-home mom and influential blogger. An obscure person can create a startup or build a charitable cause. A freelancer can decide to take a full-time job — or vice versa. Long-term employees may find their organizations restructured, requiring them to behave like entrepreneurs and create their own opportunities.

The future seems to offer little in the way of a straight-and-narrow career path — nor do most of us want one. We expect to bounce back and forth among a myriad of options, watching for chances and re-ordering our priorities. Beyond enabling you to make the most of your immediate opportunities, good writing is your best springboard for navigating from one opportunity to the next more successfully. It's often the written messages, résumés and online profiles, social presence, emails and even old-fashioned letters that enable you to be seen as credible, credentialed and creative.

Change #2 is the growing predominance of remote work. This trend has been developing over the last decade, but was sped up unimaginably by the coronavirus pandemic in 2020. Organizations of all varieties discovered that expensive office space is a whole lot less necessary than they thought. Some studies showed that at-home workers in many spheres actually became more productive at home — wherever that might be — and that many workers decided they prefer it. A scattered workforce makes good communication — especially writing — pivotal to accomplishing everyday simple tasks and long-range goals.

An allied trend is the drift toward a gig economy. Many people, especially those new to the workforce, are piecing together short-term jobs to add up to a living sufficient for their needs. If this is where you are right now, you are forever pitching for those gigs. You need all the assets of the classic entrepreneur and must be able to carry on good written conversations by email or other channels.

Change #3 is the growing degree of informality in writing for work purposes. The Internet and fast messaging channels have already played an enormous part in promoting spontaneity and even the ability to share feelings in writing via new devices like emojis, for example. Does this mean you no longer need to write well? No! It does mean knowing how to draw the lines and strategize for your audiences.

Change #4 is the growing dominance of visual media in social platforms and of course, video. Does this mean less writing? No! A good video is scripted. Moreover, writing is the essential tool for planning. Creators of print and video advertising have always known that it's challenging to produce high-quality material. Top users of Instagram and Snapchat and TikTok know this, too. We think in words. We think better when we write. If in the end product only a few words accompany the images, they must be exactly the right ones.

This is similarly true of oral and in-person communication. You may be surprised to see how much this book covers spoken media and even difficult conversations. A good speech begins with writing. Today, the oral, virtual and visual dimensions of business communication are inseparable from each other, and from writing. All must work together.

As you read this book, I think you'll be surprised by how many ways good writing can reward you. Beyond giving you the tools to handle the full range of media, building your skills will help you think strategically, solve problems and understand people — and yourself — better.

About This Book

I wrote this book to give you a high-stakes tool for accomplishing your own goals and dreams. While the ultimate aim is to sharpen your thinking, the methods I show you are totally pragmatic. Every idea and technique is ready to use and fully demonstrated. I base everything on my own decades of trial and error as a journalist, magazine editor, corporate communications director, consultant and college instructor. The methods I show you have been field-tested in hundreds of my workshops and courses for businesspeople, public relations professionals, corporate communicators and nonprofit leaders.

This book gives you a complete foundation for effective business writing as well as guidelines to instantly improve everything you write. You may wonder how a single book can teach you how to write for all media — especially since new channels materialize constantly. In fact, new communication media simply give us more ways to deliver messages. The thinking–writing process applies to all and holds steady for all, though each suggests specific adaptations.

It's like the old story about giving a person a fish versus teaching a person to fish. I can't be with you to meet every writing challenge you encounter, and truthfully, can't anticipate all of them. But I can teach you how to fish — to use your brain and your tools to figure out the message that best achieves what you want.

Foolish Assumptions

Do you assume any of the following?

>> Writing well is a talent you're born with — or not.

>> Improving poor writing is difficult.

>> Good writing is defined by correct grammar and spelling "rules."

>> Expressing complex thought demands complex language.

>> Writing dense copy with long words makes you look more intelligent and educated.

>> "New" media like social, video, chat messaging and presentations don't require good writing.

>> Reserving your best skills for "important" material makes sense.

Every one of these assumptions is false. I debunk all of them in this book. For now, the important truth is that *you can write better*, whether you need basic grounding or are already a good writer and want to become better yet. This book gives you down-to-earth, easy-to-use techniques. It's not about rules — I don't give you grammar lessons, but instead, show you practical ways to spot technical problems and fix them. Many of the ideas and thinking processes are drawn from the tool-kits of professional writers who in large part learn by expensive trial and error. I want to save you that time. My mission is to show you how to figure out what to say and how to say it, whatever the challenge.

Icons Used in This Book

To help you focus on what's most important and move it into memory, look to the icons.

These are practical ideas and techniques you can put to work immediately — and amaze yourself with good results!

This icon keys you in to guidelines and strategies to absorb and use for everything you write.

This icon signals thin ice, don't take the risk! Observe these cautions to avoid endangering your business, image or cause.

A new special feature, this icon offers time-saving strategies that were years in the making and now yours for the taking.

You'll also find sections that begin, "**Try This:**". Why leave all the work to me? Take these opportunities to try your own hand or apply an idea. Nothing builds your skills like practice.

Beyond the Book

In addition to what you're reading now, this book also comes with a free access-anywhere Cheat Sheet that gives you even more pointers on how to write effectively in the business world. To get this Cheat Sheet, simply go to www.dummies.com and search for "*Business Writing For Dummies* Cheat Sheet" in the Search box.

Where to Go from Here

Starting at the beginning gives you a foundation that applies to everything you write. But if you prefer diving right in for help on a specific challenge, by all means do so. The advice may suggest other sections for more depth and you can follow up as you choose.

Build a personal repertoire of techniques that work for you, then take this toolkit on the road with you. Doing so brings you a more successful journey, new confidence and a lot more fun along the way.

1

Winning with Writing

Learn the core elements of good business writing that equip you to create successful everyday messages and solve your most pressing communication challenges.

Adopt the professional writer's goal-plus-audience strategy that will never fail you, no matter how hard the writing challenge seems.

Discover how to make people care about your message by connecting with specific readers, highlighting benefits and showing them "what's-in-it-for-me."

Understand how to use the tools of writing — language, tone and structure — to say what you mean in a way most likely to earn respect, support and agreement.

Use everything you write to build relationships through understanding other people's perspectives and how they will perceive your messages.

Learn how to switch into the editor's role and fix common writing problems so that your messages accomplish what you want.

Chapter 1

Making Writing Your Weapon for Success

We take the ability to read and write for granted today, but human civilization started with, and depends on, the written word. Originating more than 5,000 years ago, writing empowered people to record events and share information with people beyond shouting distance. Over time it enabled us to collectively build knowledge and experience. We could think bigger thoughts and invent better ways of doing things.

For most of the time between early writing and the world we live in, writing skills were typically owned by the governing classes. A mere 50 centuries later, we can all own this magic. And as we know from Superman and his friends, when you own a power, you need to use it to accomplish great things.

But good writing is not an innate skill for most of us. It is definitely a learnable skill, but one that few people develop in school. Even if we got good marks, the academic writing we struggled with is very different from the practical writing we need for everyday and work purposes. This book shows you what this kind of writing looks like: how to do it, how to use it and how improve your own results — all in the cause of achieving what you want. It demonstrates how to create all the business staples from emails to reports to proposals to résumés; visual and oral media — presentations, video and new media — blogs, social media posts and new channels yet to be invented.

Practicing the process I show you in this chapter will lead you to clarify your thinking, understand yourself and your goals better and relate to other people more effectively.

Big promises? Yes. Let's get right to it.

In this chapter, I highlight the core elements of good business writing and introduce a planning structure that enables you to figure out what to say and how to say it in just about every circumstance. This step-by-step approach to writing works for every communication platform with some adaptation for each. You'll immediately start to see how to improve your own writing. Once you've absorbed the foundation, the chapters that follow demonstrate how to apply these ideas to all your business communication.

Putting Strategic Writing to Work for You

Can you imagine building relationships without language? Think about movies in which two people who don't speak the same language fall in love. All those soulful gazes and sighs eventually look like uphill work — and the relationship stays pretty superficial — until one person learns the other's language. Today we initiate many relationships, especially in business, through the written word. In-person contact may follow, or it may not. In many cases we continue to rely on writing to build the connection and collaborate, whether the people are down the street or thousands of miles and hours away.

From everyday email to reports, letters and digital platforms, today's working world runs on writing. Therefore, the rewards of good writing have never been more extraordinary. The Internet enables us to reach beyond our personal geographic and social reach to almost anyone we want to sell to, collaborate with or learn from. Almost anyone with time and dedication can start a business and sell a product or service, post artwork, publish a book or establish authority as an expert on a subject.

There's just one catch. Because anyone can do this, unless you are a specialist or have a private niche, the competition is overwhelming.

Consider these statistics about online platforms:

>> **Email:** Globally, 4 billion people use email, and American workers receive an average of 126 business emails daily.

>> **Twitter:** 330 million people globally are active Twitter users, sending 303 million tweets per day.

>> **Websites:** The Internet holds 1.3 billion websites.

>> **LinkedIn:** More than 660 million members in more than 200 countries use this site.

>> **Blogs:** In the United States alone, 31 million active bloggers post monthly or more.

Of course, you're not competing with all of these email messages, tweets, websites and blogs, or reading more than an infinitesimal fraction of them yourself. But people today — just like you — are extremely selective about what they choose to read because so many options vie for their attention. Your blogs, online posts, proposals and emails will be read according to how well you write them. You'll build followers according to the value you deliver.

And always, in business writing, "value" means the right content that is well expressed and shaped for the readers you want. Good writing is never "a way with words." A better maxim is "good writing is good thinking." That's why this book also focuses on how to create the right substance for your messages. Once you know what to say, how to say it becomes much easier.

REMEMBER

There are few captive audiences in today's world. Check how many messages you've recently received that you *must* read, and how many you zapped away because they did not immediately interest you. Even if you hold top-down authority, there's no assurance that your message will be read. Attention, along with respect, must be earned. Writing a message that someone will actually read is an achievement. Writing messages that people will act on demands not just writing that is clear and direct, but also content that aligns with what your readers care about. In other words, today's business writing needs to be strategic.

What is *strategic writing?* Planned communication that achieves a set of goals — the goals of your employer if you hold a job, and always, your own goals. The good news is that you already have a solid base for knowing how to write strategically. You're in command of the three imperatives:

>> **Your subject:** You are invested in your field and possess in-depth knowledge of it.

» **Your audience:** You know who your audience is, such as prospective employers, coworkers, people who share an interest of your own and target markets for your business.

» **Your goal:** You know what you want, now and in the bigger-picture future.

Here are some of the things you may *not* know yet:

» How to choose the right communication tool for the job

» How to capture and retain reader attention

» How to make people care about your message

» How to understand other people's perspective and predict their responses

» How to gauge the right degree of formality and when to convey emotion

» How to select the right content to make your case

» How to use writing techniques that make your material persuasive

» How to use every single thing you write to build relationships and advance your cause

» How to coordinate your online platforms to achieve your purposes

» How to sharpen your ear and eye so you can spot your own writing problems and fix them

This book shows you how to do all of this.

TIP

Notice that in line with my focus on the *thinking* part of writing, almost every item in this list relates to that. But of course, the technical side of writing — how you use language — matters, too, and I cover that as well. You'll find a broad resource of practical tips for improving your sentences, use of language and organization. Try out these ideas and tips to discover the techniques that work best for you.

Let's start with a planning structure that will help you figure out what you want to say and how to say it. You may be surprised at how much better your messages are received, and how much more often you get a positive response, as soon as you start applying it.

Planning and Structuring Every Message

Faced with a blank page and something to accomplish, many people freeze at the first question: *Where do I start?* The answer? Start with the three components of strategic writing. You already know them:

>> **Your subject:** What you're writing about

>> **Your audience:** Whom you're writing to

>> **Your goal:** What you specifically want to accomplish

To create a good message and get the result you want from your reader, you need to think about all of these things more systematically than you ordinarily might.

REMEMBER

You must "read" your audience in an organized way, which I show you shortly. And you benefit from visualizing your goal in a broad way. Consider that for almost every message you write, you actually have a whole set of goals beyond the immediate: communicating your own professional image, for example. When you combine your knowledge of the audience with your set of goals, it becomes easy to translate what you know about the subject into content that supports your message.

For example, suppose Jake wants to ask his supervisor, Jane, for a plum assignment on the horizon. He can simply write:

Jane, I'd like to present myself as a candidate for the lead role on the Crystal Project. You know my work and qualifications. I'll really appreciate the opportunity, and I'll do a great job. Thanks, Jake

This is may be okay insofar as it's clear and contains no obvious errors. But it's definitely not compelling. All Jane learns from the message is that Jake wants the opportunity and thinks he's qualified.

Jake would fare better if he planned his message out. *The first thing to consider with every message is your goal.* Thinking about this will show Jake that his goal is more complex than "I want this opportunity."

SHORTCUT

The best way to prompt your best thinking, especially when a message is important, is to write down the relevant facts and ideas. When you try to solve a problem "in your head," you probably find that the same ideas keep circling around and getting past them is hard. Instead, watch magic happen when you write out your thoughts. The concreteness of this action pushes your thinking forward in a natural way: You'll be surprised at how much more you know, and in many cases, can intuit. Ultimately this saves time because it avoids the inefficiency of mental meandering.

Should Jake ask himself exactly what results he wants his message to produce, his list might look like this:

I want a chance to . . .

Exercise more responsibility

Show off my capabilities — be noticed!

Expand my know-how about this project's subject

Add a management credential to my résumé

Work with an interesting team and get to know the people

But he should consider even more: the bigger picture. What could a good message accomplish longer term?

Strengthen my position for future special assignments

Remind the boss of my good track record

Present myself as a capable, reliable, resourceful leader

Build toward a promotion or higher-level job in this organization or elsewhere

From this vantage point, Jake can see the pitch itself as a building block for his overall career ambitions. This is worth a better message than the perfunctory one he dashed off.

So far Jake has really been asking himself *why* he wants the assignment on a level beyond the obvious. The next basic question to answer is, *who's my audience?*

Jake must think about Jane and see his request through her eyes. What skills does she most value? What does she care about? How does she see the job requirements? How can he match up his qualifications with the assignment's demands in a way the decision-maker will find relevant?

Taking all this into account, Jake might come up with a list like this.

Important to Jane: Collaborative teaming; people skills; independent initiative; department reputation; effective presentation; track record as team member on earlier projects. I also know she feels weak in systems planning and insecure with new technology. This is an important project she will be judged on herself, so needs all the reassurance I can give that I'll handle it perfectly.

Job requires: Leadership abilities; planning skills; ability to meet deadlines; knowledge of XYZ systems; experience in teaming and cross-departmental coordination; good judgment under pressure. A useful plus: tech and presentation skills.

And voilà, Jake has produced a blueprint for content that presents him persuasively. His email can cite his proven track record in accomplishing previous project goals and cite his people skills, ability to work independently and deliver results as a team member and leader, desire to enhance the department's reputation and confidence in using his demonstrated presentation skills to ensure the project shows effectively.

The weaknesses he pinpoints for Jane give Jake another avenue for presenting himself as the best choice. He can suggest a planning system he'll use to make the most of staff resources and/or a specific way to incorporate new easy-to-use technology. These elements are particularly apt to catch Jane's attention.

WARNING

All Jake's points must be true! I don't suggest ever making up qualifications, but rather, that you take the trouble to communicate the best of what is real and what matters in a particular situation.

TIP

Further, never assume people understand your capabilities or remember your achievements, even if they're colleagues who know you well or a boss you've worked with for years. *Other people don't have time to put you in perspective, nor, usually, the interest.* They're thinking about themselves. That's why doing it yourself has such power. But always be careful to avoid a boastful tone.

The beauty part of creating this strong strategic message is that whether or not Jake gets the assignment, he has built toward his longer-range goals of presenting himself as ready, willing and able to take on new challenges and to be seen as more valuable. Writing is an amazing tool for building your positive image over time, message by message, and recognizing the opportunities.

REMEMBER

What Jake's message illustrates is how to use a simple planning structure for everything you write. My shorthand for this is simply:

Goal + Audience = Content

When you define what you want to accomplish with a specific message, and think about the specific person you're writing to and what points will resonate with them, content decisions almost make themselves.

When you use this structured thinking to plan your messages, whether they're straightforward updates or proposals or anything in between, you move far toward the heart of good writing — real and relevant substance. Writing is not a system for manipulating words, and don't ever expect it to camouflage a lack of thought, knowledge or understanding. Good writing presents solid substance clearly, concisely and transparently in ways that make sense to your audience.

I make you a rash promise: For every fraction you improve your writing, you'll improve your thinking along with it. Plus, you will improve your ability to understand other people, which is infinitely rewarding. It will help you build better relationships and achieve what you want much more often, in every part of your life.

TIP

Chapter 2 gives you an in-depth demonstration of this planning structure and shows you how to translate it into successful messages whatever the subject, whatever the medium. While you may pick and choose which sections of the book to read and draw upon them at need, I encourage you to invest in Chapter 2. It gives you the foundation for deciding *what* to say in any circumstance. Remember that the ideas apply equally to communications that appear to be dominated by visuals or spoken language.

The other essential groundwork for successful writing is *how* to say what you want. Chapters 3, 4 and 5 demonstrate common-sense techniques that professionals use to spot problems and fix them with the least effort and attention to formal rules.

SHORTCUT

Many people find the idea of editing a cheerless prospect. But it can be done in down-to-earth ways that have almost nothing to do with mastering grammar. To give you an idea of techniques you can use, here's one for upgrading your own work immediately: the *say-it-aloud diagnosis*. When you read your own copy aloud (or whisper it to yourself if you're not alone), you'll hear immediate signals that something isn't working or can work better.

You may notice that your sentences have a sing-song cadence that denotes awkward construction, or that they are overly long and have unnecessary words. You may hear repetitive sounds or inappropriate pauses created by poor word choice or punctuation. You can easily fix such problems, and many more, once you listen to how your writing sounds. It's not a dumbing-down approach: Many professional writers use it. And read-aloud works beautifully for business writing, which should ideally have a natural, conversational feel.

No matter where you now see yourself on the writing spectrum, I guarantee there's room for improvement. Most journalists, corporate communicators, bloggers and public relations specialists are obsessive about discovering better ways to write and build their skills. They want to create material that's ever more interesting, persuasive, informative and engaging. Don't you?

REMEMBER

For people inhabiting any part of the business, nonprofit or government worlds, the rewards of better writing are often immediate. Your email and letters get the results you want much more often. Your proposals are more seriously considered and your reports are more valued. You are perceived as more authoritative, credible and capable. People accord you more respect, often without knowing exactly why. And you move toward your goals faster.

WHY YOU CAN LEARN TO WRITE BETTER AND HOW YOU'LL BENEFIT

If good writing is a skill that can be developed — and having taught hundreds of adults, I assure you it can — you may wonder why you don't currently write as well as you'd like. You already learned to write in school, correct?

Actually, unless you were lucky enough to have an unusual teacher, the people who taught you were not oriented toward practical writing. Writing in academia is usually aimed at demonstrating your understanding of what you learned, or contributing to the store of human knowledge. Traditionally, this world rewards dense, complicated, convoluted writing full of expensive words. This *is* changing, but not very fast.

Business writing, on the other hand, always has a goal and is geared toward action. Every business message is at heart "an ask": You are writing to request something. Looking at it this way, it's clear why the structure I'm giving you works every time. When you ask for something in person, you automatically frame your case within the other person's perspective and absorb that person's cues to adjust what you say. Writing lacks that advantage, so you have to consciously anticipate reader response by being more analytic.

When it comes to the technical side of writing, your own reactions are your best guide: Do you not prefer a message, whether short or long-form, that instantly communicates why you should read it? Is clear, concise, easily understood, to the point and conversational? Becoming a good business writer is based on learning to use your own common sense, with a little psychology and detective work and tricks-of-the-trade thrown in.

No matter your experience with writing so far, I bet you'll find it a lot easier (and more fun) to learn business writing than you may now think. And the rewards may come faster than you expect. Long term, you'll own a major competitive advantage that sets you apart from the crowd. Recent surveys show that across virtually every industry, good communicators are highly valued, sought and most often promoted. Good writers are in especially short supply.

Applying the Goal-Plus-Audience Strategy to More Media

You may have felt challenged at times to write differently for so many forms of communication, or may even have avoided using new or unfamiliar media. Here's the best encouragement I can give you to experiment and venture forth: The strategizing process is the same for all media, present and future. Planning a brief effective email is very much the same as planning a proposal or blog post, presentation or résumé. The Goal + Audience = Content structure will never fail you, no matter how hard the writing challenge seems.

For this reason, my early examples in this book are "small" messages like email. Once you absorb the thinking process for this everyday communication channel, you're well prepared to tackle more formal business documents and strategize your digital presence and in-person communication.

Succeeding with email, letters and business documents

Email remains the dominant everyday medium for most business communication medium, though it's increasingly supplemented by private organizational systems like Slack and online platforms. Whether you work remotely or in an office, as an entrepreneur or independent contractor, you need to do it well. If you were hoping email would go away, sorry: Surveys say its use is growing globally by 3 percent per year.

In many ways, email is also the most basic medium, so it's a natural starting point for improving how you write. Even if you don't use email much, it makes a good demonstration model. So read the guidelines and examples presented in this book and know they apply to most other writing tasks.

Once you're familiar with the planning process, I give you what you need to know about choosing the right words, creating good sentences and editing — recognizing your own shortcomings makes it easy to improve. I'll show you the fixes. I'll also cover the challenge of tone: creating the right "voice" for a written message. When do you want what you write to convey enthusiasm? Emotion — positive or negative? What degree of informality is appropriate to both your goal and audience?

Later in the book, I move into long-form materials that often feel like make-or-break opportunities: reports, proposals, business pitches, executive summaries. Your foundation with lowly old email will serve you well here, giving you a solid foundation.

Writing to present yourself powerfully

Once you're grounded in business writing basics, the book moves on to non-written formats. Communicating orally doesn't mean you dispense with writing! From a 15-second "elevator speech" to hosting a webinar to pitching live for a contract, the best system is: Plan, write, edit, rehearse, then deliver. The first stop is to explore the principles of persuasion in Chapter 8. You'll want to absorb these ideas about using persuasive language into all the media you use, along with how to communicate with conviction, identify your personal value proposition and tell your story.

Then, in Chapter 9, learn how to create a speech or visual presentation from formal to casual occasions, and adapt to the particular use of language that spoken media demand. Discover here the CEO's secret: creating talking points, a technique that enables you make your case effectively and handle challenges on your feet.

We're on the move in Chapter 10! In today's mobile and fluid world, we're always thinking of the next step. Presenting yourself as an outstanding applicant for jobs, contracts or gigs is an almost constant challenge. This chapter shows you how to define your strengths and develop your personal value proposition, which puts you way ahead in writing résumés, cover letters and successful networking messages.

Writing online: From websites to blogs to tweets

People often assume that when it comes to online content, they can toss all the old writing rules out the virtual window. Big mistake! Digital media with its lightning delivery speed and infinite reach does upend many traditional ideas about communication — top-down thinking, most notably, whereby authoritative figures issue "the word." Today anyone can market a business, entertain the world and become a journalist or author. But this democratization makes the need to write well more imperative than ever.

WARNING

There are simply too many websites, blogs, tweets, Instagram posts and all the rest to compete against if you don't provide first-rate material people want. The wide-open pioneering days of social media are in some ways over, even though new platforms keep emerging. Any digital guru will tell you that only the very best "content" gains an audience anymore.

So, in Chapters 11 and 12, I focus on how to develop content that is well-planned, well-worded, well-edited and well-aimed and exactly on target for the audiences you choose. To be most productive for you, whether you're an employee, a business owner, a freelancer or work on behalf of a social cause, the use of online platforms also demands comprehensive thinking. Impact is achieved when the pieces add up to more than the sum of their parts. You need a consistent message, adapted to each venue.

As you read this, I'm sure new technologies are emerging to dazzle and intrigue us. But the newest technology is basically one more delivery system for your messages. You will need clear thinking and good writing to succeed. The techniques presented in this book will not go out of date! But adapt them with imagination.

Leveraging your writing skills

If you're an employee on any level who wants to stand out, I've got you covered in Chapter 13. Learn to use writing to manage up, manage down and manage sideways — when you need to influence others without having formal authority. Strategic messaging enables you to establish trust, communicate professionalism and as a leader, inspire your team.

If you work remotely, whether as a contractor, freelancer, consultant or a full- or part-time remote worker, Chapter 14 focuses on your needs. Use of tools including videoconferencing and instant messaging platforms are covered as well as teaming techniques, and the chapter provides examples of how to write some of the messages that challenge many independent workers.

Remembering to think globally

This book is based on American business writing style and practice. North Americans are singularly lucky in that their English has become the international language of business, reflecting the United States' economic importance of the past century. But if you run a cross-national business or work for one, it's a mistake to assume that your audiences in other cultures will read your writing in the way you want.

Someone who learned English as a second, third or fourth language may not find your email, letters and websites easy to understand. Spoken language skills are much easier to acquire than written ones. Further, cultural differences may be much bigger than you think.

WARNING

It's often remarkably hard to realize that everyone is *not* on the same wavelength. Every country and culture has distinct values and perspectives. For writing, this means taking into account factors that include preferred degree of formality, attitude toward business relationships, priorities such as courtesy versus efficiency, specific ways of opening a conversation and an expectation of directness versus indirectness. In some countries, saying yes may mean no!

Even if cross-border communication doesn't concern you, most workplaces are increasingly diverse. People don't leave their cultural perspective at home when they come to the office. Your coworkers, partners and customers may have grown up anywhere in the world.

How can you write in ways that works for other people, in this case those with limited English-speaking skills? The second aspect is psychological: How can you communicate well with someone whose goals, values, background and experience are unlike your own, though invisible?

This question relates to the most basic premise of this book. So often we overlook how different people are from each other. You feel that you are unique — and you are. So is everyone else. We each see the world through our own filters, unconsciously constructed of innate characteristics, personal experience, cultural values and everything we grow up with and that happens to us.

Taking the trouble to see through other people's filters is what enables you to communicate powerfully in every medium, from conversation to proposals, and at the same time, to be more self-aware.

Really good business writing is not about formulas, smart responses and clever manipulation of other people. It is best based on understanding individual people and seeing the world within each one's framework. What does this person care about? Hope for? Worry about? Writing this way is especially challenging when you communicate with people you've never met and with large unseen audiences, such as through a website or blog.

The syntax of writing — the arrangement of words, phrases and sentences — is a tool for delivering your messages and must be used well. But the message is what matters. Understanding your own goals and practicing empathy enables you to build meeting points for true communication and relationships.

Improving your writing will open up your perceptions and sharpen your thinking. There's an aphorism that says, "How do I know what I think until I write it?" In my view, writing is the best imaginable way to grow your understanding of other people, foster your business relationships and work toward becoming your best and most successful self. What could be more rewarding or interesting?

You now know *why* improving your writing will benefit you and have already begun building the foundation to do it. The next chapter takes the Goal + Audience = Content formula further and shows you exactly how to strategize every message to accomplish your goals.

IN THIS CHAPTER

» **Strategizing for success before you write**

» **Understanding your goal and audience**

» **Making people care about your message**

» **Writing with the correct tone and degree of formality**

» **Using writing opportunities to build relationships**

Chapter **2**

Planning Your Message Every Time

Think for a minute about how you approached a recent writing task. If it was an email message, how much time did you spend considering what to write? A few minutes? Seconds? Or did you just hit the keyboard?

Now bring a more complex document to mind: a challenging letter, proposal, report, marketing piece, blog post or anything else. Did you put some time into thinking about and shaping your message before you began writing, or did you just plunge in?

This chapter demonstrates the power of taking time before you write to consider *whom* you're writing to, *what* you truly hope to achieve and *how* you can generate the right content.

Adopting the Plan-Draft-Edit Principle

Here is the most important piece of advice in this book: Invest time in planning your messages and reviewing them. And that means *every message*. Even an everyday communication such as an email can have a profound impact on your success. Everything you write shows people who you are.

I can't count the times I've received an email asking for a referral or an informational interview that was badly written and full of errors. I didn't respond. Would you? Or a long, expensively produced document with an email cover note that's abrupt and sloppy. A poorly written email message doesn't help the cause — whatever the cause may be.

REMEMBER

I'm not suggesting that prior to writing every email you lean back in your chair and let your mind wander into blue-sky mode to see what emerges. The planning I recommend is a step-by-step process that leads to good decisions about what to say and how to say it. It's a process that will never fail you, no matter how big (or small) the writing challenge. And it's quite simple to adopt — in fact, you may achieve surprisingly quick results. You may also find that after applying this process, you enjoy writing much more.

This strategic approach has no relation to how you learned to write in school, unless you had an atypical teacher who was attuned to writing for results. Start by tossing out any preconceived ideas about your inability to write, because in my experience, *everyone* can learn to write better.

When you have a message or document to produce, expect your time to be divided equally between these tasks:

- Planning
- Drafting
- Editing

TIP

Spend one-third of your time deciding what to say (planning), one-third writing your first version (drafting) and finally, one-third sharpening what you wrote (editing).

You probably wonder if this system helps you write faster or slower. For most people it's a time shift. When you take a write-first-then-think approach, you probably get lost in the middle, then stare at your important messages for a while with vague questions about whether they could read better or be more persuasive. Or worse, you just toss it off and click "send." Planned messages are easy to organize, and the effectiveness is built in because you've already customized the content to your goal and reader.

WARNING

What about the editing time at the end? If you don't look critically at your messages before sending them, you serve yourself badly. Sloppy writing interferes with getting your message heard, believed and acted upon. A professional writer with decades of writing experience would *never* send a business communication — even a simple-looking email — without careful review and improvements. Nor should you. The stakes are too high. You need to be your best in everything you write.

This does not mean you are aiming for formal communications with stiffly correct grammar and elaborate wording. Actually, you want nearly everything you write to feel conversational and to read fast and easy. Editing is often about removing the barriers to speedy reading and understanding and often, supplying missing links or evidence you missed with the first draft.

The real issue is less about time and more about results. Planned messages bring you what you want much more often. Try these approaches and see what happens. My money is on more success. Happily, this approach quickly becomes a habit and more — it becomes a problem solver. Practice it every day with routine messaging, and you'll be ready to field big challenges with confidence.

Fine-Tuning Your Plan: Your Goals and Audience

As outlined in Chapter 1, a well-crafted message is based on two key aspects: your goal and your audience. The following section shows you how to move inside of both more deeply.

Defining your goal

Your first priority is to know exactly what you want to happen when the person you're writing to reads what you've written. Determining this is far less obvious than it sounds.

Consider a cover letter for your résumé. If you see it as a formal but unimportant necessity toward your ultimate goal — to get a job — a cover letter can just say:

Dear Mr. Blank, Here is my résumé. —Jack Slade

Intuitively you probably know that this isn't sufficient. But analyze what you want to accomplish and you can see clearly why it falls short. Your cover letter must:

>> Connect you with the recipient so that you become a person instead of another set of documents.

>> Set up the person to review your qualifications with a favorable mindset.

>> Persuade the recipient that your résumé is worth reading.

>> Show that you understand the job and the company.

>> Make you stand out from the competition in a meaningful way.

You also need the cover letter to demonstrate your personal qualifications, especially the ability to communicate well. If you see that accomplishing your big goal, getting a shot at the job or contract, depends on this set of more specific goals, it's obvious why a one-line perfunctory message won't help you compete. Seen properly, a cover letter is in fact very important.

A cover letter for a formal business proposal has its own big goal: help convince an individual or an organization to finance your new product, for example. To do this, the cover letter's role is to connect with prospective buyers, entice them to actually read at least part of the document, predispose them to like what they see, present your company as better than the competition and show off good communication skills.

How about the proposal itself? If you break down this goal into a more specific subset, you realize the proposal must ideally demonstrate:

>> The financial viability of what you plan to produce

>> A minimal investment risk and high profit potential

>> Your own excellent qualifications and track record

>> Outstanding backup by an experienced team

>> Special expertise in the field

>> In-depth knowledge of the marketplace, competition, business environment and so on

REMEMBER

Spelling out your goals is extremely useful because the process keeps you aligned with the big picture while giving you instant guidelines for effective content. Because of good planning on the front end, you're already moving toward *how* to accomplish what you want.

To reap the benefit of goal definition, you must take time to look past the surface. Write *every* message with a clear set of goals. If you don't know your goals, don't write at all.

Try This: Invent your persona. Invariably one of your goals is to present yourself in writing as confident, professional, competent, knowledgeable, creative, resourceful, empathetic, generous, good-natured and so on, but don't let me tell you who you are or want to be! Create a list of the personal and professional qualities you want other people to perceive in you. Then remember, every time you write, *be that person.* This doesn't mean faking it — rather, it means acting as your best self. Ask yourself how that individual handles the tough stuff. Your answers may amaze you. This technique isn't mystical. It's a way of accessing your own knowledge base and intuition. You will find yourself channeling this winning persona into your face-to-face experiences, too.

Defining your audience

You've no doubt noticed that people are genuinely different in countless ways: what they value, their motivations, how they like to spend their time, their attitude toward work and success, how they communicate and make decisions, and much more. One ramification of these variables is that they read and react to your messages in different ways than you expect.

As part of your planning you need to anticipate people's reactions to both your content and writing style. The key to successfully predicting your reader's response is to target everything you write to someone specific, rather than an anonymous, faceless "anyone."

When you meet someone in person and want to persuade that individual to your viewpoint, you automatically adapt to that person's reactions as you go along. You respond to a host of clues. Beyond interruptions, comments and questions, you also perceive facial expression, body language, tone of voice, gestures, nervous mannerisms and many other indicators. A written message lacks all in-person clues, although Internet writing has developed some ways to convey feelings, like inventive punctuation and emoji. But such devices are not appropriate to all media and purposes. For your message to connect, you must play both roles — the reader's and your own. Fortunately, doing this isn't as hard as it may sound.

Unless your message is trivial, begin by creating a written profile or (portrait, if you prefer) of the person you're writing to. There's a really big payoff in doing this for people who are important to you, such as your boss or a major client. It gives you illuminating guidelines on how to improve all your interactions with that person, and clues for what to say and how to say it. You can consciously draw on this knowledge every time you write. This helps improve your face-to-face interactions as well.

When the situation involves someone you don't deal with often, or don't know at all, the depth of the profile you create depends on how important the results are to you. If you're responding to a customer query, you don't need to know the customer's decision-making style. If you're writing to the department head with a request, you might want to find out how much information this person prefers to have and what their budget and priorities are.

Before you try to build a portrait, it might seem daunting to characterize someone when so much that drives each person is invisible. Trust me, you know much more about other people than you think. In the case of someone already familiar to you, your observations, experience and intuition go a long way. It's a matter of drawing on these resources in a systematic manner, especially your memory of how they reacted to previous interactions.

Try This: Build a profile. Suppose the person is someone you know. Begin with the usual suspects: demographics. Write down what you already know about the person or take your best guess. Factors such as which generation someone belongs to and their education level may be relevant. Other factors that marketers call demographics may also matter. These include values and beliefs, attitudes, opinions, interests and leisure and volunteer activities.

But almost always, your most valuable insights relate to peoples' professional style, especially, their ways of interacting. Thinking analytically about factors that may directly affect how your message is perceived include:

>> Professional background and experience

>> Positioning in the organization: What level? Degree of authority? Moving up or down? Respected? Influential? How ambitious? Happy in the job and with the organization?

>> Leadership style: Top down? Team-based? Collaborative? Indiscernible?

>> Preferred communication style: In-person? Brief, or detailed, written messages? Telephone? Texting? PowerPoint? Social media?

>> Approach to decision-making: Collaborative or top-down? Spontaneous or deliberative? Risk-taker or play-it-safer?

>> Information preferences: Broad vision? In depth? Visuals?

>> Work priorities and pressures

>> Sensitivities and hot buttons: What makes your VIP angry? Happy?

>> Interaction style and preferences: A people person or a numbers, systems or technology person? Good team member or not?

» Type of thinking: Logical or intuitive? Statistics-based or ideas-based? Big picture or micro-oriented? Looking for long-range or immediate results?

» Weaknesses (perceived by that person or not): Lack of tech savvy? Poor people skills? Lack of education and training? Light on experience? Inflexibility?

» Type of people the person likes, feels comfortable with, trusts and respects, and the reverse. Who likes and gets along with this person?

» Sense of humor, personal passions, hobbies

SHORTCUT

Do you know, or can you figure out, what your readers worry about? What keeps them up at night? Their biggest problems? When you know a person's concerns, you can create more compelling messages. If you're pitching something, this is essential. I am not suggesting your aim should be manipulative. Taking the trouble to think within another person's framework is respectful. Wouldn't you rather be addressed in a way that acknowledges what matters to you most when you need to make a decision, for example?

And of course, your own relationship to the person matters, as well as your relative positioning and the degree of mutual liking, respect and trust — the *simpatico* factor. Notice that considering some of the points in the previous list might actually help you connect better with someone — recognizing who does well with the person, for example. I've seen clever colleagues ask a favored person how they get along so well with the supervisor and use the ideas productively. But for many of the points, your own experience serves to keep you away from the hot buttons and keep your request in a positive light — this works best when you systematize what you know with a portrait.

TIP

I'm sure you're wondering how you can possibly take so much into consideration, or why you would want to. The good news: When your message is truly simple, you usually don't. More good news: Even when your goal is complex or important, only some factors matter. I'm giving you a lengthy list to draw on because every situation brings different characteristics into play. Thinking through which ones count in your specific situation is crucial and rarely hard.

For example, say you want authorization to produce a video explaining your department's work to show at an employee event. If the boss likes the video idea, you might need to prove that you will make a good one. If not, you can appeal to other preferences. For example, perhaps this person values relationships and wants to cultivate high morale. This boss would probably welcome a way to show staff members they are valued. Or the boss may be a person who likes innovation and being first in the neighborhood. To gain approval, frame the story according to the specific decision-maker. I'm not saying you should distort the facts or omit any: The story you tell must be true and fair. But the focus and emphasis can be adapted.

Notice that the same factors matter if you're an independent contractor pitching a project, but you may lack the advantage of knowing the decision-maker well.

REMEMBER

You succeed when you take the time to look at things through another person's eyes rather than solely your own. Doing so doesn't compromise your principles. It shows that you're sensible and sensitive to the differences between people and promotes your relationships. It tells you how to frame what you're asking for.

SHORTCUT

Here's a technique drawn from psychology that lets you leapfrog into the mind of someone you know, even if not well, with less conscious analysis. Close your eyes and imagine the person as vividly as you can — if your boss is a woman, for example, see how she sits behind her desk, her posture, what she's wearing, how she looks at you, her expression and gestures. Hear her voice. Observe her environment — what's on the walls, on her desk and so on. Hold that detailed image in your mind and draft your message.

You will probably find yourself naturally thinking with the right tone and language, with a good feel for what to say. This visualization technique works because it draws on your intuition and observation. It is almost like having a live interaction with the person. In fact, you can take this one step further and imagine the conversation. Explain what you want and hear how the person responds. Then react to that, back and forth.

An imagined conversation like this can tell you what objections someone is likely to voice. You can then build the answers into your written message so it is much more persuasive. The approach is also valuable when you prepare for a tough confrontation, advocate for something, make a sales pitch and many more situations.

REMEMBER

The coronavirus pandemic in 2020 has impacted nearly everyone's role in the economy, diminishing entire industries and demanding adaptations few were ready for. In some ways the pandemic helped to flatten generational differences in the use of communication tools. People of every age suddenly needed to master videoconferencing and depend on online networks and resources to far greater extent.

This flattening has been seen in other trends as well. Twitter has become the prime vehicle for political announcements and high-impact exchanges internationally, used by CEOs and presidents alike to reach constituents without "middlemen" like the press. Expressing yourself in this medium takes good writing and editing! The price of reaching such massive audiences unfiltered can be astronomical.

GENERATION GAPS: UNDERSTANDING AND HANDLING THEM

In almost every workplace employing more than a few people, generational differences present some major challenges. These differences are equally important if you earn your living via the gig economy or as an independent contractor. Sweeping generalizations based on when people were born may seem suspect, and of course you never want to stereotype. But we are all shaped by the culture and events of the time during which we grew up. Our beliefs, communication and decision-making styles, interaction patterns and expectations of each other can be at odds. Misunderstandings flourish. Whatever age group you belong to, you will benefit from practicing empathy for the other cohorts. Supplement the following ideas with your own observations and you'll discover ways to make the people in your work life happy without compromising your own values.

- **Baby Boomers** (born 1946 to 1964) are often highly competitive and define themselves by achievement. Many are workaholics. Although Boomers wanted to change the world and fought for change (civil rights, women's role), on the whole they respect authority, loyalty, position and hard work that creates upward progress. They would like today's young people to advance the same way they did: earning rewards (and confidence) gradually over time.

  Communication style: Like in-person contact and good with confrontation; hold meetings often; like the telephone, email and detailed information; obtain general information from newspapers and television; many use Facebook, LinkedIn and Twitter, others dislike all or some.

  React badly to: Younger people's perceived lack of respect, low commitment level, expectations of fast progress, need for frequent mentoring, arrogance about their own superior technology skills and careless writing!

  React well to: A can-do attitude, willingness to work hard and overcome obstacles, respect for their achievements and knowledge and well-planned and proofed messages.

- **Generation X** (born 1965 to 1980) is a relatively small generation literally caught in the middle. They are often middle managers and must translate between those they report to and those who report to them. They are hard-working, individualistic, committed to change and seek life balance. They value opportunities to build skills.

  Communication style: Depend on email, preferably short and efficient; would prefer to skip meetings; comfortable with new technology and social media (especially Facebook) to varying degree, but without the full enthusiasm of younger people; refer to television and to a lesser extent, newspapers, for information.

(continued)

React badly to: Autocratic, unappreciative managers; an air of entitlement from subordinates and subordinates' need for constant attention, encouragement and supervision and unwillingness to go the extra mile and adapt to workplace needs; impatience; "unearned" confidence.

React well to: Resourcefulness, independence, sense of responsibility, attention to detail, willingness to take on "uninteresting" assignments, good communication.

- **Millennials** (also known as Generation Y) (born 1981 to 1996) belong to an especially large generation and face strong competition but fewer opportunities. They are highly social and communal-minded, preferring to work in teams and in close touch with everyone else inside and outside the office. They want responsibility — quickly — plus intensive mentoring. They expect to spend their careers job-hopping and experimenting with other income sources. They are non-materialistic and typically leave jobs quickly when unengaged, even without another in sight. Accord high value to active experience, inclusiveness and tolerance.

Communication style: Digital all the way; prefer to interact through texting, instant messaging and social media, especially Facebook; draw news and information from the Internet; use email only as required; unenthusiastic about telephone contact, meetings and confrontation.

React badly to: Lack of respect; insufficient encouragement, appreciation or inclusion; not being given reasons for assignments; not being accommodated in lifestyle preferences; being required to work with old technology.

React well to: Coaching, opportunities to learn and grow, sense of purpose, being valued, explanations, new experiences, constant communication, teaming, opportunities to work with other bright creative people, fast rewards and insights into the big picture.

- **Generation Z** (born 1997 to 2010) may become known as the Derailed Generation, because for many, all career expectations and plans for building a future were upended by the coronavirus pandemic in 2020. They are the most diverse generation. Many hold progressive principles and are highly educated; risk-averse; pragmatic; values-driven most notably in regard to equal opportunity and the environment. Attention span is short.

Communication style: These are the first "true digital natives" and use their smartphones for all information, entertainment and communication, but avoid phone calls. Gather news from Twitter and other online channels. Use multiple social platforms and like creative and ephemeral media like Snapchat and Instagram. Strong preference for video. Highly impacted by their peers.

React badly to: Lack of honesty and transparency, being left out of decisions, not being respected for their opinions.

React well to: Regular face time and feedback, bite-sized communication, use of video, being treated as contributors.

Brainstorming the best content for your purpose

Perhaps defining your goal and audience so thoroughly sounds like unnecessary busywork. But doing so helps immeasurably when you're approaching people with an idea, product or service that you want them to buy into.

Earlier in this chapter I talk about how to ask for something for yourself — in that case, a plum assignment at work. Here I move into how to think through a request on an employer's behalf.

Suppose you work for a nonprofit organization whose mission is to save elephants from poaching. A major new project is planned. You're asked to draft a letter to Mr. T, a one-time major benefactor who has not donated to SaveEl in two years, though he's known to have funded several other animal rights nonprofits in that time frame. What do you know, or can find out, about Mr. T?

Let's say you know he is:

>> 65 years old

>> Retired founder of a successful software development company

>> Champion of animal-related causes

>> Concerned about African conservation

>> Made the biggest donation for an orphanage for baby elephants without mothers

>> Likes his good deeds to be widely appreciated

This is pretty generic but enough to ask and answer the key question: *What is your goal and how can you achieve it?* Your first thought is to write a letter to secure a donation. This requires you to

>> Reignite his interest in SaveEl.

>> Engage him with the specific project.

>> Set the future stage for a more positive orientation to SaveEl. Should this funding plea not work, it might help achieve a better reception next time.

Now stand back and think for a minute about your main goal and the appropriate communication channel. Can you envision writing a letter that will accomplish so much? It's quite unlikely that you can elicit a return message with a big check attached. A substantial donation is a different "ask" than one requesting readers to pitch in $25, which is more of an impulse buy.

Charities, universities and cultural organizations know that "cultivating" big donors is an in-person, relationship-building process that takes time, often years. You don't need any special knowledge to realize that given many choices of where to invest their charitable funding, decision-makers need to feel trust, alignment with the cause and confidence in the organization's ability to deliver what they hope for.

Looking at it this way, a realistic goal for your letter to Mr. T is to secure a meeting, very much like the goal of a cover letter and/or résumé is to earn you an interview. And just as with a job application, *this shifts your goals to become more achievable*. The main goal of your letter can be restated as:

>> **Open the door:** Interest Mr. T enough so he wants to learn more and is amenable to a one-on-one conversation, ideally in person.

REMEMBER

This scenario demonstrates an important marketing principle that applies to many situations: A successful outcome results from combining many elements and demands comprehensive planning. Often you need to orchestrate a sequence of events or steps — in marketing terms, this is the customer journey.

Now that you've narrowed your goal for the letter and know who Mr. T is, at least superficially, you are ready to consider *content points*. Some possibilities:

>> Appreciation for past support (always say thank you, thank you, thank you!)

>> Rundown on what SaveEl has accomplished for the mission lately and in particular, with the elephant orphanage

>> Statistics on the number of elephants nevertheless lost in this recent time frame

>> Inspiring description of the project goal as helping elephant babies from being orphaned at all

>> Interesting project details:

- How it will work, very briefly

- Expected accomplishments, with stats

- Use of innovative high-tech methods

>> Expectation that this high-profile project will draw wide media attention

And finally, the ask: *May I (or a higher-up) meet with you and tell you more?*

Here are the important takeaways from this example:

TIP

>> **Know your goals clearly and know your audience.** A portrait-in-words guides you in brainstorming the points that help win your case *with that person.* Once you have a list, it's easy to winnow through the points, find the lead and organize the rest. This gives you a content blueprint.

Profiling your reader works equally well when you're writing a business request for funding; a major proposal; or business plan, a report, a client letter, a marketing piece, a blog, a presentation, a networking message or website copy. Know your goal. Know who your intended audience is and what that person or group cares about. Then think inside that perspective.

>> **Know your medium and what it can realistically accomplish.** Analyzing your goal and audience helps you figure out what communication channel will work best for the message at hand. If you want to achieve more than it can reasonably deliver, look for another channel or shift the nature of your request. Consider the medium's limitations, too. The letter to Mr. T can't be so long that it loses his attention. If a proposal is in order down the line, financials and other details are covered there.

>> **Know that good communication is often a multi-step process.** Similar to my example of asking for a donation, when you want a raise, a promotion, a new computer or an important favor, your best approach is in-person. Then the role of a written message is to pave the way for a meeting where you can make your pitch. You need to say just enough to justify the conversation. This may lead to a proposal. It's exactly the same for a salesman who is pitching a product or service. And it's the same principle you apply when you tweet to draw readers to your blog and use the blog to pull them to your website and then interest them solidly so they move to the "buy" page. Thinking through these stages puts you way ahead.

SHORTCUT

>> **Recognize that virtually everything you write is "an ask."** When you send a message or document, you automatically ask your recipients to read it. You then implicitly ask them to react or respond in some way, whether it's just to retain information about something or take an action. An event invitation asks the recipient to feel motivated to participate. A "congratulations on your promotion" note asks the lucky person to notice that you're on their side. A cover note asks the reader to pay attention to what's attached.

Try to think of a written communication that doesn't ask for something. It's pretty tough. There's an advantage to seeing every message as a request: Doing so sets you up to frame your message with the right content and tone for the person you're writing to.

>> **Personalize everything you write.** You automatically do this when you message a friend you know is on your wavelength. But don't assume everyone else shares that wavelength! Way beyond the generic descriptions like common generational differences, people are individuals. If you want people to care about your message, know what they care about and think inside that perspective.

>> **Remember that good writing demands good information.** When you write based on the process I explain, expect to find gaps in your own knowledge or understanding. When the result matters to you, fill those gaps! The letter writer can research Mr. T on the Internet to uncover additional relevant factors about him, or query coworkers about their personal experiences with Mr. T for useful tips on what motivates him to save elephants. Maybe he lived in Africa for ten years. Maybe he's memorializing a friend who loved elephants. Such information gives you the chance to create a far more compelling message.

Writing to groups and strangers

Profiling someone you know is relatively easy, but you often write to groups rather than individuals, as well as to people you haven't met and know nothing about. The same ideas covered in the preceding section apply to groups and strangers, but they demand a little more imagination on your part.

SHORTCUT

Here's a good tactic for writing messages addressed to groups: Visualize a single individual — and/or a few key individuals — who epitomize that group. The financier Warren Buffet explained that when writing to stockholders, he imagines he's writing to his two sisters who are intelligent, but not knowledgeable about finance. He consciously aims to be understood by them. The results are admirably clear financial messages that are well received and influential.

Like Buffet, you may be able to think of a particular person to represent a larger group. If you've invented a new piece of ski equipment, for example, think about a skier you know who'd be interested in your product and create a profile of that person. Or create a composite profile of several such people, drawing on what they have in common with variations. If you're a businessperson looking to improve sales, think of your best clients and use what you know about them to create profiles of your ideal prospects.

Imagining your readers

Even when an audience is entirely new to you, you can still make good generalizations about what these people are like and even better, their needs. Suppose you're a dentist who's taking over a practice and writing to introduce yourself to your predecessor's patients. Your basic goal is to maintain that clientele. You needn't know the people to anticipate many of their probable concerns. You can assume, for example, that your news will be unwelcome because long-standing patients probably liked the old dentist and dislike change and inconvenience, just like you probably would yourself.

You can go further. Anticipate your readers' questions. Just put yourself in their shoes. The dental patients may wonder:

>> Why should I trust you, someone I don't know?

>> Will I feel an interruption in my care? Will there be a learning curve?

>> Will I like you and find in you what I value in a medical practitioner — aspects such as kindness, respect for my time, attentiveness, good communication, specific skills and experience?

TIP

Plan your content to answer the questions your readers would ask and you won't go wrong. You'll save time, too. How many memos do you send or receive daily, asking for clarification or trying to sort out some kind of confusion? Careless communication is a huge concern for business leaders. One badly written email sent to ten people can waste many hours of collective work just to retrieve the situation. An even bigger worry is the impact of mistakes generated by poor communication. How often do we read about a disastrous accident because a company's engineers failed to clearly describe a safety problem? Or that a manufacturer left critical information out of its handbook for a new model? On an everyday basis, minor variations on this theme occur every minute, everywhere.

TIP

Notice that in addition to being "me"-centered, nearly all the questions asked by the dental patients are emotional in nature rather than factual. Few patients are likely to ask about a new doctor's training and knowledge. They take that for granted. They're more concerned with the kind of person the dentist is and how they'll be treated.

This somewhat counterintuitive truth applies to many situations. Good salespeople don't pitch their experience — they pitch their ability to make the customer's life better. Notice also that the questions would be essentially the same for a new accountant, a copywriter or any other service provider. People in general can't very well assess a provider's skills, since they lack the specialized knowledge. Today you can check online reviews — but notice even there, many of the comments relate to personality and quality of interaction rather than "hard" skills.

When writing, you may need to build a somewhat indirect response to some of the questions you anticipate from readers. Writing something like "I'm a really nice person" to the dental patients is unlikely to convince them, but you can comfortably include statements like these in your letter:

> *I will carefully review all the records so I am personally knowledgeable about your history when we meet.*
>
> *My staff and I pledge to keep your waiting time to a minimum.*
>
> *We use all the latest techniques to make your visits comfortable and pain-free.*
>
> *I look forward to meeting you in person and getting to know you.*
>
> *I'm part of your community and participate in its good causes such as . . .*

REMEMBER

Apply this audience analysis strategy to job applications, business proposals, online media and other important materials. Ask yourself, whom do I want to reach? Is the person a human resources executive? A CEO? A prospective customer for my product or service? Then jot down a profile covering what that person is probably like and what their concerns and questions may be.

Everyone has a problem to solve. What's your reader's problem? The HR executive basically must fill open jobs in ways that satisfy other people. The CEO can pretty well be counted on to have one eye on the bottom line and the other on the big picture — that's the CEO's role. If you're pitching a product, base a prospective customer profile on the person for whom you're producing that product.

Making People Care

Sending your words out into today's message-dense world is not unlike tossing them into the sea in a bottle. Worse, your message is now among a trillion bottles, all of which are trying to reach the same moving and dodging targets. So, your competitive edge is in shaping a better bottle . . . or rather, message.

Any message you send must be well crafted and well-aimed, regardless of the medium or format. The challenge is to make people care enough to read your message and act on it in some way. The following sections explore the tools you need to ensure your bottle reaches its target, that the target is inspired to take the message out and that the message makes the impact you desire.

Connecting instantly with your reader

Only in rare cases do you have the luxury these days of building up to a grand conclusion, one step at a time. Your audience simply won't stick around.

The opening paragraph of anything you write must instantly hook your readers. The best way to do this is to link directly to their central interests and concerns within the framework of your purpose.

Suppose you're informing the staff that the office will be closed on Tuesday to install new air conditioning. You can write:

> *Subject: About next Tuesday*
>
> *Dear Staff:*
>
> *As you know, the company is always interested in your comfort and well-being. As part of our company improvement plan this past year, we've installed improved lighting in the hallways, and in response to your request that we . . .*

Stop! No one is reading this! Instead, try this:

> *Subject: Office closed Tuesday*
>
> *We're installing new air conditioning! Tuesday is the day, so we're giving you a holiday.*
>
> *I'm happy the company is able to respond to your number one request on the staff survey and hope you are, too.*

One of the best ways to hook readers is also the simplest: Get to the point. The technique applies even to long documents. Start with the bottom line, such as the result you achieved, the strategy you recommend or the action you want. In a report or proposal, the executive summary is often the way to do that, but note that even this micro version of your full message needs to lead off with your most important point.

Notice in the preceding example that the subject line of the email is part of the lead and planned to hook readers as much as the first paragraph of the actual message. Chapter 6 has more ideas of ways to optimize your email communication.

Focusing on what's-in-it-for-me

In marketers' terms, the acronym is WIIFM (what's-in-it-for-me), meaning the audience. The air-conditioning email in the preceding section captures readers by telling them first that they have a day off, then follows up by saying that they're getting something they wanted. Figuring out what's going to engage *your* readers often takes a bit of thought.

To make people care, you must first be able to answer the question yourself. Why *should* they care? Then put your answer right in the lead or even the headline.

If you're selling a product or service, for example, zero in on the problem it solves. Rather than your press release headline saying,

> *New Widget Model to Debut at Expo Magnus on Thursday*

Try:

> *Widget 175F Day-to-Night VideoCam Ends Small-Shop Pilfering*

If you're raising money for a cause, you may be tempted to write a letter to previous donors that begins like many you probably receive:

> *For 25 years, Freedom's Path has helped incarcerated women transition to the outside world by providing job training, counseling and support services. Your donations have been essential to equipping young transgressors to . . .*

This sounds worthy but yawn-inducing. Would you respond better to a letter that opens more like this?

> *19-year-old Jenny Y. was holding back tears. "Sure, I'll get out in six months, but so what? Where's my life? No family. No high school diploma. What else can I do than go back with the friends who got me here. I don't want to. But what's my choice?"*
>
> *We gave Jenny a choice and for the first time in her life, Jenny saw a break. We picked her for the Second Chance Program and gave her a new start . . .*
>
> *We want to help more Jennys. And with your help we can . . .*

The second version works better not just because it's more concrete, but because it takes into account two factors that you can expect all recipients probably share: (1) a concern for disadvantaged young people, and (2) a need to be reassured that their donations are well used.

Persuading with benefits, not features

People care about what a product or service can do for them, not what it is:

>> *Features* describe characteristics: a car having a 200-mph engine; an energy drink containing 500 units of caffeine; a hotel room furnished with priceless antiques.

>> *Benefits* are what features give us: the feeling that you can be the fastest animal on earth (given an open highway without radar traps); the ability to stay up for 56 hours to make up all the work you neglected; the experience of high luxury for the price of a hotel room, at least briefly.

Benefits have more to do with feelings and experiences than actual data. Marketers have long understood the power of benefits, but psychologists now confirm that most buying decisions are made emotionally rather than logically. You choose a car that speaks to your personality instead of the one with the best technical specs, and then you try to justify your decision on rational grounds. You buy a dress that makes you feel beautiful, not because the seams are cleverly designed.

REMEMBER

The lesson for business writing is clear: People care about messages that are based on what really matters to them. Don't get lost in technical detail. Focus on the impact of an event, idea or product. You can cover the specs, but keep them contained in a separate section or as backup material. Approach information the way most newspapers have always done (and now do online as well). Put what's most interesting or compelling up front and then include the details in the back (or link to them) for readers who want more.

Finding the concrete, limiting the abstract

The Freedom's Path example in the previous section demonstrates that focusing on a single individual delivers a more effective message. One concrete example is almost always better than reams of high-flown prose and empty adjectives. Make things real with techniques like these:

>> **Tell stories and anecdotes.** They must embody the idea you want to communicate, the nature of your organization or your own value. An early television show about New York City used a slogan along the lines, "Eight million people, eight million stories." A good story is always there, lurking, even in what may seem mundane or ordinary. But finding it can take some thinking and active looking.

>> **Use specific examples.** Tell customers how your product was used or how your service helped solve a problem. Give them strong case studies of implementations that worked. Inside a company, tell change-resistant staff members how another department saves three hours by using the new ordering process, or how a shift in benefits can cut their out-of-pocket healthcare costs by 14 percent. And if you want people to use a new system, give them clear guidelines, perhaps a step-by-step process to follow.

>> **Use visuals to explain and break up the words.** Readers who need to be captured and engaged generally shy away from uninterrupted type. Plenty of studies show that people are much more drawn to read material like blogs, articles and social posts when there is a strong visual element. Look for ways to graphically present a trend, a change, a plan, a concept or an example. Incorporate photographs, illustrations, charts, graphs and video to suit your purpose. When you must deliver your message primarily in words, use graphic techniques like headlines, subheads, bullets, typeface variations and icons — like this book!

>> **Give readers a vision.** Good leaders know that a vision is essential, whether they're running companies or running for public office. You're usually best off framing your important messages in big-picture terms that make people believe the future will be better in some way. Don't make empty promises; instead, look for the broadest implications of what you want to communicate and use details to back up that central concept and make it more real. Will your product or service save readers time or money? Make them healthier or more attractive? Will pitching in on block cleanup day make the community better and friendlier? Those are bottom-line messages for everyone. Framing a complicated document within a broad vision also makes it more organized and more memorable.

>> **Eliminate meaningless hyperbole.** What's the point of saying something such as, "This is the most far-reaching, innovative, ground-breaking piece of industrial design ever conceived"? Yet business writing is jampacked with empty, boring claims.

WARNING

Today's audiences come to everything you write already jaded, skeptical and impatient. If you're a service provider and describe what you do in words that can belong to anyone, in any profession, you fail. If you depend on a website and it takes viewers 20 seconds to figure out what you're selling or how to make a purchase, you lose. If you're sending out a press release that buries what's interesting or important, you're invisible. The antidote: *Know your point and make it fast!*

TIP

Go for the evidence! Tell your audience in real terms what your idea, plan or product accomplishes in ways they care about. Show them

>> How the product or event improve the lives of people like themselves

>> How the nonprofit is helping people, with track record proof

>> How the service solves problems

>> How you personally helped your employer make more money or become more efficient

Proof comes in many forms: images, statistics, data, ranking, testimonials, surveys, awards, promotions, case histories, biographies, social media followers and likes, and video and audio clips. Figure out how to track success and prove it. You end up with first-rate material to use in all your communication.

Choosing Your Written Voice: Tone

Presentation trainers often state that the meaning of a spoken message is communicated 55 percent by body language, 38 percent by tone of voice and only 7 percent by the words. Actually, this formula has been thoroughly debunked and denied by its creator, the psychologist Albert Mehrabian, because it misinterpreted a very limited study. However, it does suggest some important points for writing.

WARNING

Written messages come without body language or tone of voice. One result is that humor in written messages — particularly sarcasm or irony — is risky. When readers can't see the wink in your eye or hear the playfulness in your voice, they take you literally. So, refrain from subtle humor unless you're really secure with your reader's ability to "get it." Better yet: Be cautious at all times because assuming we all laugh at the same things is dangerous.

But even lacking facial expression and gesture, writing does carry its own tone, and this directly affects how readers receive and respond to messages. Written tone results from a combination of word choice, sentence structure and other technical factors including punctuation.

Within the past few years, we've seen wide acceptance of using emoji to convey feelings like happiness or anger or disappointment, or for sending a virtual wink to tell the reader you're joking. *But as with all your writing, think about whether it's audience-appropriate to employ emoji.* Ask yourself: Will this reader (or readers) understand this? Is there any room for misinterpretation? Have I seen messages from this person using emoji? If you're writing to a boss or client or donor, hesitate to break formality unless or until the other person does.

Also important to creating tone are less tangible elements that are hard to pin down. You've probably received messages that led you to sense the writer was upset, angry, resistant or amused, even if only a few words were involved. Sometimes even a close reading of the text doesn't explain what's carrying these emotions, but you just sense the writer's strong feelings.

REMEMBER

When you're the writer, be conscious of your message's tone. *A meticulously written email, letter or proposal can fail completely if you get the tone wrong because of how it may make you reader feel.* Consistently control the tone so that it supports your goals and does not undermine your message. The following sections explore some factors to be aware of and control in all work-related circumstances and many others.

Sound positive, never negative

Who likes to receive angry or depressing messages from colleagues and coworkers? People naturally prefer being around positive, dynamic, enthusiastic, good-natured people, and they prefer receiving messages with the same qualities. Resolve not to complain, quibble or criticize in writing. People are much more inclined to give you what you want when you're positive — and they see you as a problem-solver rather than a problem-generator.

I'm not assuming that if you feel angry, impatient or resentful, those feelings aren't well-grounded. But displaying them rarely helps your cause. Nobody likes to get negative, whiny, nasty messages that put them on the defensive or make them feel under attack.

Suppose you've asked the purchasing department to buy a table for your office and were denied without explanation. You could write to both your boss and the head of purchasing a note such as the following:

> *Hal, Jeanne: I just can't believe how indifferent and ignorant purchasing is to my work and what I need to do it. I'm now an Associate Manager responsible for a three-person team and regular meetings are essential to my . . .*

Put yourself in the recipients' places to see how bad the impact of such a message can be — for you. At the least, you're creating unnecessary problems, and at worst, perhaps permanent bad feelings. Why not write (and just to the purchasing officer) this, instead:

> *Hi, Hal. Do you have a minute to talk about my request for a small conference table? I was surprised to find that it was denied and want to share why it's important to my work.*

WARNING

Bottom line: Never send a message when you feel angry, unfairly treated, exhausted or just plain "down." You've probably found that showing emotion in the workplace rarely gives you an advantage, usually the opposite. Tone conveys feelings, and if you're not in control of your emotions when you write, tone betrays you.

Never vent in writing to anyone but yourself! Words written in anger are remembered forever, and messages that feel dejected undermine the goal of communicating your best self. Avoid sounding critical or resentful or tearful, too. It undermines your professionalism.

Always, always maintain a respectful tone. Even if you must write a critical message — for example, a performance review of a subordinate who needs improvement — try for a positive and upbeat spirit in both content and style. This doesn't mean sacrificing honesty. Remembering your goal always helps: In critiquing the subordinate, you gain nothing but negatives by making your coworker feel upset and angry and hopeless. Your goal is to develop a better contributor to your own accomplishments.

TIP

To keep yourself on the upbeat track, do not send the email or report or whatever when you're in the grip of emotion. Give yourself time to recover your grip — overnight if possible. If you must write a mean-minded message, by all means do it — it's a great way to detox yourself. Just be careful not to send it. A good way is to leave off the person's email address in the To: field.

SHORTCUT

Here's a quick way to redirect your feelings on the spot: *Smile when you say it.* People whose job is answering the phone are told by customer service trainers to smile before picking up the call. This physical act affects your throat and vocal cords and your tone of voice. You sound friendly and cheerful and may help the person on the other end of the phone feel that way, too.

Try smiling before you write — it will at least help you to be conscious of your own mood and how easily it can transfer to your messages and documents.

Align tone with the occasion, relationship and culture

Pause before writing and think about the nature of the message. Obviously if you're communicating bad news, you don't want to sound chipper and cheery. Always think of your larger audience, too. If the company made more money last month because it eliminated a department, best not to treat the new profits as a triumph. Current staff members probably aren't happy about losing colleagues and are worried about their own jobs. On the other hand, if you're communicating about a staff holiday party, sounding gloomy and bored doesn't generate high hopes for a good time. The same is true if you're offering an opportunity or assigning a nuisance job: Find the enticing side.

REMEMBER

Just as in face-to-face situations, the moods embedded in your writing are contagious. If you want an enthusiastic response, write with enthusiasm. If you want people to welcome a change you're announcing, sound positive and confident, not fearful or peevish and resentful, even if you don't personally agree with the change. Strive always to write with energy, because no one will believe in what you say unless you do. I cover the technical side of energetic writing in Chapter 3.

TIP

Make conscious decisions about how formal to sound. After you work in an organization for a while, you typically absorb its culture without really noticing. In fact, most people don't realize their organizations have a culture until they run into problems when introducing change or a high-level hire. If you're new to the place, observe how things work so you can avoid booby-trapping yourself. Scan through files of correspondence, email, reports, as well as websites and online material. Analyze what your colleagues feel is appropriate in content and in writing style. What communication media are used? How formal is the tone? Are people using emoji or other creative tools? Adopt the guidelines you see enacted or differ with caution. Ask friendly coworkers for advice.

WARNING

Every passing year seems to decrease the formality of business communication. Just as in choosing what to wear to work, people are dressing down their writing. This less formal style can come across as friendlier, simpler and more direct than in earlier years — and should. But business informal doesn't mean you should address an executive or board member casually, use abbreviations or emoji your reader may not like or might misinterpret or fail to edit and proofread every message. Those are gaffes much like wearing torn jeans to a client meeting in many industries.

And you want to be especially careful if you're writing to someone in another country, even an English-speaking one. Most countries still prefer a more formal form of communication than American business English.

Writing as your authentic self

We write who we are, whether we intend to or not. *Authentic* means being a straightforward, unpretentious, honest, trustworthy person — and writer. It doesn't mean trying for a specific writing style. Clarity is always the goalpost. This absolutely holds true even for materials written to impress. A proposal, marketing brochure or request for funding gains nothing by looking or sounding pompous and weighty.

TIP

Never try to impress anyone with how educated and literate you are. Studies show that in reality people believe that those who write clearly and use simple words are smarter than those whose writing abounds in fancy phrases and complicated sentences.

TIPS FOR MONITORING WRITTEN TONE

Watch the cadence of your message by reading it aloud. Emotions like anger often translate into choppy language that sounds abrupt and rude or sarcastic:

Chuck: So when will it be ready?

versus

Hi Chuck, can you let me know when to expect it?

Expressive punctuation can create an unhelpful mood:

Chuck: So when will it be ready???

Sustained capitalizing and/or bolding comes across as yelling:

So Chuck, **WHEN WILL IT BE READY?**

Watch your use of prejudicial phrases and statements that are sure to put people's backs up, such as:

I already told you that . . .

Everybody knows why . . .

You know we always do it this way . . .

But I worked late on Tuesday!

You just don't understand the importance of . . .

Why wasn't I invited to that meeting???

Take a minute to review messages and counter an absence of positive feeling when you find it. Your written message sets the tone for the reader. In avoiding the negative, don't forget to opt for the positive!

Try This: Write in two stages. If you don't have the luxury of waiting for a good mood to hit before writing something that matters, try a method I often use. I churn out the basic document regardless of my spirits, and later when I'm feeling bouncier, inject the energy and enthusiasm I know the original message is missing. Typical changes involve switching out dull passive verbs and substituting livelier ones, picking up the tempo, editing out the dead wood and adding plusses I overlooked when I felt gray. Chapter 3 is chock-full of ideas to energize your language.

Being authentic, in person and in writing, means being yourself, right along with practicing empathy. *The writing process I show you does not mean you should constantly try to give other people what they want by anticipating what you think they expect.* Studies have shown that if you interview for jobs by trying to cater to what the interviewers presumably want, you muff the chance to show personal qualities they value and come across as vague and inauthentic.

REMEMBER

In writing too, your goal is to create a genuine connection. The mindset that helps you do that is taking the trouble to see through another person's eyes. Taking another's perspective is your best key to creating relationships in all spheres of your life. This book gives you the tools to do that: a systematic way of thinking to remind yourself that *it's not all about you.* So write — and interact in person — with empathy. You will be your authentic *best* self when doing this.

Using Relationship-Building Techniques

REMEMBER

Just about everything you write is a chance to build relationships with people you report to and even other people above them in the chain, as well as peers, colleagues, customers, prospects, suppliers and members of your industry. More and more, people succeed through good networking, especially online. In a world increasingly characterized by less face-to-face contact and more global possibilities, writing is a major tool for making connections and maintaining them.

As with controlling tone, awareness that building relationships is always one of your goals puts you a giant step ahead. Ask yourself every time you write how you can improve the relationships with that individual. A range of techniques is available, such as the following.

Showing active caring and respect

REMEMBER

Never underestimate or patronize your audience, regardless of educational level, position or apparent accomplishment. People are quite sensitive to such attitudes and react adversely, often without knowing why or telling you. In *all* work and business situations, take the trouble to actively demonstrate respect for your reader. Specifically:

>> Address people politely and use their names.

>> Close with courtesy and friendliness.

>> Write carefully and proofread thoroughly; many people find poorly written messages insulting.

>> Avoid acronyms, jargon, emoji and abbreviations that may be unfamiliar or unwelcome to some readers.

>> Never be abrupt or rude or demanding or critical.

>> Take the trouble to consider cultural differences.

>> Accord with individuals' requests to address them with specific pronouns they have asked you to use.

Apply these guidelines whether you're writing to a superior, a subordinate or peer. You don't need to be obsequious to an executive higher up the chain than you are (in most cases), though often you should be more formal. Nor should you condescend to those lower down. Consider, for example, how best to assign a last-minute task to someone who reports to you. You could say,

> *Terry, I need you to research consultants who specialize in cultural change and send me 10 names tomorrow before 1 p.m. Thnx.*

Or:

> *Terry, I need your help. The CEO called a surprise meeting for tomorrow afternoon to discuss ideas for making some organizational changes. I'd like to be ready to identify some consultants we might call on. Can you do the groundwork by morning and come up with 10 possible specialists by 1 p.m.? I'll appreciate it. —Joe*

Either way, Terry may not be thrilled at how his evening looks, but treating him respectfully and explaining *why* you're giving him this overtime assignment accomplishes a lot: He'll be more motivated, more enthusiastic, more interested in doing a good job and happier to be part of your team. At the cost of writing a few more sentences, you improve your subordinate's attitude and perhaps even his long-range performance.

TIP

Explaining how assignments fit into the bigger picture and why they matter is especially inspiring to younger generations. But whatever their age, people who report to you are doing your work and helping you perform better and look good. Why not make them feel as important as they are, in ways that matter to them? Telling people *why* you want something works magic.

Personalizing what you write

In many countries, business email and letters that get right down to business seem cold, abrupt and unsympathetic. Japanese writers and readers, for example, prefer to begin with the kind of polite comments you tend to make when meeting someone in person: "How have you been?" "Is your family well?" "Isn't it cold for

October?" Such comments or questions may carry no real substance, but they serve an important purpose. They personalize the interaction to better set the stage for a business conversation.

TIP

In any culture, creating a sense of caring or at least interest in the other person gives you a much better context within which to transact business. If you've thought about your audience when planning what to write (see "Defining your audience" earlier in this chapter), you can easily come up with simple but effective personalizing phrases to frame your message.

You can always fall back on the old reliables: weather and general health inquiries. If communication continues, you can move the good feelings along by asking whether the vacation mentioned earlier worked out well, or ask how the conference went — whatever clues you can follow up on without becoming inappropriate or intrusive. The idea works when you address groups, too: You can, for example, begin, "I hope you all weathered the snowstorm okay."

Some techniques you can use to make your writing feel warm are useful, but they may not translate between different cultures. For example, salutations like *Hi, John* set a less formal tone than *Dear John*. Starting with just the recipient's name — *John* — is informal to the point of assuming a relationship already exists. But both ways may not be appropriate if you're writing to someone in a more formal country than your own. A formal address, such as Mr. Charles, Ms. Brown, Dr. Jones, General Frank, may be called for. In many cultures, if you overlook this formality and other signs of respect, you can lose points before you even begin. Or not even get the chance to begin.

Framing messages with "you" not "I"

Embrace this basic concept: People care infinitely more about themselves, their problems and what they want than they do about you. This simple-sounding premise has important implications for business communication — actually, all human communication.

Suppose you're a software developer and your company has come up with a new template for creating a home page. Your first thought for an announcement on your website might be:

> *We've created an amazing new home page template better than anyone ever imagined was possible.*

Or you could say:

Our great new Template X helps people build beautiful home pages with the least effort ever.

The second example is better because it's less abstract and it makes the product's purpose clear. But see if you find this version better yet:

Want a faster way to create a knock-out home page in half the time, with resources you already own? Here it is: Template X.

TIP

When you look for ways to use the word *you* more, even implicitly (the first sentence of the last pitch omits the "you"), and correspondingly decrease the use of *I* and *we,* you put yourself on the reader's wavelength. In the case of the new template, your readers care about how the product can help them, not that you're proud of achieving it.

The principle works for everyday email, letters and online communication, too. For example, when you receive a customer complaint, instead of saying,

We have received your complaint about . . .

You're better off writing:

Your letter explaining your disappointment with our product has been received . . .

Or, much better:

Thank you for writing to us about your recent problem with . . .

Coming up with a "you frame" can be challenging. It may draw you into convoluted or passive-sounding language, such as, "Your unusual experience with our tree-pruning service has come to our attention." Ordinarily I recommend a direct statement (like, "We hear you've had an unusual experience with . . ."), but in customer service situations and others where you need to instantly relate to your reader, figuring out a way to start with "you" can be worth the effort and a brief dip into passive voice.

REMEMBER

In every situation, genuinely consider your reader's viewpoint, sensitivities and needs. Think about how the message you're communicating affects that person or group. Anticipate questions and build in the answers. Write within this framework and you will guide yourself to create successful messages and documents.

SHORTCUT

Before sending a message, always ask yourself: How will it make this person feel? It's easy to know — consider how you would feel if you were on the receiving end. If the answer is "not so good," take the time to remedy your material. When you care, you do the work, and it shows. And you succeed.

In Chapters 3, 4 and 5, I give you a full set of techniques to draw on for delivering your message clearly and powerfully. Discover how to use the tools of writing — words, sentences and structure — to say what you mean in a way most likely to earn respect, support and agreement.

Chapter **3**

Making Your Writing Work: The Basics

I f your writing style took shape in school, you may have been led to believe that subtle thoughts require complex sentences, sophisticated vocabulary and dense presentation. Perhaps you learned to write that way — or maybe you didn't. Either way: Get over it. The rules of academic writing don't apply to the business world or everyday writing needs.

Real-world writing is more natural, reader-friendly and easier than academic writing — especially after you learn the essential strategies covered in this chapter. They will help you write better proposals, blogs and presentations — and also personal messages to raise money for a cause, ask for a favor, request a refund for a disappointing product, qualify for a loan and just about everything else.

Stepping into Twenty-First-Century Writing Style

In work as in life, success for most of us means achieving our goals. This is how to judge business writing: Does it accomplish what you want? Some core characteristics to aim for:

>> **Clear and simple language:** Except for technical material directed at specialists, no subject matter or idea is so complex that you cannot express it in clear, simple language. You automatically move forward a step by accepting this basic premise and practicing it.

>> **A conversational tone:** Business writing is reader-friendly and accessible, far closer to spoken language than the more formal and traditional style. It may even come across as casual or spontaneous. This quality, however, doesn't give you a free pass on grammar, punctuation and the other technicalities.

>> **Accuracy in language and content:** Noticeable mistakes interfere with your reader's ability to understand you. Further, careful writing is critical to how people evaluate your credibility and authority. Every reader responds, consciously or not, to the clues that tell them whether to take you seriously. Carelessness loses you points. However, contemporary writing allows substantial leeway in observing grammatical niceties.

>> **Friendly persuasion:** When you dig beneath the surface, most messages and documents ask something of the reader. This request may be minor ("Meet me at the coffee shop at 4") to major ("Please fund this proposal; $1 million will do"). Even when you're just asking someone to provide information, frame your message to suit that person's viewpoint. This idea is introduced in Chapter 2.

All these indicators of successful business communication come into play in everything you write. The following sections break down the various components of style into separate bits you can examine and adjust in your own writing.

Writing to be understood

Clarity and simplicity go hand in hand. It means your messages communicate what you intend with no room for misunderstanding or misinterpretation. Your reason for writing, and what you want the reader to do as a result of reading the message, are equally clear. This requires using:

- >> Words your reader already knows and whose meanings are agreed upon — no forcing readers to look up words; no trying to impress

- >> Sentences centered on simple, active verbs in the present tense when possible (for example, "Jane wrote the report" rather than "the report has been written by Jane")

- >> A sentence structure that leads readers though the message and motivates them to keep going

- >> Well-organized, logical, on-point, just-enough content without anything unnecessary or distracting

- >> Clear connections between sentences, paragraphs and ultimately ideas, so your statement is cohesive

- >> Correct spelling and basic grammar

REMEMBER

Writing with the preceding characteristics is transparent — nothing stands in the way of the reader absorbing your information, ideas and requests. Good business writing for most purposes doesn't call attention to itself. It's like a good makeup job. People don't want to hear, "Great cosmetology!" They much prefer, "You look beautiful." Similarly, you want your audience to admire your thinking, not the way you phrased it.

TIP

One result of meeting these criteria is that people can move through your material quickly. This is good! A fast read is your best shot at pulling people into your message and keeping them from straying off because they're bored. These days we are all so overwhelmed and impatient that we often don't bother to invest time in deciphering a message's meaning. We just stop reading.

Creating an easy reading experience is hard on the writer. Just like a simple dress or suit is often more expensive than a fussy one, a message that seems simple is a bigger investment, but in terms of thought. When you write well, you do all the readers' work for them. They don't need to figure out anything because you've already done every bit of it. Leave out information or connections and they will leap the gap in any way they choose. So take the trouble to be unambiguous, complete and concise, because that's how you win what you want.

All these elements of good writing are covered in this chapter and the next two.

Applying readability guidelines

Guidelines for business writing are not theoretical. They're practical, and moreover, supported by research studies on how people respond to the written word. Fortunately, you don't have to read the research. Most word-processing programs and several websites have already digested all the data and offer easy-to-use tools to help you quickly gauge the readability of your writing.

SHORTCUT

More and more tools to help with grammar and language become available daily, but using a readability index remains the best tool I know to objectively evaluate your writing as you develop material or after drafting. Rather than rewriting a message for you — which robots don't do very well — it provides the clues you need to recognize weaknesses and fix them.

Several readability indexes are available (see the sidebar "Readability research: What it tells us" later in this chapter). In this section, I focus on the Flesch-Kincaid Readability Index because it's the one Microsoft Word uses. It predicts the percentage of people likely to understand a piece of writing and assigns it a grade level of reading comprehension. The grade-level scores are based on average reading ability of students in the U.S. public school system. The algorithm for a readability index is primarily based on the length of words, sentences and paragraphs.

TIP

Called "Readability Statistics," Microsoft Word's version also shows you the percentage of passive sentences in a selection, which is a good indicator of flabby verbs, indirect sentence structure and cut-worthy phrases.

Match reading level to your audience

Whatever readability index you use, your target numbers depend on your audience (one more reason to know your readers). Highly educated readers can certainly comprehend difficult material, which may lead you to strive for text written at a high educational level for scientists or MBAs. But this is never a good idea. For most practical communication, we are all lazy readers and prefer "easy" material. Don't you?

Therefore, take any calculations with many grains of salt and adapt them to your audience and purpose. And just so you know, the "average reader" in the United States is pegged at a seventh- to ninth-grade reading level, depending on which study you look at.

TIP

When you want to reach and be relevant to a diverse group, you can segment your audience, like marketers, and craft different versions for each. If a company needs to inform employees of a benefits change, for example, it may need different communications for top managers, middle managers, clerical staff, factory workers and so on. Beyond assuming varying reading comprehension levels, you often need to rethink the content for each as well. Everyone wants to know how they are affected. But a manager also needs to know the financial impact on the department and how to explain the change to staff members.

Assess readability level

Finding Microsoft's Readability Statistics varies a little based on which version of Word you use. Generally, go to Word's Spelling and Grammar Preferences screen and make sure the "Show Readability Statistics" checkbox is selected. Thereafter, whenever you complete a spelling and grammar check, you see a box with readability scores. Several other readability tests are available free online, including at www.readability-score.com. On most sites, you simply paste a chunk of your text into a box and the readability information pops right up.

My personal *print media* readability targets for general audiences, with variation based on the material, are as follows:

>> **Reading Ease:** 50 to 70 percent, meaning that between half and 70 percent of people will understand it

>> **Grade Level:** 8th to 11th grade

>> **Percentage of passive sentences:** 0 to 8 percent

>> **Words per sentence:** 12 to 18 on average (some sentences can consist of one word, while others contain a great many more)

>> **Sentences per paragraph:** Average three to five (but an occasional one-word sentence can add power)

For online media, my readability targets are tighter. Reading from a screen — even a big one — is physically harder for people so they are even less patient than with printed material. Plenty of white space and brevity are key to online readability. Sentences work best when they average 8 to 12 words, and interspersing short sentences — sometimes just a single word — adds punch. Paragraphs work best at one to three sentences.

On the other hand, if you wonder why I'm bending my own rules at times, somewhat longer paragraphs work better for books. This medium assumes a more willing concentration and thoughtful pace on the readers' part.

Try This: Apply the index. To check out how a readability index works, select a section or a whole document of something you wrote recently in Microsoft Word and run a spelling and grammar check. (Or copy and paste a selected passage into an online readability checker.) When the check is completed, review the Readability Statistics to find out if you need to simplify your writing. If the statistics say that at least a 12th-grade reading level is required (in many Word versions, the index doesn't show levels above 12), and less than 60 percent of readers will understand your document, edit. Do the same if you used more than 10 percent passive sentences. You'll find lots of suggestions for rewriting in the next section, but the stats immediately tell you to consider:

>> Substituting short, one or two syllable words for any overly long words.

>> Shortening long sentences by breaking them up or tightening your wording.

>> Breaking paragraphs into smaller chunks so that you have fewer sentences in each.

>> Looking for weak verbs that are forms of "have" or "to be" ("is," "are," "will be," and so on). These verbs produce a passive effect and complex structures.

>> Reviewing the rewrite to make sure your message still means what you intended.

Then recheck the statistics. If the figures are still high, repeat the process. See if you can get the grade level down to grade 10, then grade 8. Try for less than 8 percent passive voice. Compare the different versions. Which do you prefer? Which do you think best serves your purpose?

READABILITY RESEARCH: WHAT IT TELLS US

Serious studies to figure out what produces easy reading began in the early twentieth century and continue to be done in many languages in addition to English. The subject gained importance in the 1940s when newspaper publishers wanted to raise their circulation numbers. The researchers recommended lowering reading levels, and sure enough, newspaper readership went up 45 percent.

Savvy writers use the basic principles to ensure that their material is well-aimed for the target audience. In general, the simpler and clearer the language, the higher the readability. Here are a few examples of grade-level measurements found by testers:

- Popular music: Grades 2.6 to 5.5

- Popular authors, including Stephen King, Tom Clancy and John Grisham: Grade 7

- *The New York Times* and *The Wall Street Journal:* Grade 11

- *London Times:* Grade 12

- Academic papers: Grades 15 to 20

- Typical government documents: Higher than grade 20 (though many agencies are improving!)

Finding the right rhythm

You may wonder whether writing based on short simple sentences produces choppy and boring material reminiscent of a grade school textbook. Aiming for clear and simple definitely should not mean dull reading.

TIP

Become aware of rhythm in what you read and what you write, and you will improve your writing dramatically. Like all language, English was used to communicate orally about 100,000 years before writing was invented, so sound and rhythm patterns are critical to how written forms as well as spoken ones are received.

Think of the worst public speakers you know. They probably present in a series of long, complex sentences in an even tone that quickly numbs the ear. Good speakers, by contrast, hold your attention by varying sentence length, inflection and intonation. As a writer, you want to do the same.

REMEMBER

In everything you write, aim to build in a natural cadence. Rhythm is one of the main tools for cajoling people to stay with you and find what you write interesting. Just begin each sentence differently from the previous one and try alternating short, plain sentences with longer ones that have two or three clauses, usually marked by commas. Like good public speakers, you can also inject short punchy words and phrases, but dole them out carefully.

Fix the short and choppy

Even a short message benefits from attention to sentence rhythm. Consider this brief message:

> Kim: The video crew didn't show up again yesterday. We waited all morning. They never came. We wasted the whole day. We'll miss the deadline. Please advise. —Ted

And an alternate version:

> Kim: The video crew let us down again yesterday. Waiting all morning cost us a lot of time, and as a result, we are at risk of missing the target deadline. Do you have a suggestion on how to move ahead? Thanks. —Ted

REMEMBER

The same information can be delivered in ways that have totally different effects. Notice in this example how the tone shifts between versions 1 and 2. The choppy cadence of the original communicates blame and unconstructive anger. The writer of the alternate version sounds more professional and focused on the challenge rather than his personal resentment. Paying attention to sentence structure makes the difference.

For long documents, varying your sentence length and structure is even more critical. Few people will stay with multiple pages of stilted, mind-numbing prose.

Notice, too, that when you combine some short sentences with long ones to create an easy cadence, easy ways to improve the wording and content emerge. Ted may be inspired to go a step further and write a third version of the same message:

> *Kim: I'm sorry to report that the video crew failed to show up again yesterday. Losing a whole morning makes it hard to meet our deadline, August 14th, which keys off the annual meeting. I've looked into some alternative resources — the shortlist is attached. Do you have a few minutes to talk about how to move ahead? Thanks. —Ted.*

Notice how much more connected the thoughts seem, and how much more authoritative the overall message feels. Yes, the content shifted — but this happens when you write thoughtfully! In everything you write, *what you say and how you say it are inextricable.*

REMEMBER

Figuring out how to express something well in words often pushes your thinking to higher levels. In the first message, Ted comes across as a frustrated complainer blocked by a problem. The second moves him up to at least sound more neutral and on point. Version 3 communicates that he is a take-charge, efficient professional — someone reliable, someone who cares about the whole operation and takes initiative: a problem-solver rather than a cog who goes through the motions and waits for direction.

This is the magic of good writing. It clarifies problems. It enables you to discover solutions that didn't occur to you at first thought. It equips you to look more effective and to *be* more effective. Good writing is always worth the time it takes, and once you adopt this belief and absorb the structure I'm providing, you can become an efficient communicator as well as a powerful one.

Fix the long and complicated

Many people have a problem opposite to creating disconnected, jumpy sentences. Maybe you tend to write lengthy complicated sentences that end up with the same result: sleep-worthy writing.

TIP

The solution to never-ending strings of words is the same — alternate sentence structures. But in this case, break up the long ones. Doing this produces more accessible, energetic and enticing copy.

A number of potentially good writers don't succeed as well as they might because they fall into a pattern that repeats the same rhythm, over and over again. Here's an example taken from an opinion piece written for a workshop:

I strongly support efforts to improve the global economy, and naturally may be biased toward the author's position. While this bias may be the reason I responded well to the piece in the first place, it is not the reason why I consider it an exceptional piece of writing. Not only is this article extremely well researched, its use of cost-benefit analysis is an effective way to think about the challenges.

The monotonous pattern and unending sentences serve the ideas poorly. One way to rewrite the copy:

I strongly support efforts to improve the global economy and this probably inclined me to a positive response. But it's not why I see it as an exceptional piece of writing. The article is extremely well researched. Further, its cost-benefit analysis is an effective way to think about the challenge.

SHORTCUT

The lesson: Vary your sentence length and structure. Consciously start sentences with different parts of speech, or simply aim to alternate short declarative sentences, sentences with two commas and sentences with three commas. This technique immediately improves the message's flow and pulls the reader along. You can take liberties with the recommended short-long-short sentence pattern and use two short sentences, then two more complex ones, for example. Experiment with this tool and you'll find it super-easy to apply.

Try This: Review your own message. Identify a piece of writing you recently created, whether an email, letter, report or other medium. Pay attention to its cadence when read aloud. Does it suffer from choppiness or too much density? Adjust sentence length and structure to improve the rhythm and see if this powers up your message.

REMEMBER

Everyone has particular habits of writing that leave room for improvement. Strive to recognize your own weaknesses, because then you can counter them with one of the practical fix-it techniques in Chapter 4.

Achieving a conversational tone

New business writers are often told to adopt a "conversational" tone, but what does that actually mean?

Business correspondence written during the nineteenth century, and even most of the twentieth, seems slow, formal and ponderous when you read it now. Today's communication needs to move as fast as our lives, and we want it to feel natural.

REMEMBER

Conversational tone is something of an illusion, however. You don't really write the way you talk, and you shouldn't. But you can echo natural speech in various ways to more effectively engage your audience.

Rhythm, discussed in the preceding section, is a basic technique that gives your copy forward momentum and promotes a conversational feeling. Additional techniques to achieve conversational tone include:

>> **Infuse messages with warmth.** Think of the person as an individual before you write and content that's appropriate to the relationship and subject will come to you. The tone will be right.

>> **Choose short simple words.** Rely on the versions you use to *talk* to someone, rather than the sophisticated ones you use to try and impress. See "Choosing reader-friendly words" later in this chapter for examples.

>> **Use contractions as you do in speech.** Go more often with "can't" rather than "cannot," "I'm" rather than "I am."

>> **Minimize the use of inactive forms.** Carefully evaluate every use of the "to be" verbs — *is, was, will be, are* and so on — to determine if you can use active, interesting verbs instead.

>> **Take selective liberties with grammatical correctness.** Starting a sentence with "and" or "but" or "or" is okay, for example, but avoid mismatching your nouns and pronouns. However, this once-simple rule is more complicated today — Chapter 5 gives you updated guidelines.

>> **Adopt an interactive spirit.** As online media embodies, one-way, top-down communication is "so yesterday." Find ways in all your writing to invite active interest and input from your reader. Today's readers, especially younger ones, want to be part of the experience, not passive recipients of someone else's ideas. Many online techniques have been adapted to traditional media, and you want to incorporate them as appropriate.

If you ignore the preceding guidelines — and want to look hopelessly outdated — you can write a long-winded and lifeless message like the following:

> *Dear Elaine:*
>
> *I regret to inform you that the deadline for the Blue Jay proposal has been advanced to an earlier point in time, namely, August 14. Will this unexpected eventuality present insurmountable difficulties to your department? Please advise and inform my office of your potential availability at 3 p.m. on the 2nd to discuss. —Carrie*

Yawn — and also a bit confusing. Or you can write a clear, quick, crisp version like this:

> *Elaine, I'm sorry to say the Blue Jay deadline has been moved up to August 14. Bummer, I know. What problems does this create? Let's talk. Thursday at 3? —Carrie*

TIP

Although the second example feels casual and conversational, these aren't the actual words Carrie would say to Elaine in a real phone conversation. This exchange is more likely:

> *Hi. How are you? Listen, we got a problem. The Blue Jay deadline — would you believe — it's now August 14th. Yeah, I know, total bummer. We gotta talk about this. How's Thursday at 3?*

A chat message may read closer to the conversational mode because it is acceptably spontaneous. But for the same reason, chat doesn't work well for more "serious" matters that demand thoughtful exchange or detail — even informal networks find email better in such cases.

Online copy often works best when it carries the conversational illusion to an extreme. Pay attention to the jazzy, spontaneous-style copy on websites you love. The words may read like they sprang ready-made out of some genie's lamp, but more than likely they were produced by a team of copywriters agonizing over every word for weeks or months or years. Spontaneous-reading copy doesn't come easy: It's hard work. Some people — frequent bloggers, for example — are good at writing conversationally because they practice this skill consciously.

Similarly, do you imagine that comedians — or rap artists — perform with total spontaneity? Not so much. At the least, they draw on a repertoire of ideas developed over time and may carefully practice an off-the-cuff tone. The comedian Jerry Seinfeld shared in a video interview that one signature joke he uses in standup gigs took him three years to perfect. Preparation is critical for non-funny events as well — politicians and CEOs (or their support people) systematically anticipate all possible questions and practice answering them in advance.

Energizing Your Language

Written communication is based on words, so choose them well. But the most important guideline for selecting the best words for business writing may seem counterintuitive: Avoid long or subtle words that express nuance. These may serve as the staple for many fiction writers and academics, but you're not aiming to sound evocative, ambiguous, impressive or super-educated. In fact, you want just the opposite.

Relying on everyday wording

The short everyday words you use in ordinary speech are your basic stock for business writing. They're clear, practical, direct and concrete. They're also powerful enough to express your deepest and widest thoughts. They're the words that reach people emotionally, too, because they stand for the most basic and tangible things people care about and need to communicate about. "Home" is a whole different story than "residence"; "quit" carries a lot more overtones than "resign." Does "dumped" carry more feeling than "rejected"?

Make a list of basic one- and two-syllable words and almost certainly, they come from the oldest part of the English language, Anglo-Saxon. Most words with three or more syllables were grafted onto this basic stock by historical invaders: the French-speaking Normans and the Latin-speaking Romans for the most part, both of whom aspired to higher levels of cultural refinement than the Britons.

If you were raised in an English-speaking home, you learned Anglo-Saxon words during earliest childhood and acquired the ones with "foreign" influences later in your education. Scan these previous two paragraphs and you know immediately which words came from which culture set.

REMEMBER

For many reasons, then, readers are programmed to respond best to simple, short, low-profile English words. They trigger feelings of trust (an Anglo-Saxon word) and credibility (from the French). Obviously, I don't choose to write entirely with one-syllable words. Variety is the key — just as with sentences. English's history gives you a remarkable array of words when you want to be precise or produce certain feelings. Even in business English, a sprinkling of longer words contributes to a good pace and can make what you say more specific and interesting. But don't forget your basic word stock.

TIP

If you're writing to a non-native English-speaking audience, you have even more reason to write with one- and two-syllable words. People master the same basic words first when learning a new language, no matter what their original tongue, so all new English-speakers understand them. You know this if you've ever had a conversation in with someone whose native language is not English, in a language foreign to both of you. For example, if you converse with a Russian speaker who studied two years of French like you did, you can communicate quite well with each other.

In many workplaces today, you need to communicate with culturally diverse audiences all the time as well as with people with different educational levels. Make simple, straightforward language the general rule.

This principle holds for long documents like reports and proposals as much as for emails. They should never read pretentiously no matter how big a job you're pitching and no matter how impressive the company. And short word guidelines are also important for online writing such as for websites and blogs. When we read onscreen, we have even less patience with multi-syllable, sophisticated words. Reading (and writing) on smartphones and other small devices usually makes short words the *only* practical choice.

Choosing reader-friendly words

Using short, easy words may seem like common sense, so why do you see so much business messaging with all those long, highly educated words in dense sentences? I have no idea. If everyone wrote the way we all prefer to read, I'm sure we'd have a more collegial, efficient and productive world.

Consciously develop your awareness of short-word options. Clearer writing gives you better results. In most circumstances, opt for the first and friendlier word in the following pairs.

Use . . .	Rather than . . .
help	assistance
often	frequently
try	endeavor
need	requirement
basic	fundamental
built	constructed
confirm	validate
rule	regulation
create	originate
use	utilize
prove	substantiate
show	demonstrate
study	analyze
fake	artificial
limits	parameters
skill	proficiency
demands	necessitates

I don't mean that the longer words are bad — in fact, they can often be the better choice. But generally, be sure you have a reason for going long.

SHORTCUT

Make up your own list of words to simplify by observing your writing. Identify the three or more syllable words you use often, think about shorter alternatives and write them down as in the preceding list. An online thesaurus can help. Once you are conscious of your options, you will make better choices in all your writing.

Focusing on the real and concrete

Concrete nouns are words that denote something tangible: a person or any number of actual things, such as dog, nose, dirt, doctor, house, boat, balloon, computer, egg, tree, chair and so on. They are objects that exist in real space. You can experience them with your senses — touch, see, hear, smell or taste them.

Abstract nouns typically represent ideas and concepts. They may denote a situation, condition, quality or experience, such as catastrophe, freedom, efficiency, happiness, knowledge, mystery, fairness, observation, sadness, analysis, research, love, democracy and countless more.

REMEMBER

When you use concrete nouns in your writing, readers bring their sensory associations to your words, and this lends reality to your thoughts. Moreover, you can expect most people to take the same meaning from them. This isn't true of abstract words. Two people are unlikely to argue about what a flag is, but they may well disagree on what exactly "democracy" or "happiness" means.

TIP

When you build your writing on a lot of abstract nouns, you are generalizing. Even when you're writing an opinion or philosophical piece, too much abstraction doesn't fire the imagination. A lot of business writing strikes readers as dull and uninspiring for this reason.

Suppose at a pivotal point of World War II Winston Churchill had written in the manner of many modern business executives:

> *We're operationalizing this initiative to proceed as effectively, efficiently and proactively as possible in alignment with our responsibilities to existing population centers and our intention to develop a transformative future for mankind. We'll employ cost-effective, cutting-edge technologies and exercise the highest level of commitment, whatever the obstacles that materialize in various geographic situations.*

Instead he wrote and said:

> *We shall not flag or fail. We shall go on to the end. We shall fight in France, we shall fight on the seas and the oceans, we shall fight with growing confidence and growing strength in the air, we shall defend our island, whatever the cost may be. We shall fight on the beaches, we shall fight on the landing grounds, we shall fight in the fields and in the streets, we shall fight in the hills; we shall never surrender.*

Which statement engages the senses and therefore the heart, even three-quarters of a century after this particular cause was won? Which carries more conviction? Granted, Churchill was writing a speech, but the statement also works amazingly when read.

TIP

While you probably won't be called on to rouse your countrymen as Churchill was, writing in a concrete way pays off for you, too. It brings your writing alive. Aim to get down to earth in what you say and how you say it.

Notice how many words of the mock business-writing piece contain three or more syllables. Churchill's piece uses only three. And running both passages through readability checks (see the previous section, "Applying readability guidelines") predicts at least a 12th-grade reading level to understand the business-speak with only 2 percent of readers understanding it. By contrast, Churchill's lines require only a 4th-grade reading level and 91 percent of readers understand them.

WARNING

You may often find yourself tempted to write convoluted, indirect, abstract prose — because it's common to your corporate culture or your technical field or the Request for Proposal you're responding to. Don't do it. Remind yourself that nobody likes to read that kind of writing, even though they may write that way themselves. Take the lead in delivering lean lively messages and reap more of the positive responses you want.

Finding action verbs

Good strong verbs invigorate. Passive verbs, which involve a form of the verb "to be," deaden language and thinking, too. Consider some dull sentences and their better alternatives:

> *The whole company was alarmed by the stock market loss.*
>
> *The stock market loss alarmed the whole company.*
>
> *A decision to extend working hours was reached by the talent management office.*
>
> *The talent management office decided to extend working hours.*

The first sentence in each set represents what grammarians call the passive voice: a form of the verb "to be" followed by a word ending in "-ed." Other constructions also use non-active verbs that tell you to take a second look. One clue: sentences that rely on the phrases "there is" and "there are," which often bury meaning. Compare the following pairs:

> *There is a company rule to consider in deciding which route to follow.*
>
> *A company rule tells us which route to follow.*
>
> *There are guidelines you should use if you want to improve your writing.*
>
> *Follow the guidelines to improve your writing.*

TIP

For most dull inactive verbs, the solution is the same: *Find the action.* Be clear about *who* did *what* and then rework the sentence to say that.

You may need to go beyond changing the verb and rethink the entire sentence so it's simple, clear and direct. In the process, take responsibility. Passive sentences often evade it. A classic example:

Mistakes were made, people were hurt and opportunities were lost.

Who made the mistakes, hurt the people and lost the opportunities? The writer? An unidentified CEO? Mystery government officials? This kind of structure is sometimes called "the divine passive": Some unknown or unnamable force made it happen.

To help you remember why you generally need to avoid the passive, here's my favorite mistake. I asked a group of people to write about their personal writing problems and how they planned to work on them. One person contributed:

Many passive verbs are used by me.

REMEMBER

Take the time to identify the passive verbs and indirect constructions in all your writing. Doing so doesn't mean that you must always eliminate them. You may want to use the passive because no clearly definable active subject exists — or it doesn't matter:

The award was created to recognize outstanding sales achievement.

Or you may have a surprise to disclose that leads you to use the passive for emphasis:

This year's award was earned by the newest member of the department: Joe Mann.

TIP

Using the passive unconsciously often undermines your writing success. Substitute active verbs. They can be short and simple, such as *drive, end, gain, fail, win, probe, treat, taint, speed.* Or they can be longer words that offer more precise meaning, such as *underline, trigger, suspend, pioneer, model, fracture, crystallize, compress, accelerate.* Both word groups suggest action and movement, adding zing and urgency to your messages.

Crafting comparisons to help readers

Comparisons help your readers understand your message on deeper levels. You can use similes and metaphors, which are both analogies, to make abstract ideas more tangible and generally promote comprehension. These devices don't need to be elaborate, long or pretentiously literary. Here are some simple comparisons:

Poets use metaphors like painters use brushes — to paint pictures that help people see under the surface.

Winning this award is my Oscar.

Life: a box of chocolates.

The average human hair is 90,000 nanometers wide, compared to the width of the new polymer strand — 10 nanometers.

From 15,000 feet up, the world looks like a colorful quilt of peace and harmony.

MAKING UP FRESH COMPARISONS

Playing with comparisons is a classic schoolroom game you can use to generate new ways to express your ideas. Simply think about bringing together two different things so readers are led to see one differently.

Take a few minutes and assemble a short list of things, activities or experiences on the left-hand side of a page of blank paper or screen. For example, you can list your new project, writing your résumé, making your boss happy, the new product you're selling, playing a computer game and so on.

Think about what that item is like — how you can describe it visually or through the other senses. Think about how it makes you feel. Brainstorm about other things that have similar characteristics. Try to avoid clichés and come up with something you find interesting.

Write your idea for each item on your list on the right side of the paper. Come up with an idea for every item just to give yourself the practice, without worrying whether some of your comparisons are less than brilliant. Use your new skill when you're writing an important document, trying to explain something difficult or making your best persuasive argument.

For example, you might brainstorm for a comparison by "finishing" statements, such as:

Winning this contract is as good as . . .

This new service will change your thinking about life insurance just like X changed Y.

Saving a few dollars by investing in Solution A instead of Solution B is like . . .

Whatever device you use, effective comparisons

>> **Create mental images.** You can give readers a different way to access — and *remember* — your ideas and information.

>> **Align things from different arenas.** Using the familiar to explain the unfamiliar can be especially helpful when you introduce new information or change.

>> **Bring abstract concepts down to earth.** Express abstract ideas in concrete language so they become more real and easier to grasp.

>> **Heighten the impact of everyday practical writing.** Just as in well-written fiction, a great comparison in a business document engages the reader's imagination.

>> **Make intriguing headlines that grab attention.** A blog post caught me with the title, "How Learning to Ride a Bike is Like Working at Home." I read it just to find out what the two things have in common.

Employing Reader-Friendly Graphic Techniques

Good written messages and documents are well thought out and presented clearly and vividly, as covered in this chapter and the preceding one. But I have one more aspect to highlight. Your writing must not only meet audience needs and read well; it also must look good.

REMEMBER

Whether your material appears in print or online, every message and document you create is a visual experience. If it doesn't look accessible and inviting, your audience may not bother to read it. Moreover, readers judge your message's value and credibility by how it looks. Whether you want to write an effective résumé, proposal, report — or just an email message — the graphic appearance can make or break your success.

The following sections show you how to use various graphic techniques to maximize your message's appeal while also promoting clarity. You need not purchase special software to easily implement these good design principles — most are free and right at your fingertips.

Building in white space

To coin a comparison (see the sidebar "Making up fresh comparisons"):

Add white space to your writing for the same reason bakers add yeast to their bread — to leaven the denseness by letting in light and air.

TIP

The eye demands rest when scanning or reading. Don't cram your words into a small tight space by decreasing the point size or squeezing the space between characters, words or lines. Densely packed text is inaccessible and unwelcoming. If you have too many words for the available space, cut them down. You'll find many ways to do that while also heightening your impact with the techniques in Chapter 4.

Always look for opportunities to add that valuable white space to your message. Check for white space in everything you deliver. Factors that affect white space include the size of the typeface, line spacing, margin size and column width, and graphic devices such as subheads, sidebars and images.

Choosing a typeface

Type has numerous graphic aspects and effects. Following are some of the most significant, as well as easiest to adjust.

Fonts

For printed text, *serif fonts* — fonts with feet or squiggles at the end of each letter, like the font used in this book — are more reader-friendly because they make every letter distinct and unambiguous. They also guide the eye smoothly from letter to letter, word to word. However, *sans-serif fonts* (ones without the little feet) are often favored by art directors for marketing and online material and publications directed to young audiences, because they look more modern and classy. But some sans serifs leave room for confusion — for example, it can be hard to distinguish between a small "l" and the number "1." The sans-serif font Verdana was specifically designed to be readable on small screens at low resolution and is often used for digital media.

TIP

Choose your font according to your purpose. For long print documents, serif remains the better choice for the same reason that books still use it — ease of reading. But you can to some extent mix your faces. Using sans-serif headlines and subheads can make a welcome contrast. (For example, Times New Roman and Helvetica work nicely together.) But generally, resist the temptation to combine more than two different typefaces.

WARNING

Avoid fancy or cute typefaces for any purpose. They're not only distracting but also may not transfer well to someone else's computer system. They can end up garbled or altogether missing in action. Recruitment officers sometimes find a candidate's name entirely missing from a résumé because their systems lack a corresponding typeface and end up omitting these very important words.

And never type a whole message in capitals or bold face, which gives the impression that you're shouting. Also avoid using italics for extensive pieces of copy because it's harder to read.

Point size

The best point size for text depends on the result you're trying to achieve. Generally, somewhere between 10 and 12 points works best in print, but you need to adjust according to your audience and the experience you want to create. Small type may look great, but if you want readers 55 and older to read your annual report, 8-point type will kill you.

Online text suggests a similar 10- to 12-point range for body copy, but calculating the actual onscreen experience for a wide range of monitors and devices is complicated. Online text often looks different on different platforms. Err on the side of a generous point size.

WARNING

Never resort to reducing the size of your typeface to fit more in. And when choosing fonts and point sizes for any communication, always keep in mind that more than 60 percent of the U.S. population uses glasses.

Margins and columns

For both online and print media, avoid making columns of type so wide that the eye becomes discouraged in reading across. If breaking the copy into two columns isn't suitable, consider widening one or both margins. Also, avoid columns that are only three or four words wide, because they're hard to read and annoying visually.

Think carefully before you fool with justifying text. Justified type has a straight edge vertically. This paragraph is justified on the left, which is almost always your best choice for body copy. When text is left uneven on the right, this is called "rag right" in printer parlance. The text in this book is fully justified on both the left and right, which is good for books but can be a tricky style choice, especially for online media. Sometimes fully justified copy can visibly distort words and spacing to make your words fit consistently within a block of text.

Keeping colors simple

Using color to accent a print document makes for happier eyes, but stay simple. One color, in addition to black used for the text, is probably plenty. Typically, it's best used in a consistent way for headlines and subheads. Full color is best applied to photographs and other graphics rather than to making rainbow copy.

Even online, where you face no limit on using as many colors as you like, seeing a lot of different colors strikes people as messy and amateur these days. Designers prefer simple, clean palettes that combine a few colors at most. So should you. And avoid placing any type against a color background that makes it hard to read. This means that backgrounds should be no more than a light tint. *Dropped or reversed-out type* — for instance, white type on a black or dark background — can look terrific, but only in small doses, such as a caption or short sidebar. A whole page of reversed-out type, whether in print or onscreen, makes a daunting read.

If you're working on a major document or website with a graphic designer, never allow graphic impact to trump readability and editorial clarity. To most designers, words are just part of a visual pattern. If a designer tells you the document has too many words, listen; it's probably true and you do want the piece to look good. But "just say no" if playing second fiddle to the visual undermines your message. Graphics should strengthen, not weaken, its impact and absorbability.

Adding effective graphics

If you've got good images and they're appropriate, flaunt them. Increasingly this principle is applied to short messaging as well as long documents, because so much research demonstrates the strength of visual material in drawing and holding reader attention. Visuals are beginning to dominate relatively older online media like Twitter and *are* the story with tools like Pinterest and Instagram, not to mention video-sharing media like YouTube and TikTok.

Evaluate the appropriateness of graphics based on your purpose. A proposal can benefit from charts and graphs to make financials and other variables clear and more easily grasped. A report may include photographs of a project under way. A blog with a fun image related to the subject is more enticing. Business materials can benefit from images of successful projects to support credibility, illustrations of something yet to be built, and visualizations of abstract ideas.

When visual effect matters — to attract readers or when you're competing for a big contract, for example — take time to brainstorm the graphics. Good online resources for photographs, video, symbols, cartoons and more proliferate, and many are free. Better yet, create your own — smartphone photographs are now good enough even for publication. You can customize your own photos by cropping, shifting the color to change the mood and adding special effects. Your computer and even your smartphone offer the power to produce a good infographic, chart or graph.

WARNING

Images not appropriate to your material annoy readers. Even with websites, research shows that contrary to popular assumption, *people value the words most and are put off by images unrelated to the subject.* Ready-made clip art available online is much better than it used to be. But choose carefully and customize it when you can to avoid cheapening your message in the viewer's eye. Generally, it's best to keep visual style consistent — all cartoons or all photographs, for example.

For websites, resist the temptation to use stock photos of people: those depictions of good-looking models talking or working carefully balanced for age, gender and ethnicity. "Real" people are more interesting and convincing even though imperfect by model standards. If your business doesn't lend itself to showing people, exercise imagination to come up with other visual representations of what you do or what you mean.

Breaking space up with sidebars, boxes and lists

Today print media increasingly rely on graphic techniques to draw readers in with as much variety as they can devise. "Captive audiences" are few and far between! Interest must be captured, and kept, whatever the medium and message. Think about how we all scan to decide if an email, article, blog or book is worth our time and how easily our attention can be lost. Your tools for capturing and maintaining attention include good active headlines and subheads. Also pay major attention to creating:

>> Abstracts, which are small compelling summaries or introductions to an article, proposal or report

>> Captions to accompany photos and other images, preferably with interesting information not covered in the copy

>> Interesting quotes or tidbits used as "pullouts" or "pull quotes" in the margins or inside the text

>> Sidebars and boxes with additional background, sidelights or information or examples

>> Bulleted or numbered lists of examples or steps

>> Icons (such as the Tip and Remember icons in this book) that denote something of special interest

All these devices serve three important purposes. Along with images, they

>> **Break up unrelieved blocks of type that discourage the eye.** Traditionally, print editors used the "dollar bill test": If you can lay down a bill on a page and it doesn't touch a single graphic device, add one in.

>> **Capture reader attention in different ways.** A summary, a caption or a box may draw someone to read the whole piece, or at least some of it.

>> **Help to convey ideas and information more clearly and effectively.** People absorb information in different ways. Taking lessons from the online world, today's editors offer readers choices of what they want to read, where they choose to start and degree of depth they are motivated to pursue.

REMEMBER

Good graphic thinking should be part of your writing repertoire. Do you need these devices for every email you write? Of course not. But if you're delivering a sales pitch, they certainly provide more impact. Even many emails benefit from techniques that make what you write more clear, accessible, attractive and memorable. Simple strategies like using subheads and bullets can help get your message across. For long documents and materials whose goal is persuasion, draw on all the techniques that suit your goals, audience, nature of your message and the medium.

The next chapter introduces you to the editing stage of writing. If like most people you've never given much thought to this process, or it strikes fear into your heart, not to worry. Common sense can take you a long way and a batch of professional tricks does the rest. Once you discover how beautifully self-editing can strengthen your messages, I think you'll become a believer.

Chapter **4**

Self-Editing: Professional Ways to Improve Your Work

I f you expect to create a successful email, letter or business document in just one shot, think again. Don't ask so much of yourself. Very few professional writers can accomplish a finished piece — whether they write novels, plays, articles, websites or press releases — with their first draft. This especially includes writers known for their simplicity and easy reading.

Editing is how writers write. For them, the writing and editing processes are inseparable because they wouldn't dream of submitting work to anyone that is less than their very best. Unfortunately, many people are intimidated by the notion of editing their own work. But equipped with effective methods and techniques, many of which are based on common sense, you can edit with confidence.

Mastering hundreds of grammar rules is not necessary to becoming a good editor. Know the clues that reveal where your writing needs work, and you can sharpen what you write so it accomplishes exactly what you want. This chapter gives you the groundwork.

Changing Hats: From Writer to Editor

The writer and editor roles reinforce each other and are backed by proofreading:

» In writing, you plan your message or document based on what you want to accomplish and your analysis of the reader (which is discussed in Chapter 2), brainstorm content possibilities, organize logically and create a full draft. Always think of this piece as the *first draft* because every message, whatever its nature and length, deserves editing and will always benefit from it.

» In editing, you review your first draft and find ways to liven word choice, simplify sentences and ensure your ideas hang together. You also evaluate the "macro" side: whether the content and tone deliver the strongest message to your audience and help build relationships. Furthermore, as you make a habit of regularly editing your messages, your first-draft writing improves as well.

» In proofreading, you review your writing in nitty-gritty detail to find and correct errors — mistakes in spelling, grammar, punctuation, facts, references, citations, calculations and more as relevant to the material. Never skip this step because mistakes that look like mistakes undermine all your good thinking and damage your credibility.

TIP

Don't expect to bypass the whole editing process down the line as you further refine your writing abilities. Professional writers never stop relying on their editing skills, no matter how good they become at their craft. The following tools and tricks make you a more capable and confident self-editor and thus, a better writer.

Choosing a way to edit

You have three main ways to edit writing. Try each of the following and see which you prefer — but realize you can always switch your editing method to best suit a current writing task or timeline.

Option 1: Mark up print-outs

For about a century before computers, people wrote on typewriters, revised the results on "hard copy" by hand, and often retyped the entire document. If you were reviewing *printer's proofs* — preliminary versions of material to be printed — you used a shorthand set of symbols to tell the typesetter what to change.

These symbols offered uniformity; every editor and printer knew what they meant. The marks are still used today and remain a helpful way to communicate text changes. To find a set of these symbols with examples, just look up "printer's proof marks" in your favorite search engine.

Many professional writers still edit their work on print-outs because on-screen editing strains the eyes and makes us more error-prone. You may find physically editing your copy with universal marks to be more satisfying. Editing on paper can help you more easily switch over to the editor's side of the table. Of course, you must then transfer the changes to your computer.

Proof marks vary between the United States and the United Kingdom, and some organizations have their own special marks or special meanings.

Option 2: Edit on-screen

After you draft a document, you can simply read through it and make changes: Substitute words, fix grammar and reorganize the material by cutting and pasting with a few mouse clicks or keystrokes. The down side to this method of editing is that you're left with no record of the change process. (See Option 3 for a useful alternative.)

When maintaining a copy of your original text matters, save your new version as a separate document. Amend its name to avoid hassle later should a series of revised versions develops.

Keep your renaming simple yet specific. If the document is titled "Gidget," title the edited version "Gidget 2" or "Gidget.v2," for example, or date it "Gidget 11.13." When you edit someone else's document, tack on your initials: "nc.Gidget," for example. Title in a way that makes sense to you, but be sure it allows you to easily identify various versions to avoid time-wasting confusion later.

Option 3: Track your changes

Most word-processing software offers a handy feature to record every change you make to the text in a document. In Microsoft Word, for example, select the Review tab and you'll see a tracking pane. Click Track Changes "On" and edit away. You can delete and add words, fix spelling and grammar and move pieces around at will.

Changes will show up on the copy in a color other than black and/or in small text boxes off to the side (depending on your choice of screen view). Deletions appear as strikethrough text or off to the side. You can add "comments" to yourself, or if you're sharing the document, enter comments to the other readers.

The system takes some personal trial and error but is flexible. It's easy to change your mind about a correction or substitution and revert the text back to the original. It works well when the editor and writers are different people, too. You can easily see someone else's changes and decide whether to accept them or not.

However, when you're tracking changes on a heavily edited document, you can end up with something quite complicated. Just choose to view the document as "Final" with all your proposed changes incorporated, or opt not to view insertions and deletions, depending on your version of Word. You don't lose your edits; they're just hidden from immediate sight.

When you finish editing, save a version that shows the revisions, then go back to the Review tab and choose "Accept" or "Reject" changes. Accept all changes or go through your document section by section or even sentence by sentence. You emerge with a clean copy; save this version separately from the original. Proof the new version carefully because new errors creep in when you edit. Always.

TIP

Word's Track Changes tool can help you improve your writing process and offers a way to share refinement stages with others when needed. (Numerous online tools, such as Google Docs, also help you share document development and preserve changes.) But when you ultimately send the message to your audience, be sure your final saved version does not reveal the change process: Turn Track Changes off and make sure all changes have been accepted.

Distancing yourself from what you write

REMEMBER

The first step for a self-editor is to consciously assume that role. A professional I know keeps a special hat and puts it on to help him switch roles. Forget how hard some of the material was to draft, or how attached you are to some of the ideas or language. Aim to judge as objectively as you can how well your message succeeds in the goals you set, and find ways to strengthen it.

Your best tool to achieve this distance is the one that cures all ills: time. In Chapter 2, I suggest that you accord equal weight to the importance of planning, drafting and editing. But ideally, don't edit in the same seamless time frame as the first two stages.

TIP

Try to build in a pause between drafting and editing. Pausing overnight (or longer) is highly recommended for major business documents. If your document is really long or important, try to edit and re-edit in a series of stages over days or even weeks. Some copy, such as a website home page or marketing piece, may never be "finished." It evolves over time.

For short and/or less consequential messages, an hour or two between drafting and editing helps. A top-of-your-head email or text message that doesn't seem important can still land you in a lot of trouble if you send it out without vetting. Take what time you can to clear your mind and refresh your eyes so you can look at the words with your editor eye.

HOW "CORRECT" MUST WRITING BE?

You probably don't need the full range of sharpening tools for everything you write. But consider that you can't always know what is "important." When life and work blend closely as they do for most of us today, careless notes to a friend can cost you referrals or recommendations down the line. It may surprise you to know that your peer network is more important to your career in the long run than the people you now report to. And while a good argument can be made for complete informality and inattention to rules when you use instant messaging applications like Slack, users complain about unnecessary and confusing messages that waste their time. Half-baked thinking and sloppy writing in any venue signal a disrespect for the reader and creates inefficiency.

That said, texting and dedicated chat applications challenge the need to write perfectly. In deciding how "correct" a message or document should be, consider how important the result is to you and who will read it. Beyond these basics, each medium suggests its own guidelines. Here is my take on the varying benchmarks. These ideas are fully covered in the upcoming chapters on specific media, but a broad perspective is useful.

- **Text messaging and team chat tools:** Benchmarks for messaging applications such as Slack, Google Hangouts, Microsoft Teams, Chanty and so on, are clarity, conciseness and necessity: Is the message needed? Is it relevant to all recipients? These tools are best used to address a single matter at a time, but avoid peppering colleagues with unending questions or comments and don't ask for instant responses.

- **Email:** The degree of correctness depends. Email ranges from chat equivalent to everyday messages to formal proposals, letters, job applications, reports and so on. But even workaday messages via email are more permanent than texting — and the categories listed earlier demand your best error-free writing. Edit all email, but the degree of formality can vary.

- **Letters:** Other than the completely personal, letters are typically important and often stand-alone documents or introductions. They merit thorough editing.

- **Business documents:** Documents such as reports, proposals, white papers and résumés need to say "trust me!" They must be letter-perfect in readability, spelling, grammar and appearance. Ideally aim for a somewhat formal but confident and conversational tone.

- **Video and presentations:** A spoken script, speech or visual presentation must *sound* good with short words and sentences and have a good cadence. Sentence fragments and other rhetorical effects can and at times should skirt grammar to engage the audience and carry the message concisely and perhaps dramatically.

(continued)

(continued)

- **Online material:** Goals of material that is intended to be posted online are ease and speed of reading. A dynamic feeling helps. For websites, go for short, concrete words, sentences and paragraphs. Distill the message and take care with the visuals. Break grammar rules creatively, but beware the appearance of mistakes. This applies to blogs, online profiles and even posted comments — when viewers don't know you, they judge you and anything you're selling by how you write! Spelling counts.

Reviewing the Big and Small Pictures

Your job when self-editing is to review what you wrote on two levels:

>> **The macro level:** The thinking that underlies the message and the content decisions you made

>> **The micro level:** How well you use language to express your viewpoint and ask for what you want

Let's look at both.

Assessing content success

Start your edit with a big-picture review, leveraging the mental distance you gained by putting the piece aside for a while.

REMEMBER

Read through the entire document and ask yourself:

>> Is what I want clear from reading the message?

>> Does the content support that goal?

>> Is anything missing from my argument, my sequence of thoughts or my explanations? Do I include all necessary backup?

>> Do I give the reader a reason to care?

>> Do I include any ideas or statements that don't contribute to my central goal or that detract from it?

>> Does the tone feel right for the person or group I'm communicating with?

>> Does the whole message present "me" in the best possible light?

>> Are there any ways my reader can possibly misunderstand or misinterpret my words?

>> How will the readers *feel* when they read this? How would *I* feel? What will the readers *do*?

Consider: Based on this message, would *I* give *me* what I want?

The initial editing challenge is to drill to the core of your message. If you followed the step-by-step process presented in Chapter 2 to create the document, check now that you met your own criteria and that every element works to accomplish your goal. Your objective answers to these nine questions may lead you to partially or substantially revamp your content. That's fine — there's no point working to improve presentation until you have the right substance.

Also consider at this point whether the message *length* is right. Aim always for "just enough": Too much information dilutes impact and may lose your reader. But length often depends on the nature of the document. If you're responding to a ten-page RFP (request for proposal), for example, a one-page response is probably insufficient. But you may need to write a single paragraph summarizing your whole career for a cover letter. You may choose to do the big-picture revision right away or plan for it and proceed to the second stage, the micro-level of editing: crafting the words. It's much easier to make the language more effective when you know exactly what message you want to deliver.

Assessing your language

You have two ways to get instant, objective feedback on how well you used language:

>> **Use a readability index.** Most word-processing software can give you a good overview of the difficulty of any written piece. As Chapter 3 details, Microsoft Word's Readability Statistics box provides helpful information on word, sentence and paragraph length; the number of passive constructions; and the degree of ease with which people can read and understand your message. Use these statistics to pinpoint how you can improve your sentences and word choices.

>> **Read it aloud.** This is the favorite method for many writers. As you speak your writing quietly — even under your breath — you identify problems in flow, clarity and word choice. Asking someone else to read your words aloud to you can put you even more fully in the listener role.

In addition to telling you whether you achieved a conversational tone, the read-aloud test alerts you to eight specific problems common to poor writing (I recommend solutions to the first four of these problems in Chapter 3):

>> **Problem 1:** A sentence is so long it takes you more than one breath to get through it.

   Solution: Break it up or shorten it.

>> **Problem 2:** You hear a monotonous pattern with each sentence starting the same way.

   Solution: Change some of the sentence structures so you alternate between long and short, simple and complex.

>> **Problem 3:** All or most sentences sound short and choppy, which creates an abrupt tone and dulls the content.

   Solution: Combine some sentences to make the read smoother.

>> **Problem 4:** You stumble over words.

   Solution: Replace those words with simpler ones, preferably words that are one or two syllables long.

The read-aloud method can reveal four additional challenges. We look at each problem in greater detail in following sections, but here's a quick overview.

>> **Problem 5:** You hear yourself using an up-and-down inflection to get through a sentence.

   Solution: Make the sentence less complicated.

>> **Problem 6:** You hear repeated sounds produced by words ending in *-ize, -ion, -ing, -ous, -ly* or another suffix.

   Solution: Restructure the sentence to minimize words that end these ways.

>> **Problem 7:** You notice numerous prepositional phrases repeated or strung together — of, with, in, to, for.

   Solution: Change your wording so fewer prepositions are needed.

>> **Problem 8:** You hear words repeated in the same paragraph.

   Solution: Find substitutes.

REMEMBER

If you read your copy aloud and practice the fix-it techniques discussed in Chapter 3 and the following sections, you give yourself a gift: the ability to bypass grammar lessons. After you know how to spot a problem, you can use shortcut tools to correct it. Even better, you can track your own patterns and prevent the problems from happening.

CAN I JUST RELY ON THE COMPUTER TO FIX MY GRAMMAR AND SPELLING?

In a word, no. Thanks to AI — artificial intelligence — autocorrect software and apps are improving all the time. The problem is they're guessing at what you mean and which words you intend! And they often guess wrong. Often these programs can't distinguish between words that sound similar and will substitute entirely different words. Your smartphone "helps" you choose words and phrases via algorithms. I estimate that it wrongly anticipates the word I want to type 40 percent of the time. That's a lot of potential miscommunication! Moreover, machine-corrected grammar doesn't take account of desired tone or impact.

So, use these tools judiciously. View their grammar advice as questions and decide if you agree with the changes they suggest. Read the message through to see if the words are right. Using the wrong word when it's key to your message can be disastrous, no matter how well it's spelled.

Everyone writes with his or her own personal patterns. The better handle you gain on your own patterns, the better your writing and the faster you achieve results.

Now for some detail on handling Problems 5, 6, 7 and 8. Here is a series of shortcuts.

Avoiding telltale up-down-up inflection

SHORTCUT

"Fancy" words, excess phrases and awkward constructions force sentences into an unnatural pattern when read aloud. The effect is rather like the typical up-down-up-down cadence of the tattletale: **I** know who **DID** it.

For example, read the following sentence aloud and see what pattern you force on your voice:

All of the writing that is published is a representation of our company, so spelling and grammatical errors can make us look unprofessional and interfere with the public perception of us as competent businesspeople.

Visually scanning the sentences also tips you off to its wordiness. This single sentence contains two phrases using "of," two statements with the passive verb "is," and three words ending in "-ion." This produces an awkward wordy construction. Plus, the sentence contains 34 words — far more than the average 18 I recommend — and more than five words have three or more syllables (see Chapter 3).

You don't need to be a linguistic rocket scientist to write a better sentence. Just go for simple and clear. Break up the long sentence. Get rid of the unnecessary words and phrases. Substitute shorter friendlier words. One way:

All our company's writing represents us. Spelling and grammar errors make us look unprofessional and incompetent.

After you simplify, you can often find a third, even better way to shape the sentence. A third pass might read:

When we make spelling and grammar mistakes, we look unprofessional and incompetent.

Looking for repeat word endings

SHORTCUT

Big clues to wordy, ineffective sentences come with overused suffixes — words ending in *-ing, -ive, -ion, -ent, -ous* and *-ly*. Almost always, these words are three or more syllables and French or Latinate in origin, and signify abstractions. Several in a sentence make you sound pompous and outdated. They often force you into convoluted, passive constructions that weaken your writing and discourage readers.

TIP

Avoid using a string of these words in a single sentence. Try for one per sentence, two at most. Find these stuffy words either visually, by scanning what you write, or orally — read the material out loud and you'll definitely notice when they clutter up your sentences.

The following sections demonstrate some examples of overly suffixed wording and how to fix it. If you are unenthusiastic about grammar lessons, proceed happily: My goal is to help you develop a *feel* for well-put-together sentences and how to build them. Once you notice problems, you can correct them without thinking about rules.

Use fewer -ing words

Consider this sentence:

You may not initially find the challenge of improving your writing to be inspiring, but the result will be gratifying.

One short sentence with four words ending in *-ing!* Read it aloud and you find yourself falling into that up-down-up inflection. You can fix it by trimming down to one *-ing* word:

The challenge of improving how you write may not inspire you at first, but the results will reward you well.

Here's a sentence I wrote for this chapter:

Besides, there's something more satisfying about physically editing your copy and using the universal markings.

I didn't spot the five words that end in *-ing* until my third round of editing! Once you see a problem like this, play with the words to eliminate it. Then check that it matches your original intent. I rewrote the sentence this way:

Besides, you may find it more satisfying to physically edit your copy with the universal marks.

REMEMBER

When you're both the writer and editor, you're doubly responsible for knowing what you want to say. Fuzzy, verbose writing often results from your own lack of clarity. So, when you spot a technical problem, think first about whether a simple word fix will work. But realize that you may need to rethink your content more thoroughly. After you know exactly what you want to say, a better way to write the sentence emerges, like magic. This is how writing helps you think better.

When you edit other peoples' work, knowing the writers' intent is harder. You may not understand what they're going for, and then it's all too easy to shift the meaning when you try to clarify. You may need to ask the author to interpret the original material. Or make the changes and as appropriate, check that they are okay. Don't be surprised if the writer objects. The writer/editor partnership is often a tense one.

Reduce -ion words

The following is cluttered with *-ion* words and incredibly dull:

To attract the attention of the local population, with the intention of promoting new construction, we should mention recent inventions that reduce noise pollution.

Reading aloud makes this sentence's unfriendliness instantly clear. Also, note that piling up lots of *-ion* words leads to an awkward passive sentence structure.

The problem with too many *-ion* words can be way more subtle, as in this sentence from an otherwise careful writer:

Whether they are organizing large demonstrations, talking with pedestrians in the street or gathering signatures for a petition, their involvement was motivated by the realization that as individuals within a larger group, they had the potential to influence and bring about change.

In addition to four words with the *-ion* suffix, the sentence also contains three ending in *-ing*. The result is a rambling, hard to follow, overly long sentence that feels abstract and distant. This sentence is challenging to fix. One way:

> *They organized large demonstrations, talked with pedestrians and gathered signatures. Their motivation: Knowing that as individuals, they could influence and bring about change.*

Does it say exactly the same thing as the original? Perhaps not, but it's close. And more likely to be read.

Notice that after I cut down the *-ion* and *-ing* words, some of the cluttered phrases become more obvious:

>> Of course, pedestrians are "in the street" — so why say it?

>> The phrases "for a petition" and "had the potential" are both overkill.

TIP

Always look for phrases that add nothing or offer unnecessary elaboration — and cut them. Your writing will improve noticeably.

Downsize -ize words

Similar to *-ion* and *-ing* words, more than one *-ize* per sentence works against you. Consider the following:

> *He intended to utilize the equipment to maximize the profit and minimize the workforce.*

TIP

You rarely need these kinds of Latinate words at all. In line with the principle of using short, simple words as much as possible, shift *utilize* to *use* and *maximize* to *raise*. And you can more honestly state *minimize* as *cut*. Note how multi-syllable words are usually embedded in abstract statements that distance us from a feeling of reality.

Modern business language keeps inventing *-ize* words, essentially creating new verbs from nouns. Here's a sentence that contains two of my least favorite words:

> *He knew that incentivizing the agreement might not succeed in impacting trade in a positive manner.*

"Incentivizing" and "impacting" are among the nouns that have recently morphed into verbs through common practice. I try to avoid their use but acknowledge that living language seeks to fill in its deficits and also serve our appetite for speed. Without "incentivize," we'd need to say "offering an incentive." "Impacting" is a stronger word than "affecting," and more compact than "has an impact on."

Minimize -ment, -ly and -ous words

Words with these suffixes are usually complicated versions of words available in simpler forms.

A silly example that combines all these forms shows how using long words forces you into that unnatural rhythm, passive structure and wordy phrases full of unnecessary prepositional phrases:

Continuous investment in the anonymously conceived strategic plan recently proved to be an impediment to the actualization and inadvertently triggered the anomaly.

WARNING

Unfortunately, much modern business writing is filled with convoluted language, clichés and hyperbole at the expense of substance. When you try to edit some of it — such as this extreme example — you're left with . . . nothing at all. The fact that no one is impressed with empty writing, or likes to read it, doesn't stop people from producing it by the virtual ton. This is a mystery I can't solve.

But I'm hopeful: Research is under way to correlate good writing and communication with the bottom line. Willis Towers Watson, a global management consulting firm, conducts high-profile surveys on the financial impact of effective communication, and the American Management Association is interested in the ROI-writing connection. The *Harvard Business Review* issues a growing abundance of material on executive communication. Meanwhile, the lesson is clear: Don't write in empty business-speak — it won't reward you. Just hope that your competitors keep writing that way.

Pruning prepositions

SHORTCUT

Another way to reduce wordiness is to look for unnecessary prepositional phrases — that is, expressions that depend on words like *of, to, from, for* and *in.* Here again a good general rule is to avoid repeating the same form of speech in a single sentence whenever possible. For example:

Original: Our mission is to bring awareness of the importance of good writing to the people of the business community.

Revised: Our mission is to build the business community's awareness that good writing matters.

A sentence with unnecessary prepositions is often clumsy:

Original: He invested ten years in the development of a system to improve the performance of his organization.

Revised: He spent ten years developing a system to improve his organization's performance.

Original: Can it possibly be interpreted as a mistake by a reader?

Revised: Can a reader possibly interpret it as a mistake?

And notice that when you cut prepositions, you discover additional ways to improve a sentence. Some examples of this progressive thinking:

Original: Here are some of the imperatives of becoming a good communicator.

Revised: Here are some imperatives of becoming a good communicator.

Better: Here is how to become a good communicator.

Original: Research is needed to evaluate the potential for each idea.

Revised: Research is needed to evaluate each idea's potential.

Better: We need to research each idea's potential.

Original: Writing the proposal is necessary for clarifying your goal.

Revised: Writing a proposal will clarify your goal.

Better: Writing a proposal clarifies your goal.

TIP

Notice how weak wording generates more weak wording — passive verbs and over-use of prepositions come in bundles. Fix one problem in a sentence and you are easily able to identify and fix others. This lets you take different routes toward improvement. You can consciously look for extra "little words" in a sentence, for example, especially when they repeat. The read-aloud editing method works well for this.

Here are a few more ways to reduce your wordy phrases:

>> **Use an apostrophe.** Why say the *trick of the accountant,* when you can say *the accountant's trick?* Why write *the favorite product of our customers,* when you can write *our customers' favorite product? Each idea's potential* works better than *the potential for each idea."*

Here's a sentence I wrote and reconsidered:

The writer clearly understood the worries that neighbors would have based on their prior experiences with construction work.

Version 2:

The writer clearly understands the neighbors' worries based on their prior experience with construction work.

» **Combine two words and remove an apostrophe.** The phrase *build the community's awareness* can also read well as *build community awareness*.

» **Use a hyphen.** Rework the CEO's *fixation on the bottom* line to the CEO's *bottom-line fixation*.

Cutting all non-contributor words

Extra words that don't support your meaning dilute writing strength. Aim for concise. Use the set of clues I describe in the preceding sections and zero in on individual sentences for ways to tighten. Here's a case in point:

With the use of this new and unique idea, it will increase the profits for the magazine in one particular month, July.

Extra words hurt the sentence's readability and generate bad grammar. Even though the sentence is fairly short, it manages to jam in two prepositions (*of* and *for*), an altogether useless phrase (*with the use of*), and an unnecessary word repetition — *new* and *unique*. Of course, the sentence construction is confusing as a result. A better version:

This new idea will increase the magazine's profits, particularly in July.

Consider this explanation of Track Changes that I wrote:

Now when you make a change, the alteration is indicated in a color and any deletion is shown on the right.

The rewrite:

Your changes then show up in color, and deletions appear outside the text on the far right.

The revision works better because it eliminates unnecessary words and with them, the passive construction of *alteration is indicated* and *deletion is shown*.

TIP

Take aim at common phrases that slow down reading. Substitute simple words. Often you can substitute single words for formal, space-wasting phrases. The words on the left are almost always non-contributors; choose those on the right.

Wordy	Better
at this time	now
for the purpose of	for, to
the reason for that	because
in accordance with	under
is able to	can
it is necessary that	must, should
in an effort to	to
in order to	to
in regard to	about
in the amount of	for
in the event of	if
in anticipation of	before
in the near future	soon
on the occasion of	when
is indicative of	indicates
is representative of	represents
regardless of the fact that	although
on a daily basis	daily

Try This: Track your own wordiness. When you write, notice which wordy phrases you often use. We all do it. Begin a list and add to it for a while. Then write in more concise substitutes, as in my list. Consciously use the short more effective versions and your writing will move a big step forward.

PUTTING EMOJI, TEXTING AND INSTANT MESSAGING INTO PERSPECTIVE

Early cultures chipped their messages, whether based on pictographs or an alphabet, into stone tablets and monuments. This was such hard going that they jammed in whole strings of abbreviations and acronyms, and also depended on word shortcuts and omissions to make their point. We humans have always looked for faster and easier ways to communicate both everyday transactions and big ideas — and we're still looking. In this context, instant messaging (IM) and texting, with abbreviation and word skipping, make perfect sense. Typing on the miniscule keyboards of our smartphones more or less demands it. Language experts point out a plus — it teaches conciseness.

But you can't assume everyone understands the abbreviations and symbols or likes communicating with them. Readers who are comfortable with texting shortcuts may still expect a more formal style in other media, including email. So don't risk your effectiveness by transferring informal texting strategies to other business writing. Limit it to appropriate media and audiences that you're sure will respond well.

And emoji? In a way they bring us back to pictographs, the earliest form of writing. They were popularized by members of Generation Z (those folks born after 1997). Today many people use them to convey emotions and sentiments, traditionally absent from alphabet-based language. But like IM and texting, emoji pose a problem in terms of your audiences: Some may not understand and will misinterpret them. Generally speaking, older people tend to lag behind in adopting new communication trends. Even younger readers may not consider these forms appropriate for business use. If you like to sprinkle emoji and GIFs around your emails, first visualize your readers and how they may react. Smiley faces at least are fairly universal today, but hesitate to use even these in an initial communication with someone you don't know. And if you personally have only a light familiarity with emoji, think twice about using them to look cool — a good many have subtle implications and you may find yourself heartily embarrassed!

Bottom line: Know your audiences and "mirror" them in their use of emoji and other creative devices. If they're integral to a channel like Slack in your organization, use them insofar as you're comfortable. But remember that writing in a manner your readers may not understand or relate to never makes sense.

All that said, a trend toward general acceptance of emoji is clear. Research suggests that emails with emoji in their subject lines, for example, are opened a lot more often.

Moving from Passive to Active

Over-using the passive usually signals careless and ineffective writing. Sentences based on passive verbs — forms of *to be* — are often forced into convoluted shapes that are wordy and hard for readers to untangle. Worse, all those *to be* verbs make writing so dull that many readers don't even want to try. Let's look at passive verbs from the editing angle.

SHORTCUT

Active verbs say everything more directly, clearly, concisely and colorfully. If you want to transform everything you write — quickly — pay attention to verbs and build your sentences around energetic ones.

Thinking "action"

Active voice and action verbs are not the same thing grammatically, but for practical purposes, just remember to cut back on the following word choices:

>> **Is + an -ed ending:** *Your attention is requested.*

>> **Are + an -ed ending:** *The best toys are created by scientists.*

>> **Were + an -ed ending:** *The company executives were worried about poor writers who failed to build good customer relations.*

>> **Was + an -ed ending:** *The computer was delivered by Jenny.*

>> **Will be + have + an -ed ending:** *We will be happy to have finished studying grammar.*

>> **Would be + an -ed ending:** *The CEO said a new marketing plan would be launched next year.*

The solution in every case is the same: Figure out *who* does *what* and rephrase the idea accordingly:

>> *We request your attention. Or, pay attention!*

>> *Scientists create the best toys.*

>> *Company executives worry that bad writers fail to build good relationships.*

>> *Jenny delivered the computer.*

>> *We're happy to finish studying grammar.*

>> *The CEO plans to launch a new marketing plan next year.*

Verbs endings with *-en* raise the same red flag as those ending in *-ed*. For example, *I will be taken to Washington by an India Airways plane* is better expressed as *An India Airways plane will fly me to Washington* or *I will fly to Washington on India Airways*.

SHORTCUT

Think present tense! Changing passive-style verbs to present or simple past tense as often as possible will transform your writing. Rid a sentence of a *to be* verb, and you win a chance to bring your message to life with an active, interesting one. Many professionals work this tactic out on their own through years of trial and error (trust me on this). Writing in the present tense takes a bit more thought at first but quickly becomes a habit. Use present tense everywhere you can and catapult your writing to a whole new level.

To do this, scan your sentences to spot *is, are* and the other *to be* verbs. Often, you can find a way to use a present-tense verb. Look for the important action — "is," for example, often functions as a placeholder word without specific meaning. For example, the following sentence:

> *He is still a pest to the whole office about correct grammar.*

Is better stated as,

> *He still pesters the whole office about correct grammar.*

Or another verb may distract attention from the action that matters. This sentence:

> *Michael succeeded in breaking the pattern of expectancy.*

is more effective and engaging as,

> *Michael broke the pattern of expectancy.*

Trimming "there is" and "there are"

TIP

Big-time culprits in the passive sweepstakes are the combinations *there is* and *there are*. This problem is easy to fix — just commit never to start a sentence with either. Keep away from *there will be, there have been* and all the variations. Don't bury them inside your sentences, either.

Check out the following examples and improvements:

> **Original:** *There were 23 references to public relations in the report.*
>
> **Revised:** *The report cited public relations 23 times.*

Original: *There is a helpful section called "new entries" at the top of the page.*

Revised: *A helpful section called "new entries" appears at the top of the page.*

Original: *It's expected that in the future, there will be easier ways to communicate.*

Revised: *We expect easier ways to communicate in the future.*

In every case, using an active verb does the trick.

Cutting the haves and have nots

Like the *to be* verbs, using the various forms of the verb *to have* signals lazy writing. Find substitute words and a faster way to say what you mean as often as possible. A few examples and possible rewrites:

Original: *I have not been able to revise the proposal in time to meet the deadline.*

Revised: *I didn't meet the proposal deadline.*

Original: *Here's what can be accomplished this year provided I have cooperation from the relevant people.*

Revised: *Here's what I can accomplish this year if the relevant people cooperate.*

Original: *We have to make use of the talents we have.*

Revised: *We must use our own talents.*

Here's a sentence that uses two "haves." How would you rewrite it?

> *We have anecdotal evidence that it works, but in order to get the clinical community interested, there's a robustness of data we need to have.*

Often there is more than one way to fix a sentence, just as with any problem. Here's my version — yours may be different and as good or better:

> *Anecdotal evidence suggests it works, but to interest the clinical community, we need robust data.*

Using the passive deliberately

Despite all the reasons for minimizing passive sentences, passive verbs are not "bad." You need them on occasions when the "actor" is obvious, unknown or unimportant, or is the punchline. For example:

The computer was developed in its modern form over a number of years.

After long trial and error, the culprit was finally identified as the Red Toad.

You can also make a case for using the passive voice when you need to frame a message in terms of *you* rather than *we* or *I*. When writing to a customer, for example, you may begin more effectively,

Your satisfaction with the product is what we care about most.

Rather than,

We care most about your satisfaction with the product.

The second statement gives the impression that "it's all about us." Of course, don't write an *entire* letter like the first opening — just the first sentence.

The passive is also useful when you don't want to sound accusatory. *The bill has not been paid* is more neutral than *You failed to pay the bill.*

Sidestepping Jargon, Clichés and Extra Modifiers

Relying on words that have little meaning wastes valuable message space and slows down reading. Overused expressions also dilute impact, and "insider" language can confuse "outside" readers. Jargon, clichés, buzzwords and unhelpful adjectives are hallmarks of ineffective business writing.

Reining in jargon

Almost every specialized profession has its *jargon:* terminology and symbols that shortcut communication and in some cases, make group members feel more professional and "inside." If physicists write to other physicists, they don't need to spell out the formulas, symbols and technical language. The audience shares a common knowledge base.

Similarly, lawyers can write to colleagues in the peculiar language they mastered through education and practice. A musician can exchange performance notes with other musicians in a way that means little to non-musicians.

The risk arises when people talk or write to anyone other than fellow-specialists and use inside jargon. They forget that the general public does not share their professional language. If, for example, you're a scientist who needs to explain your work to a journalist, report on progress to company executives, order supplies, negotiate employment or chat at a party, it's best to skip the scientific jargon entirely or tactfully explain it.

Outside of our own specialized fields, we are all generalists. We want to be addressed in clear, simple language we can immediately understand.

But business writers face an additional challenge. A specialized, jargon-laden language flourishes full of buzzwords that means little — even to those who use it. For example, a technology company states in a publication:

> *These visible IT capabilities along with IT participation in the project identification process can drive the infusion of IT leverage on revenue improvement in much the same way as IT has leveraged cost cutting and efficiency.*

What does it mean? Who knows? All too often, corporate executives and consultants string together sets of buzzwords and clichés that communicate little beyond a reluctance to think. I know many editors who make good money saving some of these people from their worst utterances, but they sure don't catch them all.

Of course, sometimes a writer or organization deliberately chooses to bury a fact or a truth behind carefully selected words and phrases. Then you might argue that a message built on empty business jargon works well. But I don't recommend deliberately distorting the truth, writing without substance or masking either situation with bad writing. Doing so just doesn't work and it may boomerang.

This widely circulated Citigroup press release a while back (`www.citigroup.com/citi/news/2012/121205a.htm`) makes the company look ridiculous:

> *Citigroup today announced a series of repositioning actions that will further reduce expenses and improve efficiency across the company while maintaining Citi's unique capabilities to serve clients, especially in the emerging markets. These actions will result in increased business efficiency, streamlined operations and an optimized consumer footprint across geographies.*

Translation: *We're firing a lot of people to improve our numbers.*

To avoid producing empty business-speak, beware of using words and phrases such as the following — some are perennials, others come and go:

360-degree view	move the needle
bandwidth	optimization
bleeding edge	scalable
boots on the ground	shiny objects
core competency	swim lane
curate	take it offline
dialog (as a verb)	take it to the next level
granular	unpack
incentivize	vertical
learnings	

SHORTCUT

If you're writing a press release, website or other promotional copy, check it for buzz-wordiness by asking yourself: Could this copy be used by any company, in any industry, to describe any product or service? If I substitute down-to-earth words for the clichés, does the message have meaning? Will my 17-year-old nephew laugh when he reads it?

Cooling the clichés

Jargon can be seen as business-world clichés. English, like all languages, has an enormous trove of "general" clichés, expressions that are so overused they may lose their impact. A few random examples that can turn up in business communication: *All's well that ends well, think outside the box, barking up the wrong tree, beat around the bush, a stitch in time, read between the lines.*

Clichés are so numerous they often seem hard to avoid. Often, they're idioms, and they are found in every language. They're popular for a reason — they communicate a meaning in shorthand. And they can be used well in context. But it pays to stay on the lookout for any that don't carry your meaning or trivialize it. Instead, say what you want more simply, or perhaps develop an original comparison, as I explain in Chapter 3.

WARNING

Never forget that English idioms and clichés are sometimes confusing to non-native English speakers, so try to avoid them altogether when writing to these audiences. In fact, speakers of British, American and Australian English use different idioms, so take care with their use cross-culturally here, too. A surprisingly high number are based on sports, and different sports predominate in the various countries.

Minimizing modifiers

The best advice on using descriptive words — adjectives and adverbs — came from the great nineteenth-century American novelist Mark Twain:

> *I notice that you use plain, simple language, short words and brief sentences. That is the way to write English — it is the modern way and the best way. Stick to it; don't let fluff and flowers and verbosity creep in.*

> *When you catch an adjective, kill it. No, I don't mean utterly, but kill most of them — then the rest will be valuable. They weaken when they are close together. They give strength when they are wide apart. An adjective habit, or a wordy, diffuse, flowery habit, once fastened upon a person, is as hard to get rid of as any other vice.*

Twain wrote this advice in 1880 to a 12-year-old boy who sent him a school essay, but he's right on target for today's business communicators.

If depending on buzzwords and clichés is Sin #1 of empty business-speak, overuse of adjectives is Sin #2. Consider, for example,

> *The newest, most innovative, cutting-edge solution to the ultimate twenty-first century challenges . . .*

What, another solution?

Adopt whenever possible the fiction writer's mantra: Show, don't tell. Adjectives generally communicate little. In fiction, and especially scriptwriting, writers must find ways to bring the audience into the experience so they draw their own conclusions about whether a character makes bad decisions, is unethical, feels ugly or pretty, is suffering pain and so on.

In business writing, "show, don't tell" means giving your audience substance and detail: facts, ideas, statistics, examples — whatever it takes to prove they need your product or idea, or you. Stating that something is innovative proves nothing. Adding an adverb, such as "very" innovative, just multiplies the emptiness.

Welcome opportunities to replace empty rhetoric with substance! There's no substitute for good content. Use good writing techniques to make that content clear, straightforward and lively.

Energizing What You Write

Like everyone, you probably had the experience of creating a message or document carefully but finding on review that it's simply not very interesting. You want important material to have impact and lead people to keep reading, and ideally, buy-in. How can you accomplish that?

The right content for your chosen audience is critical. When you relate to their interests, people find you interesting. Examples, anecdotes and comparisons can bring a message to life. But good substance needs support from effective language. First consider tone. In many cases, enthusiasm is probably the highest card to play. When you apply for a job, for example, or an assignment or contract, coming across as enthusiastic gives you an edge and may even trump formal qualifications to some degree. Energetic writing carries enthusiasm and helps you present as a positive, optimistic person. Here are some of its attributes (I cover more of them in the chapters that follow):

>> A natural, logical organization with good transitions

>> Simple sentences that move the reader along quickly

>> High percentage of short, concrete words mostly drawn from basic English

>> Use of active rather than passive verbs

Almost always, I direct my last editing effort to the verbs: Can I liven them up to make the writing more engaging?

SHORTCUT

Substituting strong verbs for drab, placeholder verbs gives you the most value for time invested. Here, for example, is a sentence that offers alternatives to the bolded words:

*The U.N. is trying **formulate a deal** between the two warring factions.*

That sounds rather stuffy, so you could instead say *arrange a deal.* Better but dull.

More informal is *work out a deal,* or even more, with *pull together a deal.*

Another option is **broker a deal,** which is less commonplace and more graphic.

Yet another choice is one I saw used in a similar sentence, stating the thought this way:

*The U.N. is trying to **midwife a deal** between the two warring factions.*

Which word choice is best? Well, that depends: Who are you writing to? What is the nature of the document? You'll probably prefer one of the more common terms for an email or business document, but one of the more graphic options for an article or opinion piece. When you need to persuade others to a viewpoint, expressive wording is your ally.

How do you find strong evocative verbs? Nothing could be easier: Use an online thesaurus. As an example, consider the word *initiate*. Entering "initiate syn" (for synonym) in my search engine, I find dozens of choices that include *launch, trigger, intro, originate, pioneer, kick off, lead, break ground, embark on, set in motion, plunge in, jump into, get the show on the road* and so on.

You need not be a poet to write colorfully. Yes, the words on the list all have somewhat different meanings. So pick the one that accurately communicates what you want to say and works in context of that message's tone and purpose.

In Chapter 5, I move from focusing on sentences to creating solid paragraphs, solving organization problems, using strong transitions and fixing the technical problems that most often bedevil business writers.

Chapter 5

Fixing Common Writing Problems

As you explore in Chapter 4, good self-editing requires you to review your writing from two perspectives: your content and the presentation. This chapter drills down to specific editing issues: how to organize material, improve language and build your messages' energy and impact.

REMEMBER

Every one of us has our own writing demons, persistent problems that show up in everything we write. Happily, most of these issues fall into common categories that you can correct with common-sense approaches. This chapter gives you a repertoire of practical techniques for recognizing and addressing your own weaknesses. After you absorb them and begin putting them into practice, they enable you to head off problems *before* they pull you off-message or undermine your success.

If you need more motivation than to dramatically improve all your written communication, remember that *the process of thoughtful writing sharpens your thinking.* When you trouble to distill your meaning into direct, concise, compelling language, you clarify it for yourself as well as your readers. In a number of examples, I show you how this works. Starting with a poorly written sentence, I move it through three or four successive editing stages. All the versions may be "correct," but I think you may agree that the final one works best.

Notice as you edit your own material that each improvement opens the door to more improvement opportunities. They add up to increase the impact of your messages and documents. Editing is a powerful tool. Once you absorb this truth, you may find it well worth your time — and more fun than you may expect.

Organizing Your Document

Many people, including a number of experienced writers, say that organization is their biggest challenge. If you follow the process outlined in Chapter 2, which shows you how to plan each message within the framework of your goal and audience, you can sidestep the organization challenge substantially.

But this may not altogether solve your problems, especially when documents are lengthy or complicated, are written by more than one person or are just plain confusing. You may need to review organization at that point and reshuffle or recast material. The following techniques help. Implement them at the writing stage — or at the editing stage.

Paragraphing for logic

You may remember being told in school to establish a "thesis sentence" and develop each paragraph from that. If you found this advice a little dumbfounding, you're not alone.

TIP

Here's a much easier way to look at paragraphs. Start with the idea that each chunk of text should contain no more than three to five sentences. If you write your document that way, you avoid falling into a morass of confusing thoughts and easily achieve a logical flow of self-contained units — otherwise known as paragraphs.

If you routinely produce uninterrupted strings of sentences, don't despair: You can make the fixes later, during the editing stage. Read over what you've written and look for logical places to make breaks.

Can't decide where to insert breaks? Use the following technique:

1. **Scan your text to find places where you introduce a new idea or fact or where you change direction.**

    Break the flow into paragraphs at these points.

2. **If your paragraphs are still more than three to five sentences long, go through the whole piece again and make decisions on an experimental basis.**

   You'll check later to see if they work. The three- to five-sentence guideline is a general one that applies to print material. But an occasional one-sentence paragraph is fine and adds spark. When you write for online reading, shorter paragraphs work better, as I explain in Part 4.

3. **Look carefully at the first sentence of each newly created paragraph.**

   See whether the new first sentence makes sense in connecting with what follows or whether it connects better with the preceding paragraph. If the latter, move the sentence up a paragraph and then break to a new paragraph.

   If a sentence seems not to belong with either paragraph, it may need to stand on its own or be rephrased.

4. **Look at your paragraphs again in order and check whether any wording needs adjustment.**

   Pay particular attention to the first and last sentences of each paragraph. You want each paragraph to link to the next. Using transitions helps with this — read more about these in "Working with transitions" later in this chapter.

   If when you scan the whole message you don't like the sequence of paragraphs, fool around with shuffling them. Working with paper helps with longer documents like reports and proposals: Print the whole piece out and cut it into paragraphs, then experiment with moving the paragraphs around. Once you have a good order in place, adjust the language as necessary so that your paragraphs clearly relate to each other. You often find repeated words or whole ideas during this step, so make the necessary cuts and smooth everything out.

REMEMBER

The point of paragraphing is clarity. You want to deliver information in absorbable or usable chunks that lead from one to the next, rather than a single, long, confusing word dump.

Sometimes the reason you have trouble organizing your material is because you don't yet understand it well enough to effectively present it to others. Ask yourself: What *is* my point? What are the components of my argument? Number or list them if you haven't yet done so — you can omit the numbers later if that's better for your purpose. Also ask, am I missing critical pieces and need to add information or ideas?

Building with subheads

TIP

Another strategy for organizing, useful on its own or to supplement the paragraphing strategy described in the preceding section, is to add informative subheads. I mention subheads as an excellent graphic technique in Chapter 3. They are also useful guideposts for planning what you write, and help clarify your message applied in the editing stage.

Suppose you're a department manager writing to tell your staff that a new customer relationship management system will shortly be introduced and they are required to attend training workshops. You realize that this will be met with resistance because everyone is used to the old system, and many people resent training events.

Brainstorm the points to make (see Chapter 2) and write them as a series of descriptive subheads. Perhaps:

>> New CRM system changes how we work

>> Everyone must use it

>> System will save us time

>> System will encourage information sharing

>> Mandatory workshop training schedule to come

>> Rollout date: March 6

>> Department Q&A meeting: February 1

Arrange your subheads in a logical order. In line with the principles laid out in Chapter 2, aim to instantly engage readers by signaling that the message directly relates to them and that it's important. So, shuffle "rollout date" and "everyone must use it" to the top, and probably cover both ideas in the subject line. Then just fill in the relevant information under each heading. As you do this, additional topics may occur to you — for example, that creating support subgroups would help people adapt more easily to the new system.

Also, you want to motivate readers by appealing to the what's-in-it-for-me (WIIFM) viewpoint, so you might add a subhead like "how you will benefit." Find logical places in your sequence of subheads and add the new ones.

In your final message, discard the subheads if you wish — or polish them to read more actively, and use a consistent style. Subheads created from the brainstorming list might read, "New CRM System Rolls Out March 6," and "How CRM-2 Will

Save You Time." Subheads work well to pull your readers through a message and keep them organized as well. They'll pick up the main points even if they just scan the message and the subheads will help readers focus on the information that matters to them.

Moreover, there's a psychological effect in presenting a clearly organized message. Readers feel you've got the situation well in hand and have thoroughly thought everything out. This feeling alone inspires greater confidence in both you and the new system, making people more receptive to the change.

REMEMBER

Long, complex documents benefit from the subhead strategy, too. For a report or proposal, for example, identify the necessary sections and, rather than subheads, write a headline for each. Then write a set of subheads for each section. *This system works best if your subheads and headlines are specific and descriptive rather than just labels.* For example, a subhead that says "Treasurer's Report" will remind you to include it, but "Treasurer's Report Shows Downward Trend" delivers information that orients you — and the reader — to what's important.

Drafting headings and subheads is a great way to be sure you cover all the right bases, identify missing pieces early on and build in good organization from project start. You also break up the writing process into doable bits so it's far less formidable. Be sure to use a consistent style for all your headings. Your word-processing program offers built-in styles, so it just takes a click to apply one.

Working with transitions

Transitions, those low-key words and phrases, are like the connective tissue that holds your skeleton together and empowers you to move where you want. Transitions tell readers how all the ideas, facts and information in a piece of writing connect to each other. They grease your writing and pull people along in the direction you want to take them.

TIP

Good transitions signal good writing and good thinking. They help you organize your own ideas as a writer. And for the reader, they promote the feeling that your argument is sensible and even unassailable. Transitions are important tools for all writing — and for persuasive copy, good ones are essential.

Transitions can consist of single words, phrases or sentences. They can be put to work within a sentence, to link sentences and to connect paragraphs. Think of them in the following categories.

To continue or shift a line of thought, or indicate agreement or addition:

additionally	conversely	mainly
also	despite	nevertheless
alternatively	for example	on the other hand
and	furthermore	originally
but	however	so
consequently	in other words	sometimes

To establish a sequence or time frame:

as soon as	for now	to conclude
at the moment	later	ultimately
finally	next	
first, second, third	to begin with	

To indicate examples or emphasis:

for this reason	namely	significantly
in other words	often overlooked	surprisingly
in this case	on the positive side	

To reinforce a desired focus or tone:

at the same time	I'm sorry to say	of particular interest
counterintuitively	in the hope that	provided that
disappointingly	invariably	unfortunately
equally important	it sounds good, but	unless
given that	luckily	

Notice that the last set of words and phrases are prejudicial — that is, they orient a reader or listener to feel a certain way about what follows. Use them with awareness.

Transitions give you a good way to begin paragraphs or sections, while putting that information in context of the full message. The following are examples of whole sentences that serve as transitions:

Based on this data, we've made the following decisions.

We've considered all the information and have reached some conclusions.

We should pay special attention to the sales figures.

A number of issues need to be addressed. Our priorities:

Notice how these introductory statements set up a super-simple way to organize subsequent material, including within long, complicated documents.

As with all writing principles, there can be too much of a good thing. When you give your writing the read-aloud test and it sounds stilted and clumsy, review your transitions — you may need to remove some. Do so and you still have a well-organized, convincing message.

Working in lists: Numbers and bulleting

Lists offer an excellent way to present information in a compact, to-the-point manner. They suit readers' Internet-trained text-skimming habits, and most people are attracted to them. They also automatically promote graphic variation, another plus for your document (see Chapter 3).

Numbered lists

Use numbered lists to present sequences of events, procedures and processes. For example, a numbered list can guide readers on how to do something:

Follow these steps to sign up for the online workshop:

1. Go to the November workshops section of the company Intranet.

2. Choose "November Options."

3. Check the workshop and start date you want.

Scout actively for opportunities to organize a sequence by dates or milestones:

1. Jan. 10, Deadline 1: Submit project proposals

2. Feb. 10, Deadline 2: Finalize working plan

3. March 10, Deadline 3: Submit final budget

Numbered lists bestow a clarity that is so unambiguous, few people can misinterpret your meaning — no matter how hard they try.

TIP

You can also use numbered lists in more sophisticated ways. Bloggers use them, for example, to present blog posts in a popular and reader-friendly style: a number-centered headline followed by each numbered point, spelled out. For example:

5 Insider Secrets of Tripling Your Conversions Overnight

As I discuss in Chapter 12, many experienced bloggers think up a headline like that first, brainstorm for related ideas, and then write the copy. The Part of Tens at the end of this book follows the same pattern. This format appeals to readers and channels your knowledge in a different way, helping you uncover ideas you didn't know you had.

When I wrote "Ten (or So) Ways to Grow Your Personal Power with Writing (Chapter 15), for example, I committed to the topic because I had a few ideas to share. Then I brainstormed a list of possibilities, angling in on my knowledge base from a new perspective. I ended up with a lot more ideas than I started with.

Numbering is also a staple for presenters:

I'm going to give you five reasons why using this strategy will transform your life.

Here are 7 reasons why there will not be a war.

The technique works every time because audiences like knowing how much is ahead of them, and love ticking off the speaker's progress. It gives them easier-to-remember takeaways, too. But for a speech, limit your numbered items to avoid losing people's attention.

TIP

Make items in your lists parallel in structure — begin them with the same part of speech. And they work best visually when they're approximately the same length. Both points apply to bullets as well and are illustrated in the following section.

Bulleted lists

Between on-screen writing habits and PowerPoint-type presentations, reading has become a bullet-heavy experience.

Like numbering, bulleted lists convey information tightly and neatly. They're appropriate for summaries, checklists and information-at-a-glance. What's more, readers like them — but only up to a point. Used incorrectly, bullets can kill. Audience interest, that is.

TIP

To successfully use bulleting, take account of the guidelines outlined here.

DON'T USE TOO MANY

Research shows that people can't absorb more than about seven bullets at one go. They tune out after that because each bullet typically makes a separate point and gives little logical connection to hold onto. If you must present more than seven bullets, break them into more than one list and intersperse some narrative material.

USE THE SAME SENTENCE STRUCTURE FOR EVERY BULLET

Start each item similarly. Sentence structure must be parallel so as not to confuse readers. You can begin bullet points with action verbs, for example, such as when you present accomplishments in a résumé:

- *Innovated . . .*
- *Generated . . .*
- *Streamlined . . .*
- *Transformed . . .*
- *Mentored . . .*

Or you can compose a bullet list that starts with nouns, such as:

When you weekend in Timbuktu, be sure to pack:

- *Tropical microfiber clothing*
- *Sunglasses with a good UV coating*
- *Sunhat with extra-long visor*

WARNING

Don't be lazy and create bulleted lists of unrelated mix-and-match thoughts, like this:

Here are goals to aim for in business writing:

- *You want a conversational but professional tone.*
- *When you quote numbers, check that your readers use those systems.*
- *Don't be emotional or make things up.*
- *Jane is trying to standardize a similar look on charts and graphs.*

You can refine this list by rearranging points two through four to start like the first one:

- *You want to check that all numbers quoted are in line with systems your readers use.*
- *You want to avoid emotion or making things up.*

But that approach produces an annoying repetition of *you want*. The solution: Find an introductory sentence that covers the points you want to make. For example:

In business writing, try to use:

- *Conversational but professional style*
- *Non-emotional tone*
- *Number systems familiar to your readers*
- *Consistent style for charts and graphs*

Or, just issue orders with verbs:

In business writing:

- *Use a conversational style*
- *Avoid an emotional tone*
- *Adopt a familiar number system*
- *Include real facts and anecdotes*

PUNCTUATE AND FORMAT BULLETS CONSISTENTLY

You can choose from a number of variables. In this book, the first phrase or sentence in a bulleted list is sometimes set in bold, and I don't use periods at the ends of bullet points that aren't complete sentences. In some bulleted lists, each item begins with a capital letter (that's the *For Dummies* style). In others, they're all lowercase.

The styles you choose for punctuation and formatting depend on specific situations and your organization's style guide, if it has one. Many organizations develop style guides that cover most aspects of writing and graphic presentation because consistency is important to branding. Without a guide, or if you're on your own, achieve your own consistency with a commercial style guide. *For Dummies* uses a combination of its own style and the *Chicago Manual of Style,* which is suitable for books. The *AP Stylebook* (Associated Press) is also commonly used and because it is based on journalism practice, I find it better geared to the speed reading most business writing should aim for.

GIVE BULLET POINTS CONTEXT AND CONNECTION

WARNING

Don't use bullet points as independent statements that don't relate to each other, especially if you're trying to convince people of something or want them to remember your points. Tell readers what your bullets mean with good narrative writing or a quick introduction that puts the bullets in context. In a bio or résumé, for example, using all bullets to describe your assets defies readability. Begin with a well-written overall description of your current job followed by a list of your accomplishments, putting the information in context. For example, a job description can say "Consistent performance beyond company goals for three years," followed by your bulleted evidence (but no more than five to seven, and stated in sentences with parallel construction).

Don't take the lazy way out and use bullets and numbered lists to share information that needs to be persuasive — which applies to most material you write. These formats may be fast to draft, but they're best used to support an idea or significant statement. Take a hard look during the editing stage to see if your material might present more persuasively in narrative form, either in part or whole, or by translating some portions into a visual, such as a table or graph.

Catching Common Mistakes

Unlike the common cold, common writing problems can be treated and even prevented. The prescription is simple: Know your own mistakes, which you will find to be surprisingly consistent once you start to develop your awareness.

Improving your grammar is somehow a personal thing, so if you want more technical grounding, I recommend you scout what's out there in books and on the Internet. Choose a resource compatible with your learning style and dig in.

My grammar-related goal in this book is to

>> Raise your consciousness so that you recognize your own problems and fix them with practical approaches that minimize the need to master grammar.

>> Save you from making mistakes that may undermine the authority of your writing.

>> Relieve you of some of your worries. What you're doing may be perfectly okay for today's less formal communication.

Infinitely more can — and has — been written about writing it right. See the sidebar "The journalist's grammar guidelines" later in this chapter for what may be the most succinct rundown ever created.

SHORTCUT

You can easily fix writing mistakes once you recognize them, but here's a general guideline to help you relax: When your own writing confronts you with a technical problem that's hard to resolve, or you just can't figure out what's wrong, write the sentence differently and sidestep the challenge altogether. For example, you write:

Do either of these options present a problem?

Then you wonder if the first word should be "Does." Rather than delving into tricky grammar issues, reword. Perhaps:

Would either option present a problem?

Fine-tuning punctuation

Commas, periods, question marks and other punctuation signals matter a lot: They tell people how to read your writing. Often, they substitute for the tone of voice, inflection, gestures and body language we naturally use when delivering a message in person. Some marks — like commas, periods and question marks — are essential.

But other punctuation indicators go in and out of style. Here is my personal take on current punctuation style for practical business writing. Take them to heart or not based on your own preferences and each writing situation. I have found that once I looked into it, punctuation is more interesting than I expected, so see if you think so, too.

Using comma sense

No need to stress about commas! If visual cues don't work for you, use oral ones. The reading-aloud trick I recommend in Chapter 4 works surefire to tell you when you need a comma. Note the difference:

Eat Grandpa!

Eat, Grandpa!

Love, me

Love me

If you read the first example aloud to say what you presumably intend — that Grandpa should eat — the first option sounds this way:

Eat (downward inflection and pause) *Grandpa*

A long pause with a change in inflection signals the comma is needed. And definitely, this sentence needs the comma. Try reading the second example aloud and note whether the difference in inflection is similar.

Too many commas can also be a problem:

Secretary of the club, Mark Smith, was also present.
Reliance on the Internet, as the source of all information, produces problems for the connected generation.

Read these sentences and you hear that they work better without pauses where the commas are placed. They interfere with smooth reading and should be cut.

Badly placed commas in cases like this often signal a wording problem. A better version of the second sentence could read:

Using the Internet as the source of all information creates problems for the connected generation.

Do use commas if clarity is at stake. For example:

I think I may take more morning walks when I have the energy.

If a comma is inserted after "walks," the sentence has a whole different meaning.

TIP

Reading aloud can also cure runaway or run-on sentences that typically depend on misused commas. Here's one that emerged from a writing seminar:

Grammar is something that everyone can always touch up on, the writers should use simple punctuation, properly place the punctuation marks, things like too many commas and semicolons can confuse the reader.

The read-aloud test shows that the long, sustained pause after *touch up on* calls for starting a new sentence. The comma between the two middle thoughts doesn't work either because an *and* should connect them. Insert that conjunction and it's then clear that you need a period after *marks,* because to read meaningfully demands another sustained pause. The result:

> *Grammar is something that everyone can always touch up on. Writers should use simple punctuation and properly place the punctuation marks. Things like too many commas and semicolons can confuse the reader.*

Another way of fixing this paragraph is to connect the whole second part with a transition and cut some redundancy, as in:

> *Writers should use simple punctuation and properly place the punctuation marks, because too many commas and semicolons can confuse the reader.*

SHORTCUT

Train your ear and with a little practice, you'll be comfortable with commas. I once argued with the best grammarian I know about the reading-aloud method, running through a whole list of examples. Finally, she said, "The problem is it only works 97 percent of the time!" I figure I'll take my chances with the 3 percent and you may also prefer to.

More punctuation tools

Colons are helpful when used to precede lists and examples. They can also produce special effects when you want to emphasize something: *The CEO called for great new ideas that involve no risk to the company: The silence was deafening.* Depending on your style guide, the part following the colon should be capitalized if it is a complete sentence, or not.

Quote marks are a bit tricky and writing testers like to trip people up with them. The basic rule: In the United States, periods and commas always go inside the marks. Question marks and exclamation points only go inside if they are part of the actual quote. But in the United Kingdom, single quote marks have traditionally been used, and periods and commas go on the outside.

The *semicolon* should be used sparingly in business writing, at best, because it usually accompanies complexity — long sentences that demand deciphering.

Parentheses are similarly unpopular because they're distracting and slow down reading. The modern slant is "stick to the point" and don't confuse people with more than they need to know. Generally speaking, decide whether what they contain is worth including in the message or else omit the statement altogether. An exception is when you refer to something specific, as in "(see Chapter 4)," a phrase that appears often in this book. Parentheses remain useful to denote an aside; just be sure they don't interfere with reading.

The *em dash,* on the other hand, is quite popular and as you probably noticed, I'm partial to it myself. It carries a tight telegraphic feeling and saves space. But too many will kill the broth, so keep the number down and resist using them to save yourself from thoughtful writing. And remember that generally, you need two of them, one before and one after the comment.

Along with emoji, *exclamation points* illustrate the living language idea best of all. They were until recently identified with "childish enthusiasm," and business writers scrupulously avoided them. But today, because we depend so much on written communication in our work lives, the emotional deficit of written language often makes itself felt. Exclamation points have risen to the occasion.

To equip our contemporary media with a little emotion on demand — enthusiasm, excitement, surprise, intensity — exclamation points have been called back into service.

WARNING

Exclamation points can also communicate a higher level of importance — *Pay attention!* But just as with revealing emotion on the work scene, exclaim in writing with discretion. More than one or two per message and they rebound on you. Emoji potentially give you far more emotional content, but as I cover in Chapter 4, using more than a smiley face may be inappropriate for some of your key audiences.

White space should also be seen as a punctuation tool. It signals readers to stop between paragraphs or sections and instills necessary breathing space on your page, whether print or virtual. Thinking of it as punctuation helps you deploy it productively and use it to make your messages more welcoming.

Expressive punctuation is another way to convey more than basic information. Capitalization, bold and italic font and repeating punctuation marks are tools that are more universally understood than emoji, but you need to judge their appropriateness on the same old basis — your goal and audience. Look what you can do with this sentence:

I will not consider it.

I will. not. consider . . . IT!

I . . . will . . . not . . . consider . . . it . . .

I will not consider it!!!!!

*I will **NOT** consider IT!*

Bottom line: Correctness — and emotional response — is in the eye and mind of the beholder. Consider your readers.

Using "however" correctly

As with commas, reading aloud gives you the clue about how to use *however* in your writing.

Many perfectly decent writers embarrass themselves with sentences like these:

I planned to write the report over the weekend, however, my dog ate it.

Expense filings are due on January 15, however, exceptions can be made.

Reading these sentences aloud shows that long pauses are necessary before each *however*. You can break up both statements into two sentences with periods after *weekend* and *January 15*. The second sentence in each case starts with *However*.

You can also separate the thoughts quite correctly by adding a semicolon before *however* in both sentences. But generally speaking, semicolons seem old-fashioned in business writing. They have a literary air and are falling out of favor.

TIP

Alternatively, you can sidestep the "however" problem and also refine your wording in one of these ways:

» Replace the *however* with *but*. If this substitution works, go with the *but*. It's correct and less stuffy as well.

» Use *however* only to begin sentences.

>> Move a *however* that falls in the middle of the sentence to the beginning and see whether the meaning holds. For example:

He agreed with Jane, however, she was wrong.

He wants to know, however, so he can plan his vacation.

Moving *however* to the front makes nonsense of the first sentence. With the second sentence, however, the move retains the basic meaning.

Weighing "which" versus "that"

Almost always, choose *that* rather than *which*. The latter word refers to something specific. When you're not sure which to use, try using *that* and see whether the sentence has the same meaning. If it does, keep *that*. For example:

The report that I wrote at home is on John's desk now.

But if you find that *that* doesn't reflect your meaning, you may mean *which*.

Note that you can write the sentence this way:

The report, which I wrote at home, is on John's desk now.

The second version calls attention to *where* you wrote it. And observe that you need two commas to set the clause off. *Which* always requires two commas unless the phrase appears at the end of the sentence. Another instance:

We provide afternoon breaks which, we know, help reduce stress.

You're using *which* correctly if you can eliminate the phrase inside the commas *(we know)* without changing the sentence's basic meaning. It becomes:

We provide afternoon breaks that help reduce stress.

Does this sentence carry exactly the same meaning as the original? Not if the "we know" is important. A lot of the effort in writing is to become clear on what you want to communicate.

Considering "who" versus "that"

For reasons I can't understand or explain, contemporary writing is chock-full of *thats* and very few *whos*. People have become depersonalized into objects. Speaking for myself, I find this practice disrespectful. The following sentences are all incorrect:

The new office manager that started on Monday already called in sick.

New customers that want to use the discount must register.

I don't like a person that never changes her mind.

As a favor to me, please use *who* when referring to people. Inanimate objects and ideas are *that*. You may choose to refer to animals as *who*, but some prefer *that*.

Choosing "who" versus "whom"

This is foggier territory. Grammar enthusiasts insist that you differentiate between the word used as a subject (*who*) and as an object (*whom*, as in *to whom*). But adhering to the rule can land you in some pretentious places.

To whom should I address the package?

With whom should I speak?

To whom it may concern . . .

In the first two sentences, the less correct version works better for general business writing — reflecting the natural conversational style you're aiming for:

Who should I address this package to?

Who should I speak to?

In the case of the last example, don't use an archaic phrase like *to whom it may concern* at all. Always find a specific person who may be concerned, and use that person's name. If that's impossible, use a title (*Dear Recruitment Chief*) or a generic address (*Dear Readers*).

Beginning with "and" or "but"

Like other wording choices addressed in this section, grammatical standards have relaxed, and only the rare individual complains about sentences that begin with *and* or *but*. *The Wall Street Journal* does it, the *New York Times* does it. I do it, a lot. And so can you.

But not so often that it loses its effect. Starting sentences with these conjunctions adds to your rhythmic variety and gives you a way to add a little verve, especially to online writing. It works best with short sentences.

Because can be used the same way, although I still hear people repeating the schoolroom mantra against starting sentences with that word. And you can start an occasional sentence with *"yet," "or,"* and *"so."*

Using sentence fragments

You probably recall your grade school teachers drilling this idea home: "Every sentence must be complete! Noun, verb, object!" Technically this remains true, but as our pace of life speeds up, so must our written language. For example, it's fine — except when writing the most formal documents — to say:

> *Here's the summary. Pretty long, I know.*
>
> *Do I like following the rules of grammar? Not so much.*
>
> *Use good grammar in everything you write. Unless breaking the rules makes sense and doesn't look like a mistake.*

REMEMBER

Fragments carry the business-casual tone that works for most practical writing. They give you short punchy bits that speed up reading, help promotional copy sound breezy or even cheeky and break up sentence rhythm neatly: "Never again!" "Maybe next time." "Yes, tomorrow."

When you write online copy, unless the material is really formal, use fragments to keep people engaged. On-screen reading is more strenuous so speed readability is especially important. But keep fragments interspersed with full sentences and be sure your copy remains crystal clear. Notice in the three examples that the fragments wouldn't make sense without the preceding sentences.

Ending with prepositions

An often-quoted piece of wit attributed to Winston Churchill underscores the silliness of strictly obeying some rules:

> *This is the sort of bloody nonsense up with which I will not put.*

Obviously, it's more natural to say,

> *This is the sort of bloody nonsense I won't put up with.*

Similarly, sentences such as these that end with prepositions are fine:

Leave on the horse you rode in on.

He's a man I can't get along with.

We didn't know where he came from.

Who is the decision up to?

TIP

Many stock phrases end with prepositions and there's no reason not to use them wherever they fall in a sentence. This especially applies if writing "correctly" requires an unnatural-sounding manipulation of language. The general guideline for business writing is: Use what feels comfortable in conversation.

Fielding Pronoun Challenges

Pronouns have a simple function — to stand in for nouns so you don't have to keep repeating them. Misused pronouns are the culprit in many cases of unprofessional-looking writing, so I devote considerable space to them. If you ever take a writing test for a communications-related job, or others that require good thinking, many of the questions are pronoun-based and look to trip you up. So be prepared — it's not hard with the techniques that follow.

Match nouns and pronouns

A major cause of confusion is when to use a plural pronoun (like *their*) as opposed to singular (*his, her, its*). Here is the traditional advice: Stay alert to the original noun and match it. A singular word like "anyone" requires a singular pronoun — such as him or her. However, this set of guidelines is shifting. For example:

A journalist must always be attuned to their readers' interests.

According to the rules of grammar most of us learned, this sentence is wrong because *journalist* is singular and *their* is plural. But language gurus, stylebooks and dictionaries are starting to endorse the use of "their," "them" and "they" with singular nouns when the alternative would be awkward (such as requiring "his and her" in the sentence about journalists). Accordingly, the sentence is fine. It reflects natural conversation and sidesteps the need to identify gender and default to using "he" when gender is unclear. It is also inclusive of individuals whose gender identity is nonbinary. (More on that in the section that follows.)

But what if you're writing formally, or to someone you expect will perceive the use of "their" as a mistake? I can't give you a universal guideline for making these decisions. Change of this kind can be slow to penetrate. Your choices are:

>> Stay traditional:

   A journalist must always be attuned to his or her readers' interests.

>> Switch back and forth between the masculine and feminine so the manager, for example, is sometimes female with attendant pronouns and at other times male.

>> Workaround! Change the subject noun to plural or rework the sentence:

   Journalists must always be attuned to their readers' interests.

   Better:

   Journalists must always be attuned to reader interest.

   When you've altered the sentence this far, if you take one more look, you'll see an option for making it more concise and dynamic:

   Journalists must always attune to reader interest.

That's the present tense trick referred to in Chapter 4. *Be attuned* sounds passive and like a state of being rather than action. *Must attune* feels like an imperative and an active process. It even provokes some curiosity: How *do* journalists attune to their readers?

Here's another sentence demonstrating a workaround. It's correct in the framework of the "new" rules, but risks being perceived as an error:

   Everyone should use their discount when ordering online.

If you want to sidestep, you might write:

   Use your discount when ordering online.

   Everyone should apply the discount when ordering online.

   When you order online, use your discount.

All will work. They say marginally different things, so your choice depends on the message context and medium. If you're writing a print piece like a flyer or advertising circular, you'd probably use the first statement. If you're writing a blog about leveraging discounts, probably the second seems most natural. If the statement was destined for a website that sells the product, *ordering online* becomes extraneous — it is obvious people are ordering online — so you'd be better off with:

Use your discount when you order.

REMEMBER

Some pronoun issues reflect cultural differences. In the United States, an organization is considered singular, so you say:

The company is widely criticized for its actions.

But in the United Kingdom, the plural is used:

The company is widely criticized for their actions.

Be mindful of personal pronouns

With the increased visibility of the transgender, genderqueer and gender nonconforming community, a broad effort has begun to reflect diversity in language and neutralize the use of binary (*he, she*) pronouns. One result, as mentioned earlier in "Match nouns and pronouns," was to advance the diversification effort and at the same time, remedy some of the English language's awkwardness with handling personal pronouns.

Having one common neutral pronoun that covers all genders — like "their" — can solve this challenge for writers. Similarly, "they" and "them" can be used even when the subject is singular. In fact, for these reasons, "they" was Merriam-Webster's word of the year in 2019.

Because English lacks "non-binary" pronouns, an effort to create new words is also under way. This was successful in a twentieth-century instance, when the title "Ms." was created to promote equal treatment of women. The list that follows demonstrates some current variations for new pronouns. Note that at least five words are being suggested to replace "he" and "she," for example:

>> **He/She:** Zie, Sie, Ey, Ve, Tey, E

>> **Him/Her:** Zim, Sie, Em, Ver, Ter, Em

>> **His/Her:** Zir, Hir, Eir, Vis, Tem, Eir

>> **His/Hers:** Zis, Hirs, Eirs, Vers, Ters, Eirs

>> **Himself/Herself:** Zieself, Hirself, Eirself, Verself, Terself, Emself

An example:

Jordan went to the cafeteria because zie wanted zir lunch, and took it back to zir office so zie could eat by zieself.

To speak and write inclusively and considerately, keep in mind some basic human considerations:

>> **Don't make assumptions about people.** In the case of a new hire, for example, you can matter-of-factly ask how the person wants to be addressed. Or, make it comfortable for people to take the initiative and tell you this. If you're a person with such a desire, you might say something like "Hi, I'm Leslie, and my pronouns are zie and zim." Some people have begun to include this information as part of their email signatures and on their business cards.

>> **Ask about your organization's policy and best practice.** A growing number of companies, nonprofits, government agencies and universities have created guidelines on the use of pronouns or may be in the process of doing so.

>> **Practice being comfortable with using "they" and "them" and "their" with singular subjects,** as in:

Who is the person in charge of the Jones account? I need to email them. Their assistant asked for a report.

You will be grammatically correct and respectful to all individuals.

>> **Create respectful workarounds.** While you should not avoid using people's personal pronouns when you know them, it's often a positive in any case to employ people's names as much as possible and use words like "you" and "everyone." Use "humans," "human beings" and "people" rather than "men," "women" and "men and women." Rephrase sentences. You might for example write:

I need to email the person in charge of the Jones account. Do you know who that is?

>> **Develop your awareness of exclusionary terms and avoid them.** Titles like "chairman" are often inappropriate: Choose "chair" or "chairperson." Use "police" instead of "policeman," "firefighter" instead of "fireman," "actor" instead of "actress." Use "spouse" rather than "husband" and "wife."

>> **Don't start messages (or meetings) with salutations like "Hi guys!"** And don't center multi-gender conversations on the latest football or other game: Even people who like sports may see this as a male-dominance tactic.

REMEMBER

If anyone asks you to refer to them in particular ways, naturally, honor these requests in good spirit. Remember to sustain this with group messaging as well as one-on-one.

Spot common pronoun errors

Pronouns present more challenges yet for writers of English, alas. Perhaps no other parts of the language demonstrate such a wide difference between how we speak and grammatical correctness.

I versus me

One cause of confusion is when to use *me* instead of *I*, *he* rather than *him*, and so on. For example:

> *Just between you and I, Jean was correct.*

> *Mark, Harold and me will go to the conference.*

Both sentences are wrong. *I* is a subject pronoun — used when that person is the "actor": *I plan to give a speech tomorrow.*

Me is an object pronoun — *He gave me a good idea.*

One way to figure out whether you need *me* or *I*: Switch some of the wording so the correct pronoun becomes obvious. In the first sentence, if you substitute *us* for *you and I*, it works fine. But if you substitute *we*, the sentence sounds absurd and you're clearly wrong. *Me* is therefore correct.

Or, just reverse the order of the subjects. *Just between I and you* is blatantly wrong, but you could say, *Just between me and you."* This signals that "between you and me" is correct.

In the second sentence, you can choose to say *We will go to the conference*, and because the singular for *we* is *I*, using that pronoun is correct. Or, you can eliminate Mark and Harold from the scene altogether, in which case you obviously must say *I*, not *me*.

As a general rule, go with what seems natural; but check yourself out as in the preceding examples.

I versus we

I is singular, *we* is plural, but if you're not a king, when is it okay to use *we* instead of *I*? You can choose to do so as a writer of website copy, an opinion piece or marketing material — even if you are a one-person team and there is no *we*. If you have a fledgling enterprise and no help, you can still use the corporate *we* — as in *we give you the best vacuum cleaner service in Oakland.* No need to make up fake people to fill the pages.

Who versus whom?

Who is a subject: *Who is knocking on the door?*

Whom is an object: *To whom shall I give the present?*

However, these days, *whom* comes off as pompous in all but the most formal of documents. In most other cases it's fine to say, *Who shall I give the present to?*

Fixing Common Word Confusions

A number of word confusions are amazingly common. Here are a few that seem to happen most often. Like pronoun misuse, they are favorite "gotcha" items on writing tests.

It's or its

It's is a contraction of *it is*: *It's cold out there.*

It also means *it has*: *I'm happy it's been a good summer.*

Its is a possessive pronoun: *My iPhone has its crazy moments.*

Their, there and they're

They're is short form for *they are*: *They're meeting on Friday.*

There denotes a place that is not "here": *The meeting room is over there.*

It is also used abstractly: *There is something I forgot to tell you.*

Their is a possessive pronoun for more than one person: *They left their papers on the desk.*

It is also is increasingly used for a single person as well: *Someone forgot their coat.*

Your, yours and you're

Your is a possessive pronoun: *Did you know your shirt is stained?*

Yours is a possessive adjective: *This dirty shirt is yours.*

You're is the short version of *you are*: *You're wearing a dirty shirt.*

THE JOURNALIST'S GRAMMAR GUIDELINES

Business writers can learn a lot from journalists, whose full-time work is figuring out how to present ideas and information in the clearest, most succinct and interesting way possible. Unfortunately, as the newspaper industry shrinks, it provides an ever-smaller training ground for writers.

This classic list of rules was originally taken from a bulletin board at Denver's *Rocky Mountain News* and has appeared, with different add-ons, in a number of journalism books. The *Rocky Mountain News* stopped publishing in 2009, but many a writer keeps this demonstration of grammar pitfalls on hand.

1. Don't use no double negatives.

2. Make each pronoun agree with their antecedent.

3. Join clauses good, like a conjunction should.

4. About them sentence fragments.

5. When dangling, watch your participles.

6. Verbs has to agree with their subjects.

7. Just between you and I, case is important too.

8. Don't write run-on sentences they are hard to read.

9. Don't use commas, which aren't necessary.

10. Try to not ever split infinitives.

11. It's important to use your apostrophe's correctly.

12. Proofread your writing to see if you any words out.

13. Correct speling is essential(!)

14. Avoid unnecessary redundancy.

15. Be more or less specific.

16. Avoid clichés like the plague.

Affect versus effect

Affect is a verb that means to have an impact on something: *The message affected Jack badly.*

Effect is a noun meaning result or consequence. *The effect on his coworker was even worse.*

Reviewing and Proofreading: The Final Check

Before sending out your message or document into the world or to its target audience of one, review it at both the big-picture macro level and the close-in micro level.

WARNING

Editing is essential, but almost always, the process can unintentionally shift meaning and introduce new mistakes. Plan to review any passages you reworked at least one extra time.

Checking the big picture

Once you've edited your message or document, it's time to return to the big picture and assess your overall message in terms of content, impact and tone. A technically perfect message may not be ready to accomplish what you want!

DOESN'T MY COMPUTER CATCH GRAMMAR GOOFS?

I said this before, but it's worth repeating: Microsoft Word and other word-processing programs have grammar- and spell-checking features that identify possible mistakes and indicate potential fixes. Although these tools can help, accepting the corrections unquestioningly is like trusting a smartphone's word-guessing function. The more sophisticated this gets, the more potential for mayhem. Just in the past hour my own computer translated "They had a passion for sharing their ideas" into "They had a passion for sharing their disease." Pay attention to the corrections and changes your word-processing program wants to make, in both spelling and grammar, and evaluate them thoroughly. Always reread after the check.

Forgetting all the work and the decisions that went into what you've written and edited, look at your text as a self-contained piece and consider:

>> Is my *purpose* — what I want to accomplish — absolutely clear?

>> Does the piece support my personal agenda? For example, does it promote the relationships I want to build, represent me in the best professional light and contribute toward my larger goals?

>> Do I get to the point quickly and stay on message? Does every element of the message support the result I want?

>> Does the message move well and smoothly from section to section, paragraph to paragraph?

>> Is the level of detail correct? Not too much, not too little, just enough to make my case?

Step even further back and read your document from your recipient's viewpoint.

>> Will the reader know what I want and exactly how to respond?

>> Is the message a good match in terms of tone, communication style and audience characteristics? Does it focus on what's important to the reader?

>> If I were the recipient, would I care about this message enough to read it — and respond?

>> Did I provide appropriate evidence to support the case I'm making? What unanswered questions could the reader possibly have?

>> If I were the reader, would I give the writer what he wants?

>> Can anything in the message possibly be misinterpreted or misunderstood? Could it embarrass anyone?

>> How does it look: Accessible? Easy to read? Plenty of white space? Good graphic devices? Visuals as called for?

And finally,

>> Will I feel perfectly fine if this document is forwarded to the CEO, mailed to my grandmother or shared online with millions?

Correct any problems using ideas and tips in this book, plus your own common sense.

Proofreading your work

In professional communication circles, proofreading is seen as separate from writing and editing. But in these economically tight times, copywriters, journalists and even book authors often wear all three hats. Many publications now outsource their proofing services or eliminate them altogether.

TIP

On a daily basis, obviously proofreading is all up to you. But you can still reach out for help. Many writers use a buddy system to back them up on important material, and you can, too. A colleague, friend or partner may be happy to supply editing advice with you in exchange for the same help. As the saying goes, two sets of eyes are better than one.

Cutting to fit

Sometimes you may realize that you've written too much for a given amount of space or longer than the subject justifies, which may lose the reader. Or you may suspect your text is too wordy, but it's difficult to cut it back. Here's a way to become more comfortable with cutting.

Try This: Cut to a specific word count. Choose a piece of your existing writing that is at least 250 words long. Go ahead and cut it by 25 percent. Eliminate words, phrases and sentences that are not absolutely necessary, or even whole paragraphs. Condense ideas to state them more succinctly. Tinker with what's left so it holds together. Then evaluate: Is the shorter message more effective? Assuming so — and I bet on it — go back to the original message and now reduce it the same way by 50 percent. Assess honestly if it works better yet.

If you like the results of either round of cutting or both, try it on the first draft of a new message. You may surprise yourself. It's a good technique for keeping your everyday and more major materials tight, and also works well for translating print-style copy to online forms that need to be minimalist.

WARNING

But, avoid editing the life out of a piece of writing when you condense, especially if you want it to be interesting or persuasive! It may be more important to keep certain details, examples and anecdotes and cut back the generalities or background information. This especially applies to writing that must be interesting or persuasive: an opinion piece, speech, article, sales pitch or website, for example. For another take on cutting techniques, see the section on "pyramid style" in Chapter 12.

Of course, you need not count the words each time you exercise your cutting skills — your Word program does that for you under "Tools." Click on that for an instant word count of the message, or of any part of it you highlight.

SUREFIRE PROOFREADING TIPS

Here are some ways to do the best job proofing your own work, or someone else's. They're based on my own hard-won experience and I share them, like everything in this book, to save you all that trial and error.

1. Use one of the systems I explain at the beginning of Chapter 4 so your proofreading is systematic and clear.

2. Make sure in the case of a major document to keep an original unedited version.

3. Try to proofread when your eyes and mind are fresh, and take frequent breaks.

4. Proofread more than once — ideally three times — and allow some time between sessions.

5. Carefully check sentences before and after every change you make, because editing usually generates new errors.

6. Pay special attention to the places where you find an error, because errors often clump together (perhaps you were distracted when you wrote that part).

7. Look for words that are often misspelled. Every grammar book has these lists or you can easily find one online; keep a copy on your desk.

8. Examine all the "little words," including *on, in, at, the, for, to*. They may repeat or go missing without your noticing if you don't pay attention.

9. Look up all words you aren't sure about. Choose a dictionary you like or just Google the word.

10. Triple-check names, titles, numbers, subheads and headlines.

11. Rest your eyes regularly, especially if you're proofreading on-screen. Looking out a window into the distance helps. So does setting your computer screen to a comfortable brightness.

12. Try enlarging the on-screen type for easier viewing — but not so much that you don't see the whole sentence, paragraph or section.

13. Read challenging portions of text backwards. This approach helps a lot with material that is highly technical or contains numbers.

14. Resist relying solely on your computer's or smartphone's auto-correct feature. The more aggressive these systems get, the more you risk big mistakes and potential disasters.

15. Recheck all the places where a mistake would prove most embarrassing: headlines, lead sentences, quotes.

Creating your personal writing improvement guide

Most writers are highly consistent in the errors they make, so creating a list of your writing shortfalls helps you sharpen up — and ultimately speed up — your writing.

Try This: Create your own improvement plan. Treat yourself to an in-depth session to review either a major document or a batch of smaller messages. Or gather information and insights over time. Better yet, do both. Start by thoroughly editing your selected work using the various criteria I explain in this book. Look for patterns of errors and less-than-wonderful writing. Addressing these particular problems will really benefit you.

Record the challenges — and the solutions — systematically. For example, in editing the chapter you're reading now, I made notes about where I needed to improve. That list appears on the left. Then I wrote down the solutions on the right.

My Problems	Solutions
Too many words ending in *-ing*	Find substitutes for most and rewrite as necessary.
Too many long sentences	Break them up or tighten by cutting.
Need to fix sentence rhythm often	Read the sentences aloud and add or cut words so they move better.
Too many sentences per paragraph	Break them up.
Too many long words	Replace with short ones, mostly.
Too much passive voice	Substitute active more interesting verbs.
Repeated and boring words	Replace them. To do this quickly, look up the word to find synonyms in an online thesaurus (for example, search for *"boring" syn*).
General wordiness	Keep an eye on Microsoft Word's Readability Statistics, and rely more on strong verbs that promote an action feel and help minimize "filler."
Too many qualifiers (such as *you might, you can, you should*) and extra phrases	Cut, tighten and/or rewrite. Cut the hedge words and write in present tense!

This analysis produces a road map I can use to review everything I write, from an email to a home page to a proposal.

TIP

Get even more specific and add categories, like words you often misspell or incorrect use of possessives. Scout for solutions in this book and other sources, and equip yourself with tools to lick the problem.

What about my personal style?

Although it might seem that writing well for work and other practical purposes will lead you to sound like everyone else, this is far from the case. First of all, you will have a personal style whether you want to or not, just like you have a personality. There's a saying among musicians that "you play who you are." In written communication, you write who you are. Second, I am equipping you to write better than most of your colleagues and competitors: more concisely, more clearly and more compellingly. My goal is for you to write as yourself — but your best self.

To care about what you write may be a different way of thinking for you. Do you really need to plan, draft, edit, cut, rewrite, add, subtract, edit and proofread everything you write? You be the judge. But before you decide most of the process isn't necessary, consider whether or not your reputation and effectiveness are on the line nearly every time you write. I bet they are.

Try This: Start using the plan-draft-edit process. Track whether your everyday messages achieve what you want more often. The good — no, great — news is that when you practice the plan-draft-edit process on the small stuff, you're ready to use it for the big stuff: proposals, reports, articles, websites, blogs and marketing materials. Ultimately you will save time and plenty of headaches.

Now that you're ready to apply all these ideas to your workday writing life, in the next chapter I focus most immediately on email messaging. This short-form communication is the lifeblood of most organizations and has become a central staple for marketing, overshadowing its more glamorous cousin, social media. Don't overlook its value or pass up honing your skills with email. I then extend this know-how to letters and in subsequent chapters, the full range of business materials.

HOW DO I KNOW WHEN IT'S OKAY TO BEND THE GRAMMAR RULES AND WHEN IT'S NOT?

A good rule of thumb: Does it look like an unintentional mistake? Or can a reader possibly interpret it as a mistake? If either is possible, it's not okay to bend the rules. You don't want to look careless or like you're trying to be cute or clever. It's just too expensive in terms of credibility and authority. And errors disrespect the reader. In such cases, even if it hurts to be more formal, bite the bullet and rewrite more sedately. This principle applies to general tone as well as language. Irony and sarcasm can be downright dangerous in written communication, where there's no inflection or smile to deflect the edge. Don't assume a smiley face will do the trick.

2
Applying Your Skills to Business Messages and Documents

Understand why email matters in the business world and how to make the most of this everyday communication tool.

Learn techniques for creating clear, concise email messages that fast-forward your agenda and build good relationships incrementally.

See why long-form business documents like reports and proposals remain make-or-break materials and how to produce them efficiently and effectively.

Learn how to create strong and interesting executive summaries by giving perspective to complex material, determining what matters and putting headlines to work.

Learn to adopt the entrepreneurial mindset that promotes success for both employees and independent workers in today's business world.

IN THIS CHAPTER

» Understanding why email matters and where it can take you

» Writing email messages that achieve immediate and long-range goals

» Using strategies and techniques that work — and avoiding pitfalls

» Creating effective letters for business purposes and beyond

Chapter 6

Writing Email and Letters That Get Results

ove it or hate it, you can't leave it — email is the central nervous system of business life all over the world. Companies may declare "e-free Fridays" or add newer media like instant messaging or social networks to communicate, but whether you're an employee, consultant or professional specialist, I bet you still find that your work life centers on managing your email inbox and at least some of your personal life too, as a consumer.

The volume and omnipresence of email in your life gives you the opportunity to accomplish your immediate and long-range goals or screw up both. This chapter shows you how to make the most of this powerful medium and sidestep the traps.

Fast-Forwarding Your Agenda with Email

If you wish for a way to show off your skills, judgment, competence and resourcefulness and have decision-makers pay attention, *shazam* — email is *the* opportunity. Yes, everyone is overwhelmed with too much email and wants most of it to go away. Consider your own inbox and see if you agree: Most of the email you receive is unrelated to your interests and needs, and most of it is badly thought out and poorly written.

Then take a look at your outbox. Ask yourself how many messages you carelessly tossed off without planning or editing. You may feel that this is the nature of the medium — here one minute, gone the next, so not worth time and energy. But email is the tool you can depend on to get things done, day in and day out.

Moreover, email has become the delivery system for many forms of communication. In earlier times, you'd write a cover letter to accompany a résumé, for example, and today you send it electronically. But a cover letter for a job application is still a cover letter — no matter how it's delivered. A business proposal may be sent by email, and because often there's no personal contact involved, it must be exactly right in content, tone and language. This demands your best thinking and writing.

REMEMBER

Good email messages bring you the results you want more often. Moreover, writing good messages every time — no exceptions — brings you amazing opportunities to reach the people you want to reach with a message *about you:* how resourceful and reliable you are, for example, and how well you communicate. Even those humdrum in-house email messages contribute incrementally to your positive image as an efficient professional, and give you a long-range advantage way past accomplishing your immediate goal.

EMAIL'S EVER-WIDENING REACH

Despite many premature claims that email is a "yesterday" tool, it's more important than ever. Email is the basic tool of global communication and grows steadily by 3 percent yearly. The technology market research firm Radicati Group anticipates that 4.4 billion people will use it by 2024, sending and receiving 361 billion emails per day. It's also estimated that today's workers spend 28 percent of their workday managing email. And, email has come to the fore as a major marketing tool. So don't minimize its value to your work life.

Send relevant, direct, concise email that has a clear purpose and respects people's time, and you get respect back. People notice and respond to well-written messages. In many cases without conscious thought, they equate good writing with intelligence.

TIP

The higher you go in an organization's hierarchy, the more people tend to recognize good writing and value it because they see so little of it these days. Executives are acutely aware of how badly written email, even on mundane matters, can create

>> Misunderstandings that cause expensive mistakes

>> Needless dissent among employees and departments

>> Inefficiency, because countering unclear messages demands much more communication

>> A staggering waste of collective time and productivity

Smart leaders are even more aware of how poor email messaging can affect an organization's interface with the world at large, resulting in

>> Weakened company image and reputation

>> Disaffected customers

>> Missed opportunities to connect with new customers

>> Long-term damage to relationships with the public, investors, suppliers, lenders, partners, media, regulators and donors — directly affecting the company's bottom line

REMEMBER

Take email seriously and you will be more highly valued. In addition,

>> **Email offers unique opportunities to develop relationships in the course of doing business.** To build and sustain a network of trusted colleagues and contacts in-house and out can only benefit you over the long term.

>> **Email gives you access to the loftiest heights.** Fifteen years ago, the idea that you could directly write to your CEO, or the hiring manager of your dream employer, was unthinkable. Now you can, and they may read it and even respond — if you make your message good.

>> **Email is your ticket to connecting with people all over the world.** Without it, international trade would depend on mail systems and faxes for initial contact and following up. Surely email is the unsung hero of globalization.

TIP

If you're an entrepreneur, consultant, freelancer or outside contractor, know that well-written email can help generate what you need: in-person meetings, opportunities to compete for business, new agreements, relationships of trust and ways to promote what you do. If you're new to the job market, good email will help you beat out the competition.

SHORTCUT

Practicing your email smarts is in itself a shortcut to developing your communication skills. The guidelines also apply to writing messages such as memos and letters and chat via workplace messaging tools like Slack. Email further serves as a kind of writing microcosm: The same principles guide you through proposals, reports, presentations, video, social campaigns and more. Build your skills here and you know most of what you need for every business writing medium. And — a promise that may sound rash but really isn't — whatever does replace email someday, these same ideas will make it work for you.

Here is the process to use, A to Z.

Starting Strong

Your first imperative in drafting an email is to draw your reader to open it and read it. Sound easy? Not at all, given the sheer volume of messages that motivates most people to press the Delete key for any excuse they can come up with. That's another reason why every email you send must be good: Why court a reputation for pointless, hard-to-decipher messages that lead people to ignore the important ones that you craft carefully?

With email, the lead has two parts: the subject line and the opening sentence or paragraph. The following sections explore each in depth.

Writing subject lines that pull people in

Take another look at your inbox and scan the subject lines. Note which ones you opened and why. Most of them probably fall into one of these categories:

>> Must-read because of essential information

   Subject: June 6 meeting rescheduled!

>> Want-to-read because you like the writer (in which case, the "From" matters, too)

   From: Neville Medhora

   Subject: 24 psychological triggers (for buying)

>> Want-to-read because the information may be valuable

Subject: Free tools to recover deleted files

>> Want-to-read because it looks like a good deal

Subject: Two iPhones for price of one!

>> Want-to-read because it makes you curious

Subject: How to make a 5,000-year-old energy bar

>> Want to read because you're in the market for whatever it is

All furniture: 20% off and free shipping

REMEMBER

Few messages are required reading. In the preceding list, only one subject, the first, was a must-read for me. Your challenge in writing email subject lines is to connect what you want with what's most likely to concern or interest your reader: not all readers — the readers you want. But always be fair. Don't promise something in the package that isn't actually there upon opening.

To create a good subject line that keeps fingers off that Delete key, follow these steps:

1. **Figure out what's most relevant to your reader in the message — why the person should care.**

2. **Think of the most concise way of saying it: Three to eight words should do it.**

3. **"Load left": Put the core of the message — the key words — as far to the left as possible so your recipient understands it instantly.**

Subject lines work best when they're *as specific as possible.* Here are examples of email messages I didn't open because the subject lines were too vague to capture my interest, although the alternative versions that follow would have enticed me to take a look.

Poor: *Important question*

Better: *When does Tuesday meeting start?*

Poor: *June newsletter*

Better: *Learn new Twitter strategy in June issue*

Poor: *Please contribute!!*

Better: *Community Food Bank Needs Donations!*

Poor: *Are you wondering when we'll discount your favorite boots?*

Better: *15% off Enzo boots today!*

The last example demonstrates why cute and drawn-out subject lines backfire. Even if a scanner keeps reading, the important words may be cut off in their inbox window, especially on smartphones or other small devices where the majority of emails are read. Few people pay attention to this simple principle, so building this habit reaps you an advantage.

Investing in accurate, informative subject lines always rewards you. Craft them to communicate the main point of your routine, everyday emails as well as your important business messages so they will be read! Even for a marketing message, there's rarely a need to be clever. It's better to pull target readers in by appealing to their self-interest: the WIIFM principle (what's in it for me).

WARNING

When you can't come up with a tight subject line that communicates the core of your message, consider that either you are packing too much into one message, or your message lacks a core — or any relevance at all — to your target reader. Review both the subject line and what follows to see whether you're perfectly clear on why you're writing and what outcome you want.

It's smart to review your subject line after you write the whole message. The writing process can nudge you to think through your reason for creating the email and how to best make your case, so you end up changing tack. Drafting the message first and then distilling the subject line is often easier.

TIP

Don't be lazy about changing the subject lines of long message threads. If you don't, people may overlook your new input. Later on, both you and the recipient may be frustrated when looking for a specific message. Try for some continuity, however, so it doesn't look like a whole different topic. If the first email of a series is identified as "Ideas for Farber proposal," for example, a new subject line might say "Farber proposal Nov. 3 update." Keep the subject lines obviously relevant to everyone concerned.

Many people use email as their personal database to draw on as needed, so always use the subject line to make messages findable. This applies even when you write a note to friends. You may have a friend like I do, who titles every message with "Hi!" Her emails are hard to find — and easy to miss.

Using appropriate salutations

The greeting you use is also part of the lead. Draw on a limited repertoire developed for letters:

> *Dear . . .*
>
> *Hi . . .*
>
> *Hello . . .*

You can use "Greetings" or something else, but be sure it doesn't feel pretentious.

Traditional advice is to follow with first name or last name as appropriate, using the person's form of address (Miss, Ms., Mrs., Mr.), but as you may know from your own experience and as covered in Chapter 5, these can be exclusionary.

Workaround 1: For groups, come up with an aggregate title as appropriate, such as "Dear Software X Users," "Dear Subscribers," "Hi Team," and so on. Don't be homey or quirky. Using "Folks," for example, can grate on people sooner or later. Also, avoid generalizations like "Dear Customer" if you're writing to an individual. These days, customers expect to be addressed by name.

Workaround 2: Use the person's name. If it's not suitable to write "Dear Chris" to someone you don't know, say: "Dear Chris Cooper"; or "Hello, J.T. Thomas." Use a similar approach if you're addressing actual envelopes: Simply omit the binary titles of "Mr.", Miss", Ms." and "Mrs." Using titles like "Professor" or "Dr." is fine, of course, when the title is merited.

TIP

Often, people who know each other well or are transacting business in an email series simply start the message with the person's name — for example, "John." That's fine if doing so feels comfortable. Generally speaking, don't omit a name altogether and plunge right into your message. You miss an important chance to personalize. You can, however, build a name into the opening line, as in: "I haven't heard from you in a while, Jerry, so thought I'd check where things stand."

Drafting a strong email lead

REMEMBER

The first sentence or two of your message should accomplish the same goals as journalists aim for with the lead of an article: Keep your readers' attention, present the heart of what you want to say and give them a reason to care. In addition, for business messages, you must tell readers the reason you're writing: what you want.

Try not to repeat the same wording or exactly the same information in the subject line and lead. Email copy occupies valuable real estate. Your best chance of enticing people to read the whole message is to avoid repetition and keep a fast and tight forward motion.

Your email lead can consist of one sentence, two sentences or a paragraph, as needed. When the subject line clearly suggests your focus, you can pick up the thread. For example:

> *Subject: Preparing for August 8th meeting*
>
> *Hi Jenn,*
>
> *Since we need the materials for the Willow conference in less than a week, I'd like to review their status with you ASAP.*

Often you need a context or clarifying sentence before you get to your request:

> *Subject: Timing on design hire*
>
> *Hilary, you mentioned that you'd like to bring in a graphic designer to work on the stockholder report ASAP. However, I won't be able to supply finished copy until April 3rd.*

TIP

Note how quickly both of the preceding messages get to the point. Do this with all in-house messages whether you're addressing colleagues, subordinates or supervisors. But never sacrifice courtesy. The right tone is essential (see the sidebar "Finding the right tone for email" later in this chapter).

When you write to people who are outside your own department or company, you often need to frame more explicitly so they know who you are, or the context from which you write. Suppose you're responsible for buying supplies and are looking for a new source of grommets:

> *Subject: Query re grommet purchase*
>
> *Dear Ellen Black*
>
> *As the Purchasing Officer of XYZ Inc., Michigan's largest eyeglass distributor, I'm in the market for a new grommet supplier.*
>
> *I will appreciate information about your pricing of the following items, along with quantity discount options:*

If your goal is to sell something or obtain an appointment to pitch a product or service, a "yes" is obviously harder to achieve than when you're the buyer. Your opening becomes critical and needs to tap into the triggers that lead people to buy or make a decision. Chapter 14 addresses these writing needs and others that are key to entrepreneurs and independent workers.

Good subject lines and leads rarely just happen: You achieve them by thoughtful planning. If you prefer to figure out the main point through the writing process itself, be sure you leave time to edit your opening and subject line before sending.

Building Content That Achieves Your Goals

You build a successful email message at the intersection of *goal* and *audience*. Intuition can take you part of the way, but analyzing both factors in a methodical way improves all your results. Knowing your goal and your audience is especially critical when you're handling a difficult situation, trying to solve a problem or writing a message that's really important to you.

Clarifying what you want

Email seems like a practical tool for getting things done, and it is. You write to arrange a meeting, receive or deliver information, change an appointment, request help, ask or answer a question and so on. But even simple messages may call for some delving into what you really want.

Consider Amy, a new junior member of the department, who hears that an important staff meeting was held and she wasn't invited. She wrote the following:

> *Tom, I am so distressed to know I was excluded from the staff meeting last Thursday. Was it an oversight? It makes me feel like you don't value my contribution! Can we talk about this?*

Bad move! Presenting herself as an easily offended childish whiner with presumptions undermines Amy's true goal — to improve her positioning in the department. Instead of using the opportunity to vent, Amy should take a dispassionate look at the situation and build a message that serves her much better:

> *Tom, I'd like to ask if I can be included in future department meetings. I am eager to learn everything I can about how we operate so I can do my work more efficiently and contribute more. I'll very much appreciate the opportunity to better understand department thinking and initiatives.*

Knowing your goal for an external communication is equally important. For example, if you're responsible for answering customer complaints about defective appliances and believe your goal is to make an unhappy customer go away, you can write:

> *We regret your dissatisfaction, but yours is the only complaint we have ever received. We suggest you review the operating manual.*

If you assume your job is to mollify the customer on a just-enough level, you may say:

> *We're sorry it doesn't work. Use the enclosed label to ship it back to us, and we'll repair it within six months.*

But if your acknowledged goal is to retain this customer as a future buyer of company products and generate good word of mouth, and maybe even positive rather than negative reviews, you're best off writing:

> *We're so sorry to hear the product didn't work as you hoped. We're shipping you a brand new one today. I'm sure you'll be happy with it, but if not, please call me right away at my personal phone number . . .*

For both Amy's and the customer service scenarios, keeping your true, higher goals in mind often leads you to create entirely different messages. The thinking is big picture and future-oriented. In Amy's case, the higher purpose is to build a relationship of trust and value with a supervisor and gain opportunities. In the unhappy customer case, you want ideally to reverse a negative situation and cultivate a loyal long-term customer.

TIP

Be the best person you can in every message you send. Every email is a building block for your reputation and future. And email is never private: Electronic magic means your message can go anywhere anyone wants to send it — and you can't count on erasing it, as so many public figures are shocked to discover.

Assessing what matters to your audience

After you're clear on what you want to accomplish with your email, think about your audience — the person or group you're writing to. One message, one style does not fit all occasions and individuals. As Chapter 2 details, when you ask someone for a favor in person, you instinctively adapt your message as you go along according to the other person's reactions via words, body language, expression, tone of voice, inflection and all the other real-time clues that tell you how the other person is receiving your message.

An email, of course, provides no visual or oral feedback. Your words are on their own. So your job is to think through, in advance, how your reader is most likely to respond and base what you write on that.

SHORTCUT

Use your imagination to anticipate your reader's reaction. You'll probably be able to do this more easily than you expect. Try holding a two-way conversation with the person in your head. Observe what they say and how they say it. Note any areas of resistance and other clues. Frame the questions they might ask and integrate the answers into your message.

Here's another surefire way to predict your reader's reaction: Systematically consider the most relevant characteristics of that person or group. Chapter 2 gives you a comprehensive list of factors that may relate to what you want to accomplish.

Do you need to consider so many aspects when you're drafting every email? No, if your goal is really simple, like a request to meet someone you're already on good terms with. But even then, you're better off knowing whether this particular recipient needs a clear reason to spend time with you, how much notice they prefer, if they already have set feelings about the subject you want to discuss and so on. It makes a difference if you're writing to someone higher up the ladder with a crushing schedule or your colleague next door. You can tilt the result in your favor — even for a seemingly minor request — by taking account of such things.

The more important your message is to you, the more carefully you must think it out and consider your reader's perspective. Sometimes just one facet of the person's situation or personality may matter, like attitude toward new technology. The person's age may be relevant to shaping both content and tone. Politically incorrect as it may sound, different generations generally have different attitudes toward work, communications, rewards, authority, career development and much more.

If you're a Millennial (born after 1980) or Gen X'er (born between 1965 and 1980), you need to understand the Boomer's (born between 1946 and 1964) need for respect, hierarchical thinking, correct grammar, courtesy, in-person communication and more. "Goal" and "audience" are the planning guideposts that never fail you. Chapter 2 covers this in more depth.

Try This: Write a portrait of your VIP. I often ask participants in writing workshops to create detailed profiles of their immediate supervisors. Pretend that you're an undercover secret agent and you're asked to file a report on the person you report to. Take ten minutes and see what you can put together. First scan the characteristics outlined in Chapter 2 and list those you think relevant to explaining that person (for example, generation, position, information preferences, hot buttons, decision-making style). Then fill in what you know or can surmise about the person under each category. Take the idea one step further and work this information into a narrative, adding what you know from experience and listening to your intuition.

You may end up with ideas you hadn't voiced before even to yourself. To illustrate:

> *Carol Johnson is the Marketing Department head I report to and she reports to VP Mark Blue — he is a tough boss and doesn't always support her decisions. This makes her nervous and sometimes irritable. But she's a good mentor and takes time to help me learn . . .*

Invest in this exercise and I promise you'll find you understand far more about your VIP than you think. The process works equally well for a client or prospect you plan to pitch. I promise you'll see major clues on how to communicate better with the important people in your life, as well as how to work with them successfully and increase your value. You may well uncover ways to strengthen your relationship or even turn it around.

Here's a practical example. Suppose you're inviting your immediate supervisor, Jane, to a staff meeting where you plan to present an idea for a new project. You hope to persuade Jane that your project is worth the resources to make it happen. First clarify your goal or set of goals. Perhaps, in no particular order, you aim to

>> Obtain Jane's buy-in and endorsement.

>> Get input on project tweaks sooner rather than later.

>> Gain the resources you need for the project.

>> Demonstrate what a terrific asset you are (always, always a constant).

You know Jane is heavily scheduled and the invite must convince her to commit the time. What factors about her should you consider? Your analysis may suggest the following relevant factors:

>> **Demographics:** Jane is young for her position and the first woman to hold that job. You've noticed that she feels pressured to prove herself. She drives herself hard and works 60-hour weeks.

>> **Personality/communication style:** She likes statistics. She likes evidence. She's an impatient listener who makes decisions when she feels she has just enough information. Her hottest button is being able to show her own manager that she's boosted her department's numbers. How to do that probably keeps her up at night — she's angling for a promotion. She takes risks if she feels reasonably sheltered from negative consequences.

>> **Positioning:** She has the authority to approve a pilot program, but probably not more. She's probably being groomed for higher positions and is closely monitored.

>> **Predilections:** She is famously pro-technology, a true believer and early adaptor.

Presto! With these four points, you have a reader profile to help you write Jane a must-come email — and even more important, a guide that enables you to structure an actual meeting that accomplishes exactly what you want.

Determining the best substance

You now have the groundwork in place for good content decisions. You know how to judge what information is likely to lead the person or group to respond the way you want. (See Chapter 2 for guidance on how to address groups and construct a reader who epitomizes that group.)

TIP

To figure out what you need to say, play a matching game: What information, facts, ideas, statistics and so on will engage the person and dispose them to say "yes"?

FINDING THE RIGHT TONE FOR EMAIL

In everyday email, your tone contributes heavily to coming across as empathetic, so never overlook it. Tone is discussed as it applies to all writing in Chapter 2, but here is how to look at it for email in particular.

Think in terms of "business casual" in general, with variations according to your subject and audience. When you know the person, you can key in more closely by visualizing them for a moment. Imagine yourself in conversation with that person and determine where their work-life personality falls along the spectrum of formal and reserved to casual and friendly, and also, the atmosphere and professional relationship you have with them. Your email tone should correspond.

If you're writing to someone you don't know or to a group, edge toward the more formal, but avoid sounding stilted or indifferent. Conveying a degree of warmth and caring is nearly always appropriate because who doesn't like that? We all want to feel we matter and that we're respected.

Strive for positive energy in all your email unless for some reason it feels inappropriate to the subject. Granted, you have limited ways to express enthusiasm and must balance word choice and content to achieve a positive tone. You can use an occasional exclamation point to communicate excitement, but don't scatter them everywhere and make yourself look childish. And unless you know your reader well, do not use emoticons, except for possibly a smiley face, to indicate a shared joke, for example. Keep in mind that older people especially may regard you as lightweight if you do this a lot. And some graphic emoticons don't translate between various technologies and may be auto-replaced with . . . who knows?

Also, before sending an email, consider whether it might be forwarded up the ladder to colleagues or to anyone else. If so, the highly casual tone you'd use to a simpatico boss may need to be tempered toward the more formal.

Think about audience *benefits.* This important marketing concept applies to all persuasive pitches. Benefits speak to the underlying reasons you want something. A t-shirt with a team logo, for example, may be well made, easily cared for and comfortable. But you buy it to identify with and feel part of a favorite team. Your underlying goal is to feel a sense of belonging.

When you're planning a message and want it to succeed, think about the audience and goal and write down your first ideas about match points and benefits.

For example, to draw Jane from the preceding section to that meeting, based on your analysis the list may include

>> Evidence that the idea works well somewhere else

>> Information on how cutting-edge technology will be used

>> Potential for the idea to solve a major problem for the department

>> Suggestion that company leaders will be interested and impressed

Many other ideas may be relevant — it's great for the environment, it gives people more free time — but probably not to Jane.

Structuring Your Middle Ground

Think of an email message like a sandwich: The opening and closing hold your content together and the rest is the filling. Viewed in this way, most email is easy to organize. Complicated messages full of subtle ideas and in-depth instructions or pronouncements are unsuited to the medium anyway.

Email's typical orientation toward the practical means that how you set up and how you close count heavily — but the middle still matters. Typically, the in-between content explains *why* — why a particular decision should be made, why you deserve an opportunity or why the reader should respond positively. The middle portion can also explain in greater detail why a request is denied, provide details or technical backup or offer a series of steps to accomplish something.

Try This: Use a step-by-step structuring. Here's a recap of how to plan a message demonstrating how the middle works. Take a message you wrote recently or are in process of writing. Figure out the basic content by brainstorming what points will accomplish your goal in terms of your target audience, as outlined in the preceding sections. Then do the following:

1. **Write out a neat, simple list of the points to make.**

   One example is the list I created to convince Jane to come to a meeting with a positive mind-set in the "Determining the best substance" section.

2. **Scan your list and frame your lead.**

   Your lead is the sentence or paragraph that clearly tells readers why you're writing and what you want in a way most likely to engage their interest.

   Starting with the bottom line is almost always your best approach for organizing a message. Remember the reporter's mantra: "Don't bury the lead."

Skipping the subject line for now, a get-Jane-to-the-meeting message can open like this:

> *Hi Jane,*
>
> *I'm ready to show you how using new social media platforms can help us increase market share for our entire XL line. After checking the online calendar for your availability, I scheduled the demo for March 5 at 2 p.m. Can you meet with me and my team then?*

To structure the middle, consider the previously identified points that are most important to Jane:

» Evidence that the idea works well somewhere else

» Opportunity to use cutting-edge technology

» Potential to solve a major problem

» Potential for wide company interest

You then simply march through these points and connect them with your project or other subject to build the body of the message. For example:

> *My research shows that two companies in related industries have reaped 15 to 20 percent increases in market share in just a few months. For us, using the emerging media I've identified can potentially move XL out of the sales doldrums of the past two quarters.*
>
> *Further, we'll be positioning our department at the cutting edge of strategic social media marketing. If we succeed as I anticipate, we may lead the way for the whole company to follow our model.*

The thinking you did before you started to write now pays handsome dividends. With a little reshuffling of the four points and attention to how they connect, you have a persuasive memo that feels naturally organized and logical. You know the right content and how the points fit together. Your simple invitation has an excellent chance of bringing Jane to the demonstration with an interested and positive attitude.

This process may sound easy to do with an invented example, but actually, working with real ideas, readers and facts is even easier.

SHORTCUT

Your biggest strength in building a successful message in any format — even "big" material like a website, proposal or book — is to know your story. Organizing a clear email message is rarely a problem after you pinpoint your content. You simply need to spell out for yourself the *why*:

>> Why the person you want to meet with will benefit by seeing you

>> Why your recipient will find your report or proposal of interest

>> Why the employment manager should read *your* résumé

Review the list you assemble, decide which points best serve your purpose and put them in a logical order. Your list may include more thoughts than you need for a convincing message, and you can be selective. That's fine. Cross them out and hold them in reserve. "Just enough" is better than too much.

Closing Strong

TIP

After you write your lead and the middle, you need to close. When you use the guidelines in the preceding sections to begin messages and develop the middle, your close only needs to reinforce what you want. An email doesn't need to end dramatically. Often, it works to circle back to the beginning and add any necessary information to the "ask."

>> If requesting a decision, say something like, "I look forward to knowing your decision by October 21st."

>> If you're delivering a report, your close may be, "I appreciate your review. Please let me know if you have any questions or if you'd like additional information."

>> In the case of the memo to Jane, the closing might be simply, "Please let me know if March 5th at 2 p.m. works for you. If not, I'm happy to reschedule."

Sign off with courtesy and tailor the degree of formality to the occasion and relationship. If you're writing to a very conservative person or a businessperson in another culture, a formal closing like "Sincerely" is often better. The same is true for a résumé cover letter, which is essentially a letter in email form and should look like a letter. But in most situations, less formal end-signals are better: *Regards, Jill.*

But best of all is to think of a way to say thank you because psychologically, this is almost always the most effective close. As in, "I look forward to hearing from you. Thanks, Jane!" Or according to the situation, "Thank you in advance." "I appreciate your attention to this." "Thanks for bringing this to my attention." "Thanks for reading this." Or just, "Thank you." Then add your name — first name if you know the person or are comfortable establishing informality. Even if your readers hear from you all the time, using your name personalizes the message.

Now your finished message needs one more thing: finalizing the subject line. Consider at this point the total thrust of your content. Then decide what words and phrases work best to engage your audience's interest. The "Jane" subject line, for example, needs to get across that your message is a meeting invitation, suggest what it's about, and emphasize that it is worth her time. Perhaps:

Invitation: May 3rd Demo, Proposed Social Media Project

Polishing Your Email

Email deserves your best writing, editing and proofreading skills. Often the message is *who you are* to your audience. You may be communicating with someone you'll never meet, in which case the virtual interaction determines the relationship and degree of success. At other times, crafting good email wins you the opportunity to present your case in person or progress to the next stage of doing business.

REMEMBER

People look for clues about you and draw conclusions from what you write and how you write it. Even if your ideas are good, incorrect grammar and spelling lose you more points than you may suspect no matter how close your relationship with the recipient feels.

The following sections run through some of my top tips for crafting copy that particularly suits email.

Monitoring length and breadth

Generally speaking, keep email to fewer than 300 words and stick to one idea or question. Three hundred words can go a long way (the memo I wrote to draw Jane to the meeting in the preceding section ended up 138 words total).

WARNING

Such limits are hard to consistently observe, but you're wise to remember how short people's attention spans are, especially for online reading. That's why you benefit from knowing your central point or request and opening with it. Don't bury it as a grand conclusion. Nor should you bury any important secondary questions at the end.

TIP

Aim to make email as brief and as tight as you can. If your message starts to grow too much, reconsider whether email is the right format. You may choose to use the message as a cover note and attach the full document. Or you may want to break the message up into components to send separately over a reasonable space of time.

Simplifying style

Choose words and phrases that are conversational, friendly, businesslike and unequivocally clear. Email is not the place for fanciful language and invention. You want readers to understand the message the first time they read it. If they are left to figure out your meaning, they will either stop reading or fill the lines in themselves and may end up elsewhere than you intended. This is where a lot of that expensive confusion comes from in every organization. Put your energy into the content and structure of your message and express what you want to communicate in unambiguous and straightforward language.

Try to make your writing transparent, eliminating all barriers to understanding. Your messages may end up less colorful than they could be, and that's okay. I've never seen anyone criticized for writing clear concise messages.

Going short: Words, sentences, paragraphs

The business writing guidelines in Chapter 3 apply even more intensely to email. You want your message to be readable and completely understood in the smallest possible amount of time. Draw on the plain old basic word-stock and use mostly one- and two-syllable words. Use longer words when they're the best choice and serve a real purpose.

Short sentences work for the same reason. Aim for 10 to 15 words on average. Paragraphs should be one to three sentences to support comprehension and build in lots of air.

Using graphic techniques to promote clarity

These graphic techniques don't require special software or a degree in fine arts. They're simply ways to visually present information and make your writing more organized and accessible.

TIP

Do everything you can to incorporate generous *white space* (areas with no text or graphics) into your writing. Don't crowd your messages and leave them gasping for air. White space allows the eye to rest and focuses emphasis where you want it. Short paragraphs with double returns between them instantly create white space.

Add subheads

Subheads are great for longer email. You can make the type bold and add a line of space above it. Subheads for email can be matter of fact:

Decision point close

Advantages of new system

Step 1 (followed by Step 2 and so on)

Special considerations

Project pros and cons

This technique neatly guides the reader through the information and also enables you as a writer to organize your thinking and delivery with ease.

SHORTCUT

Try drafting all your subheads *before* you write. This can be a terrific way to organize an email. Pick a message that you already wrote and found challenging, or one you'd like to write but needs some nerve. Think the subject through to come up with the major points or steps to cover and write a simple subhead for each. Put the subheads in logical order and fill out the relevant content under each. Now check if all the necessary information to make your point is there — if not, add it. Your message is sure to become clearer, more cohesive and more persuasive.

If you feel that you have too many subheads after drafting the entire message, just cut some or all of them out. You still have a solid, logically organized email message. Just be sure to check that the connections between sections are clear without the subheads.

Bring in bulleted and numbered lists

Bullets offer another good option for presenting your information. They are:

>> Readily absorbed

>> Fast to read

>> Easy to write

>> Useful for equipment lists, examples, considerations and other groupings

WARNING

However, observe a few cautions:

>> Don't use more than six or seven bullets in a list. A long stretch of bullets becomes mind-numbing and hard to absorb.

>> Don't use them to present ideas that need context or connection.

>> Don't mix and match. The items on your list must be *parallel,* so that they begin with the same kind of word — a verb, a noun or an adverb.

Never use bullet lists as a dumping ground for thoughts that you're too lazy to organize or connect. If you doubt this advice, think of all the bad PowerPoint presentations you've seen — screens rife with random-seeming bullets.

Numbered lists are also helpful, particularly if you're presenting a sequence or step-by-step process. Instructions work well in numbered form. Give numbered lists some air so that they don't look intimidating — skip a space between each item.

Consider boldface

Making your type bold gives you a good option for calling attention to key topics, ideas or subsections of your message. You can use bold for lead-ins:

> **Holiday party coming up.** *Please see the task list and choose your way of contributing.*

You may also use bold to highlight something in the body of the text:

> *Please see the task list and choose your way of contributing* **by December 10.**

Of course, don't overload your message with boldface or it undermines its reason for being. Keep in mind that boldface doesn't always transfer across different email systems and software, so don't depend on it too much for making your point.

Underlining important words or phrases is another option, but it tends to look old-fashioned.

Respect overall graphic impact

REMEMBER

Avoid undercutting your content through poor graphic presentation. Plain and simple is the way to go with plenty of white space. Use short paragraphs with plain text or the simplest HTML — no tricky, cute or hard-to-read fonts. Don't write whole messages in capitals or italics and don't use a rainbow of color — that's distracting rather than fun for readers. Don't vary the font size: Use one that's readable for most people, in the 12- to 14-point range.

It's a good idea to check how your messages look once in a while by sending one to yourself — it may morph during its trip through cyberspace. Avoid a crammed-in feeling. People simply do not read messages that look dense and difficult. Or they read as little of them as possible. Like everything else you write, an email must look inviting and accessible.

Using the signature block

Contact information these days can be quite complex. Typically, you want people to find you by email or telephone. Plus, there's your tagline. Your company name. Your website. Your blog. The book you wrote. The article you got published. Favored social media. Professional affiliations and offices. And potentially much more, perhaps including your pronouns (see Chapter 5).

Decide on a few things you most want to call attention to and refrain from adding the rest. Better yet, create several signature blocks for different audiences. Then you can select the most appropriate one for the people you're writing to. Don't include your full signature block every time you respond to a message, especially if you incorporate a logo, which arrives as an attachment. Check your email program's settings so the automatic signature is minimal or altogether absent.

PRACTICING EMAIL SMARTS

Email's "easiness" can lead you to inappropriate use.

DO NOT:

- **Present complicated issues or subjects.** Of course, you can attach a report, proposal or other long document to an email, but don't expect an email in itself to produce an investment, donation or other high-stakes buy-in.

- **Wax philosophical or poetic.** Readers look to email for practical communication and are annoyed by windy meanderings — even (or especially) if you're the boss.

- **Amuse.** As for most business correspondence, generally avoid sarcasm and irony, and most humor unfortunately, because it can be misinterpreted against your interests. And sense of humor differs among individuals, regions and countries.

- **Spam.** Send email only to people directly concerned with the subject and don't send unnecessary replies. Don't forward cute anecdotes or jokes unless you're absolutely sure the particular person welcomes that. And don't forward chain letters: They can upset recipients. Don't forward anything without reading it. Thoroughly and carefully.

  Is it considered spamming to respond to a message chain with a minimalist confirmation, like "Yes, the meeting is at 3," or "I received your input"? Not when it feels necessary to close the communication circle. If your reader may feel left hanging, or any uncertainty can linger, then follow up with the last word. Better safe than . . . you know what.

- **Fail to respond promptly.** Most matters covered in email have an immediacy and people expect to receive answers promptly, within 24 to 48 hours — but sooner is better. When you can't supply the information or meet a request quickly, it's often smart to send an acknowledgment saying when you'll get back to the person.

- **Respond to poorly considered and written email with poor email of your own.** You don't know who else may see them, and even those who write badly — perhaps through a feeling of executive privilege — may disrespect you for doing the same. Enjoy feeling superior (without expressing it, of course). Your classy, effective email is likely to reward you over the long run more than any other business communication medium.

Using Email for Marketing

It may surprise you to know that email, the oldest online communication vehicle still in use, is considered a far better marketing tool than the glitzier social media platforms. A few recent statistics:

>> Almost 72 percent of small businesses use email to communicate with customers compared to 60 percent for Facebook, by far the most heavily used social channel for business.

>> Eighty-one percent of businesses say that email drives customer acquisition and about the same percentage depend on it for customer retention.

>> Every dollar spent on email marketing generates $32 in return on investment.

>> Conversion rates (from click to purchase) for email is higher than for social media and search.

>> Fifty-nine percent of consumers say that email marketing influences their purchasing decisions.

>> Some studies show that people spend an amazing two and a half hours per day checking personal email at work.

The effectiveness of email holds true even if your targets are as young as college students. They pay regular attention to email because it's necessary to their schoolwork, while their social media attention is typically divided among five or six accounts. Plus, younger people typically use social accounts for fun rather than serious decision-making.

All this said, email marketing works best when woven together with a social media strategy and perhaps traditional channels, all within a well-thought-out comprehensive marketing plan based on thoroughly knowing your audiences, goals and "value proposition" — the heart of what you offer.

In a way, email marketing is a newer branch of direct-mail marketing, which — despite being hugely more expensive — is in itself far from dead, judging by my own mailbox. Like direct mail, it is a demanding kind of specialized writing beyond this book's scope. But here are some tips to help:

>> **See email messages as one step in your marketing effort.** Coaxing a purchase via a single message is unlikely. You goal is narrower: to capture attention and persuade the reader to proceed to the next step in the chain, like clicking to your website or blog and/or becoming receptive to future emails in a planned chain.

>> **Be sure your website, blog and other vehicles shows you off well.** Ideally, provide a specific landing page so an interested reader can jump from the email straight to your specific pitch rather than having to scout your site from its home page. You can continue making your case on the landing page and ideally close the deal, or lead the prospect to something else (for example, a quiz, allied product, more detailed specs and so on).

>> **Target your audiences closely.** Research says that almost 70 percent of users delete commercial emails without reading them. To increase your chances of being read, you must reach people who need — or are at least open to — your pitch, and make the connection through well-planned and written messages, personalized if possible. Developing that email list is a primary need. Keep in mind that even a small list with the right people can be worthwhile. And that segmenting your market pays off very well because it helps personalize your message to reach different people.

>> **Give people a good reason to relate to your message instantly and stick with you along the marketing chain.** Are you offering a discount? That is the biggest click-inducer. Free gift or sample? Free webinar or event? Cheat sheets or templates? A free consultation? Subscription to your blog or newsletter? Insider information? Chance to win something or join something? Or connect with people they want to know?

>> **Invest in crafting a strong subject line.** Forty-seven percent of recipients are found to open emails based on subject lines alone. It draws people to open the message or junk it. Go straight for the benefit your audience stands to reap by using what you offer and *crystallize the message in three to eight words*. How will their lives be better with your product or service: What problem will it solve? Will it save them time or money? If you're offering an incentive like a discount, put it right up front, but if you're an unknown quantity or the product is unfamiliar, you need to cover that ground, too.

Here are a few subject lines drawn from my inbox that demonstrate some of the possibilities. I didn't open most of them because the content failed to sound relevant to me, or I was not currently in the market for it. As in many endeavors, timing is everything — which is why most promoters send a constant stream of messages. But don't send so many that people are annoyed and block you.

See what you can do with AI in Photoshop

15 luscious lemonade desserts

When Someone Wrongs You at Work Say This

1 more day to enjoy 25% off!

>> **Keep it short.** Use the language of your prospects and a friendly tone that leans, generally, toward the informal. Avoid buzzwords and empty biz-speak that turns readers off and earns you a quick trip to the junk box. Email marketing benefits from creative ideas, but the writing itself need not be clever and certainly not poetic. Craft concrete, simple, clear, straightforward language. Base it on short everyday words and be sure to instill a good forward-leaning rhythm (all this is covered in Chapter 2).

>> **Include *one* clear call to action.** What do you want the person to do upon reading the message? And be sure to think through what exactly you do want. Click onto your website? Try your blog? Subscribe to a newsletter? In many cases garnering readers' email addresses is the goal. This enables the sender to keep communicating with them. Nothing could be cheaper than promoting by email, but don't communicate so much that people unsubscribe. Drawing the line on how-much-is-too-much is a challenge.

Composing Effective Letters

You may be under the impression that you don't write business letters and never need to in today's fast-paced world. Think again. You are probably writing letters without realizing it. Don't be fooled by the fact that you're using an electronic delivery system and don't need a stamp. Acknowledge that your missive is a letter, and you do a much better job of achieving your goal.

When something important is at stake recognize that what you produce merits extra care in terms of its content, language and visual impression. This doesn't necessarily mean you need to find your old stationery. In many cases, it's perfectly fine to send your letter as an email. In other instances, a physical letter serves you better. If you're a nonprofit manager writing to elderly donors, for example, relying on email is risky. As always, consider your goal and audience in deciding on the best mode of delivery.

Here are some of the business-world occasions when you should think "Aha! This calls for a letter!"

>> **Introducing yourself:** If you're the new veterinarian in town writing to the patient list, or need to explain why a VIP should give you ten minutes of their time, or why people should vote for you, you're courting the reader and must make the best possible first impression in order to secure what you want.

>> **Making a request:** If you want a referral, a recommendation, an invitation, an informational interview, a special assignment, a corner office, a favor of any kind, write a letter.

>> **Pitching something:** If you sell a product or service, one effective way is with a sales letter, either via the post office or email. When you market anything, you must apply your best strategizing and writing.

» **Presenting formal applications:** When you apply for a job, submit a proposal or compete for an educational opportunity, nine times out of ten, you need a cover letter. If it's optional, leaving it out is a mistake. Sometimes the letter must accomplish the goal on its own — when a job posting specifies a letter and no résumé, for example.

» **Saying thank you, I'm sorry or expressing sympathy:** Such messages are important and should be carefully personalized and meticulously written and presented. If they don't look as if you have given thought to such a message and taken trouble, they don't communicate that you care. A personal letter is much more effective than a greeting card.

» **Expressing appreciation:** If someone gives you a wonderful break, takes a chance on you, offers significant advice or makes an introduction for you, a letter from you to that person will be treasured — trust me. People so rarely do this. And it's worth considering a retrospective thank you to anyone in the past who inspired or helped you, too.

» **Congratulating someone:** Supervisors, coworkers, subordinates, colleagues, suppliers — everyone welcomes a graceful congratulatory note when reaching a milestone or achieving something significant.

» **Documenting for legal purposes:** Letters can be called for as official records in relation to job offers, agreements, performance reviews and warnings. These formal records may have legal implications now or in future. A binding contract can take the form of a simple-looking letter, so must be scrupulously written if you want them to protect you. And know what you're agreeing to when you sign those written by other people!

» **Seeking redress:** If you have a complaint about a product or service, how you've been treated or how a print or digital publication has misrepresented you or your organization, to be taken seriously, write a letter.

» **Expressing opinions and concerns:** Yes, Virginia, just as there is a Santa Claus, newspapers and other publications still run Letters to the Editor — and those editors know that this section is usually the most read feature of all. But it takes a good letter to be heard. Letters to local government and legislative offices reap a lot of attention, too.

» **Inspiring people to care:** If you want friends and colleagues to actively support a cause you believe in, with money or time or connections, a letter bears much better testimony to the depth of your own commitment.

» **Valuing privacy:** Letters carried by the postal system are privileged documents protected by the "secrecy of correspondence" principle. In many countries, it is illegal to open letters in transit. The privacy of digital communication remains murky, and you obviously risk disaster by communicating private information in an email or social post or text. Printed-and-delivered physical letters offer a last bastion of privacy.

WARNING

If you search online, you'll find a ton of prewritten and preformatted letters for every occasion. You may draw some ideas from them, but almost never will a cookie-cutter template work as well as your own well-crafted letter. Often the tone is wrong and the content is bland and impersonal. This totally undercuts the reason you're writing a letter.

Therefore, I won't give you a formula for every letter. Some specific types of letters, such as marketing messages, job application letters and networking notes, are covered in the relevant chapters ahead. Right now, I want to stimulate your imagination as to what a good letter can accomplish for you in your professional life and beyond. I have personally used this skill in situations ranging from a need to establish my (at the time, somewhat uncertain) credentials for a major purchase, build ongoing relationships with VIPs, and more than once, obtain a refund for a disappointing purchase or when a major deposit was withheld.

To show you the impact a letter can have, here are some actual examples (with details altered). In each case, instead of leading you through the planning process that leads to a good message, I first give you the final product and then follow with the analysis.

Situation 1: You hear a major renovation is to commence on a house down the street — a peaceful, well-kept, private-feeling street where children play outside and residents share a community spirit. You find the following letter on your doorstep.

Dear Neighbor:

As you may be aware, the Bennet family will be venturing into a home renovation/ addition project shortly.

As the family's general contractor and representative, I wanted to take a moment of your time to introduce myself. My name is Allan James and for the most part, I, or one of my project managers, will be on site every day. Having completed numerous projects in the area over the years, I am familiar with the town and sensitive to the effects a project of this scope can have on the neighborhood.

It is my intention not only to deliver a quality, on-time project to my customer, but to ensure the least amount of impact to your environment. My subcontractors are very much aware of my expectations in regard to respect for your neighborhood, the town by-laws and the need for utmost common courtesy and respect.

It is inevitable that there may be some minor damage to the town-owned grass strips between the sidewalk and the street. Any such damage will be restored at the end of the project. To ensure that this occurs, a surety bond has been levied with the town.

Please feel free to contact me in person, by cell phone or email if some aspect of this project is affecting you adversely.

With best intentions,

Allan James, AIBD, CPBD, UCSL

President, AJ Builders, Inc.

How would you react as a resident? It's hard to imagine a negative response. However, even though the business strategy is so effective, I have never seen or heard of another contractor taking the trouble to write and deliver such a letter. Even if the idea does not seem relevant to you right now, notice how this letter aligns with the planning process, which is the heart of this book:

Goal: Smooth the way for a process that is naturally disruptive and forestall likely complaints.

Audience: Homeowners who fear damage to the street and a potential flood of unsupervised workers and subcontractors to the quiet neighborhood they value.

Content points: Communicate . . .

>> High sense of responsibility and caring as company owner

>> Active direction of workers and subcontractors

>> Knowledge of protective bylaws and commitment to them

>> Acknowledgment of probable damage and commitment to repair it

>> Ensurance of legal protection via surety bond

>> Credentialed company president (no matter what the acronyms stand for)

Accountability: Direct contact information is given in case of a problem (or should readers want to inquire about services for themselves!).

Tone: Low-key, respectful, sincere.

Why it works: The writer understands the neighbors' worries based on their prior experiences with construction and directly addresses those fears. In doing so he generates trust: He makes the coming interaction personal. He reassures residents that he will respect the street they share and care about. But there's more: *the thoughtfulness of the letter conveys that this is a caring, capable and intelligent person who will do an excellent construction job.* That's the magic of what you can accomplish with good writing. Of course, the writer must follow through on all counts.

Outcome: Beyond accomplishing a collegial environment to work in and forestalling complaints, the contractor received several queries from other local homeowners who were inspired to pursue their own renovations.

Situation 2: Here's an example of how good business writing carries over to non-work needs. You are relocating and have put your house on the market. Happily, you soon receive a number of offers that move over the asking price. You're ready to accept the highest bid when this letter arrives:

> *Dear X:*
>
> *My name is Donna Whitman and I am writing to you to express how important it is for me to purchase your lovely home. I have dreamt of living on a lake for more than 20 years. When I was transferred from Minneapolis to Charlotte this past year, I hoped to make my dream come true.*
>
> *I have spent time with colleagues in the Arborville community and knew it would be exactly right for me. When I saw your home listed, I knew I had to see it! And when I walked in the door, I told Jim, my broker, that this was the home for me!*
>
> *I love the location, layout and of course, the lake. My 15-year-old cat, Cappy, will also love your home. She will have so much happiness sitting with me on the splendid deck (her joints don't allow her to sit on windowsills any more).*
>
> *I'm excited that the dining-room set I inherited from my dear grandmother will fit perfectly. And I love that my parents will have a beautiful place to stay when they visit in March, should I be lucky enough to purchase 45 Lakewood.*
>
> *I truly hope I will be chosen to be the new owner of your home and finally have my dream become a reality!*
>
> *With the utmost sincerity and gratitude for your consideration,*
>
> *Donna*

As the seller, how would you react to receiving this letter? Donna may not consciously have followed the process I recommend for all your writing, but here is why it succeeds as a message.

Goal: To win the bid, without knowing what other offers were received.

Audience: Someone who has loved the home herself, apparent in its cared-for condition, furnishings and decoration.

Content: To accomplish this goal, with this reader in mind:

>> Personalize the interaction to stand out from other potential buyers.

>> Express high enthusiasm for the chance to live there.

>> Communicate appreciation for potentially being "chosen."

FORMATTING YOUR LETTERS

What letters have in common is the need to look good. They may be delivered electronically and can even be signed online in most legal situations today. But in many cases, they should look like a letter, not an email. If your letter is being delivered by post, use a standard business format. If delivery is electronic, take pains to make the message look as much like a letter as possible so readers take it more seriously. Lots of books and websites present letter-formatting details, but here are the essentials:

- **Use block style.** Start every element flush left, but run it rag right (uneven rather than a straight line).

- **Eliminate indents.** Instead, skip a line space between paragraphs.

- **Choose clear, simple fonts.** Try Times Roman in 11 or 12 point or a sans-serif face like Helvetica if the message is short and need not look conservative.

- **Add graphic elements judiciously.** A headline, subheads and color and type variations can be appropriate for sales letters; include just a few or none for other letters unless helpful for clarity.

- **Use letterhead with your logo if you have one.** You can create the look of letterhead on your computer. Incorporate a small digital file of your logo in messages you send electronically.

- **Supply contact information.** Make it full and complete, using the letterhead and signature block.

- **Pick proper paper.** Stick with white paper (or other light color that doesn't interfere with reading).

- **Sign your name,** preferably in blue, which looks formal, but also makes your signature stand out rather than appearing to be mass-produced as part of the letter.

These points are backed by citing specific benefits to the writer and communicate a personal vision — Cappy the arthritic cat on the deck . . . the beloved grandmother's dining-room table in place . . . the happy visiting parents.

Tone: Enthusiasm!

I suspect your reaction in this scenario would be similar to the seller's: a little skepticism at so much excitement, overridden by feeling gratified that her long-term home will be appreciated, enjoyed and cherished.

Outcome: The writer had not in fact made the highest offer, but the seller wanted her to have the house. Donna agreed to meet the slightly higher price of the offer above hers and everyone left the table feeling very good.

The point: Think about what well thought-out letters could accomplish in your own life. Adopt that mindset and the opportunities will come.

Consider at times the value of a real letter — the kind that you can hold in your hands, reread at will and keep with your important or treasured documents. Do you have a shoebox of letters that connect you with important events or people of your past personal life? Letters relating to our professional lives can also have strong associations for us, especially if they make us feel good. Digital messages are fleeting — some are even meant to disappear in a few minutes. But a physical letter is real and tangible and (relatively) permanent, like a photographic print. I know several professional colleagues who make a habit of handwriting their messages to clients and other important connections on notepaper: thank you for the help or referral, happy holidays, happy birthday, congratulations on your award or your son's graduation. These savvy professionals look for opportunities to write notes like these. Don't laugh. When they visit these recipients' offices and see these notes prominently displayed on the contact's bulletin boards, the strategic value of this small effort is reinforced. These friends are all very successful.

Moving on, Chapter 7 explains how to apply the basic writing principles to the big make-or-break business documents: proposals, reports, grant applications and more.

Chapter **7**

Creating High-Impact Business Materials

Today, we all need to think like entrepreneurs. This applies even if you're not among the growing number of people who earn their living as consultants, freelancers and professional specialists, or hope to run their own full- or part-time business. Even established employees need to keep proving their value, pitch their own ideas and compete for good opportunities on the job. More and more people must contribute to their organizations' marketing in some way, too.

Bottom line is that writing successful business documents such as reports, proposals and funding applications is on almost everyone's agenda for tomorrow if not today. They often present make-or-break opportunities. Building on the principles of everyday communication, this chapter shows you how to create major business materials that fly you high above the crowd.

Creating Valued Reports

I find that many staff people are short-sighted about the value their reports have for those who read them, and thus, overlook what good reports can accomplish for themselves. Independent workers such as consultants and entrepreneurs are well aware of their worth — or soon learn. In this section I start from the ground up and offer guidelines for writing effective reports in a wide range of situations.

You may be called on to report on activity and/or projects small to large. Many reports cover both. *Activity reports* (also called *status reports*) describe what you accomplished during a set period, whether weekly, monthly, quarterly or annually. They include personal reports on how you spent your time and what you achieved. Consultants may also need to report to similarly report to clients.

Project reports explain how an initiative was carried out, the results and perhaps recommendations. Scientists report on their experiments and long-range studies this way and so do people responsible for overseeing a campaign or rollout. These reports may contain complex information, such as a technical white paper or an actuarial report analyzing probable outcomes of different decisions.

Writing activity reports

Activity reports basically inform the reader of how you spent your time during a defined period. For most people, they typically occasion the biggest groans of any paperwork except perhaps filing for expenses. Most in-house workers especially see them as a distraction from their "real" work and treat them as busywork imposed by inconsiderate, tradition-bound managers.

Resist that feeling! If you think writing reports is boring, you're bound to produce dishwater documents that serve you badly. Consider *why* someone wants the information involved. Yes, a supervisor may want you to keep proving that your job is justified, but a smart one wants to know some or all of the following:

>> Your progress (and everyone else's) in carrying out the current initiative

>> Possible need for course corrections to meet goals and deadlines

>> Surprises: Unexpected problems, obstacles, connections

>> How well the team is coordinating tasks and whether things are humming along smoothly, on time and on budget

It may surprise you to know that many employers want to know what their staff members think, as well as what they're doing. Especially when a staff consists of more than a few people, it's hard for the big-picture decision-makers to keep track of what's happening under their watch. Written reports as well as team meetings become essential to keeping track of the action.

Managers base decisions on staff reports more often than you may suspect. Ideally, reports collectively add up to the larger perspective their roles demand and provide clues to help them deploy their resources more successfully. When you contribute informed observations and ideas, they're valued because you're closer to the action, whatever that is, and speak for that piece of reality. Reports keep those further from the ground in touch.

Keep in mind, too, that bosses need grist for their own report mills. They must in turn report to their superiors, and need information from their team members to do so. Good material from their staff enables them to write better reports. And some of your own input may rise all the way up the ladder.

Many lofty leaders find it frustrating to receive dull, dense, unorganized reports that bury the facts and insights they need under a barrage of undiscriminating verbiage. Even high-up executives often write meandering reports that waste the time and energy of all who use them.

Use reports to communicate your capabilities and value. Take the trouble to make them well-organized, well-strategized, informative and well-written. Make them as interesting as you can. If you suggest your own boredom through a rote delivery, what does that say about how you feel about your job and how you do it?

Just as with writing email, which is covered in Chapter 6, start with the perennials: goal and audience. Your *goal* is to provide useful information and perspective to the reader, and no less important, to present yourself as the thoughtful, skilled, resourceful, creative professional you are. Your *audience* is the manager who asks for the report as well as the whole crew of managers above them.

Look at your report from your supervisor's viewpoint to gauge the appropriate content, level of detail and style of writing. Take their informational preferences and decision-making style into account (see Chapter 2 on how to do this). A report's orientation also varies according to company culture and your role.

If you manage a unit or department, you're responsible for reporting on the team's performance as well as your own. Some of the advice that follows may be more relevant to a report on a department, or other area of broad responsibility, rather than yourself as a single individual. But notice ideas that will help you make your reports stand out.

Focus reader attention

You can easily get lost in detail when reporting on an activity period or project. Remember that the reader doesn't care much about how you spent every second, but does care about what you accomplished, any problems you encountered and, in many cases, your recommendations. The higher-ups depend on you to analyze what occurred and filter out what matters.

SHORTCUT

If reports are a regular part of your work, take the time to develop a set of questions based on what you seek to accomplish and the nature of your work. Start with the following list. Cross out those that don't relate to your situation, adapt others as necessary and add more questions so you end up with a customized list that leads you to know your story and helps you present it, time after time.

>> The most important thing that happened this month was ____.

>> The most important thing I/the team accomplished was ____.

>> What progress did I make toward my goals?

>> What initiatives did I take or what new approaches did I use? What resulted?

>> What management and colleagues should know about is ____.

>> My core message about the ups and downs of the last period is ____.

>> The problem I really need help with or support for is ____.

>> The good news is ____. The not-so-good news is ____.

>> After reading this report, the resulting decision, action or feeling I want from readers is ____.

>> What I want most for myself is ____.

TIP

A report's substance should not center on what you did ("I spent five hours scouting for new clients and wrote email to three prospects"), but rather on what your efforts accomplished ("I secured two new agreements and I'm currently working with three interested prospects"). Writing a good report requires you to clearly know how your project, assignment or initiative relates to the organization, department or client. This in turn means knowing the ultimate goals and challenges of the organization employing you. Align your perspective with this big picture by posing additional questions to yourself, such as:

>> What did I contribute to immediate and long-term goals?

>> What's changed from the previous month(s)? The impact?

>> What has progressed, held steady or regressed?

>> What comparisons are relevant — last month, last year or another time frame?

>> Did I see any opportunities? Did I act on them or refer them to someone else? Any results?

To go one step further, offer insights and data-based opinions. This is often expected from managers. Some questions to help with this:

>> What surprised me?

>> What occurred that should be taken into account in the future or bears watching?

>> Did the general climate of the past period offer challenges or advantages? Risks or dangers?

>> Is the team moving in the right direction? How or what would I change if I could?

>> What would be fun or thought-provoking to share?

>> What do I recommend based on the information in this report?

>> Do I see opportunities for collaborative action?

WARNING

Of course, decide on content judiciously. Consider company culture, your own role and your relationship with superiors before making broad recommendations and sharing personal viewpoints. Keep this in mind when assembling your own list of questions. They should be appropriate but also give you scope to more proactively present yourself as a thinker and problem-solver.

Know your story

An activity report may have a prescribed format or you may have some degree of leeway in how you present your information. Either way, first figure out your story by answering the questions you developed in the previous section. If you have a prescribed format use that as a guide, but don't get lost in the format: Know what you want to say and figure out how to do so in the required configuration. Often you can set the perspective you want by beginning with a brief executive summary, which can be as short as a single introductory paragraph.

SHORTCUT

Even with guidance from a series of questions, it can be hard to distill your experience to find a perspective for a report. Here's a shortcut: Imagine a good friend asks you, "What did you (or your team) do the past month (or the past three months or year)? What happened? What mattered?" Think of what you would spontaneously say to your friend, and you may find your summary crystallizing nicely for you. Then use this perspective to frame the report and write the opening. In transferring your ideas from the oral to written medium, adapt as called for, but don't overly complicate the storyline and language.

Try This: Use the subhead method. If you're creating your own format for a report, use the subhead method I describe in Chapter 5. For example, if you're a department or unit head, you might structure your report this way:

Executive summary

Old initiatives, progress, results

New initiatives, progress

Staffing changes

Unexpected challenges/stumbling blocks

Environment scan — relevant big-picture factors

Bottom line: Gains/losses

Projections

Resource or assistance needs

WARNING

If the categories for your reports are predetermined or you inherited them through long company traditions, honor them. But don't turn into an automaton. Even though the powers-that-be may insist on a given format, their eyes tend to glaze over the fastest. Nothing makes for a duller report or application than filling out each section of required information as a rote task, in the number of words that seem called for. Doing so produces a lifeless litany that makes you look like a hack.

After you have a reasonably organized set of categories and spend some time thinking about your overall message, start working with one category or section at a time. Do this in sequence or not, according to your personal preference. Some people like to start with what's easiest for them. The beauty of sectionalizing the document is that you can choose your working method while knowing in advance how the pieces fit together.

Draft the report

When you're ready to pull the whole report together, start at the beginning with the first section after the executive summary. For each section, open with a good summary statement — the *lead.* As with the lead for many kinds of writing, aim to capture attention and explain what information is coming. For reports and other business documents, a good generalization that puts the information in perspective works well. A section on staffing changes in a manager's quarterly report, for example, might begin:

The department successfully added three new well qualified specialists in high-need technical areas this period, while losing two mid-managers by attrition. This improves our positioning and enables us to better upsell technical services to current clients. Only one of the managerial jobs needs to be filled.

Then go on to fill in the details on the level you deem appropriate. Stay organized painlessly by identifying subsections for each major part. To follow up the preceding lead, your subsections might be:

New technical hires

Expanding service capacities

Manager attrition

Overall staff situation/outlook

REMEMBER

Stay conscious of how each section contributes to your overall message, as well as how you're relating to the company's problems and priorities. Know thoroughly how things fit together and make sure you clearly communicate that to your readers.

WARNING

Stick to your storyline — the big perspective — and use everything in the report to back that up. Don't bury what matters. To avoid overwhelming people with information, analyze what you can leave out. Providing too much detail may trivialize the important things you want people to absorb. If you don't provide a strong perspective, you leave readers to make assumptions. Lawyers routinely confound the other side by dumping tons of unsorted documents on them that they are forced to wade through. Don't information-dump your readers, especially if they pay you. If necessary, you can put the data into an appendix.

Reporting project results

While the process for writing project reports is similar to writing activity reports, a project report may call for a different structure according to the subject. Here, too, aim to tell a story with a logical beginning, middle and end.

WARNING

Often the challenge of a project report is how to present an abundance of data and concepts in a way that holds together for readers. Faced with masses of poorly sorted information, most people will either stop reading or jump to undesirable conclusions. Neither outcome is good for you. Take the time to determine your central message — and how you want your reader to react. Use the questions you draft in "Focus reader attention" earlier in this chapter to guide you, but start with these:

> What was the reason for undertaking this work?
>
> What did I want to find out and why?

Identify the project's goal as closely as you can. For example, did you want to supply a basis for decision-making? Provide support? Question a current position? Predict outcomes from various scenarios? Justify an action? Or just keep specific audiences updated? A basic reporting sequence like this one suits many purposes:

> What we wanted to know and why (the problem or mission)
>
> What we did and how (abbreviate if this may not interest key readers)
>
> What happened
>
> What we learned and evidence and/or outcomes
>
> Discussion of important points, perhaps pros and cons
>
> Conclusions (what we recommend, problems, next steps)

Section by section, create an engaging lead based on your most important result from the reader's perspective. When you have good news, flaunt it, don't bury it. On the other hand, don't obscure any bad news so it's overlooked or comes as a shock.

REMEMBER

A good report, like any major document, doesn't happen overnight. Don't position yourself to start from scratch when the deadline is tomorrow. Consider collecting information for the report gradually in a folder or on your computer or desk (or both), for each section. Add to the folders over time so you're not overwhelmed at the last minute desperately trying to remember what happened, where the figures are and what it all means. Before you draft, give yourself time to read through all the material you gathered and decide on your message.

SHORTCUT

Here's a good way to cut through complex masses of information to the bottom line: After scanning your material, put it away for a few hours or days. Then without referring to it, summarize it orally or in writing. You may find that given a little distance, your brain filters out what matters.

Fast-Tracking Your Proposals

If the futurists are correct, you may have more proposal writing ahead of you than you suspect. Every year, many companies and not-for-profit organizations maintain smaller staffs and hire more consultants and independent contractors. Even if you stay in-house, you may find a growing need to pitch in writing for new assignments or responsibilities.

Sometimes you may need to prepare formal proposals in a format either prescribed by an organization or the occasion. For example, if you're aiming for investment capital, you need to meet your audience's expectations of content and style. In many cases, however, a far less formal proposal can succeed and may even be preferred by your target reader. More and more consultants I know use brief proposals to sell their services. Here, I show you how to write both varieties.

Writing formal proposals

Most RFPs (request for proposals) require formal, standardized responses. This is true in most big-business situations and also for many grant applications. You may have a list of specifications to meet and a prescribed format. If you do, follow those specifications to the letter, especially if you're bidding for a government contract. At other times, you may have more leeway to organize your document as you like, or to interpret a set of guidelines.

TIP

For help with preparing a long-form, high-stakes proposal, check out Internet resources and business management books. You can find abundant good advice on formatting but not much about the process of writing the proposal itself. Not to worry. Here are several tips for answering RFPs that can make the difference between winning a bid and losing out:

>> **Tell a story.** Even if the prescribed format makes storytelling tough, use the space to communicate a cohesive picture of what you recommend and why, what you'll do and why you're the best person or company to do the job. True, specialists may scrutinize only a few sections, but key readers review the whole document and want it to make sense cumulatively — with as little repetition as possible. (See Chapter 8 for storytelling tips.)

>> **Demonstrate your understanding of the problem and goal.** If you're pitching for a complex contract, take time to know the company and the problem its decision-makers need outside help to solve — it's always there. Read the RFP exhaustively between the lines and research the organization to see how the requested work fits into the company's overall needs — and by extension, how you can fit in. In doing this, you'll pick up keywords to incorporate and better understand the company's "voice" so you can respond in kind and show you're on the same wavelength.

>> **Give your audiences what they need.** Include content and details that specifically match audience expectations. Remember that most businesspeople want to increase profitability or efficiency. All reviewers want to know a project's timetable, how you measure success, the budget and how it breaks

out, who will do the work and their credentials and your track record and specific qualifications for the job.

>> **Write simply and conversationally in third person.** Use a slightly more formal tone than you'd use for everyday communication — fewer contractions, for example — but don't sound overly academic and stuffy. Avoid using first person ("I," "we," "us"). Make the company the entity, even if you are the only person involved (for example, "Bluebird Audio will provide a complete sound system . . ."). Make your language lively but jargon-free unless totally unavoidable. See Chapter 4 for more tips about how to do this.

>> **Speak their language.** Notice any statements that are emphasized or repeated in the RFP or other communication. These are clues to the organization's hot buttons and perhaps sensitivities honed by experience. Incorporate key phrases and ideas in your responses, but don't come across as if you're parroting back their words rather than providing the answers they hope for. And be sure to explain how you'll measure outcomes!

>> **Remember the decision is about you.** Whatever you're proposing, you're asking someone to choose you and your team. Never skimp the biographical section. Show why each team member is right for the role, how the team works together, its accomplishments, and why you in particular can be trusted to deliver on time, within budget and to specification.

>> **Go for the proof.** Don't say "the team is creative, reliable and efficient." Cite examples, case histories, statistics and testimonials that demonstrate these points, as appropriate. Impress with substance rather than empty claims. "Tests show that our concrete lasts 16 percent longer than other varieties" is better than "our concrete lasts forever."

>> **Edit and proof your work.** After writing, review and correct your document in several stages. (See Chapters 4 and 5 for more about this process.) One error costs you your credibility. Ask a friend with sharp eyes to proof for you, too. If you fail to showcase your ability to communicate well and correctly within the document itself, you lose ground regardless of what you're trying to win.

>> **Make it look good.** Your competitors will. Use all the graphic options to help your proposal read well and easily. Give your readers opportunities to rest their eyes. (See Chapter 3 for advice on using graphic tools.) Include relevant graphics — images, graphs, charts, infographics — but they must never be extraneous. If a lot rests on this document and you're on your own, ask a friend with a good eye for advice. Or find a good model or online template and adapt elements of its design or the whole layout.

Always do a big-picture review of your document before sending out a proposal. Ask yourself (or a colleague) the following questions:

REMEMBER

» Did I demonstrate my understanding of the problem or goal?

» Did I explain who we are and why we're the best choice?

» Did I clearly state what I will do to address the problem and the expected outcomes?

» Did I clearly spell out what "success" will look like and how it will be measured?

» If different people worked on the proposal, has the whole piece been edited to read consistently and well?

» Would *I* give me this opportunity based on this document?

TIP

Many candidates focus proposals on *process* and short-sell *results*. For example, a training proposal to update staff technology skills should talk less about how many workshops the program includes and more about the gains that result in efficiency, problem-solving and error-reduction after the training. When possible, give the client a vision of how much better his people will function, or how his processes will improve, or how life and the world will be better if you are awarded the opportunity. But the vision must have "feet" — a solid grounding in your ability to achieve concrete results, not pie in the sky.

And, remember the professional proposal writer's mantra: Be SMART — Specific, Measurable, Achievable, Realistic and Time-sensitive.

Writing informal proposals

The foregoing section addresses formal proposal writing, typically in response to an RFP. If you're vying for a government or big-industry contract or a grant, you usually have no choice other than to follow the given specifications. But creating formal proposals can be intensely time-consuming, and understandably, few consultants or contractors want to do more than necessary to win the job. In many situations, you can save yourself a bundle of time by opting for an informal proposal. And almost always the prospective client is perfectly happy with a concise, readable document.

One way is to build the proposal into the selling process and make it a simple agreement — confirmation of a plan already discussed. You can create a logical sequence to cover what's necessary, or even use a letter format. This approach requires a different selling process because it builds on a personal discussion of the job at hand rather than analysis of a written request.

The first step is to achieve that conversation. As any sales professional can tell you, aim for a face-to-face meeting or if that's not possible, a virtual one. Then write the proposal based on what you discover. Proposals based on phone conversations, or worse yet, written exchanges, are harder sells. Ideally, you want to gain a second appointment to present your solution — that is, your proposal.

TIP

At the first meeting, rather than aggressively selling your qualifications, hold a conversation. Encourage the prospect to talk. An opener that works well for crack salespeople is, "I'd love to know how you came to this position." Listen very carefully and use friendly prompts to keep the person talking and gently steer the direction to cover what you need to know. Ask open-ended questions that will yield answers to the following:

» What single problem would you most like to solve?

» How is this problem affecting your business?

» What difference would solving it make for you?

» What has been tried so far and why didn't it work?

Watch for clues as to how you really can help the organization and the value, to them, of fixing the problem at hand. Experienced consultants watch for chances to expand the perspective within which the challenge is viewed. For example, exploring the inability of units to meet their sales figures may reveal an underlying problem — unsupportive management policies rather than insufficient training, perhaps. This could mean a bigger job for you, or a mismatch if it doesn't suit your skill set. It's better to find this out before you're invested.

If the conversation is positive, you can follow up with your informal written proposal. This can cover, in sections:

» The problem you propose to address ("I heard that your sales figures have plummeted 6 percent . . .")

» Why that problem is important ("These losses have forced you to lay off three employees and . . .")

» What you recommend ("Shangri-La Consulting will develop a plan to . . .")

» How you will carry out the program ("Our step-by-step plan is . . .")

» What will result ("The result will be . . .")

» Mutual obligations and time frame ("Our mutual obligations, time frame of deliverables and so on . . .")

» Financials ("My fee [broken down if and as appropriate] is . . .")

You can also work in why your firm is the ideal choice to undertake the job or add a separate page with your credentials and qualifications, tailored to the project.

Here's an example of a common-sense proposal that a business communications consultant might draft. Notice that the title does not refer to "communication training," but more important, the reason improved communication will benefit the client.

A Workshop Proposal by CCW, Inc. for Whiteflag, Inc. to Improve Customer Relations

CCW is pleased to propose a series of workshops to help Whiteflag customer service representatives handle customer complaints more effectively and actively build customer relations through more positive interactions and correspondence.

The Problem: Alienated customers

Your recent review of 24 representatives' interactions with customers showed:

- An 18 percent increase over the past six months in customer complaints with how their problems were handled
- An abrupt, sometimes rude tone characterizing many outgoing messages to customers
- An unprecedented number of social media posts criticizing Whiteflag products and service

(This list can be longer, but generally, keep it to no more than four or five.)

Impact of the problem on Whiteflag:

The situation is adversely affecting your company. In your own analysis, it is a major factor in a recent 4 percent decline in your customer base. This has created a downturn of 2.6 percent of gross volume.

CCW proposes:

A step-by-step outline of the proposed workshop series — specific but very concise — goes here.

Outcomes:

The workshop series will achieve . . .

List the outcomes you aim for that correspond to the problems and note how results will be measured.

How we will work together:

Describe the collaborative planning, time frames and obligations of each party.

The facilitators:

Indicate who will deliver the program and their credentials.

Fee structure:

State your project fee or hourly rate, which should protect you from "scope creep"; for example, cite extra charges for work that exceeds the parameters you set.

Agreed to by: _____

The entire document can be just a few pages. It may be fine to format it as a letter that begins with a salutation — "Dear Jane" or "Dear Ms. Brown," as appropriate. Or assuming email delivery, present the proposal as an attachment to a note written as a cover letter. Some more standard sections, like the "presenters" section that describes staffing and credentials, can be done as a separate add-on.

TIP

Your tone and language for an informal proposal are just as important as for a formal one. You've spoken personally with the person or group who might hire you. You've also seen how they present and communicate, what sparks their interest and concern and how important the problem is to them. Be alert to all these signals and picture the decision-maker in your mind as you write.

Ultimately, most contracts and assignments are won in person, but writing is the essential first step toward most opportunities. You rarely get in the door without a first-rate proposal. Good writing and the good thinking it reflects can be a great leveler. I know personally many cases where a small David beat a smug Goliath to win stellar opportunities, and companies that have built their entire success on very good writing. This happens more than ever given the growing dependence on virtual media.

A good letter introducing yourself — another kind of proposal — can work wonders in many circumstances. This may seem like a simple task, but often, the less room you have to frame an "ask," the better you need to think it out.

TIP

If you're writing a straight-out pitch for funding, the basic proposal ideas apply, but remember the priorities: Anyone asked to finance your idea or business primarily wants to know how much money you want, how you will pay it back and what they will gain from the investment.

Writing a business plan

If you're writing a business plan, the same fundamental structure applies as with writing a formal proposal, but with some reangling. Traditional business plans cover:

>> The great idea tightly presented and, preferably, captivating. This is your value proposition expanded (see Chapter 8).

>> Market analysis — why your product or service is needed and will sell, backed by facts and statistics.

>> How you'll structure and build the enterprise.

>> Service or product details and benefits to customers.

>> Marketing and sales — your strategy for finding customers and delivering.

>> Financials — costs, profitability prospects and financing sources.

>> Why you are equipped to succeed.

Even if your vision is for a random set of gigs with you working in the attic, a business plan often spells the difference between failure and flourishing. Especially if no one else reads and responds to the plan but you. Online advice and standard templates abound, but excellent free help is available from the Small Business Administration (www.sba.gov), the Small Business Development Centers (https://americassbdc.org) and SCORE, which offers free mentoring by experienced businesspeople (www.score.org).

Applying for grants

In most ways, applying for grants is similar to answering business RFPs. Grants bestowed by government agencies, foundations and large corporations typically involve completing very explicit questionnaires that must be followed to the letter. Smaller grant-givers, such as volunteer-run organizations that award modest amounts to local nonprofits, typically supply their own application forms. These vary widely in both the nature of the information required and how to present it. However, following some common-sense guidelines will maximize your chance of winning a grant.

REMEMBER

If the grant giver offers a session on how to apply, by all means be there. Many businesses and nonprofits that give grants use their own idiosyncratic processes to evaluate applications. But again, a common-sense set of strategies can ground you in almost every case. Start with the guidelines for RFPs and add the following, which are specific to grant proposals. I am assuming you want to apply for project funding because most funders prefer to invest in a new project or extend a successful program, rather than contribute to operating expenses like staff salaries and facilities.

>> **Align with the funder's mission.** Thoroughly understand "what's in it for them." Why is this company or foundation or government agency investing in

this set of projects? Each giver has its own mission to accomplish. A foundation focuses on one or many causes, carefully articulated in its print and digital materials, so always scour these. Many companies support causes that align with their own commercial interests. An eyeglass manufacturer, for example, may choose to help vision-impaired children live fuller lives; or it might adopt a community cause or one that resonates with its employees. A governmental entity typically identifies unmet needs of its citizens.

TIP

Once you identify the funder's mission, align with it as closely as you can. How will your activity help the giver fulfill its own mission? Build your application on the answer to that question. If you can't do this, you may not be applying to an appropriate funder.

>> **Aim not to bore your reader.** I've written grant applications and also screened them. Both processes are hard work. Whether the readers are paid professionals or volunteers, plenty of red-eye activity is usually called for. The requestor pile is big. When a reviewer becomes bored, the application gets a skimming at best. Therefore, consider these guidelines:

- *Frame your information as a story.* Know your core message — what you want to achieve, who you are, what you will do and what this will accomplish. Even when using a formal prescribed format, figure out how to tell the story in that framework, even if it must be told in increments by answering questions in the order given. (See Chapter 8 for story-building approaches.)

- *Let your conviction shine through.* As in every sales situation, your own belief in your cause, and the project you want funded is your greatest selling point. Don't mask it with complicated abstract writing. Write with enthusiasm. Show heart and energy. If you don't feel that for your project, why should anyone else?

- *Avoid information repeat.* Don't start all over again for every question if there's any way around it. Different people may or may not evaluate various parts of your proposal, but it works better to assume one or a series of readers will evaluate the whole document. If you must repeat, find another way to angle the idea or reword it. The dull repetitive proposals typically lose.

- *Establish the need clearly without dwelling on it.* If hundreds of children live in your community and need help with vision aids, certainly say so, with good documentation. But write about the program that will address this challenge rather than unnecessary details that crowd out your solution.

- *Stress outcomes, not process.* Funders are usually more interested in what will change or improve than in the details of how you will do it. If you want to train the children to use special devices, for example, do explain how you'll accomplish that — for example, with a series of free small group workshops — but don't over-present the logistics: where the workshops will be held, how the instructors will be hired and so on. Rather, paint a full picture of how 175 children's lives will be improved.

- *Show if possible that the project results will be sustainable in some way.* For example, beyond helping the initial 175 children, will the program train nurses to help them after the project people are gone? Will they leave equipment for them to use?

- *Use good graphics to support your words.* Well-presented material is always more closely read and bestows credibility. Take the trouble to make your application look good. Charts, graphs or tables can make data more easily understood. Relevant photographs and video can be effective for many good causes — but they may be prohibited on the application, so always check.

>> **Think long range.** You're asking a funder to choose your project from among many and give you money that may have been challenging for them to raise. *It's up to you to create trust!* Good writing is your best friend here. Be sure you represent your own organization effectively in everything you write. In addition to any correspondence with the grant-giver, and the application, be sure your online presence is in good order and backs up your group's credibility and relevance. Posting success stories has helped many a cause do this.

TIP

A good application that doesn't get funded may still be a door to future support. You may well get a better reception next year or the year after. Reviewers do notice your persistence and sustained interest. In many cases, it's acceptable to inquire why your project wasn't chosen and how you might do better next time. Some funders supply this information routinely, and if so, scrutinize it carefully.

WARNING

If your proposal is funded, don't number among the great majority of grant recipients who fail to say "thank you." Express appreciation. And follow up! The people who gave you money want to know how well your program succeeded and they deserve to, whether they require this reporting or not. In practical terms, demonstrating results is much more likely to help you qualify again in the future.

Writing an Executive Summary

Readers are summary-mad these days. Whether scanning the capsule-size rundowns at the beginning of articles, or digesting multipage introductions to complex content in reports and proposals, people love summaries. Don't you?

And no wonder: Summaries save so much time. They tell you quickly if you need or want to read the actual material. Even if major decisions hinge on a report or proposal, many people may never read the entire document. CEOs make untold numbers of decisions based on executive summaries alone.

TIP

When a piece of your future hangs in the balance with a long-form business document, take the trouble to write a first-rate executive summary. Always reserve time to think them through as documents on their own. Never dash them off after meticulously writing the larger document. Write them as original, complete, logical and interesting statements. See them as a way to get people on your side by communicating what's most important and, perhaps, what you recommend.

Every summary has its own set of goals, but first know its role and what it needs to accomplish. Almost always, aim for summaries that

>> Generate interest — excitement, if possible — to lure readers into reading the report, proposal or other material.

>> Integrate the document's main points into a cohesive narrative that readers can easily understand.

>> Put the larger document in perspective for your target audiences so that they know why it matters to them.

>> Write throughout with energy and lively language.

>> Use a reader-friendly format that is *not* based on bullets.

>> Create a call to action if appropriate, rather than a pile of passive information from which readers are left to draw their own conclusions.

Giving perspective to complex material

Good reports, proposals and other business documents are read and often acted upon. Bad, boring ones are trashed faster than yesterday's fish. They may be used to wrap the fish. A strong executive summary makes the difference. It starts you off on the right foot with your audience and can keep you there by establishing interest in the rest of your material.

TIP

A helpful writing sequence is to first write your document, then write the executive summary, then review the main document to ensure that it lines up with the summary and thoroughly supports it. Or, you can write your executive summary first and then back it up with the full document.

Both processes work because developing the summary helps you figure out your real story. This truth applies to a range of reports and proposals as well as white papers, grant applications, business plans and most other business documents.

Your aim in the executive summary is to predigest the information and give the reader a meaningful perspective. You accomplish these goals by understanding your own material in depth.

SHORTCUT

Suppose you're reporting on what you did last month. Two quick tricks presented earlier in this chapter can trigger your thinking for the summary:

>> Without looking at the already-written report, ask yourself: What settles out as important, interesting, provoking, promising or enlightening about what I covered? Write that down.

>> Imagine your partner or a good buddy was away for the last month and upon return asks, "What happened in your work while I was gone?" What would you say? Write that down.

If you're following a report format that your company or department prescribes — with preset categories (trends, new projects, profits and losses and so on) — try one of these shortcut processes for each category. Also, take time to determine what matters with a bigger-picture brainstorming so that you know what perspective to give the full report.

Determining what matters

WARNING

Your executive summary should not march through a series of mini-versions of the larger document's sections. After the opening statement — think of it as the summary of the summary — follow the document's sequencing and integrate the material and ideas for a crystallizing statement.

TIP

Figure out what's important — what is most worth sharing — especially in terms of your readers' interests. If you're writing a report, review your answers to the questions presented in "Focus reader attention" earlier in this chapter; if it's a proposal, look back at "Writing informal proposals."

TIP

For models of how to handle an executive summary, check out the best. Warren Buffett, the financier, is justly famous for his crystal-clear communication of tough material. His "To the Shareholders of Berkshire Hathaway" letters strike readers as honest, but at the same time, present a point of view very persuasively. Back in 2007 when the U.S. housing market was beginning to implode, his letter began:

Our gain in net worth during 2007 was $12.3 billion, which increased the per-share book value of both our Class A and Class B stock by 11 percent. Over the last 43 years (that is, since present management took over) book value has grown from $19 to $78,008, a rate of 21 percent compounded annually.

Overall, our 76 operating businesses did well last year. The few that have problems were primarily linked to housing, among them our brick, carpet and real estate brokerage operations. Their setbacks are minor and temporary. Our competitive position in these businesses remains strong, and we have first-class CEOs who run them right, in good times or bad.

Some major financial institutions have, however, experienced staggering problems because they engaged in the "weakened lending practice" I described in last year's letter. John Stumpf, CEO of Wells Fargo, aptly dissected the recent behavior of many lenders: "It is interesting that the industry has invented new ways to lose money when the old ways seemed to work fine."

Buffett goes on to explain the housing crisis in a paragraph, then moves on with sections titled: "Turning to happier thoughts, an acquisition"; "Finally our insurance business"; and "That party is over," warning investors to anticipate lower insurance earnings and more.

The whole introduction occupies seven paragraphs. It sets readers up to read the full report, with all the statistics, charts and financial detail — in the frame of mind Buffett chooses.

REMEMBER

Notice how Buffett's quoted statement aligns with the principles of good writing as shared in this book. His goal is obvious: to reassure his investors that his company is on solid ground despite troubling financial events. To make that view convincing, he takes account of the negatives as well so the picture he presents appears to be balanced. Understanding his audience — Hathaway investors — makes obvious why he chose a fact-rich lead as his first paragraph. While not catchy, the comparative numbers are nevertheless riveting to those whose eyes are glued to his (and their own) bottom line.

Buffett's use of colloquial language helps everyone relate to his subject. His assurance that "we have first-class CEOs who run them right, in good times or bad" is both conversational and confident. The 2007 letter ends with a paragraph about how lucky he and his partner feel: "Every day is exciting to us; no wonder we tap-dance to work." You're never too successful or sophisticated to share your passion and enthusiasm. In fact, it's essential if you aim high.

Try This: Look at how Buffett does it. Check out a bunch of his shareholder letters at www.berkshirehathaway.com/letters. Even if you have no interest in the financial details, observe his clear, concise word choices and organized presentation style. This complex information is delivered at a tenth-grade reading level. Notice too how he creates each letter's tone. Spend ten minutes analyzing what makes him such a credible writer and how he conveys trustworthiness, even when reporting bad news.

One more recommendation for executive summaries: Don't call it "Executive Summary," which is sleep-inducing. Give it a real headline that says something concrete about your content, positions it and promotes reader interest. You can still use the words but amplify them:

Executive Summary: How the Audit Shifts Company Priorities for Next Year

The next section looks specifically at using headlines and subheads.

Putting headlines to work

To make all your business documents more engaging and reader-friendly, adapt some good journalism techniques. One energizing approach is to stop thinking of section headings as labels and to start writing these elements as headlines.

The difference is that labels are static, dull and uninformative. Headlines, on the other hand, tell readers what's happening right now and pique curiosity for what they're about to read. Headlines have a feeling of action and movement.

You can use headlines to begin sections of reports, proposals, white papers and business plans. They are easy to write when you think about delivering information rather than naming a category. Here are some labels transformed into headlines:

Label: *Admissions: Results compared to forecasts*

Headline: *September admissions exceed forecast by 10%*

Label: *Calumet Program case history*

Headline: *How the Calumet program turned an oil company's image from black to green*

If you're responding to given categories and must use them, simply add a headline after the label. Adding a colon at the end of the standardized label line works fine:

Admissions Performance:

This year's enrollment leaps 19 percent over last

Most reports, proposals and business plans benefit enormously from working in subheads as well as headlines. Use this method to solve problems with organization. As I suggest in Chapter 6, write a series of subheads before drafting the material itself and then add the appropriate information and ideas under each.

Breaking long sections of big documents into sequences of smaller sections with subheads pulls readers along and helps them make sense of what you're presenting. Plant these guideposts to help focus your audience on what is most important for them to know, and what you want them to know.

If you have a multipage section on financial indicators, for example, write a headline to capsulize the whole picture and then a set of action subheads for each topic. For example:

March Indicators Promise Much, Move Little

Skilled worker recruitment loses traction: down .5 percent from plan

Stock price climbs to 126, up 2 percent

Sales jump to 2012 levels, led by Jumex breakthrough

Company economists feel cautious confidence for April

You may question whether the preceding headlines and subheads are too specific, encouraging readers to not look past them. Actually, the more specific and compelling you can be, more of the "right" readers — the ones you target — will read the material. And you'll have a ready-made Table of Contents, which most business documents that are longer than two or three pages should have.

REMEMBER

The more clearly you signal where you've located specific types of information in your document and why that information matters, the better the response. People are extremely selective about investing their energy and time. Helping them choose what to read is an excellent technique. Further yet: The headline/subhead technique makes your material look more interesting and communicates that you are a take-charge, action-oriented leader. This is true even when the news you're delivering is bad!

Writing Tips for All Business Documents

For your own line of work, you may need business materials that differ from the specific types I cover in the preceding sections of this chapter. Most of the ideas still apply: to white papers, RFPs, survey reports and all the other document challenges you may encounter. Some general writing guidelines and techniques are helpful to keep in mind whatever the format.

REMEMBER

Finding the right tone is critical. Important business communications must come across as authoritative, objective, credible and confident. You're trying to persuade someone to do something, so don't sound ponderous and dull. The more lively and engaging your document, the more likely people are to respond with what you want. Given the mounds of boring material most recipients face, they may actually be grateful for a good read.

If you compete for a high-stakes opportunity like a really big contract and someone tells you to write expensive-sounding, verbose, grandiloquent prose, shut your ears. You want a transparent writing style that showcases your thinking, not fancy or puffy language that calls attention to itself. Employ all the good writing techniques at your disposal. Chapters 3, 4 and 5 cover a bounty of useful strategies, but pin this list to the top of your proposals file:

Minimize use of:

>> First person voice: I, we, us

>> Stiff pompous tone

>> Arrogant or self-aggrandizing atmosphere

>> Passive indirect statements

>> Long complicated words

>> Jargon, acronyms and clichés

>> Meandering sentences that demand two readings

>> Abstractions

>> Empty hype, including flowery adjectives and unproved claims

>> Hedge words and qualifiers: *might, perhaps, hopefully, possibly, would, could* and the like

>> Extra or extraneous material that doesn't support your point

And take pains to avoid mistakes in grammar, punctuation or spelling.

Maximize use of:

>> Third-person voice as your organization ("RX Global delivers on time . . .")

>> Conversational but respectful style

>> Quiet low-key confidence

>> Straightforward clear sentences, average 12 to 18 words

>> Short basic concrete words and action verbs

>> Short paragraphs of one to five sentences

- » Rhythmic flow of language (read it aloud)
- » Creative comparisons
- » Proof/evidence: Facts, statistics, images and examples
- » Positive language that doesn't qualify or hedge
- » Story line: Have one, support it and stick to it throughout

Now that you know the basics of creating high-impact business materials, learn how to make these documents — and everything you write — more persuasive. This is the subject of the next chapter.

3

Writing to Present Yourself Effectively

Learn the techniques of persuasion that enable you to communicate with conviction and connect with your audiences.

Develop your own "value proposition" to express the qualities, accomplishments and vision that make you special.

Find out how to craft your own powerful "elevator speech" for effective networking and teaming.

Discover how to find and tell a personal or business story that crystallizes what you offer and humanizes you with your chosen audiences.

Apply your writing skills to develop presentations, speeches and talking points that prepare you for any situation.

Learn how to create winning résumés, cover letters and networking messages that get your foot in the door and give you an edge over the competition.

IN THIS CHAPTER

» **Writing to reach heart and mind**

» **Using the language of persuasion**

» **Discovering your core message**

» **Finding, shaping and using stories**

» **Translating words into visuals**

Chapter **8**

Building Persuasion into Your Writing

P
revious chapters demonstrate that every message is "an ask." Your audiences must be persuaded to read your messages and then convinced to respond to what you want, whether your request is minor or major. Success demands careful attention to both content and use of language. This chapter focuses on specific techniques of persuasion that help you write better everyday materials like emails, letters and reports, and are essential for high-stakes challenges like writing sales and marketing materials, negotiating and advocating. I show you concrete ways to make all your writing more persuasive and offer some big-picture ideas to amplify your toolkit for marketing yourself, an enterprise or cause.

Connecting with Your Readers

Essentially, when you need the tools of persuasion, you are asking people to change in some way. The challenge is that human beings don't like change. We may enjoy deciding whether to travel to Paris or Rome, but change a long-held conviction? Give up a skill we took years or decades to develop in favor of the new? Cheerfully accept a company reorganization that transforms patterns and habits and relationships we're used to?

Even talking people into changing their brand of coffee is an uphill battle, let alone asking them to take a risk. We are emotionally invested in the choices we've already made, from our coffee to our political leanings to our work patterns. No wonder persuasion is hard. Let's start with some general ideas about that art and a few fun shortcuts to generate your own enthusiasm, because your own conviction is a first essential.

Drawing from psychology

From the golden age of Greece on, persuasiveness has absorbed plenty of attention. The philosopher Aristotle described the formula for a great speech as combining *ethos* (establishing authority), *logos* (logical argument) and *pathos* (swaying an audience emotionally). Today, techniques of persuasion obsess marketers, communicators, psychologists, neuroscientists and even economists, who created the field of behavioral economics with breakthrough analysis of how humans make decisions. Their opinions are backed by research that ranges from brain imaging to big data crunching.

Consensus is that Aristotle knew what he was talking about but according to today's thinkers, the balance of factors — logic, authority and emotion — has shifted toward the last. The key takeaway: While we may believe we make choices based on information and logic, in truth, our decisions are usually driven by emotion and then justified with rationality. Analytic thought consumes enormous amounts of brain energy, so we typically call on it only when we more or less force ourselves to take the trouble.

TIP

For business writing, the key lesson is: *Whenever possible go for both the heart and the mind.* When it's important that readers respond to your message in a particular way, create an emotional connection. Relate to your audience's hopes and aspirations, or perhaps feelings like worry and anxiety. Use language that produces positive associations, builds trust and shows empathy. Find ways to capture people's imagination. Give them a vision. But back it all up with evidence that speaks to your claims and your own authority or expertise.

The emotional connection draws people in and encourages them to stay with you, but most people will look for backup information that justifies trust. Also, some people typically approach decisions more rationally, so the facts, and signals of authority, are dealmakers for them. In short, covering all three elements makes perfect sense.

Drawing on the resource of techniques and strategies that follow can improve all your communication, from emails to proposals, presentations to interviews, websites to speeches to sales pages. I can't cover every need you encounter to write or speak persuasively. So read this advice with an eye toward adapting it for your use according to the goal and situation.

Communicating with conviction

Every section of this book stresses the importance of identifying and understanding your audience. It is the key to succeeding with every message. But the other side of the equation is *you*. You must speak and write from a sense of your own value and the value of whatever you're pitching. When persuasion is in order, your own belief is your best friend.

REMEMBER

One corollary of the self-belief principle: When you craft an important message to introduce yourself in person or in writing, remind yourself of your own value and relevance. If you're pitching a product or service, soliciting a donation or asking for peoples' votes, take a minute to reinform yourself of why you believe that what you represent is worthy and why (I presume) you're making it your life's work.

What drew you to do what you do? Why does it matter to you? Is it a passion? A commitment to solve a problem or help people? Why are you certain that knowing about your service or product or yourself will benefit others and/or their own audiences? Why are you the ideal person for the opportunity?

A popular quote often attributed to Theodore Roosevelt sums it up this way: "People don't care how much you know until they know how much you care." Enthusiasm is the best convincer. Few will review your facts and figures if you don't project enthusiasm and generate it in others. If you aspire to a leadership role, few will follow you if they don't sense your enthusiasm.

SHORTCUT

To bring confidence to your writing as well as to face-to-face situations, experiment with techniques that actors, presenters and salespeople commonly use to set the stage for a good performance. When you're about to work on an important message or make an appearance, energize yourself by assuming an assertive but comfortable posture and walk around that way for a few minutes. This technique exploits the mind-body connection, signaling to your mind that you are capable, resourceful and knowledgeable.

Another strategy from the psychologist's repertoire: Choose a photo or other image that's associated with a proud moment in your life when you felt on top of the world, and relive that moment as vividly as you can. Perhaps you won an award, were congratulated on something, finished a marathon or celebrated another personal achievement. Employ all your senses to re-create how you felt, stood, held your shoulders, moved. Practice re-creating this glow in your mind and body several times and you'll be able to trigger your confidence just by calling up the image!

Strategizing in Many Dimensions

Especially if you're writing a sales page, advertisement or marketing-oriented email, consider all the ways you can capture the heart, address the mind and prove your authority.

For "mind," think evidence, statistics, research, examples and voices of authority. To reassure readers that you're to be trusted as an authority or expert, cite appropriate track record, awards, testimonials and reviews. Create a concise but sparkling rundown of your credentials and your team's credentials if others are involved.

"Heart" may take more imagination. A personal story and anecdotes often work. In other cases, try directly connecting your service or product with an audience's problem: "Give us three hours and you'll double your profit margin." And of course, images offer a powerful tool for bypassing logic. Nonprofits are especially adept at using photographs to connect potential donors with their cause, whether that involves helping people, animals or the environment.

Advertisers often use images of children, puppies or glamorous people for their magnetic pull even when the visuals don't much relate to the pitch. But a clear relationship between image and subject is always better. It need not be a literal connection. An image can epitomize a situation, problem or feeling, an approach explored in the last section of this chapter.

TIP

Note that tapping into "heart" does not necessarily mean creating an association with strong emotions like love or fear. It can mean connecting what you offer to the way it will make a difference, however small, in your readers' lives — something that matters to them. A pillow that will help them sleep better . . . a more elegantly designed smartphone . . . an online system that records pilfering. Fortunes have been built on such solutions and a vast majority are on a much smaller scale of importance.

Centering on benefits

Technical specifications and other features do matter, more to some people than others. Certainly, you need them if you're marketing a gizmo to engineers — but even for technical folks, put the focus on *benefits* rather than features because they reach everyone on the emotional level. Rather than *Gizmo XYZ has 14 ABC connectors,* try *Gizmo XYZ cuts charging time by three hours.* A useful tactic is to connect features with benefits with statements such as, "this feature helps you do X" or "this feature solves Y problem."

To find benefits, ask the "why" question. Why might someone want a car with twice the power of an ordinary, less expensive one? Perhaps it makes them feel more powerful themselves, or they love *the idea* of zooming along the highway at a speed few will actually practice. Or they anticipate the thrill of impressing friends with their showpiece. So promote the dream; use the specs as backup.

Try This: Translate your product's or service's features into benefits. For example, rather than just saying,

The new Caliber X120: four cylinders and a 360 HP engine.

Try something more like,

Become the fastest animal on land and leave the slow lane world behind.

If you are promoting a service, you might say,

Our training firm is the only one in the tri-state area to employ a psychologist.

But instead of or in addition to this line, complete the sales point for the reader:

Our staff psychologist helps create every New Way seminar so we know exactly how to engage busy professionals and deliver practical strategies.

To return to the engineering gizmo, combining feature with benefit works as well:

Gizmo's 14 ABC portals cut charging time by three hours.

In a single line, you've gone to the heart of the audience's concern and given a nod to the mind as well.

Creating a friendly and reasonable tone

Especially if you're advocating for an idea or decision, present your argument with an objective voice. Let your passion for your subject show — but in a controlled way. Aim to communicate enthusiasm and at the same time, a feeling of impartiality.

TIP

In fact, rather than offering a one-sided harangue, choose to convey objective open-mindedness to other arguments and preferences. A favorite technique is to figure out the major opposing arguments your reader is likely to come up with and build in the rebuttals in a cheerful, fair-minded spirit. When you take account of opposing ideas rather than ignoring or dismissing them, you are more credible and persuasive. Some examples:

1. You might be concerned that the system requires adapting to a whole new technology. With a single half-day workshop, we will train your key people and be on call for a full month should questions arise.

2. You may recall that we experimented with this strategy ten years ago, but at that time, we couldn't tap big data analysis tools to fine-tune each step.

This approach gives you good openings to cite evidence, too.

> *Yes, you can produce a new website less expensively. But our Second Window site generates twice as many leads for our clients than any of their previous sites. The data shows . . .*

Try This: Use the Talking Points strategy. See "Composing Talking Points for Live Interaction" in Chapter 9, which shows you how to brainstorm for the content you need. Use the process to surface reasons why your reader or listener might resist your ask. Then build those rebuttals into your message. This can be done in subtle rather than overt ways. For example, rather than saying,

> *Our competitor's product needs expensive servicing every four months.*

You could write,

> *No expensive servicing! Unlike similar products, our G-machine is designed as a closed system that self-maintains for a full year.*

REMEMBER

Of course, everything you say must be true. The idea is not to make up facts or describe something you can't implement, but to present the truth in the best light for your chosen audience. This leads you to frame your message in a way that accomplishes the result you want. As the words on my favorite coffee mug say, in the novelist Jack Kerouac's words, "It ain't watcha write, it's the way atcha write it."

Giving people time

REMEMBER

When you sell a service, product or new way of thinking, it's wise not to expect overnight miracles. Decisions are grounded on trust. Think "one step at a time." A good letter can gain you entrée to meet with someone; a well-crafted email pitch draws people to your website; an interesting tweet leads someone to read your blog; a free webinar brings in people ready to pay for a service; effective blogs lead readers to trust you enough to buy your book. The process of capturing readers and channeling them stage by stage to purchase is called *funnel marketing*.

Good teachers aim for incremental learning. They start where their students are and take them, step by step, toward more knowledge and understanding. Experienced marketers aim to build trust in a similar way. Persuading someone to buy a different product or adopt a new idea takes sustained effort and a consistent message across platforms. That's what integrated marketing is about: knowing your core message and using it to frame all your communication. I explore that later in this chapter.

Planning Your Persuasive Message

Before you start writing, plan. This is especially important when the stakes are high and call for strategizing. The step-by-step method I explain in Part 1 of this book will see you through every time and is worth your review. Here is how to use it when building a persuasive message.

Step 1: Clarify your goal to yourself

What is your basic intent? If you're announcing a company or office reorganization, is your goal simply to deliver cut-and-dried information, like this?

Dear Staff: As of March 21, by Leadership Team directive, our department will be reorganized on a team basis. Reporting systems will be adapted accordingly. Stand by for specific assignments and guidelines. Your cooperation is appreciated.

Realistically, such a message could prompt some employees to start a job search and others to just stay put dispiritedly, expecting their own hammer to fall. Not good outcomes. The writer overlooked the real intent: to deliver news in a way that at least maintains morale and encourages employees to see the change as potentially positive.

TIP

Always consider how the message will make your readers feel. If the potential is negative, brainstorm your content and find ways to counter natural concerns by addressing them through content choices, tone and use of language, all covered in this chapter.

TIP

Before you shape an important message — whether a three-paragraph email or 20-page report — remind yourself that your goal is not just to deliver information but to orient your readers to feel a certain way about it. Once you know your intent, the challenge is to know your readers.

Step 2: Characterize your audience

Imagine the readers you want to reach and think about the message you're delivering, through their eyes. Other than asking people in advance, this is the only way to gauge how they will react to what you write or say. Take the necessary time to relate to their possible fears, worries and concerns regarding your subject. Find the emotional connection by remembering the WIIFM principle (what's-in-it-for-me). The more you know and understand your audience, the more effective you can be in persuading them to a viewpoint. Scan the extensive rundown of audience characteristics described in Chapter 2 and decide which are relevant to the specific situation.

Step 3: Determine the best content

Step 3 of the planning process is to brainstorm based on your understanding of your goal and audience. To deliver an upbeat message about a staff reorganization, for example, you might list points such as:

>> The realignment will promote collaboration which makes work more productive and enjoyable than the current structure.

>> The teaming approach will give you more opportunity to use your strengths.

>> You will have more autonomy and have a say in which assignments you take on.

When you think in this structured manner, new relatable ideas occur to you — for example, that the department could sweeten the pot by offering more opportunities for growth, with company-sponsored programs to learn or sharpen a skill. Also, it becomes clear that for this level of change, a written message is best viewed as preamble to one or more meetings where everyone can ask questions and perhaps contribute to the planning.

SHORTCUT

A good planning device is to begin with subheads. Take three pieces of real or virtual paper and label one "heart," another "mind," and the third "trust-building." Start your brainstorming by filling out one category at a time. Once all three lists are done, scan them to identify your lead, which ideally is your strongest most engaging point — it's probably on the "heart" list. Then juggle the rest to find a logical arrangement. You can interweave the three categories or run the technical backup and/or your credentials in a box or sidebar so they are available but don't interrupt your main appeal. If you end up keeping all or some of the subheads, readers can quickly see the points that most matter to them and your coverage will be balanced.

Rather than using labels, write action statements in your subheads to make a stronger case. For example:

Label: *The new thingymabob*

Subhead: *Our newest thingymabob measures temperature at 40 feet*

Step 4: Create action headlines that relate to your audience

Drafting a preliminary headline helps because it leads you to crystallize your main point and orient everything to it. Later you may identify a better headline, or not.

Try This: Review your own response patterns. Whether you're asking for an appointment, writing a blog or sales page or developing a report, you must fight to get your message read. To get a feel for how quick decisions about whether to read something are made, scan your inbox. In emails, the headline is your subject line, and good ones are essential (as covered in Chapter 6). If you're like most people, it takes you four seconds to decide to "open" or "delete." It's not a lot different for other materials. While you're checking this out, look carefully at what kind of subject lines draw you in.

Bottom line: Craft a good action-style headline for almost everything you write. Headlines needn't be catchy, but must be to the point and *hone in on how your content relates to your readers.* Why should they read this? Can you come up with a must-read angle? What follows the headline must further cement reader attention.

Step 5: Develop a compelling lead that connects content and reader

Focus on what is most interesting, useful or relevant about your subject. What problem will you solve? How will viewers' lives be better? Why should your target audience care about your product, service or idea? Answer that question yourself to find your best opening. An anecdote might work, an interesting fact, a rhetorical question, an example. Professional writers probably spend 20 percent of their work life on constructing good leads. It's well worth the time.

Step 6: Draft the rest of the message

Draw on the lists you created for heart, mind and trust to build the body of the message. Don't forget to call readers to action — be perfectly clear on what you want them to do next. In many selling situations you may want to provide an incentive: Sign up for my newsletter and get my free e-book on how to do X . . . Order now to receive a 15% discount . . . Read my blog to discover inside information about your . . . Send a photo of yourself enjoying our product and we'll send you a free gift . . . Take this workshop and become a member of our Advice Whenever community, and so on, according to the nature of your message.

Using the step-by-step planning process is thoroughly covered in Part 1, including the review, edit and proofing steps, which are the same for all writing so

I don't repeat them here. Let's look now at language choices to support a persuasive intent, whatever the medium.

Using Persuasive Language

So far, this chapter has concentrated on how to create persuasive messages by planning the right content. Of course, the content must be expressed in language that supports the viewpoint you want to communicate and connects with your audiences. Accomplish this by following the "Goldilocks" formula — aim to say just enough: not too little, which leaves your readers unconvinced, and not too much, which buries them with more than they want to know and turns them off.

Work for clarity and simplicity. Persuasive writing is instantly comprehended and does not bog your audience down in ambiguity, confusion or wordiness. Persuasive writing at its best seems transparent, underscoring the ideas rather than calling attention to the writing itself. But at the same time, messages work best when they are vivid and energetic.

Because writing persuasively is a key factor for all business writing, every chapter includes relevant advice, particularly Chapters 4 and 5. Here are some specific guidelines for using language and message structure that will reinforce persuasiveness in all your communication.

Choosing words that persuade

Build sentences on action verbs. Take time to substitute lively verbs for dull passive ones (an online thesaurus helps you do this in an instant). In addition to energizing your language and bringing your ideas to life, basing sentences on active verbs helps you eliminate wordiness and unnecessary phrases that dilute impact.

Use short, common words that are tangible rather than abstract — things you can see, touch, measure. They're the words we most often use in everyday speech. What if you're trying to communicate complex, abstract ideas? Then it's especially important to find concrete ways to express them. Simple one- and two-syllable words connote honesty, reality, transparency and conviction.

Avoid the use of meaningless hyperbole. Exaggerated statements and clichéd words and phrases add nothing and turn readers off (such as, "innovative, cutting-edge, state-of-the-art breakthrough"). Often this means eliminating all or most descriptive words — adjectives and adverbs. Using them as camouflage for empty thoughts doesn't work.

Skip the wishy-washy. Don't hedge with qualifying words, such as "maybe" or "perhaps," and hesitant phrases, such as "I hope you will find this idea of value." Be positive! Show conviction! Communicate energy! Demonstrate faith in your own product or service — or yourself. Using some exclamation points support this cause, but don't go overboard and sound childish.

Create comparisons — similes, metaphors and other imaginative devices — to build pictures in readers' minds. They attract attention and help make complex and abstract concepts more real. There is a fine line between a metaphor and a cliché, however. "To sow the seeds" and "bear fruit" don't add much to everyday language and may even hurt your cause. Here are two I noticed that livened up two humdrum reports recently:

Depending solely on the XYZ technology is like standing on one leg.

We want to grow the economy so the cake is bigger and everyone gets a slice.

Comparisons need not be a sentence. They can take the form of a phrase ("enthusiasm is contagious"), a paragraph or even a whole document. Try experimenting with comparisons — similes are easiest — by writing down something you want to express. For example, to explain what handling a tough project feels like, you might say "X is like . . .", and play with what conveys the difficulty of the effort (for example, "Managing Project X is like trying to keep a river from overflowing").

Here's one related to our subject: "Write headlines as if they're flags to wave at passengers speeding by in a train." And another: "A big vocabulary is like underwear — everyone should have it, but they shouldn't show it off."

Avoid words that carry negative feeling. Often, it's a matter of how you choose to put something. If you're eliminating a service, "canceling" is negative, "streamlining our operation" is positive. But don't resort to sugarcoating facts when they must be delivered. If "streamlining" involves laying people off, you must say so because it's honest, and everyone will find out anyway. But you can say it tactfully and regretfully, and mention how the company is helping those people.

Build in words that evoke positive emotions and associations. For a sales page, words like *first ever, guaranteed* and *reliable,* make people feel more secure in making a choice. *Youthful, serene* and *glowing* connote happy states. If you want to convey peacefulness, words like *carefree, radiant, unhurried* and *natural* may find a place.

TIP

For a unique and exhaustive reference guide to words associated with the eight basic emotions, as well as positive and negative sentiments, download one of the free NRC Emotion Lexicons (https://nrc.canada.ca/en/research-development/products-services/technical-advisory-services/sentiment-emotion-lexicons). These lexicons are produced by the National Research Council of Canada and are invaluable to serious marketers.

Employ magic words. When you want to entice your readers to take the next step, whether it's to click from a landing page to "order now," or give you permission to use their email address, make them an offer they might be unable to refuse. Some words that resonate with most people: "Free." "This week only." "Offer ends today." "Proven." "Tested." "Free returns." "Free sample." "Biggest discount of the season." "Free gift." "Bonus!" "One left."

Structuring material to support persuasion

Use mostly short sentences but develop a good rhythm by working in some longer sentences. But not too long — lengthy complicated sentences are hard to follow on first reading and may lose many readers instantly. Hesitate before using more than one clause in your sentences, which usually translates as no more than two commas. Avoid a choppy, stilted cadence and try for one that pulls readers along in a forward motion.

SHORTCUT

Read the copy aloud to immediately identify its cadence. The human mind is most responsive to oral arguments, because speech preceded writing by eons. *So when the aim is to persuade, think of what you're writing as a speech.* Edit until the read-aloud test shows you a smooth, easy-to-say, hitch-free ride.

Build in plenty of white space. Keep paragraphs short, perhaps three sentences long, each focused on a single idea. But vary their length. Work in occasional single-sentence paragraphs. Material that looks approachable and easy to absorb gets read, understood and more readily accepted.

Use sentence fragments to add punch. But be sure your meaning is completely clear and they cannot be interpreted as mistakes. For example, the first sentence in the following set feels incorrect. But we are used to statements like the second (and sentences starting with "And, "But" or "Or," like many do in this section):

Has the Miseramobi ever left anyone stranded in the desert? Has not.

Has the Miseramobi ever left anyone stranded in the desert? Never.

Single words are useful, such as "Always." "Ask." "Problems?" "Questions?"

Edit for correct spelling, punctuation and basic grammar. Yes, you can take liberties in the interest of rhetorical impact, but if it looks like carelessness or a mistake, you've shot your credibility.

Employ rhetorical devices. Approaches drawn from speech-making offer powerful options for presenting ideas effectively. Posing rhetorical questions is one such device, and devising comparisons is another, both covered earlier in this chapter. Here are a few more to experiment with (note the Latin names: The Romans were an argumentative people):

>> *Alliteration:* A sentence or phrase that repeats a sound, the initial consonant: *The market's dreary downward dive . . . .*

>> *Anaphora:* A repeating word or phrase. *We looked at X . . . We looked at Y . . . We looked at Z.*

>> *Onomatopoeia:* Words that sound like what they mean: whizzed, plunged, plopped, hooted, drummed, mumbled, shrieked, clumped.

>> *Rule of Three:* Citing three main points, three reasons, three examples, three fragments — this technique resonates with us. We came, we saw, we conquered. We identified the problem, explored the issues and found a solution.

And here's my own secret sauce for using language effectively:

Pay close attention to all transitions between information points, counterpoints and conclusions. A few examples of these valuable words and phrases:

Furthermore, besides that, equally important, similarly, however, significantly

Instead, on the other hand, in spite of, considering that, nevertheless

In final analysis, in the end, for this reason, on balance, ultimately, in conclusion

It can be helpful to add extra transitions between sentences, paragraphs and sections to help you clarify your own logic and see if you've left out anything. It also helps you judge whether you've said too little about something or too much. You can always cut some transitions in final editing. When you show clearly how each idea relates to the next, you create a progressive argument that strikes readers as reasonable, logical and unassailable.

REMEMBER

The concept of persuasive messaging carries ethical issues that can be complicated. Remember that when you consciously use persuasive techniques, your goal is to find the positive and build on that. A thoughtful writing process helps you do this and may also uncover gaps in strategic thinking.

This situation often occurs for public relations experts when they develop an important communication on behalf of decision-makers. They may see not only gaps in the information, but an inattention to how the messages will make readers *feel.* Contrary to popular opinion, the PR job is not to cover negatives by fudging the facts with language. Rather, it's to explain the risks a poor message can create and also suggest *actions* that will counter or mitigate a negative situation and improve it. Be your own PR specialist and review what you communicate in this big-picture perspective.

Knowing what language to choose and what to avoid

To close this discussion of persuasive techniques, I return to a central idea of this chapter and this book: Remember that practicing empathy will always help you handle difficult situations. Remember that everyone owns a personal history and set of experiences that shaped their attitudes and beliefs. Remember to be *kind*.

When your goal is to persuade, avoid prejudicial thinking that leads you to undercut your intent with statements that put others on defensive. You are more likely to say things like the following in conversation, but be aware of betraying such sentiments in writing as well:

> *"I can't believe you feel that way."*
>
> *"Frankly . . ."*
>
> *"With all due respect . . ."*
>
> *"How in the world can you think that . . ."*

Choose positive language that tells people they are heard:

> *"Tell me more about that."*
>
> *"You make some good points."*
>
> *"Help me understand how you see that."*
>
> *"I wonder if you've considered . . ."*
>
> *"Can we agree that . . ."*

And a sentence that's useful if you reach a stalemate and want to move on in good spirit, at least for the moment:

> *"You could be right."*

TIP

Yet one more technique for your persuasion arsenal is your own personal experience. Nothing can be more powerful than explaining why you changed your own mind, came to a belief, decided on your career path or founded a company. Accordingly, I show you next how to crystallize your own experience with a "value proposition" and employ it in telling your own story or that of an enterprise.

Finding Your Core Business Message

If you're in business for yourself or intend to be, the key to all communication from marketing campaigns to sales pitches, proposals and websites comes down to owning a core message. This applies equally if you run a nonprofit, government office or one-person operation of any kind. And it applies to freelancers, gig workers, authors and consultants. Even employees on staff need to self-market in some way. And whatever your field, when you compete for a special opportunity like a grant, appointment, elected office or especially attractive job, you need to self-market.

More formally, in marketing and sales terms, the core message is called the *value proposition* or *unique selling proposition*. It is an organization's central statement that defines its uniqueness and provides the substructure upon which its marketing and branding are built. Smart enterprises invest in their creation and use them to frame all communication. The value statement keeps them attuned to what matters most when making pivotal decisions and assures that all employees are tuned to the same frequency.

Does that sound like the job of a mission statement? Ideally, a mission statement would accomplish these goals, but too often it's a superficial identity concocted for public relations that bears little relation to reality. However produced, they are often too general to mean much. In contrast, the whole *reason for a value proposition is to be specific.*

I won't kid you: Creating a meaningful core message is real work. Big businesses often hire expensive agencies and teams of consultants to help them. The guidelines I give you (at no extra cost!) are based on the business model, adapted to more general use. Adapt them further yourself according to your own needs and aspirations.

REMEMBER

"Audience" is the heart of the value proposition thinking process. You're not aiming to tell other people how fabulous you are, but rather, how fabulously you align with *their* problems, hopes and dreams. Or convenience. To shape this message, dig down and scan wide. Figure out your truest value to those you want to connect with. This leads you to identify your bestselling points and shows you the essence of what you want your target audiences to know. Whether you're writing a speech or a website, a sales letter or tagline or story, you'll have an invaluable head start.

Your goal is a statement in down-to-earth language that can be a single sentence, or better, a paragraph. This can be amplified with bullet points or more copy, but the basic statement should stay clear and compact and memorable — not necessarily word by word, but in essence. I find it helpful to frame it in terms of "you," meaning the audience, to automatically orient toward the client base from the outset. But you can initially use the third person to identify your company and your clients (for example, *National Haptics helps college professors . . .*). Either way, know who your audience is, thoroughly.

Don't imagine a core message is a matter of juggling words. Here's the difference between wordsmithing and developing a message that directly speaks to customers. Suppose I own a consulting firm that helps businesses create their core messages. I can say:

> *Keystone Messaging helps you tell your story to the world so it resonates with customers. We find the right words to liven up your sales pitches, website and networking messages. We bring a full set of creative skills to this challenge and free you to focus on your mission. The results energize your sales team, attract more people to your website and brighten all your presentations.*

Not that terrible? But suppose I start this way:

> *Keystone Messaging works with you to find your company message — the message that crystallizes what you alone offer and aligns you directly with your customers' bottom line.*

This concreteness suggests a different follow-up from the first one's vague claims. It sets you up to cite evidence. As an example, for a sales page or website, the second version could continue on with:

> *Research shows that organizations that communicate well are 1.7 times as likely to outperform their peers. Our clients in your industry document that using the core messages we help them build generates a 10 to 20 percent increase in website traffic . . .*

The original version of the message may read okay but it's just words: "resonates," "livens up," "creative," "energizes" and "brighten." These are *process* words rather than results words, and clients don't care about them. They don't want to know what you do — but what you can accomplish *for them*. The second message addresses your customers' likely agenda: improve the bottom line.

Here is a value proposition that is widely admired:

> *Uber is the smartest way to get around. One tap and a car comes directly to you. Your driver knows exactly where to go. And payment is completely cashless.*

This statement is deceptively simple, because in four short sentences it compares the Uber experience with that of its main competitor, taxicabs. Notice how the entire orientation is "you." A lot of time-consuming drilling down may well have been involved. With a headline added — "Tap the app, get a ride" — this statement was used on the company home page (before the 2020 coronavirus pandemic, when it was replaced with a "we care about safety" message).

Searching for true value

If you run a business of any kind — or a nonprofit, consultancy or government office — you can get in touch with its true value in a variety of ways:

>> **Ask your customers or clients what you have accomplished for them and what they most value.** Try for specifics, especially in bottom-line terms. They may be more prepared to deliver this information than you think; if you're a repeat or long-term supplier, they may be quite aware of their ROI (return on investment). For ideas on how to frame good questions, see the section, "Questions to ask your clients and customers."

>> **Brainstorm with an internal group.** Working with your immediate colleagues or representatives from different departments gives you the advantage of advance buy-in from different stakeholders. Or work with a business-savvy person or two whom you trust. The section, "Questions to ask your team and yourself," gives you material for this process.

TIP

If you choose to use the inside team approach, consider supplementing it with at least a few outside opinions. This gives you a reality check on whether you're moving in the right direction and staying aligned with your clients. More often than not, organizations are surprised with the disconnect between what they *believe* their clients value and the actuality.

>> **Do it yourself.** Ask yourself probing questions — or create a small circle of colleagues from other organizations who can also benefit from exploration within a group setting. CEOs from top companies meet this way to share problems and solutions and you can, too. Focus on building a core value statement for each of you, one at a time.

>> **Work with a business counselor.** If you're an entrepreneur or want to be one, a professional business counselor can save you a lot of trial and error. Free workshops and counseling are available in many U.S. locations from the Small Business Development Center (https://americassbdc.org) and SCORE (https://core.score.org), a national network of volunteer mentors for entrepreneurs. Many colleges offer low-cost courses and programs as well.

Questions to ask your clients and customers

If you currently have clients, solicit their insights to help craft your core message. Use written questionnaires, hold telephone conversations or conduct in-person or teleconference meetings. Interpret the following questions to fit your operation, adding some and subtracting others to align with your particular operation.

In addition to a base for your core message, plan to emerge with great testimonials for your website and other materials. (Gain customers' permission to use their words, of course.)

TIP

And while you're at it, pay scrupulous attention to any performance shortcomings that emerge and be prepared to follow through and improve. When you ask people for input and acknowledge its merit, you're obliged to respond with action!

» What do you most value about our product or service? Why?

» Have we helped you increase profitability? How? Can you quantify that?

» Have we helped you increase market share? By how much?

» Have we saved you money? How much?

» Did you use the money saved another way? What resulted?

» Did we help you cut costs? How?

» What problems have we solved for you?

» Have we helped you reach new markets or audiences? Which?

» Did we increase efficiency? Systems?

» Did we help you reduce mistakes and errors?

» Did we improve relationships between staff members? Does this prevent conflict? How does that matter?

» What do you like about working with us? What don't you like?

» Did anything surprise you while working with us?

» When would you call us in the future?

» What would you say about us to a colleague?

» Did we meet your expectations? How can we improve? What can we do better?

» Did you know we also offer service X?

» Should we add to our services in any way?

REMEMBER

If you approach clients in the spirit of checking on their satisfaction level and seeking their suggestions, they're almost certain to respond positively. Don't see the research as an imposition, but as a relationship-building opportunity. And don't be surprised if what you discover differs from what you expected.

Questions to ask your team and yourself

Uncover insights that can contribute to your core message by brainstorming with partners or collaborators and if your organization is large, with representatives from different parts. Or work with a business counselor or a team you create — colleagues, partners, friends — who can amplify your perspective. Without outside input, you risk overlooking your best opportunities or may reinforce a misdirection.

The following questions will help you explore. Focus on those that relate to you and your enterprise. The goal is to tease out what makes *your* organization unique and how to position it powerfully. Skip questions that don't apply, but invest some time in brainstorming ones that do.

>> What makes us special?

>> What do we do that's different from our competitors?

>> What sparked the idea for this enterprise?

>> What's unusual, interesting or surprising about our history?

>> Do we feel a sense of mission in what we do? What is it?

>> Do we have a philosophy or company culture that distinguishes us? What is it?

>> Is this a satisfying place for our employees to work? Do we actively developed their capabilities and help them grow?

>> What are we most proud of (achievements, problem solving, creative thinking, collaborative skills, industry leadership, reliability and so on)?

>> Does a particular person epitomize our history and values? How?

>> What does our total body of work say about us?

>> What's the best example of our extraordinary service?

>> Do we have a high satisfaction rate? How many of our clients come back?

>> What was our toughest, most complex project so far?

>> How do we help clients solve the problems that keep them up at night?

>> How can we prove how successful we are in carrying out our mission?

>> How might the world (or industry) change if everyone hired us or used our product?

>> Has our growth pattern been steady? What has affected it?

>> Why are we better than our competitors and should be chosen?

>> Where would we like to be in a year? Five years? Ten years?

>> What would we most like our customers to say about us?

>> How does what we do make the world a better place in any way?

Notice that a thoughtful process will inevitably identify shortcomings as well as competitive advantages. When you clarify what you are trying to accomplish on a basic level, you also clarify the criteria that tell you how well you're doing. Many successful organizations use truth–telling exploration to help chart next steps and identify deficits to plug.

Making your case in business terms

Your true value statement must connect with your customers and prospects, and this may take some translation. Reaching businesspeople in their own terms is not really rocket science. It's often about dollars and cents and time. Use this truth to make your core message more powerful.

SHORTCUT

Start developing your core message by looking into work you or your company has done that solves problems. Look for ways to show that you can:

>> **Increase revenue and profitability.** For example: Grow market share, retain customers, find new markets, reach a wider audience, make marketing initiatives more productive.

>> **Cut costs and streamline.** For example: Reduce expenses, increase efficiency, cut redundancies, reduce mistakes, redeploy staff, reduce turnover, minimize product returns, cut red tape.

>> **Improve positioning.** For example: Build the client's or product's cachet, improve public or customer perception, raise company profile, minimize complaints, increase customer satisfaction.

>> **Change behavior.** For example: Train staff to work in teams or communicate better, promote adoption of organization's core mission and values, shift unproductive systems and behavior to productive ones.

REMEMBER

Important as it is, money isn't everything. Identify your clients' pain points and think about how you address those, especially in different ways from your competitors. Perhaps you have evening office hours to accommodate those who work; wash dogs in their homes; train those who buy your equipment; or provide free ten-year warranties. If you're in business, you probably already offer specific amenities. The idea is to think about value more systematically so you can communicate about what sets you apart and sharpen your own focus.

Every industry is different but all share the same imperatives, though they may take different forms. Increasing revenue for a nonprofit may mean upping donations, sponsorships or grants or recruiting more volunteers. A government agency typically wants a larger share of the tax revenue pie, which requires that it better articulates the need for its service, demonstrates new efficiencies or expands its client base.

A good general rule of thumb for your marketing: Identify your value and then move on to prove it. Your business may be less abstract than my Keystone Messaging example, or your product may lend itself to quantifying results more easily than a service. Whatever your business, your customers may be able to give you real numbers for ways that you helped them. If not, or your venture is new, do some research and cite industry statistics. Or cite one outstanding example of how you helped a customer. Or do all of these things.

TIP

Don't overlook the "good citizen" part of your organization's message. Most people today, especially the younger generations, value enterprises that support and contribute to good causes in the community and beyond. Are you helping people? Making the world better in even a small way? Nurturing your own employees? These may be important elements of how you do business and deserve to play a role in your communication. Research shows that a company's association with a cause such as saving the environment, promoting social justice and fighting poverty may not provably impact the bottom line. But it does demonstrably attract employees of the Millennial generation and younger who will work longer, more enthusiastically and more capably for such employers.

Equipped with your own core message, you are prepared to experiment with one of the most persuasive techniques of all: storytelling.

Finding, Shaping and Using Stories

Let's start with some perspective on why stories matter and then focus on your own story: the story you tell about yourself or your enterprise — to yourself as well as the world.

Our modern technological society has come full circle to value storytelling, the oldest communication art, as the best way to deliver messages. Experts in marketing, branding, advertising, public relations, sales and education now advocate stories to communicate ideas, values, aspirations and competitive advantage.

The idea makes sense: Human beings have told each other stories for millennia, and as neurological science now demonstrates, we're hard-wired to respond to them. Specific areas of the brain process stories, and when vividly told, these tales excite the same circuitry as actual experiences, making us feel we are living other people's actions and emotions ourselves. Or just as powerful, we feel the storyteller is living *our* experience.

Stories bypass our logical side and grab our emotions, which as discussed earlier in this chapter, determine our decisions and most other actions. Poet Ann Bracken puts it like this: "The way people change their minds is not with facts, but a story they connect with."

REMEMBER

For children, stories make sense of a complicated world and at best, are inspiring. They serve the same purposes for adults. Given the chaotic and random environment we find ourselves in, it's no wonder we crave good stories that put things in perspective and have a beginning, middle and end.

In practical terms, stories bring presentations alive, create a bond between teller and listener and stay with the audience. They can make abstract ideas real and vivid. They offer endless opportunity to individualize and humanize an institution or enterprise or leader.

What's not to like? Naturally you want to harness the power of stories for yourself and your enterprises. The problem comes in applying the idea. Where can you find a good story that embodies your mission: Can you buy one online? Should you take a fiction writing course? Or hire a novelist to create one for you? The short answer: None of the above.

TIP

Here's a simple and practical way to think about stories: They tell what happened. Sometimes they tell what *can* happen. Your story is implicit in the way you chose your career, made your discovery, built your business, helped other people and much more.

In terms of your business message, you can build a story that communicates the heart of who you are, crystallizes your unique strength and connects with the people you want to connect with. We all own a story line and once discovered, it explains us to ourselves. It gives you a perspective on what you've already done and experienced and where you want to go next.

I focus on story-making for entrepreneurs and freelancers because they most clearly need them. But the ideas are applicable whatever your current role. Stories are highly adaptable for purposes that include:

- » Wesbites, especially the "About Us" page

- » Elevator pitches and formal introductions

- » Job application cover letters

- » Pitches for investment or other support

- » Brochures and marketing materials

- » Speeches and presentation openings

- » Media features and interviews

- » Special event promotions, like a company anniversary

- » Exhibit handouts for trade shows and other public events

- » Blogs

I recently saw several good stories told on restaurant placemats. Each basically relates who the founders were, where they came from, how the restaurant was born and evolved, which descendants are running it now and what makes it so great. These sorts of stories are hard not to read while you're waiting for your food! Look for suitable opportunities (not necessarily on dinner placemats) to share and tell your own stories. Tailor them to the medium and occasion.

TIP

Stories are also prime tools for corporations. They communicate a shared history or vision that keeps people on the same track and keeps inspiring leaders, generation after generation. They also serve well for carrying a message about the firm's good works, such as the charitable causes it supports or its efforts toward inclusiveness, sustainability, green building and conservation. Demonstrating corporate responsibility is a must for all businesses today, and telling stories is a great way to do that.

REMEMBER

For nonprofit organizations, stories can provide the best key to fundraising, volunteer recruitment and more. They can make the mission real and important, even exciting. Some nonprofits do this through the "founder" story, effective when that person is famous or charismatic. Often, charitable causes tell moving stories about the people who need their help and/or success stories about individuals they have helped.

Many nonprofits are good at embodying their sense of purpose and accomplishment in stories. Companies can learn a great deal from them about humanizing abstract ideas to touch people and make their organizations important and memorable.

Finding your business story

If you're in business for yourself, the *lodestar story* — one that epitomizes your business and guides how you think and communicate about it — often evolves over time and must embody the core value idea, explained in the previous section of this chapter.

Stories can take many shapes, but it's helpful to think about four basic types that work for many organizations:

» **Discovery:** How I discovered my talent or passion, found my mission, developed a way to match my values to my work, started my business.

» **Bumpy road:** Obstacles I faced, mistakes I made, weaknesses I encountered, my turning point, how I overcame challenges and grew the business.

» **Success story:** How I used my skills, product or service to help someone else, or an enterprise, achieve what they wanted or solve a major problem.

» **Big vision:** How much better things will be, the benefits resulting from accepting my idea or product or service.

TIP

For any business-oriented purpose, your story must relate to the specific people you want as your audience. If you're explaining why you're passionate about your work, it must be work that relates to your readers. A bumpy-road story must have a message your audience cares about — perhaps how you equipped yourself to solve *their* problems. A success story is best centered on somebody just like your audience so those people can relate. A big vision should connect with your audience's needs — perhaps by promising a solution to an important perceived problem.

WARNING

Framing your experience and practicing selective memory is legitimate when you build a story, but *never tell a story that is not fundamentally true*. First of all, you're unlikely to tell it well, and moreover, you kill your own authenticity at the outset. Trust that the materials are there.

SHORTCUT

A good way to develop a story is to start with the point you want to make. Then methodically scan your experience for a piece of history that illustrates that point. If nothing presents itself immediately, think your way back in life year by year and notice when something stops you. There is usually a reason something grabs your attention, so explore this memory. Does it lend itself to one of the story formats mentioned in the preceding sections, or another that speaks to you?

Building your story

For fiction writers and playwrights, just as for journalists, the hard part is the lead: where to start. Don't be surprised if your story presents the same challenge.

A good beginning is not usually a chronological one. That generally produces a narrative, which is quite different from a story, and will probably wander all over the place and bore your audience. When you start at the first event and proceed forward in time, a story lacks suspense and doesn't provoke the curiosity that keeps people reading or listening.

TIP

Look for an interesting "in." A surprise or a built-in contradiction is a good way to start. The fact that Steve Jobs dropped out of college and built Apple fascinates. Similarly, the story of how Facebook was born in a college dorm and how a 17-year-old sold his software for $37 million grab people's attention. Of course, such stories are only interesting because the people have already hit the big time. You don't have to blow away your audience. Discovery and turning points in your own life or career make good lead material, too.

SHORTCUT

Try the tell-it-to-someone technique. I often find that people will naturally deliver the heart of their message orally but then turn it into a dull abstract statement and/or bury it in a mountain of claims that make them sound just like their competitors. For example, I heard a restaurant owner and chef tell a group, "I worked in three different Latino restaurants for ten years but was always unhappy that none of them served the real Salvadoran food I grew up with and cook at home. So we saved up to open our own family restaurant and we serve things that people never ate before!" Yet on the business's website, this was expressed as "offering authentic Latino cuisine."

Similarly, the owner of a local wellness business told me that in her extensive experience as a master physical therapist, she was constantly frustrated by having to send patients all over the city for other services, knowing the hardships this presented them. So she determined to build a practice that brought many specialists together working under one roof, and has done so very successfully. Calling this approach "integrated services" loses the story.

So, see what happens when you tell your story informally and out loud. A single sentence may do it. J. K. Rowling wrote her first Harry Potter book after looking out the window of a train and thinking, "Boy doesn't know he's a wizard, goes off to wizard school."

If you're an entrepreneur, I know you can find your storyline, because if you didn't have a "eureka" moment of some kind, you wouldn't be in business. It can be a quiet one. A colleague who teaches presentation skills opens by sharing her first day of teaching. She felt awkward and uncomfortable, and she knew she was not connecting with her students. At the first break, one young woman approached and quietly gave her the magic clue she needed — "just be yourself." She then briefly recounts how she gradually learned to become a strong speaker and is now equipped to help other people become their own best selves as presenters.

Story-writing tips

The following ideas come from the fiction writer's side of the writing spectrum, but they can help the business storyteller, too. Use these approaches with both written and oral communication:

>> **Show, don't tell.** Rather than sticking to straight narrative or piling on the descriptive adjectives, pull readers right into your scene so they can draw their own conclusions. Paint a detailed picture of the situation, event, place or person.

>> **Engage the senses.** Use vivid, graphic language to activate readers' sense of smell, hearing, sound, touch and sight and make them feel as if they are there themselves. Research shows that specific areas of the brain light up if you say a surface is "splintery," for example, rather than "rough."

>> **Try telling the story in present tense.** Instead of writing in the past tense, the present tense brings it more immediate and alive for you as well as the reader or listener. Immerse yourself in the detail and speak from inside the re-created experience.

>> **Use dialogue and first-hand quotes.** Rather than, "My sixth-grade teacher told me I could be a success," try, "One day, I'm sitting at my desk thinking about my new video game, and suddenly there's Mrs. Dime, my sixth-grade teacher, staring down at me. She says, 'Jeremy, I know you have a lot to contribute but I ever hear your voice. I want to hear what you have to say. Will you do that?' From that moment . . . ."

>> **Be concrete and specific.** Take time to pin down details and the right words. Abstractions don't resonate with people. "I teach people to improve their writing" accomplishes less than "I show entrepreneurs how to create messages that win more hearts, minds and contracts."

>> **Use simple, say-able language.** Rely on short words, short sentences and plain structures. This especially applies to written stories because you're tapping into an oral tradition that generates its own expectations. Who doesn't listen up when you hear, "Once upon a time . . ."? Think about that natural story cadence and try echoing it. Or try using the words to spark your brainstorming, and perhaps even keep them in your delivered message: "Once upon a time I put on my first tie and went out on my first sales call . . . ."

>> **Stay positive.** Highlighting your mistakes and setbacks along the way is effective; people relate to this sharing and even mentally cheer you on toward success. Jokes you tell on yourself are usually well received. But be sure your story has a happy ending — one that leaves the audience with a good impression of you. Think carefully about sharing ironic jokes that undermine how you want to be perceived.

>> **Connect your point.** Be sure you know why you're telling your story and that this moral aligns with the point you want to get across. In fact, many experienced business storytellers write the ending first and then build the rest of the story toward it. You might bring the point home, as in "I know now that following those side roads is what prepared me to set you on the right track." A big-vision story might end, "I see a world where no one has to struggle for clean air and all children are healthy" or "My idea will solve the industry's data storage problem and save millions of dollars, millions of trees." Or you may decide to let the story make the point on its own.

SHORTCUT

Another way to explore story ideas and close in on a promising one is to identify something that has stuck in your mind, whether an experience or small incident any time in your life, and then tell that story to someone orally and record it. You may find you can immerse yourself in a specific place and time and relive what happened to a surprisingly detailed degree. See where the story takes you. It may shed more meaning than you expect on your career or a particular decision, action or idea. Then create a written version. (A useful app that records and quickly produces a transcript, keyed to the oral version for easy editing, is https://otter.ai.)

You can also showcase yourself by telling someone else's success story — for example, a customer or client who benefited from your help or product. In addition to supplementing your own story, these are useful case histories for your website or sales materials.

Stories are everywhere around us. Develop your awareness of good storytelling techniques in presentations you attend, what you read and what you listen to. NPR and the BBC both have storytelling programs, and it's especially illuminating to hear well-crafted stories read aloud well. On a more down-to-earth level, take a look at Quora, "the best answer to any question," at www.quora.com. On this site, anyone can pose a question and have it answered by interested people ranging from "ordinary" to celebrities in their fields. You may be surprised at how effective popular answers are in setting the stage with a line or two, drawing thousands to click on the rest.

Translating Words into Visuals

Is a picture worth a thousand words? Images can tell their own stories or support yours: the "lodestar" one that crystallizes who you are and what you offer, and the smaller ones that support your everyday communication in social media, blogs and proposals. A large part of the human brain is dedicated to visual processing. We respond to images instantly: The human brain can recognize a familiar object in only 100 milliseconds, bypassing our efforts toward logic.

Further, research studies say that the visual cortex — the part of the brain that processes images — can actually make decisions for us. One study at Iowa State University found that a rotating photo of salad in a cafeteria caused children to take some 60 to 70 percent more often. This reinforces what marketers have always known, that the right pictures sell products.

Marketing research backs the academic studies up with plenty of statistics for online media, since they are so trackable. For example:

>> Social posts with images are ten times more likely to engaged audience attention engagement than text-only posts.

>> People are 85 percent more likely to buy a product after viewing a video of it.

>> Tweets with images earned up to 18 percent more clicks, 89 percent more favorites and 150 percent more re-tweets.

How to handle such a visual revolution in your own messaging?

It's undeniable that images attract attention, engage people and help them visualize facts and ideas better. They entertain us, while reading often feels more like work. But do not think that visual materials replace words in most messaging situations. They enliven what you write and make it more fun. They translate an idea or need into visual terms that reach our heart. But in themselves, without words, they usually do not communicate all that much.

WARNING

Also, some of the statistics are to be taken with a grain of salt (a cliché but useful). A number of studies claim that emails with emojis in the subject line are opened far more often than those without, while others found that using emojis this way has no such effect, and that recipients feel that messages with subject-line emojis have less value than those without.

As usual, the key is to know your audience and what will trigger a negative or positive response. It's smart to track your own data, such as open rates and unsubscribes in the case of email to adjust your course. But where images will support your message, practical possibilities and resources abound.

Many younger readers are moving toward speaking through pictures via platforms like Snapchat, Instagram, Pinterest and current short-video apps. These are essentially social channels, geared to entertain or for general information-sharing in the case of Pinterest. However, many organizations work to capitalize on their popularity by using them for business messaging sometimes quite successfully. Like all components of communication, visuals are best used strategically and within a firm framework of "audience."

In the wide perspective, the value of using images in business communication derives from their ability to

» **Attract attention.** Visuals instantly engage. In a digital world that's more and more competitive, you want readers to choose your particular tweet or post or blog from a million choices and not only read it, but find it worth sharing with their networks.

» **Reach us emotionally.** A photo of a high-fashion shoe triggers a visceral reaction from its target audience — impossible with even the best description. However, the shoe photo on its own probably won't close the sale, unless the reader is already a fan of the designer and trusts the distributor. The buyer wants information about quality, fit, ease of returns and so on. The image gains the audience's attention, but the copy must talk them into action.

» **Save a lot of words.** They're invaluable for any kind of how-to material. They can substitute for a mountain of dull descriptive detail in many situations — to describe the fashion shoe, for example, or explain a set of complicated factors as a chart of graph. As I say throughout this book, promoting speedy comprehension is always a good idea.

» **Make things real to people.** Not long ago we bought all our shoes in stores. We touched them, checked out the colors, tried them on, held them alongside other options. We directly experienced how they made us feel: Comfortable? Beautiful? Young? When you buy your shoes online, you have no tangible experience with them. Photographs are as close as you can get. Selling a charitable cause, or an online course, is similar. We want to see what we're getting: the result of our charitable giving, what people say about the course.

» **Create trust.** Establishing relationships — so much of what the Internet is about — is also not so different from our experience buying products we can't touch. We make friends digitally, hire virtual workers and collaborate with people around the world whom we will never meet. Photography or video does this better than just words. And seeing is believing — watching a video on how to do something, or seeing a speaker in action, is a lot more effective than reading the credentials.

» **Present abstract and complex information with impact.** Businesspeople and scientists have always used charts and graphs and tables to report and persuade, but technology makes it easy now for anyone to create lively, colorful material that entertains us as they inform. Witness the rise of the infographic, to explain everything from how to make a cup of tea to why water quality is declining in different parts of the word. The format makes the data easier to grasp and invites interesting comparisons.

If you're a blogger or marketer, you know your copy will draw more readers and be better read when you include images: but how to illustrate something abstract, like how to cut red tape in the office? Adopt a "show don't tell" mindset. You may know the term "objective correlative" from a literature course. It means conveying an emotion, or something abstract, by representing it in a physical dimension. Rather than saying "I'm really mad," for example, a character in a play or book shows fury by smashing a precious vase. Rather than saying "I'm cutting myself off from a world I can't handle," a character burns all their shoes.

Try This: Look for an objective correlative. When you're presenting something abstract, look for something real to represent the idea. Say you want a visualization of too much red tape. Would you like an image of people trying to push a boulder made of paper bound by red ribbon up a hill? An office worker at his desk surrounded by darkness, with a single lamp to illuminate a toppling pile of paper? Files overflowing a cabinet and colliding on the floor? Or maybe you want to represent "solution": a scale of justice with a ton of paper weighing down one side and a tiny hard drive on the other.

The remarkable thing is that all the visual approaches mentioned are within reach of us average folks. In addition to the good photos we can shoot on our smartphones, we can access unending resources of free or reasonably priced photos, illustrations, gifs and video clips. Check out Unsplash (`https://unsplash.com`) for free high-res photos cleared for social media.

One useful service of online image libraries is that they categorize their holdings not only by physical objects, like "apple" and "keyboard," but also by emotions and concepts. You can enter words like "anger," "love," "disappointment" or "optimism" in the search box and pages of candidates come up with a choice of photos, cartoons, symbols and illustrations. Or enter descriptive words like "irrevocable" or "incomplete." Browsing through such collections is also a good way to trigger new ideas for blogging or marketing, and you'll already have the perfect illustration.

Chapter 9

Speaking Well for Yourself

Most people overlook two central truths when preparing speeches, presentations and scripts:

» They need to be written.

» They need to be spoken.

That may seem ridiculously obvious, but take these rules seriously and you're way ahead of the game, whatever yours is. Many people assume they'll rise to the occasion and wing much of what they say when they're on stage or just introducing themselves. Or, they write a speech as if it were a piece of literature and then are surprised at how hard it is to deliver it well.

Whatever the length or importance of your spoken piece — from an elevator speech that lasts just a few seconds to a formal presentation — the planning and writing process I cover in this chapter gives you the foundation you need. It will help you script yourself in formal situations and ground yourself in the essentials when the interaction is more informal. I also show you how to give yourself the edge when you need to think on your feet.

I start with a basic tool of your communication arsenal, the elevator speech. Take time to review this section whether or not you now attend in-person meetings and events where you must introduce yourself to new people. A strong elevator speech for telephone and video conferencing is also necessary. So is the constant need to introduce yourself well to collaborators and teams and when you interview for jobs and gigs, explain yourself to a new boss and connect with potential buyers or collaborators in any venue.

And it's an indispensable tool for defining yourself to . . . yourself. Further yet, developing an elevator pitch is a micro version of how to prepare for every kind of speaking opportunity.

Building Your Elevator Speech

The name of this mini-speech, also called *elevator pitch*, comes from this challenge: If you found yourself in an elevator with someone you want to connect with, how would you introduce yourself in the time it takes to travel from a low floor to a high floor? What would you say to the other person to make a good impression, find common ground and advance your cause?

Even if you don't envision an elevator ride in your immediate future, remember that opportunity knocks when you least expect it, as well as when you have a make-or-break appointment or appearance in person or on camera, or even on the telephone. So, adopt the old Boy Scout motto: Be prepared. Plan it, write it, edit it, practice it, adapt it. Most successful businesspeople and professionals obsess about this self-introduction and work constantly to evolve it.

Much of the advice that follows is based on the "classic" use of the elevator pitch to introduce yourself at a business-oriented meeting or event. But once developed, it becomes an all-purpose tool for connecting with the people and communities you want, in any venue. It will be the heart of all your work-related communication and well worth the time a deep dive takes: into yourself and the value you offer.

Your endpoint is a super-concise spoken statement that tells other people who you are, what you do, why that's valuable and how it relates to them. It's a different version of the question we encounter in writing all business messages: Why should the audience care? But in this case, rather than meaning why should someone care about a particular subject, it means why should they care about *you*?

Not that long ago, the usual recommendation was to create a pitch about 30 seconds long. Then 20 seconds became the preferred norm. But things keep speeding up. Including elevators. My best current advice is to aim for 12 to 20 seconds. You can keep an additional 10 seconds or more in reserve and use it if you sense a good audience reaction. But the basic version must stand on its own. Some trainers teach people to have their say while holding a lit match. If they haven't finished by the time the match burns down, well . . . .

REMEMBER

Drilling down to your core message is hard, but the benefits are many. Effective elevator speeches are conversation starters. If you can provoke a little curiosity and generate a question, you hit the mark.

To create a new elevator speech or improve an existing one, start by answering the same questions as for a written message: What is my goal? Who is my audience? How can I best connect the two? Essentially you need to crystallize your competitive advantage and communicate what you uniquely offer. The process leads you to internalize your value. For more help on finding your value, see Chapter 8, which focuses on identifying your personal value proposition, and Chapter 10, which shows you how to assess your skills and express your value in job-hunting situations.

The following sections apply the ideas to suit the style and demands of spoken communication.

Defining your goal

Every person and every situation may differ, but generally, aim to connect through your elevator speech with someone you don't yet know — or sometimes more important, *someone that person knows* — who may share an interest or link you to an opportunity you want. A good self-introduction is part of your overall marketing. It helps you build connections over the long run.

You may have noticed that when people are asked to introduce themselves at live meetings, an elevator speech delivered even in a low-key way can result in one or more participants approaching particular speakers later and exchanging business cards. The introduction was well geared to connect with a need. And a memorable pitch — one that's right on the mark for the audience —may be acted upon by more people later. Use the process I lead you through to generate this kind of interest yourself.

WARNING

Remember that an elevator speech is only a first step in building relationships. If the scene is an industry event, for example, trust that there is nothing you can say that will land you a job or consulting offer on the spot. Rather, aim to relax and find meeting ground. Contact points may be purely professional or more personal (like a shared interest in opera or antique cars). If the outlook is promising, look for a way to pursue the acquaintanceship.

Defining your audience

Think through your audience's perspective: what interests them, what they want to know, their pain points and why they should want to know you. A good introduction is intrinsically as much about "them" as it is about "me." It should explain why they need you.

For this reason, expert networkers always encourage someone they've just met to speak first. They listen intently and look for ways to adapt their own introduction so it highlights their potential benefit in becoming acquainted.

Of course, when creating an elevator pitch, you seldom have a single person in mind. Start by thinking in terms of group characteristics: what its members are likely to have in common. The concerns of bar association members are very different from those who belong to a medical or architects' association, for example. If a group consists of your peers or customers, you know a lot about them and can easily create a useful profile of the group.

SHORTCUT

A good way to spark a group profile is by visualizing your ideal client or connection: those you have now or would like to have. Think about what they are most interested in and how you align with that. What keeps them up at night? What are their problems and how can you help solve them? This will give you good ideas for putting yourself in focus with prospects in that line of work. (Chapter 2 shows you how to define audience characteristics in depth.)

TIP

Analyzing your goal and potential audience gives you a big bonus: It shows you where to show up — the places, events and occasions that enable you to network with the people you want to tell your story to. This strategic thinking leads you to avoid a mistake many businesspeople make: investing all their time with people similar to themselves. If you're a real estate agent, certainly you can learn a lot from your fellow agents and enjoy their company, and perhaps form strategic partnerships. But if you want to market, it's smart to go where your buyers are.

Take time to figure out where your prospects congregate. A good information source is www.meetup.com, which exhaustively lists interest groups in your geographic area by subject, covering virtual as well as in-person events. Online research will also turn up business and professional associations relevant to you.

Strategizing your content

To begin developing your pitch, it's helpful to take a detour to Chapter 8 and read the section on creating a personal value statement. Scan through your core message to find a statement that comes close to expressing the single most important point you want to get across. Then reimagine it in words that work for the ear. For example, here is Jed's value statement, which I use as a demonstration in Chapter 10:

Artist, art historian and administrator with experience and advanced training in archiving, preservation and photography. Special expertise in designing computer systems to accomplish administrative work more efficiently and economically. Excellent interpersonal skills, adept at training people to use new technology cheerfully.

If Jed met with a group of museum administrators, he might adapt this to say:

Hi, I'm Jed White. I'm a consultant for museums. I build custom computer systems so they can digitize their collections inexpensively and train people to use them. I just finished a project for the Canadian-American War Museum.

Jed's task here was to recycle the content into a conversational, easy-to-say, specific statement that centers on his most important asset for this audience. I clocked this speech at about 15 seconds — delivery speed varies depending on the region where you grew up, which influences your speech. Note how much you can get across in that time.

REMEMBER

The first imperative of a good speech, whatever its length, is to *write it* — on paper or your computer. This lets you look at, rethink, edit and refine it. The second imperative is to *say* it. There's no substitute for speaking it aloud, because it's ultimately an oral communication and must be polished based on sound.

Of course, you want your speech to seem spontaneous, especially if it's an elevator pitch, so there's a third imperative: *practice.* When you think you're ready, try it out on friends and see how they react. Then refine it further.

But you don't necessarily need to recite what you crafted word for word. More important, you need to completely internalize your message so without stress, you can listen to your conversational partner with all antennae out and adapt it on the spot.

SHORTCUT

Whether you've worked on a core value statement or are starting on your elevator speech from scratch, think intensively about whom you help. Whatever your product or service, ultimately someone benefits. Figure out how and what those benefits are. Think also about what in your work you're passionate about and what makes you feel proudest.

Tailor elevator speeches to the audience and occasion. A search engine optimization expert may tell this to an audience of marketing directors:

I'm Marian Smith, and my consulting group is SEO-Plus. My mission is to get businesses right on top of Google search results. I'm the marketing department's secret weapon.

While to a roomful of entrepreneurs, she may say:

> *I'm Marian Smith of SEO-Plus. My company is a one-stop shop for online marketing, websites and social media support. We level the playing field for small businesses — and know how to do it on small budgets. We're whizzes at SEO.*

Here are a few more representative elevator pitches to stir your thinking:

> *I'm a personal trainer, and I work with older women who feel out of shape. I design custom programs they're comfortable with and teach them to do it on their own. I love seeing how just a few sessions can make an amazing difference in their lives.*

> *I'm a financial planner. I know how important financial planning is for everyone and believe it shouldn't be a service only rich people can afford. So, I consult by telephone and it works really well — I help people decide how to pay for college, finance retirement, buy a house — whatever their goal is.*

TIP

Note how a brief elevator speech can generate questions. Keep the answers in your mental pocket. A sample exchange that might happen at a business or social event:

> Speaker: *I'm Melanie Black. I'm a dentist and I specialize in preschoolers. I love giving them a good experience so they won't be scared of going to the dentist. That way they'll be happy to take care of their teeth all their lives.*

> Audience: *Hmm . . . how do you do that?*

> Speaker: *I take plenty of time to show them all the equipment, which is painted in bright colors. We give them a playset of tools to take home. We minimize any pain, of course, but tell them the truth if something might hurt for a few seconds. Almost always they accept that. Would you like a business card if you know someone with small children who would appreciate how we work?*

TIP

Actively observe what works well in your own industry environment and what you respond to. Experiment with your own mini-pitches and evolve what works best. Here are some surefire strategies:

>> Be specific and concrete about what you do and who it benefits; generalizations make you sound like everybody else.

>> Use short words and sentences, and craft them to sound like natural speech, not a memorized statement.

>> Make your pitch memorable and easy to repeat.

>> Rev up your spirits and voice to sound positive, enthusiastic and lively.

>> Infuse your words with your passion for what you do and who you help, as appropriate.

>> Support your message with good body language and facial expressions.

>> Practice it to the point where you sound spontaneous and can adapt it on the spot. It's the idea you want to communicate — you can express it differently every time to suit the conversation and occasion.

Welcome the questions your listener may ask and be prepared to answer: "How do you do that?" "What kind of opportunity are you interested in?" "How does it work?"

Using your mini-speech

REMEMBER

Elevator speeches lend themselves to closing with a direct question of your own. To any of the examples I cite, you can with suitable variation say, "Do you know anyone who needs that?" "May I give you my card?" "May I have your business card?"

In many situations, it's perfectly fine to ask for what you want. If you're looking for a job or a career transition, add that to the end of your introduction or bring it up earlier, but not at the beginning. Help your listener by being specific about your need. "I'm looking for a marketing job" is far less likely to gain a nibble than:

I'm a five-year vet of the financial services industry. Right now, I'm working on an extra degree in marketing because that's what I really want to do. I'm looking to move into marketing now at a place where my unusual experience would be appreciated. Can you think of anyone I might talk to?

No guarantees, but the person you're speaking with may well glance around the room or mentally review his contact file to find you a match or give you a lead.

TIP

If you're brand new to the job market or almost so, or currently out of work, it's also perfectly fine to say that. But be aware of your own assets and speak from strength. And talk about yourself as a professional!

I'm a marketing specialist and I'll graduate from Tennyson in May. I've worked as an intern at several companies. Last summer I worked at PepsiCo with a team developing ways to integrate social media with traditional marketing. I'd love to continue with work like that — can you suggest anyone I might talk to?

Most young people underestimate the value of in-person networking and the enthusiasm with which professional associations and groups customarily welcome them. Many associations are developing programs to connect with students, who they see as vital to the industry's future and the association's. They often have a reasonable student membership rate, and in many cases, you can go to meetings without paying for membership at all.

TIP

Many associations sponsor a growing number of virtual events to keep members involved, so don't overlook those opportunities. The plus side of teleconferenced events is that they can extend your geographic reach beyond your own location, which would be hard to do in the case of live events. So, if you'd like a job in a new area, or are open to going anywhere, look for videoconferences in whatever locations you choose and participate. You may not be able to directly interact with someone who impresses you, but you can follow up in writing!

REMEMBER

In any networking situation, the people you talk to are just as eager as you are to make a new connection and to be heard. Listen with both ears. When you detect an opportunity to follow up by helping someone else in even a small way, take it, without necessarily expecting a return favor. After a meeting with someone of interest, great networkers develop relationships by sending a relevant clipping or link, or information about a travel destination or something else that came up. Or if the exchange is mutually promising and common ground is clear, they suggest further conversation or getting together in whatever way is practical.

Representing your organization and yourself

When you introduce yourself as a representative of your company or other organization, you speak for it. Often focusing on yourself isn't appropriate when you're talking to potential customers or industry groups. Introducing the organization is first priority. But do identify your role. For example:

I'm Nancy Williams and I'm the head of business development for Brash and Brumble. We're a local company that helps attorneys develop their branding through new social media strategies. I work with the team that creates the visuals for the client campaigns.

Your description of the organization should ideally be a 15- to 20-second expression of company core value created in much the same way as a personal elevator pitch. It should meet the same criteria — memorability, sharp focus, enthusiastic tone. Your company may have a ready-made pitch, a way of explaining the organization that you can adapt.

If you're a consultant or the owner of a one-person enterprise, you can speak in your own name or the company's and use the editorial "we" if you wish:

I'm Mark Smith, and my company is Four Legs on the Move. We transport horses all over the country for races and competitions . . . .

Distilling who you are through an elevator pitch gives you a great focus for all your communication, including your website, online profiles and the "about" credit when you write a blog or article. It gives you the best kernel for creating a tagline. Some people use a version on their letterhead or email signature.

And you've practiced the same methodology that will serve you well for all the presentations you may give that are more than 20 seconds, which I discuss next.

TIP

The magic of learning good communication techniques is that they work for everything you're called on or choose to write, and everything you write well helps you tell other people who you are and what you can do. And never think that what you do (or want to do) is too dull or limited to feed an interesting elevator speech. Dig deeper: Why did you choose your focus? Who needs it? Where do you want to take your skill? Know who you are, and the rest follows.

WARNING

While it may be in order to use a version of your introduction at social occasions, don't use it indiscriminately and label yourself a self-promoting bore. On the other hand, one of the most successful sales coaches I know routinely starts conversations when waiting in lines in any situation and remarkably often, ends up with good business leads.

Preparing and Giving Presentations

As presentation coaches often point out, many people view public speaking as literally worse than death. But effective presenting is more and more essential to today's business culture, so if you're among the fearful, you need to get over it!

Opportunities to speak directly to your audiences abound as never before. Anybody can mount a webinar, a teleseminar or online workshop via video, Skype, Zoom or other emerging software. You may need to give speeches or conference presentations. Or you may be invited to appear on seminar panels or share your expertise or viewpoint less formally.

Generally, the more truly interactive a presentation, the more on-the-spot thinking is needed as opposed to when you deliver a monologue. But you need to be even more prepared in order to carry it off because you don't want to be surprised by the questions you invite. Therefore, I focus on the most demanding presentation mode that readers are likely to encounter: delivering information and ideas, or sharing your know-how, with a large or important audience. You're not necessarily standing on a platform: You may deliver your message in a conference room or corner office or by video. But whatever the channel and formality, when the occasion matters, be ready to be your best.

The tried and true classic way to present well and comfortably boils down simply: preparation followed by practice. Adapt the ideas to the situation. They center (of course) on how to strategize content and use writing, but you'll find some delivery tips as well.

Planning what to say

Just as for an elevator speech, make decisions for a presentation based on your goal and your audience. What do you want to do: Motivate? Inspire? Sell something? Share information? Impress with your expertise? Change people's opinions or behavior? Each goal calls for different content, whatever the subject. And the advice that follows should be adapted to the format — speech, workshop, business pitch, presentation — and venue.

REMEMBER

The more closely you define your *goal,* the better the guidance you give yourself. For example, when you want to share information, think through *why* you want to share it. Helping your audience work harder and smarter is different from aiming to sign audience members up for one-on-one coaching. The first goal demands that you motivate the audience and deliver practical how-to information. To accomplish the second, you'd calibrate how much information to give away so that audience members are enticed to want more.

The *audience* to whom you're giving the information is the other half of the planning equation. If you're a scientist, you naturally present different material to other professionals as opposed to a lay audience interested in something useful or fun. Give real thought to what your listeners wants to know, what they worry about and what they care about. How will what you say solve problems? Or make life better, even if just a tiny bit?

WARNING

Unless you are a technical professional talking to people just like yourself, presentations are not usually the medium for deep, detailed, complex material. Despite how most teaching is still done, oral learning by itself is not very effective. And on-screen visuals and video in the way that most people use them don't help much.

Always the best rule of thumb: Keep it simple. When you plan a presentation, start at the end. What do you most want your audience to walk away with and remember? The best teachers aim to increase their students' knowledge and understanding incrementally rather than in giant leaps. It's best not to be overly ambitious and try to pour everything you know into 15 minutes of fast talk.

It's critical to know the time frame for your presentation. If half an hour is allocated, remember, according to the situation, to allow some of that time for you to be introduced, and to leave time at the end for questions. This probably brings

30 minutes down to 20 at best. Obviously if you have 15 minutes, or an hour, your content planning will be substantially different. You may need to narrow down your subject for smaller time frames.

TIP

Try to articulate a *theme* for your presentation — a basic message. Framing your material with a point of view, and putting things into perspective, is far more effective than giving people "just the facts." Most of us feel we're already drowning in information. We want to be told what the data means; what the product or service does for us; what will be different if we adopt the idea or invest in the belief.

SHORTCUT

To crystallize your basic message, try it the Hollywood way: Figure out how to express it in a single sentence. In fact, billion-dollar movies may be funded based on pitches such as, "Boy robot and girl robot fall in love and want a baby." A business equivalent? Perhaps for an audience of talent management specialists, "Managers who take our cross-cultural workshops perform 19 percent better." For a new product, your theme can be as simple as "Buy this gizmo because it shaves 11 percent off your electric bill." For a charitable cause, "Five dollars per week will buy food for 20 orphaned llamas."

Beginning well

Build your talk with the classic, simple structure — beginning, middle, end. As with most written materials, the lead — how you open — is the most important piece. It sets the tone and audience expectations. Aim to engage people and capture their attention. An opening anecdote is one way to do that. Other options include a startling fact, a rhetorical question or a briefly stated vision: "What if . . .?" But your opener must be relevant to your audience.

A good approach is to find a useful anecdote in your own experience. Or try what many professional speechwriters do: Ask all your friends if they have a good anecdote about the subject, the venue or your audience's profession. Be careful with jokes — never tell one that can be interpreted as laughing at the audience or taken as an insult by someone. Much better: Laugh at yourself.

REMEMBER

Often, however, you don't need to be super-clever. You can rivet your audience and generate an attentive mood by simply telling them directly why they should be interested: "My goal today is to show you how to find treasures in your basement you didn't know you had." "You'll be happy to hear that we expect the dividends for the next quarter to go up 12 percent."

Or might paint a picture of the problem you'll address and entice them with your solution: "Workplace misunderstandings cost businesses $15 billion last year. How could that happen? Poor communication! Today I'll show you how . . . ."

You can't really miss if you know the heart of your message and the biggest benefit the specific audience will reap by paying attention. But do your audience homework! Recently I was asked to talk about new techniques for teaching business writing to an audience of teachers. But in decoding preliminary conversations, I saw that student apathy was the biggest problem, and that both students and teachers first needed to feel that learning to write better was valuable. So I opened with, "I find that a lot of students are bored by learning business writing because they don't understand how critical it is to their careers. Here's how to wake them up and keep them engaged." This start generated useful conversation without making the teachers feel criticized. Introducing new techniques could follow more effectively than if I had started with them.

Remember to practice the WIIFM principle — what's-in-it-for-me (meaning "them") — and frame your presentation within this understanding.

Middling well

Just as for an email or other document, brainstorm the solid middle content that will accomplish your goal with your audience. Keep to your theme and organize the material in a logical, easy-to-follow sequence. Remember that you don't need to deliver the universe. There can definitely be too much of a good thing, *so know how much time you will have and set limits for yourself in terms of content.*

One organizational method that works well for presentations is to create a list of the areas relevant to your subject, much like creating a list of subheads for a written piece, which I explain how to do in Chapter 6. If you were a doctor pitching a new medical device to an audience of investors, for example, you might list:

1. *The problem Device X solves: Why needed?*

2. *What we're asking for and why*

3. *Who the device will help: The numbers*

4. *What it will replace and its advantages*

5. *How idea originated and was developed*

6. *Where things now stand*

7. *Next steps: Financing we need, how it will be used, how it will be repaid with profit*

8. *Future vision: Anticipated market and company growth*

If you were presenting your new device to fellow doctors, you'd omit the financial information, but might add more technical data, pros and cons and detailed trial results. "Future vision" would center on offering a bigger toolset to help their patients. If you were addressing senior citizens who might benefit from the new device, you'd talk about how it will help them, who would qualify and how they can follow up. "Future vision" in this case would be the better life they could enjoy and when and how that can happen.

As with every presentation and written piece, the more interesting you can make your information the better, no matter the audience. For the medical device, there might be anecdotes, examples, "fun facts" or surprising discoveries to incorporate along the way. For many subjects, a numbered approach works well and keeps you organized: "Here are the six most important changes that will affect your future in the advertising industry." Or "Four ways this new software will help you better handle project management." Most audiences love this strategy because they can tick off the items as you move along. Numbering gives them a sense of accomplishment and is easier on the brain.

TIP

Staying attentive for a length of time is hard work for adults! One research group claims that the average human attention span today is eight seconds — a little less than a goldfish's. For this reason, unless you're giving a speech, use some imagination to build interactive elements into what you present. Can you invite your listeners to do something active? Or break for a Q&A session once or twice during the course of a long presentation? Or you might ask an interesting question for audience members to answer and spend a few minutes having volunteers share their answers.

If your event is really long — like a workshop or seminar — it's helpful to "assign" a group project on the spot and have them report back in. For a large audience, break the group into smaller ones and ask each to work on something and report back.

Visuals can of course help you maintain audience attention, but they must always support your message and take second place in your planning.

Ending well

As appropriate, state your grand conclusion, sum up what you said and reinforce the takeaway you want. You might bring home to your audience why your subject matters to them and, if relevant, how to take the next step or put it to work in their practical lives. If appropriate, close with an energizing vision of the future as it relates to your talk. But don't rehash the entire speech and bore your listeners. Keep your ending brief.

REMEMBER

As the saying goes, it ain't over till it's over. A good ending often requires that you prep for questions. Preparing for the Q&A session afterward helps you deliver more confidently, too. If you inspire tough questions, see that as a plus. But have answers ready. Brainstorm, with colleagues as possible, to figure out the likely questions. Especially try to anticipate the one question you hope no one will pose, and know what you'll say. Use the "talking points" process I give you later in this chapter to do this.

Crafting your presentations with writing

Other than rocket science and brain surgery, perhaps, no thought is so complex that you cannot express it in clear, simple language. If you find it a challenge to be simple and clear, take it as a signal that you may need to understand your subject better. Or rethink it entirely.

SHORTCUT

If you have trouble homing in on your message or start to lose track of it, tell it to somebody: Explain what you want to get across and go on to detail the major relevant ideas, facts and points you want to make. Record what you say and build on this plan.

Writing helps you think through your presentation content and approach, so start with a piece of paper or your computer screen. Depending on how you work best, you can:

>> Draft a full script, based on subheads if this method works for you, or create an outline that covers all your main points. Many people recommend building on no more than three main ideas.

>> Identify a set of idea chunks and sequence them in a natural way so you can deliver your content in logical order, but plan to create the actual language on the spot.

Spelling it all out with Option 1 may seem more secure, but consider that you'd either have to read it verbatim — the worst presentation technique — or completely memorize it. This is extremely hard, and struggling to remember what you memorized is sure to turn off the audience. So, you'll need to boil your script back down to cues that remind you of the points you want to make.

TIP

Option 2, then, is often the best way to go. You must be totally comfortable with your material: Know your stuff and know your audience. Think through each area you want to cover and speak to it one piece at a time. You can remind yourself of your topics with an index card or two or what you put on the screen.

Delivering this way makes your content seem fresh — and it is, because you're framing the words as you speak and responding to your audience's expressions, gestures, body language. If as you talk it sounds like you're figuring it out, that's fine, unless you're really slow: A thoughtful delivery brings the audience along with you and typically matches their learning speed.

SHORTCUT

A useful compromise between memorizing-the-whole-thing and creating-it-as-you-go is to script and carefully rehearse your opening section, over and over again, so you start off with maximum confidence and create audience trust in the value of paying attention. Experiment with friends before the event and adjust the script if the input is helpful.

Maintaining maximum eye contact with your audience is essential. Therefore, do not depend on reading a draft or outline. If the event is so formal you need to read the whole speech, find out if there's a teleprompter — but understand that using it well takes real practice. This is also true of teleprompter apps you can use on your smartphone or other device. Another approach is to type the speech in a large font with pauses built in so you can look up often. For example:

> Four score and seven years ago
>
> our fathers brought forth
>
> on this continent . . .

However you achieve it, always remember that audience contact is much more important than remembering every word or even every thought. Expect that you may leave things out. No one but you will know. A U.S. president once gave a famous speech built around four points, an organization he spelled out at the beginning. He only delivered three points, but they were so well presented, no one appeared to notice.

Techniques to keep in mind at the planning stage:

>> Use basic, natural language as you do in conversation: short words, short sentences. You want to be instantly understood and trusted.

>> Build in natural pauses — the oral equivalent of white space — between ideas, sections and important sentences to help people absorb what you say.

>> Say your words aloud as you write and listen for an easy flow; when you find awkward hard-to-say patches, or you run out of breath, rewrite and check the sound again.

>> Avoid using too many statistics or numbers, because they dull the senses and numb the brain.

>> Use metaphors and other comparisons to make your point: "The applicants could have filled half a football field" is better than citing a figure.

>> Use graphic language and action verbs to engage the emotions and paint pictures. Check a thesaurus for alternative high-energy words to spark things up.

>> Time your presentation to fit the expected space and identify areas to skip should you run on too long to avoid shortchanging your close. Also have some extra material in your head should you run short (usually not the case).

>> Have a few content options in mind: When you see your audience losing interest, switch tracks and move on to something else.

Integrating visuals

It's not accidental that I've not yet mentioned Microsoft PowerPoint, Prezi, Keynote, Google Slides or their proliferating younger cousins. And for good reason: Despite all too common practice, visuals should always be treated as support for your message, not the main show.

Don't use a presentation system to plan and write what you'll say. Your message becomes distorted when you try to jam it into a limiting, structured format. Resist making decisions about what to include or omit based on preallocated pieces of space or flashy templates.

Plan and write your presentation as a speech, and then think about supporting visuals. Or work out possible slides simultaneous with the copy as you go. When you prepare the slides, don't cut and paste onto them the editorial content you wrote: Treat each slide as an individual communication and figure out what (few) words should be included and what visuals help make the same point. Avoid throwing your whole speech onto the screen.

You are — or should be — the central focus when you speak. People tune in to see and hear you, not stare at a screen. Never read from your slides. And don't distribute your handout before you speak, because it distracts your listeners, who leap ahead to the end and then wait impatiently for you to catch up.

Here are a few basic guidelines for integrating visuals into slide presentations:

>> Keep every slide simple and easy to absorb at a glance: no long lists of bullets and sub-bullets, no complex charts and graphs, no sets of statistics.

>> Translate important data or statistics into visualizations — for instance, if you're trying to explain the size of a nanometer, show comparisons such as a human hair and other objects.

>> Keep fonts simple and BIG so an in-person audience can read the material from anywhere in the room. How big depends on the size of your room and audience, but generally, don't go below 24 points. If your presentation is for virtual delivery, you may not need font that large but check readability on various platforms, including smartphones.

>> Keep graphics simple and consistent in format, style, colors and type of illustrations. Mixing photographs with cartoons, for example, is usually jarring. Check for legibility *before* you present to an audience to be sure the text projects well and is easy to read.

>> Use the "action" feature of presentation systems for dynamic visuals to show change — for example, how one element of a graph line moves over time. But use animation features sparingly so they are not distracting.

>> Incorporate video clips as available to liven things up, but be sure they're worth the watching time and support your message. Short is usually better. You want to stay the main focus of attention.

>> Test everything out before show time to make sure the technology is working, especially if you emailed the slide deck or are using unfamiliar equipment. Video clips in particular may come undone. The savviest presenters stand ready to deliver without their slide decks and Internet access because you just never can absolutely depend on them.

SHORTCUT

Don't drive yourself crazy by spending inordinate time on the mechanics of presentation. Focus on the substance. In fact, a good way to stay grounded as you speak is to use your slides as an organizational tool. Set up headlines and subheads that key you to remember important points. This keeps your audience with you, too. For example, build a succession of slides that just say minimal things like: The Problem, What We Did, How it Worked, Our Conclusions, What's Next — each with maybe just a few lines of copy. Wouldn't you rather they listen to you for the answers rather than trying to read them?

Or, phrase the ideas as questions: Why did X become a problem? How did we figure it out? How does this help 7 million people?

Standing and delivering

When you do your homework and shape your message to audience expectations and your own goals — first in writing and then by practicing the message to internalize it — you have the right content and have earned confidence to boot.

Practice is how dancers, musicians, actors, athletes and CEOs remember what to do when they're on stage or other performance arena. Rehearse as many times as necessary to master your own material and feel entirely comfortable with it. If you can't speak without notes, use cue cards as reminders, but don't stare at them for minutes or rustle through them to find your place.

Try This: Use prepping techniques. A great many elements are involved in creating and giving effective presentations, which you realize if you know an actor, have worked with a voice coach or have given a formal speech. Practice won't make perfect, and doesn't need to. But some useful techniques can go a long way. Following are my ten favorite ideas for feeling professional and confident:

>> Warm up. Many professional speakers have an easy exercise routine they do before presenting to help them feel relaxed and limber and get the energy flowing; many warm up their voices as well.

>> Stand, don't sit — even for an elevator speech and video conferencing when practical.

» Keep your posture straight and balanced, but not stiff; no rocking or fidgeting or pacing (but natural hand gestures and natural body movement are excellent).

» Breathe deeply, from very low in your diaphragm. This takes practice.

» Radiate positive energy and pleasure at being there.

» Vary the pitch and tone of your voice and be conscious of pacing: Avoid speed. The best pace may be a little slower than in a natural conversation.

» Maintain voice energy. Don't trail off at the end of sentences or end with an upward inflection that sounds like you're asking a question. Pause before and after a major point.

» Focus on one person at a time as you speak, perhaps for five-second intervals — don't let your eyes dart around or look to the sky for help.

» Notice how people react. If eyes glaze over, or half your audience is looking at their smartphones or toward the exit, slide into a new direction.

» Don't sweat what you forget. Even if you skip a major point, you're the only one who knows. Just focus on saying the rest with conviction.

TIP

Public speaking is an excellent way to grow your business. If it's important to you, give yourself some solid grounding. Many good speakers value their experience with Toastmasters International (www.toastmasters.org). And workshops in voice and presentation techniques are often available through local colleges, other educational centers and private sources.

Composing Talking Points for Live Interaction

So far, this chapter has covered techniques for preparing presentations, whether an elevator pitch or speech, as one-way communication. Basically, you talk, they listen. But writing is also an invaluable way to prepare for interactive situations. You don't want to give a great speech and then flub the Q&A. If you ever wonder how CEOs and politicians equip themselves to win debates, be good interviewees and prepare for press conferences, the answer is *talking points.* Many organizations also use talking points to ensure that all executives, or the whole staff, are on the same wavelength with a consistent message when talking for or about the company.

Talking points give you a beautiful personal tool for any kind of confrontation, including a media interview, job interview, sales meeting, Q&A session, cross-examination or any situation where you need to think on your feet.

TIP

The method is simple: Preferably with a colleague, friend or small group, sit down and brainstorm the main points you want to communicate for a given scenario. Write them down in telegraphic form. For example, if you're preparing for a job interview, think through your best matching points and examples. Then write them out, preferably just a line or two for each, limiting yourself to a single page total. Someone applying for a sales manager job might list:

Seven years' experience in a similar industry; know many people

Achieved 14 percent increase in my territory's sales over previous person by . . .

Appointed assistant sales manager a year ago

Named local "Salesperson of the Year" three times because . . .

Hold business degree from Martial U.

Captain competitive sailing team

Active in community: Board member of local Heart Association, former school board member, play Santa Claus in school pageant every year

TIP

Of course, you have more to say on each point, but the idea is to *know in advance the essentials to get across* during the course of the interview and write just enough for each item to trigger your own recollection of the full idea. Then you can draw on this thought-through material to make points in your favor and answer questions well.

There's no need to cover points that turn out not to fit the actual situation, but with a checklist of your "advantage" points in your head, you can draw on them to answer questions that give you appropriate opening. You're also ready to compose a good "who I am" explanation on the spot, and gracefully add a major point that didn't come up at the interview's end ("You might also like to know that . . .").

You can also use a politician's trick to "bridge" past a question you'd rather not answer, or can't, to something you do want to say (for example, "I don't have direct experience with that strategy, but for two years I used the Marigold Method to . . ."). However, take care not to appear evasive if you bridge this way. Most people have become very aware of this politician's technique and it provokes suspicion. It's important to convey that you are straightforward and honest. A "soft" version might work: "I haven't yet used the Marigold Method but look forward to doing so, and I'm sure my experience with the Primrose version applies . . . ."

TIP

The talking points approach helps you plan for any situation where you may be asked difficult or hostile questions. Say you're advocating for something and expect to be questioned, or even attacked, by people who disagree. Look at the situation from your opponents' perspective and brainstorm: What questions can they possibly ask? What are the nightmare questions? Be sure to include those you most dread. Once you have a full list and can't think of anything else, march through, question by question, and figure out the best concise answer you or the team can produce.

This systematic preparation gives you invaluable confidence for handling whatever follows. You're able to listen more intuitively to the other side and create good responses as needed. Moreover, it enables you to communicate in the calm, assured, non-defensive manner that so often helps win the day.

REMEMBER

Another significant use of talking points is to drive agreement. Government agencies, for example, forge talking points around an issue, often involving a combination of stakeholders in the process. Once a consensus is formulated, the page is distributed to everyone concerned with the expectation that they will act in accordance.

Similarly, a corporation under pressure creates talking points and supplies them to all representatives so they align with the expressed position. In a high-risk situation, the result may be distributed to a number of employees so that everyone speaks in the same voice. Sales departments often prepare talking points for the people in the field so all are well informed with the pros and cons of the product or service, and can tailor their pitch around the positives and gracefully respond to any negatives that are raised.

Keep in mind that talking points often evolve through several versions if reviewers are given the chance to contribute input or raise questions.

Try This: Develop talking points for a current need of your own. Talking points are immensely versatile. When you intend to ask for a raise, hold a difficult conversation, sell an idea, air a problem, disagree with a position or recommend an unpopular course of action, underwrite your success by developing them thoughtfully. *But don't take them into the conversation with you!* Review them before the event to remind yourself of what you want to communicate.

REMEMBER

My last word on public speaking: *Smile when you say it.* You can write the best elevator speech or presentation or sales pitch in the land, and answer tough questions deftly, but if you deliver without conviction and enthusiasm, you don't succeed. Write what you believe — and believe in what you say.

The oral communication techniques covered in this chapter will help arm you to compete for jobs effectively. But most often, you must first deploy your writing strength to earn those interview opportunities. The next chapter shows you how to create strong written materials for the job hunt.

Chapter **10**

Writing for the Job Hunt

I f the U.S. Bureau of Labor Statistics is correct, today's average worker stays at each job for a little more than four years and most Millennials keep jobs for about two years. If you were born after 1980, that means you may hold 20 or more jobs in your lifetime. Moreover, you may switch among a number of different fields over the course of your career because whole industries appear and disappear so quickly.

These predictions don't take account of the 2020 coronavirus pandemic. Its reverberations amplify the need to be a smart and well-equipped job applicant. Interesting jobs that require good thinking and communication skills are more competitive than ever. Whatever your industry, you must be able to demonstrate these abilities, a challenge that starts with your written résumé and cover letter. This chapter helps you showcase your abilities and personal strengths through these written formats.

If your application materials stand out, you gain an interview. Handling this well may be especially daunting if the interaction is virtual rather than in person. The best way to prepare? Use the tools of writing to define your value and communicate them. I cover how to do this as well.

Also: Be aware that in times when the number of job-seekers far surpasses the number of attractive jobs, writing may be part of the application process in yet more ways. Depending on your occupation, you may need to provide your best work samples and this usually means written material. Even when a job description does not specify good writing, a growing number of employers use writing for insights into how a candidate thinks and reacts to handling an assignment in a given time frame.

You may be asked to write materials on the spot. Typical assignments are to propose new ideas for the industry or organization; explain how you would handle a problem or have dealt with one in the past; evaluate existing materials; describe how you overcame an obstacle or would handle a difficult colleague or client, and so on, according to the business and the hiring specialists' imagination. This entire book is devoted to helping you approach this challenge with confidence.

But first things first. Especially because job hunting will be a constant part of your life in an evolving workscape, your first imperative is to have a solid sense of who you are and what you offer. Even when you're on the job, you may have to keep demonstrating your value and compete for the opportunities you want, so this self-assessment always matters. Therefore, let's start by talking about how to identify and describe your value.

Knowing and Expressing Your Value

Marketers call a message that expresses your or a company's value a "value proposition" or "core value statement." For an organization, this message is the crystallization of what the enterprise contributes to its customers, and the world in general, that no other entity provides. A company might, for example, offer extraordinary service in its domain, a 50-year history, an innovative or superior product in its niche, or a unique way of solving a problem. A nonprofit or government agency typically tries to communicate that it serves a specific segment of the population with services that would otherwise be unavailable.

REMEMBER

The most effective branding is based on this concept. An organization communicates its central value in a systematic and consistent way, using the channels it judges to be best — websites, ads, social media, print materials and all the rest. You can use the same thinking. A personal core value message clarifies your sense of identity. Just as a core message guides an organization, a personal one helps you always know who you are, what you're doing and why. It keeps you on track toward your goals and enables you to identify opportunities that support your progress.

TIP

Holding fast to your central identity is especially important in a flux-dominated world that demands chameleon-like responses. You may need to bring different parts of yourself to the fore when applying for particular jobs. Knowing your own uniqueness gives you a solid grounding in on how to communicate in résumés, cover letters and online media.

This sense of self empowers you in-person as well. Imagine going into a job interview with a secure conviction of what makes you valuable. Owning an effective message about *you*. Believing in this message gives you the confidence to deliver it well. You're prepared to answer interview questions without floundering and can field whatever is thrown at you. You can listen well and easily make the connection between employer needs and your own capabilities.

Consider, too, that when you hold a job you want to keep or advance in, you are bound to encounter new department heads or a manager who's looking for people to cut — or promote. How can you justify the company's investment in you? Show you're capable of more? If you start with an internalized core value statement, you're certain to fare much better than your colleagues. Here is how you can develop one for this moment in your life.

Pinpointing your personal strengths

One way smart leaders work toward their company's value proposition is to ask their executives, employees, clients, customers, themselves and perhaps the general public questions that reveal what the various stakeholders value about the organization. Then they analyze and distill all this input to determine the company's central value and find the language to communicate it.

I offer you here a process that adapts this corporate approach to your personal needs. Don't view this as an assignment worth a casual ten minutes. Good answers may take shape over time. I recommend experimenting seriously with this process because it can produce a perspective that radically improves the content of your job-hunting communication. Good substance is always the first imperative of good writing!

TIP

A good way to engage in this process is to work with one or two other people you trust and feel comfortable with. You can focus on yourself or give everyone equal attention so everyone emerges with their own core value statement. I guarantee you'll be happily surprised at what you learn about yourselves.

Try all or some of the following approaches:

>> **Explore your past history as a story.** Imagine someone asks you, "So, how did you get here?" What would you say? Think about your life overall as well as your career path so far. Try answering orally. Notice what comes to the fore. Jot it down. (Chapter 8 offers more specific guidance on finding your story.)

>> **Analyze your experience in writing.** This pushes you to think more deeply. Start at the beginning of your career or close to it, with facts such as where you were born, your family situation, your education, your first and subsequent jobs. Can you identify turning points? Milestones? Obstacles you overcame? Connections between your personal life and work choices? Write down achievements, recognition and honors of any kind in all of your life arenas.

>> **Focus on your assets.** What natural skills did you bring to the table? What skills have you developed? What assets do you value in yourself, and what do you believe others value in you? How would you describe your ideals? Write these things down, too.

>> **Ask other people for input.** If you're working solo, frame some questions to ask people who know you from various standpoints: friends, ex-colleagues, partners, maybe a former supervisor. For example:

- *What do you think I'm good at?*

- *What do you like about being my friend (or colleague or boss or partner)?*

- *Do you believe I have any qualities that make me different from anyone else?*

- *What would you say about me to a prospective employer (or friend or colleague)?*

- *Does knowing me benefit you in any way? Make your life different in any way?*

>> Then ask yourself:

- *What am I passionately interested in? What do I care about? Read about?*

- *What am I most proud of?*

- *What is my highest ambition?*

- *How do I want other people to see me?*

- *What have I accomplished so far for my employers?*

- *What have I contributed to friends? Family?*

- *How do I want my work and life to fit together?*

- *What activity, endeavor and/or pastime has been a constant in my life?*

- *What do I want to contribute to the world?*

SHORTCUT

Here's a fun activity to bring some useful ideas to light. With a group of perhaps seven to ten people, choose a scribe. Then focus on one person at a time. Each person in turn quickly says a single word or short phrase that they feel best captures that person. The scribe scribbles each contribution down on a single sheet of paper and at the end, everyone receives their own page with the full group input.

You may see a surprising consistency, and equally probable, a set of personal qualities or assets you would not have attributed to yourself.

Pulling your ideas together

Review the results of the exploratory work you did. What patterns do you see? Are there more correlations between your personal life, background and career than you expected — or fewer? How closely does your self-image accord with how others see you? Has your career path been straighter than you thought and moving in a direction you like? Can you see yourself as more persistent and effective in overcoming obstacles than you imagined?

WARNING

As human beings, we share a tendency to dwell on negative aspects of our self-image and discount positive experiences. Psychologists tell us this is built into our brains and that learning to accentuate the positive is a challenge. So, if you find yourself taking a negative slant on your history and value, think again! Give yourself permission to see the positive and you will. Look past "mistakes," missed opportunities and setbacks that bog you down. Psychotherapy and business coaching too depend on the idea that we can shift perspective on how we interpret the past and see the present. And we can fashion new endings to our own story.

When you've reviewed your findings, write a one-paragraph statement. There isn't a specific formula for doing this: Every one of us truly is unique. The statement is just for yourself, and it's provisional, so don't get stuck in the wording. Here are a few general considerations to take stock of:

>> **The light that other people's input sheds on your personal qualities, assets and skills that you haven't recognized, take for granted or tend to discount:** What did they uncover about you that you didn't see in yourself?

>> **The proofs of success you identified in different parts of your life:** In terms of work, did you find a way to save your employer time or money? Manage or contribute to a successful project? Are you the go-to person for something? The natural coach at work and in your personal life?

>> **Degree of alignment with your work:** Do you now have the scope to exercise your ideals, talents and abilities? Use your best skills? Do you see progress toward your goals or a need to correct course?

>> **Personality factors:** Often, they are more readily recognized by other people: for example, a sense of humor, adaptability, kindness, resilience. What are the qualities that make you special to the people in your life?

>> **Your passionate interests:** Do they find expression in your work? Do you want them to? Note that when you can feel a passion or even a deep

enthusiasm and curiosity for something that can relate to a job or career, you stand out. Can you see connections between different parts of your life, abilities and experience so far?

TIP

Here's a practical lens for reviewing your own experience: Identify a combination of skills and interests that make you unusual. I know a psychologist who combined her love of horses and skills as a therapist to develop a practice in which her clients work with horses. Another acquaintance was a college athlete who studied graphic design and after a few years of basic experience, landed a job as chief designer for a national sports league. Other success stories: A musician who studied business management, a dancer with an avocation for photography, a chef who studied business management. A set of disparate-seeming skills makes an individual unique and especially marketable, leading to a satisfying career.

Even an unrelated passion is worth thought. Do you have a hobby or strong interest that relates to the job even indirectly or has helped you build your "hard" or "soft" skills? Make that connection in your materials. Think also about what you might learn that could give your expertise a whole different dimension. Employment specialists always advise investing in yourself this way in periods when the job market is limited.

Assessing All Your Skills

Don't overlook things you're naturally good at! Many of us tend to take for granted what comes easily. If we learn languages quickly, we think math is a higher calling, for example. It's fine to take on challenges, but don't cheat yourself by underestimating the value of an innate ability — or the value of enthusiasm. Curiosity, the drive to know more, is the force that enables many people to excel in challenging careers.

WARNING

And don't overlook your "soft skills." Traditionally employment managers have distinguished between two types of skills: "Hard skills" are the technical abilities that enable you to perform the specific requirements of a role: edit a manuscript, analyze a profit and loss statement, write computer code and so on. "Soft skills" are those that relate to personal qualities and aptitudes. The lines between the two types of skills are blurring as more employers acknowledge that "people skills" are paramount to success in nearly every endeavor. As a case in point, in many circles writing has moved from being identified as a soft skill to a "core skill."

To spark your thinking, here are the basic soft skills categories and some of their elements (note their usefulness as keywords):

- >> **Communication:** Always the first on the list! Includes interpersonal relations, verbal communication, negotiation, public speaking, presentations and of course writing — know-how with reports and proposals especially.

- >> **Critical thinking:** Analytic thinking, resourcefulness, decision-making, problem-solving, creativity, research, troubleshooting, innovation.

- >> **Teamwork and leadership:** Collaboration, mentoring, conflict management, supervising, project management, planning, big-picture thinking, strategic thinking.

- >> **Attitude and work ethic:** Reliability, resilience, self-motivation, enthusiasm, energy, respectfulness, readiness to pitch in and go above and beyond, working well under pressure.

How should you incorporate such abilities in your self-presentation? Some of the concrete ones may have explicit places, such as writing, public speaking, mentoring, supervising, problem-solving. Preferably, demonstrate such abilities through specific accomplishments. Less tangible skills — like reliability, energy, creativity — should play an infrastructure role: The goal is to find ways to communicate such assets in how you write and speak about yourself.

TIP

To help you highlight your best self, when cataloging your personal assets, consider the times we live in. One impact of the 2020 coronavirus pandemic that sustains in many ways is to upend many standard practices of the business, nonprofit, government and education sectors alike. Most enterprises keep scrambling to find new footholds and ways to function, even survive. "Agility" is the watchword.

Can you demonstrate and speak to your own adaptability, flexibility and ability to think out of the box? To work with or even thrive on the challenges that surface as the ground keeps shifting? Can you appreciate the difficult decisions leaders must make amid constant uncertainty? Communicate such qualities to put yourself ahead of the pack.

Resiliency has become an especially valued personality trait. If you've been undermined by a terrible job market but found ways to survive, even if they have nothing to do with the work you want, don't hesitate to tell this story. It's likely that your prospective employer will appreciate your initiative and resourcefulness. In today's climate, that can give you even a better narrative than the traditional career progress.

SHORTCUT

A straightforward way to follow up your exploratory thinking is to write a simple list. Create headings such as:

My deepest abiding interests

My technical skills

My accomplishments and successes

My proudest moments

My experience overcoming obstacles

My curiosity: what do I want to learn?

My talents and potential skills I would like to develop

My vision for the work and life I ultimately want

Cut or add categories that relate to you and fill them out in as much depth as you choose. This brings you well on the path to understanding your value and potential. What could be more interesting? Inspire yourself!

Let's look now at the job-hunt components one by one.

LEVERAGING YOUR PERSONAL VALUE STATEMENT

In the workaday world, your value statement gives you a healthy advantage as a job-seeker. It's a compass for making good decisions about what jobs to look for, how to match your strengths against job specifications and how to present your qualifications. Here's how one young man leveraged two skill sets to find a career path and present himself.

Jed has always wanted to be an artist and earned a set of degrees in the fine arts. He also had an affinity for computers and took practical courses in their use. This brought him an assignment helping a historian archive photographs. Later, ready to launch an independent life, Jed needed a full-time job that would support a good life, which full-time painting could not do. Jed used the process described in the preceding section to review his abilities and experience. He consulted other people to collect their observations of his assets and composed a simple list of his interests and strengths. His goal immediately clarified: Find a job within the art world that would both expand his thinking about his avocation and give him a base for a career he could enjoy. Jed soon spotted a posting for an administrative job in a museum. He reviewed the job specifications and adapted his core value ideas to align with the opportunity this way:

- *My background and interests make me completely comfortable with the museum world and its people. I bring training and experience in archiving, preservation and photography.*

- *I have a special skill with applied technology. Everywhere, I become the go-to person when computer problems crop up. I can assess technology systems quickly and create better ones to do the work. Example: my recent project for an image archiving company, where I showed them how to digitize and organize their materials more efficiently. The system I designed does in minutes what used to take staff hours to do by hand.*

- *I like training people to use new technology in friendly ways that help them feel good about using it.*

Jed built his application cover letter around this idea, backed up his claims in the résumé and was able to speak well for himself in a series of interviews. He won the job and this additional credential helped him obtain the next opportunity and further prove himself. He's become a well-rewarded technology specialist for an international art gallery. And paints on his own time.

Writing Résumés That Win the Race

If you like to imagine that résumés are no longer necessary in an employment market where online search and hire is the norm, sorry — that remains a fantasy. Employers need a standardized way of evaluating candidates because good jobs draw a flood of applicants. Moreover, when in-person interviews are difficult to arrange, neither side can count on personality and simpatico connection to make the best choice.

An outstanding résumé is your best offensive. Let's see how analyzing the usual suspects — *goal* and *audience* — can help.

REMEMBER

Your résumé's *goal* is not exactly to get a job — rather, it's to move you past the first filter to the next step of the hiring process. What can you put "on paper" to make you stand out and get you to the next step?

You must show in writing that you

>> Understand the organization and the job's demands

>> Offer a good match for that job and will bring value to the company

>> Can prove your qualifications with proof of accomplishment

Beyond these basics, you must communicate that you are an energetic and proactive person who can be relied on to solve problems, take the initiative, work well with others, rise to challenges and perhaps lead. On a technical level, you must meet tangible demands by using the right keywords to survive prescreening by computer algorithms or clerical review.

TIP

To accomplish all this, your résumé needs your best thinking and writing skills. In fact, employers judge whether you have these in-demand abilities, consciously or not, by how well your materials communicate.

In considering *audience*, note these three points:

» **Making the match is your responsibility as an applicant.** This means that the employers' needs matter more than yours. Face it: They don't care that you require "an interesting position in the field I love that will use all my skills and help me grow." They want to know what you can do for them.

» **Customizing every résumé to the specific job and employer is essential.** One size doesn't fit all. You can create a general résumé that's adaptable to different purposes. You can produce two or more résumés that are slanted differently if you're open, say, to either a marketing job or a public relations spot. But always, if a job is worth an application, you need to customize it. This includes using the right keywords for the role.

» **Doing your homework is smart.** Inform yourself as well as you can about the organization: its history, products, industry standing, challenges and problems. Infinite information is available through the company's own website, its social media presence, online conversations by employees, career sites such as Glassdoor (www.glassdoor.com) or a simple Internet search. And don't forget to scour the job ad for all the clues it offers as to company needs and candidate qualifications.

WARNING

Consider also what else your target is reading about you! Do you have a LinkedIn profile that paints a different picture of your experience and interests? Do you have inappropriate photos of yourself partying on Facebook? Does your Twitter feed include nasty remarks to or about people you don't like? (Chapter 12 offers advice on cleaning up your virtual act.) Assume the people hiring will search all this out, as might your current employer.

Let's look at concrete ways to produce the winning résumé you need.

Choosing a format

Traditional résumés, with variation, generally cover your life this way:

Contact information (name, email address, home address, telephone)

Job objective, or more often today, your self-identification (for example, "Senior Project Manager, Nonprofit Sector")

Summary statement of your qualifications

Reverse chronology of your work experience with title, overview of each position, achievement highlights, dates

Education

Skills: knowledge, certifications (may also be called "key competencies")

Other categories as relevant: honors, awards, recognition; special interests; publications; volunteer experience; affiliations; certifications

Additional contact information: How to reach you easily, plus perhaps a few of your online links if they relate to the job or desired skill set. If you wish to share your personal pronouns, this is the place to do it. (This is discussed in Chapter 5.)

Generally speaking, your résumé should keep to a single page unless you have eight to ten years of relevant experience or you're applying for a position in a field that demands detail, such as academia.

Functional résumés, often used by freelancers but useful in many situations, open with a much more detailed version of the summary statement — perhaps half a page — that highlights skills and capabilities rather than specific employment experience. This approach also works well for consultants, gig workers and other non-staffers because someone hiring for a project wants to know what candidates can do, right now, rather than their work histories. Depending on the industry, an independent worker might supplement the résumé with an online portfolio.

Even if your goal is a staff job, adapting aspects of the functional résumé can solve a host of planning problems if the traditional format doesn't showcase your strengths. A functional résumé is organized this way:

Contact information

Title and/or company name if there is one (for example, "Mark Brown, Freelance Copy Editor"; "ABC Associates, Inc., Social Media Marketing")

Full summary overview that specifies relevant skills

Sampling of most significant clients and projects

Relevant background experience (for example, former positions that relate to the project, described in narrative form)

References, preferably relating to the gig at hand

Sidestepping presentation problems

Adapt elements of the functional résumé format if it helps put the emphasis where you want it. It's a good way to minimize any perceived deficits. You can also juggle the traditional résumé format to put you in the best light. For example:

>> **Right out of school?** If you lack relevant work experience, put the education section first and amplify it with your coursework and any honors. Focus on what relates to the job. Include notable experience such as leadership activities, sports, debate team, hands-on projects, assisting teachers.

>> **Long-term unemployment or gaps in your work history?** Use the expanded functional résumé version of the summary statement and write a good narrative about your capabilities and achievements. But you do need to explain the gaps and indicate your activity during that period (more on that later in this chapter).

>> **Worried that you're "too young" or "too old" for the job?** Minimize the dates visually by adding them in parentheses after the job description rather than placing them in the margins. If you're on the older end and want to avoid making the point, no law says you have to include all the jobs you've held. But don't undersell yourself: Communicate your experience and expertise with pride. And if eventually you'll have to show up in person or virtually, it's shortsighted to mislead the reader too much.

>> **Trying to transition to a new field or role?** Adapt the functional résumé approach and produce a strong summary statement that translates your practiced skills to the prospective job's demands. Back this with specific experience, focusing on the most relatable elements of each position.

>> **Is your current or most recent job less relevant or impressive than previous ones, or does it veer off your intended career path?** To keep reviewers reading past the current job description, create a more detailed summary statement to communicate the strengths that relate to your current goal.

>> **So many jobs you look scattershot?** Find a category for whole groups and cover them with a single time frame. For example, the job title might be, "Retail Job Experience, 2012 to 2015." Below that give each job a line of its own, such as "Managed Icy Treats Shoppe for two summers, coordinating staff of three, operating cash register, tracking inventory." Part-time work and internships can be grouped this way, as well as summer and temporary jobs, and present a strong collective impression.

Bottom line: Customize every résumé you send out to match you up with the job specifications and play to your strengths and assets.

REMEMBER

Styling Language for Résumés

Because conciseness is a critical need for a résumé, you need not write in full grammatically correct sentences. Good résumé writing technique has a telegraphic quality, saying just enough to clearly communicate. This style's characteristics are:

» Simple sentence structure that reads instantly

» Omission of the "little" words like prepositions and conjunctions (and, but, or, the, a)

» Minimal use of first person ("I")

» Minimal jargon and business-speak

» Eliminating most modifiers (adjectives and adverbs)

» Simple concrete everyday words, except for necessary technical terms

» Bulleted details

» Minimal repetition of words and facts

TIP

Most important, *build your résumé on action verbs*. Use them to prove how you've made a difference in the job. Launched, streamlined, originated, chaired, generated, instituted, rejuvenated, mobilized, originated, revamped . . . there are hundreds of high-energy verbs to choose from, and you can easily find them by doing an Internet search for "action verbs." They're even broken down by industry. Avoid phrases such as "responsible for" or "duties include." They convey that you were there, but so what? Go for accomplishment and facts. "Managed purchasing for office" can be better stated as "systematized departmental buying and saved 3 percent of total budget." Of course, tell only the truth.

REMEMBER

The tone to aim for is confident and positive. You want résumés to breathe quiet self-assurance and capability. Avoid hedgy, wishy-washy words like "sometimes," "might," "seems," "probably," "almost" and "possibly." They diminish your stature and raise doubt about your value. And keep away from empty descriptive words like "extremely," "incredibly" and "amazing." Communicate a quiet strength.

Here is a job description exemplifying how *not* to use language when writing a résumé:

Manager of Infrastructure Services, Rising Architects LLC

I performed a very diverse set of responsibilities for this architecture firm company that included leading my department's meetings, carefully preparing quarterly reports and supervising five staff members and consultants sporadically as called for. I stayed in this job for four years and saved them a lot of money.

Here's a better example of résumé language. Notice that it begins the description with a big-picture narrative statement and then uses bullets to provide specific backup, citing tangible results where feasible (more on this later):

Manager, Infrastructure Services, Rising Architects LLC (2015-2020)

Directed five-person department for Tulsa's largest architectural firm, specializing in building projects for schools, laboratories and libraries. Analyzed project specification data, managed client communication systems, deployed and coordinated consultants.

- Originated new computer system to assess project requirements, reducing staff time 7 percent

- Created client-department teaming strategy to improve working relationships, reducing constructions reworks by 70 percent

- Built digitized resource to streamline assessing, hiring and managing specialized consultants for landscaping, interior design and materials analysis

- Directed communication program to reach client prospects, honored by Universal Architects Association in 2019 as Silver Level-Outstanding

- Member of Leadership Team, participating in firm's major decision-making; developed and headed Customer Relations Taskforce, which spiked 12 percent growth over first 18 months

Using keywords: An essential

Always remember that your first reviewer in 70 percent of cases is a machine that scans your written material based on rigid algorithms. In other cases, a junior-level employee or an HR specialist who may not be familiar with your field, may be tasked with the initial screening. In only a very small operation will the decision-maker read what comes in without screening. So, a résumé's initial goal is to get past the machine or relatively uninformed screener.

Therefore, do not expect anyone to translate your experience, abilities, skills or other qualifications to the needs of the job. That's why you need to figure out the match points: keywords and phrases. Typically, they are nouns describing hard skills, such as presentations, safety, certification, logistics, programming, CRM, supply chain, coding, Oracle, writing. They may be more specific depending on the field and particular job. Soft skills are also represented by key words, as referred to in the "Assessing All Your Skills" section earlier in this chapter.

Also, keywords make you findable. Recruiters routinely search the Internet using their pet search terms. So, spend some time brainstorming the wording that typifies the industry and role you want. The job posting gives you the best resource. Notice the words they use and echo them. You can also look at similar ads, online industry materials, social media sites and the free Occupational Outlook Handbook published by the U.S. Department of Labor (www.bls.gov/ooh). This exhaustively describes everything each type of job requires.

WARNING

Do not just add keywords to your résumé. Rather, work to translate your own descriptors into the common industry wording. And it's legitimate to adapt your own job titles in the same spirit. On the other hand, avoid jargon and biz-speak language that readers may not necessarily understand. It often leads you to empty rhetoric that dilutes your impact.

Writing the summary statement

To guide readers to review your qualifications in the light you want, begin your résumé with a strong three- to five-line narrative capsulizing why readers should be interested in you. Rather than telling your readers what kind of job *you* want, tell them why you match what *they* want.

Effectively done, the summary embodies your job target and makes you eminently qualified for it. This can take a lot of thought so don't be surprised if that is the case. But if you worked out your core message, as I recommend in "Knowing and Expressing Your Value" earlier in this chapter, you can easily adapt it to the purpose. For example, my young friend who applied for the arts administration job might write:

Arts Administrator, Art Historian, Practicing Artist

Experience and advanced training in archiving, preservation and photography. Special expertise in designing computer systems to perform administrative work more efficiently and economically. Adept at training people to use new technologies cheerfully. On every job, recognized as the go-to person when computer glitches happen.

What if you're nearly or altogether new to the job market? Give serious thought to how you have prepared for the opportunity you want and what you will bring to it. Then figure out what in your life to date demonstrates these claims. Typically, you compete with other novices, so how you frame your own qualifications helps you stand out. An example of how a beginner might apply for a job as lab assistant:

Medical Lab Technician

Lab assistant with hands-on clinical skills gained through two years part-time work at New Rochelle's Orient Technologies, concurrent with earning BSc with Honors from Candida University and maintaining 4.4 average. Strong computer skills and developed writing abilities. Fluent in Spanish.

TIP

A helpful way to develop your self-summary is to start with the job you're aiming for — *not the one you already have, if you're already employed.* Describe it as specifically as you can. If you don't have a help-wanted posting in hand, scan online to find some in your field and look carefully at the requirements. This tells you what matters to the employer and provides you with the keywords you need. Then review your own experience and see how well you can align it with those skills and qualifications.

SHORTCUT

An interesting tactic is to invent an ad for your ideal job. Put yourself in the head of the hiring manager and describe the opportunity in detail — the role, responsibilities and challenges; essential "hard" and "soft" skills; desired experience and other qualifications. Then answer the ad you wrote. Besides giving you some useful insights into your résumé content, this helps you define what you want more closely. And in turn, this helps you recognize the right opportunities and identify ways to get there, such as learning something new or networking with a particular set of people.

TIP

The best résumés make it look as if the candidate has been preparing for the job all of their life. You achieve this not by misrepresenting your skills and qualifications, but by looking at them within the perspective called for. Strategize what deserves the most emphasis for each job, and which factors count in your favor. Often you must creatively translate the value of a skill learned elsewhere for this job. Never expect the reader to do this for you.

Discriminate among the parts of your own experience. In Jed's case, for example, he knew that his personal avocation — painting — was not what would connect with his target job market, but rather, his practical skills. Yet the fact that he is himself an aspiring artist is relevant, because it means he will relate to the community that serves artists. He mentions this clearly, but doesn't elaborate.

REMEMBER

The summary statement is almost always the first — and perhaps last — part of your résumé that will be read. Use it to communicate your value to reviewers so they will be drawn to read more and orient the rest of the résumé as backup.

Building your work history section

Whether you call it Professional Experience, Employment or Work History, this section must prove the claims of your summary statement. A reverse chronology is standard. Start with your current or most recent job and present it more or less in the following order (I point out variations you can choose):

>> **Job title, company name and location, employment dates:** You can take some liberty with titles — for example, if you were officially Third Assistant Manager for Technology, but your main job responsibility was troubleshooting, you are justified to call yourself Technology Troubleshooting Specialist. If you feel guilty about this, user lower case letters to make it generic.

You can also choose to use a title that closely matches the job you're applying for, assuming you can back it up. This will help keep you from being screened out by the machines. If you're questioned on the difference between your actual title and the one you used, explain that you were trying to communicate the reality of your job functions.

Regarding dates: If for any reason you do not wish these overly noticed, put them quietly at the end of this line or the end of the description, rather than thrusting them into the margin in bold face.

TIP

Include a phrase explaining the places you've worked as necessary and helpful. If it's a company few will recognize, identify it. For example, "Whitehead Hats, largest Midwest wholesaler of top hats with $200 million revenue." If it's GE, sure, people know the name, but not its scope, or the specific piece that employs you, so put that in.

WARNING

>> **Narrative overview:** Don't start a job description with bullets! You first need to provide a succinct perspective on your main responsibilities and overall achievement. Follow with bullets that present notable accomplishments. If you have trouble writing the overview, write the bullets first and then look for the most general and encompassing bullet you wrote to expand on. For example, a magazine editor might write:

Directed editorial, design and production of the martial arts supply industry's leading publication. Produced 12 120-page monthly issues, overseeing a staff of nine. Increased ad revenue 19 percent over five-year tenure.

>> **Bulleted accomplishments:** Each bullet should provide a detail of the job and whenever possible, be achievement oriented. It's not being there that counts — the responsibilities you carried out that nobody complained about — it's about how you made a difference. The editor might say:

- *Responsible for coordinating work of sales and editorial departments.*

But shouldn't. This is better:

- *Created integrated team of sales professionals and editorial staff to collaborate on issue themes and facilitate ad sales.*

That sounds a whole lot less passive and boring. But better yet:

- *Introduced collaborative sales/editorial team system to create issue themes, securing 11 new advertisers in the first six months.*

REMEMBER

The last version is better because it *quantifies an achievement*. Do this every time you can because it speaks every manager's language — call it *bottom line-ese*. Did you save time or money? Increase efficiency? Solve a problem? Introduce something successful or innovative that accomplished a specific goal? Flaunt it! If you've done a decent narrative overview of your current job, as described in the preceding section, you can use bullet follow-ups to highlight your best contributions.

"Soft skills," described earlier in this chapter, give you more ammunition for citing achievements. Some are hard to quantify, but being specific in some way helps. For example, "successfully worked on 90% remote basis for two years." "Mentored 14 new hires and adapted onboarding processes to virtual communication." "Oversaw transition from computer system A to system B." "Reorganized files to speed access and decrease staff time for all departments."

SHORTCUT

Mentally brainstorm your time at the job to identify those crystallizing specifics that prove your value. One good way is to review projects you've led or been part of, because those typically start with a problem and end with a successful resolution. Also look at everything that produced a tangible result: "Built a landing page that doubled the conversion rate in three months."

Try also asking yourself, "What would have been different in my unit or organization had I not worked there?" Some of your accomplishments will be hard to translate into time or money. Get as close as you can — sometimes an anecdote or testimonial will work. For example: "Office restructuring idea identified by the CEO as among the ten best ideas of the month"; "Class op-ed writing assignment published in regional newspaper"; "Managed intern program rated 92 percent effective by participants."

Treat earlier jobs similarly, with a short opening narrative amplified with bullet points. Logically, each previous job merits less territory than the more recent one, but don't short-shrift an earlier job if it relates best to the role you want.

Showing off strengths

Here are a few more ways to adapt the presentation to your strengths and the job's demands:

>> **Create a Professional Highlights section.** This is especially useful if you want to minimize the impact of your chronology. To focus on your capabilities, make this Highlights section a star attraction by putting it right up front before listing your jobs. This approach enables you to work in your soft skills gracefully and provide a substantial perspective on your assets. A simple rundown of the positions — in effect, where the experience was developed — can follow. This is a good tactic for a highly experienced job-seeker, a career switcher or someone reentering the job market. See the section on choosing a format earlier in this chapter to help with this.

>> **Work in testimonials.** If a professor said you were the best accounting student he ever had, or a former boss agrees to acclaim your contributions, use the accolades to strengthen your hand. Sometimes even a coworker or friend who looks to you for related help can add spice. Give some thought to graphic presentation for testimonials. You might add a statement at the very bottom or box it in a good place.

>> **Add an Areas of Expertise or Professional Skills section to clearly communicate your capabilities.** Include certifications, licenses and languages you can speak or write. Or, add a Professional Development section if you're in a fast-moving field like technology. Even if you're in a slower-changing field, indicate that you care enough about your field and skill building to take advantage of courses, workshops and training opportunities.

>> **Include pastimes and hobbies.** These are helpful to cover if they're relevant to the job, like flying model airplanes if you're an engineer; if they speak to your perseverance, like winning dressage competitions or climbing mountains; or if they speak to leadership and initiative, like starting an astronaut fan club. If you think they're interesting, they may help you connect with reviewers as conversation starters, but be sure they are not controversial (for example, a political affiliation or gun club).

>> **Include a Community Service section.** This has become a valuable part of people's credentials in our socially conscious world. Activities not job-related can help you come across as a caring, involved person, and who doesn't respond to that? Such a section is also useful if you've been out of work for a long time, or if thus far it's what you mainly have to show rather than work experience. Unpaid work does count! If you taught free classes in tax preparation while out of work as an accountant, that's a lot more impressive than looking like you sat around the house. But don't call it volunteer work. Call it *community service*.

>> **Incorporate an Honors section.** Scan your school years as well as job history and personal life for these. Use your judgment about what to include — if you're applying for an engineering job the employer might not want to know you were the champion seller of Girl Scout cookies in your troop, but they well might care if they're hiring a salesperson or PR specialist.

>> **Include a Personal Assets section to present your soft skills.** Some examples include your ability to work without supervision, handle remote communication media, adapt to fast change, maintain poise under pressure, learn new skills quickly. This works well if you're relatively new to the world of work, but tie the claim to facts as much as possible.

>> **Explain employment gaps.** Why leave those unaccounted-for years open to interpretation? Basically, tell the truth. Most employers are entirely open to erratic career paths today knowing that so much is out of the individual's control. If the coronavirus pandemic in 2020 derailed your career, say so. If you were caring for a child or relative, say so. If you tried your hand as an independent consultant, that's fine, no matter that you didn't wildly succeed. But be prepared to speak of the experience and outcome, as well as why you now prefer a staff job. Explaining gaps may be better done in a cover letter rather than résumé, but if your résumé shows holes that may provoke serious questions, consider including a line such as, "occupied with family needs."

>> **Make the most of your progress.** If you were promoted after three months, say so. If you were the youngest regional manager ever appointed, say so. Especially if you've held one or more long-term jobs, it's important and inspiring to make your progression obvious. You can incorporate these successes in the job narratives or in a highlight statement.

WARNING

Do not include any information that trivializes your experience. If for example your administrative assistant duties included organizing meetings, overseeing supplies and filing, leave out filing, unless you're going for a job where it's important or you can cite some specific accomplishments related to that work. You do not need to include everything you've ever done or every detail of a job. Doing so tells the résumé reader at the least that you can't discriminate the wheat from the chaff. Worse, including the least significant tasks distracts readers from absorbing the higher-level work and may lead them to value you less than they otherwise would.

One more piece of advice: Make it look good. Aim for an inviting, accessible presentation that reads easily. This means:

>> Keep good margins and plenty of white space rather than cramming in more information that few will read.

>> Use a plain, legible typeface in at least 10-point type for body copy and a bigger version of the same font, or one other coordinating typeface, for headings.

>> Don't use fancy fonts that may not even translate between platforms, especially for your name.

>> Arrange your elements in a logical way; most reviewers prefer a standard format so you don't need to get creative and invent your own, unless you're a graphic designer who needs to show that skill off (but still do not sacrifice clarity and accessibility).

If a video résumé is appropriate to your industry, check out Chapter 12 for guidelines.

Succeeding with Cover Letters

TIP

How important is the cover letter? It depends on the industry, the organization and the decision-maker. My advice: Take time to write a good, original, targeted cover letter for every job application you submit. These days, a cover letter is often delivered by email, so don't think an online submission exempts the need. This applies even if you're responding to an ad that say cover letters aren't necessary.

This is especially true if you're applying for a job that requires good thinking, leadership experience or potential, creativity or of course, communication skills. Or if your self-presentation will benefit from an introduction that orients the reader to view your credentials in a particular light. (Exception: If the posting says "absolutely no cover letters," obey.)

A cover letter is your chance to talk in the first person — "I" — about yourself as an individual. Use the letter to supplement the basically dry information of an application form and résumé and create the perspective you want. You can provide a context for your accomplishments, point at what's most relevant, add depth to a noteworthy qualification. You can create a friendly positive tone.

Sometimes a simple but carefully correct message serves your purpose: You must judge when this is appropriate. In many other instances, only the best cover letters make the cut — I know a number of employment managers and small-firm CEOs who only read résumés if they like the cover letter, and file the rest you-know-where. If you can't decide whether simple and straightforward is called for or a deeper introduction, go for deep. In short, approach the letter as if it's the only thing the decision-maker will read — which may be the case.

Planning a cover letter

The basic decision-making system I introduce in Chapter 2 and apply to email in Chapter 6 works for cover letters, too. Start by focusing your goal. While your ultimate purpose is to get a job or secure a contract, as with the résumé itself, you rarely achieve this result from paperwork alone. *The letter is best viewed as a personal introduction to your résumé.* Or, in some cases, it may serve as the whole application.

Your audience is critical, so think about what will connect with the particular person you're writing to. When you give some thought to what someone on the employer's side worries about and hopes to find in a candidate, it's surprisingly easy to figure it out. In all cases, envision harried, pressured professionals facing hundreds of applications and happy to say no to as many hopefuls as they can, the sooner the better.

WARNING

Never treat the cover letter as an afterthought. Most of your competitors invest all their energy into résumés and tack on careless, perfunctory notes rather than letters. Take advantage of this. The bonus is that the process of planning a letter yields insights on how to stand out.

Use the strategy outlined in Chapter 6 for email: Brainstorm a list of the points you may want to make. Consider the following questions to find content ideas:

>> What personal facets are you unable to include in the application that would animate your bid?

>> Do you have any connection with your reader or the organization worth referring to — a common acquaintance or alma mater, for example?

>> What key qualifications and qualities is the organization looking for — and what are your most salient match points?

>> Does your personal story give you an anecdote that epitomizes your enthusiasm for the field or how you prepared for it, overcame major obstacle, applied out-of-the-box thinking, used a relevant skill, learned something and so on? (Chapter 8 shows you how to develop your own story to draw on.)

>> How can your cover letter embody the qualities the organization seeks (for example, leadership, initiative, adaptability, creativity, attention to detail)?

>> Why do you want this opportunity? Can you say something genuine and positive about your motivation? Show enthusiasm?

>> What can you say that is genuine and positive about the person or organization you're applying to? And why do you think this is a good match?

Opening with pizzazz

It's always worth taking trouble with your letter's opening sentence and paragraph. Like email, letters should get to the point as quickly as possible and focus on what most matters to readers so they are enticed to keep reading. But often, letters need context. If you're responding to a job ad, you're probably impelled to begin along the lines, "I'm writing in response to your ad for an SEO specialist in the *Daily Techie*'s July 1 issue, page 13."

TIP

If you're delivering the letter as an email, use the subject line to identify your reason for writing: "Application for Software Engineering Job #1465." But if it's a physical letter, avoid a boring lead this way: At the top of the letter, preferably on the right-hand corner, type "In application for the SEO specialist job, *Daily Techie* July 1." Then you can begin the letter more like this: "I began inventing computer software at the age of 9 using a flashlight in the dark because I was supposed to be in bed." Or, "For years my goal has been to work for Soapstone Unlimited because . . . ." Or a simple, straightforward statement can work (use your judgment): "As a Topsy Software developer with seven years' experience, I see your job opportunity as an ideal match."

To create a strong opener, look for clues in the brainstorming list you assembled based on the preceding section. If you've developed your story, as demonstrated in Chapter 8, look to it for a special nugget that's yours alone. Then review the job description exhaustively to find match points.

Consider: What do you most want the reader to notice in your résumé? What will make you more "real" to the reader, more individual? What's your best selling point for this particular job? If you have trouble honing in on a special asset or need more to work, identify three things in line with the "rule of three" idea, which has rhetorical power.

TIP

Avoid repeating word for word statements in your résumé. That wastes people's time and bores them.

WARNING

Another caution: Be scrupulously courteous. Always address a specific human being if you possibly can, using their last name and title. Never demand something of the reader — for example, "Please call me at 2 p.m. on Thursday, February 5." Close respectfully and considerately: "I look forward to learning about the next step for pursuing my application," "I can be available for a conversation at your convenience any time after 2 p.m." End with letter-style formality: "Sincerely" is fine. "Thank you" is better: "Thank you for considering me," "Thank you for reviewing my credentials," or other variations.

Another caution: Edit and proof the letter ten times. It requires your best effort — full sentences that relate to each other, for example, unlike the résumé. Ask a friend to review it. Read it backward. Let it sit overnight and read it again. A spelling or grammar error in a cover letter comes across as even more disrespectful than in a résumé, and may keep you out of the starting gate altogether.

Networking with Messages

You may often send spontaneous messages for online networking, but when you're job hunting, see such messages as letters that deserve TLC. If you're requesting an informational interview, reference or introduction, you're usually asking influential people to give you valuable time or stake their own reputation on you. If you're writing a thank-you-for-your-time note, you will be judged upon its merit, perhaps just as much as how you interviewed. You must write such messages thoughtfully with all your empathy feelers out.

Requesting informational interviews

When you ask for any kind of favor in writing, your message represents *you* to the reader, whether they've met you or not. What you say and how you say it determine how they react. If you send careless, sloppy requests for informational interviews, don't expect people to do you many favors. If you ask in the right way, most people are extraordinarily willing to help. People may choose to spend a half-hour telling you about their experience, for example, either in person or by telephone, if you

>> Target the appropriate person

>> Define and limit your expectations

>> Show respect and appreciation for the prospective conversation

>> Demonstrate that you will be a credit to the person, company and industry, when you interact with others in their circle

>> Come across as someone worth knowing in the future

TIP

Ask the classic "what's-in-it-for-me" question to frame content for any request. If you're asking for informational interviews from a relatively young people, they may be pleased to know you consider them knowledgeable and influential. More established people are often motivated to "give back" — to their alma maters, their professions or simply in recognition of their good fortune. They may recall someone who reached out on their behalf at an earlier time in their careers. And, many successful people take satisfaction in helping young people.

In addition to altruistic motives, smart businesspeople like making connections and bringing worthwhile people together. They value being known for their networking skills. When you craft your messages, you rarely address such "what's-in-it-for-me" factors directly. But being aware of probable motivation guides you to the right tone and content.

If you share a connection, use that entree early in your message — in the lead, if possible. For example, "Our mutual friend Pat Jones suggested I contact you because I'm aiming for a career in your field, biomedical engineering, and would deeply appreciate your advice."

If you don't have a ready-made connection, research the people to whom you're writing and see if you can find one. For example, do you have a college, career path or professional association in common? Did you hear the person speak at a conference or read their blog? Do you have a reason for admiring the person?

TIP

Do your homework and make sure it shows in your request. You need to have a good reason to write to a particular person and organization. An individualized message has an entirely different impact from a hit-and-miss email that could be addressed to anyone.

To see what I mean, think about your reactions to the following two messages.

Message 1

Dear Rob Walker:

I'm a new grad with a degree in Business Admin and think I might like to work for an international nonprofit. I see that you do that now. I'm in your area next Thursday available from 2 to 4. OK for me to come in then? Thanx much. —Mark

Message 2

Dear Mr. Walker:

I write at the suggestion of Allison James, who interned with your office this past summer and spoke highly of the experience. I hope very much you might find the time to talk with me about my career path — ten minutes would mean a lot to me.

I've just graduated from Marshall State with a degree in nonprofit management. During the past five years, I've held internships with four international development agencies and feel confident that this is the work I want to spend my life doing. I've spent several months in Nigeria, Sri Lanka and Peru.

In hopes of preparing for work like yours, directing overseas field volunteers, I see several possible career routes and would appreciate your perspective.

Would you consider scheduling time for a brief telephone interview? I can be available at your convenience almost anytime next week.

Thank you for considering this request.

Sincerely, Melanie Black

If you think the politeness of Message 2 is exaggerated, perhaps so. But if you were Rob Walker, would you talk to Mark or Melanie? Which one sounds like a good investment of your time — not only because of how much the candidate may value the opportunity, but because of that person's relative long-term prospects? Melanie comes across as someone worth helping.

To succeed with network messaging, think through your content options, draft a message tailored to the particular reader, then carefully edit and proof. You may be amazed at what opportunities and people move within reach. If you're performing a virtual introduction between two people, spell out what's in it for both parties — why you're suggesting the connection.

WARNING

Don't use the power of written networking, whether via email messages or social media, to replace or avoid in-person networking or human contact unless there's no choice. You can sit at your computer all day and exchange written messages, but that's no substitute for a conversation or live interaction. When an in-person meeting is not an option, try for videoconferencing or telephone.

TIP

If you want the best assignments, job leads and relationships, *show up* whenever it's practical to do so. The benefits of networking face-to-face within an industry and through professional associations are huge. Use your writing skills to achieve one-on-one opportunities.

Saying thank you

Suppose you achieve the informational interview you want and speak to the person. Should you write a thank-you note? Don't even ask: The answer is not "yes," but "always." That applies even if you didn't find the person all that helpful, and it applies every time someone gives you information, advice, an interview, a contact or an introduction. If you don't write, the discourtesy may be held against you.

A good thank-you note is notoriously challenging. I often ask graduate students in public relations to thank, in writing, a special guest who participated in a seminar. Most are surprised at how much thought a brief note takes. Those who didn't pay attention found it especially hard, because they had little substance to work with.

TIP

To the writing rescue once more — the idea of defining goal and audience! To thank someone for an informational interview, a job lead, a reference or other favor, your *goal* is to express appreciation and also to keep the door open for future interaction or help. In considering the *audience*, decide:

≫ What did the person do that you appreciate?

≫ What feedback would this person value?

Consider Roger, whose client, Jen, has referred him to one of her own clients in need of services in his province. Roger sends this note:

Jen, followed up the referral to your client Bob Black, went well! Thanks. Roger

You're probably not impressed because major elements are missing. The information is vague and gives no concrete idea of the interaction or outcome between Roger and Bob. Second, the tone is careless. Added to minimal feedback from Roger, Jen (who staked her reputation on Roger) is likely to feel uneasy about making the connection and reluctant to reach out on his behalf again. Here's a version that works better:

> *Dear Jen,*
>
> *Thanks so much for connecting me with Bob Black. I met with him at his office this morning, and we had a good conversation about his technology update program and how my group is equipped to help.*
>
> *Bob asked me to prepare an informal proposal for review by his team. Of course, I'm delighted to have the opportunity.*
>
> *Jen, I really appreciate your opening this door for me and will keep you updated on developments.*
>
> *Sincerely, Roger*

Besides being carefully constructed and written — itself a necessary tribute to Jen's generous spirit — the note reassures her that Roger made a good impression on her client rather than flubbing it. In this instance, what's-in-it-for-Jen is creating a connection that benefits both parties and makes her look and feel good.

Depending on the situation, consider too whether a more definitive thank you is called for: offering your favor-giver a cup of coffee or lunch, for example, if practical. Surprisingly few people actively reciprocate a good turn. Returning the favor at some point is the most effective response, of course. Each thank-you situation deserves individual thought.

TIP

If your thank-you note is written in the wake of a job interview or pitch for a project, it probably becomes part of your application package. Treat the thank-you note as a test of your communication skills and a chance to customize what the decision-makers know about you. If you spoke to someone on site or experienced the environment, you have new insights on what qualifications the organization most values. Or perhaps you realize you didn't mention something important in writing or in person. Such additions are first-rate material for thank-you notes. The note is also a good way to reinforce your belief in how good a match you see between the company and what you can do for it.

Odd as it may sound, take the time to thank someone for the opportunity even when you don't win the job, contract or grant. The same people are likely to make the decision next time, and your positive attitude may pay off. Thanking someone for the opportunity underscores your professionalism and makes you a bit more memorable. Many people positioned to bestow jobs, projects and other awards find the world discourteous. Act as the exception and see what happens.

With the next two chapters, I move on to the digital world. Discover how to strategize your online life to support your goals and dreams.

4

Writing for Online Media

Learn how to build the online presence you want whatever your business goals by strategizing your content and "persona" to your goals.

Decide which digital platforms are right for you: websites, blogs, social media, LinkedIn and/or Twitter accounts and how to adapt your writing to each channel.

Learn techniques for writing long-form digital content that is fast-reading, engaging and convincing.

Understand the strategies for building a website from the ground up or reviewing a current site.

Determine whether to blog and what to blog about, and how to capture the right tone and style for both blogs and articles.

Find tips for networking with Twitter, writing online profiles and engaging with other social media sites.

See how you can leverage video as a marketing tool and learn how to apply professional approaches to creating videos.

IN THIS CHAPTER

» **Positioning yourself online**

» **Choosing your platforms**

» **Applying your know-how of "goal" and "audience"**

» **Adopting guidelines for online writing**

» **Working with Twitter and LinkedIn**

Chapter **11**

Writing for the Digital World

The Internet is like a magic door that opens up the world for everyone who uses it. More than was commonly imagined even a decade ago, it has transformed how we do our jobs and are hired, whether as employees or independent workers. It is our most important source of advice and information and a prime resource for how we buy and sell, learn, engage socially, form communities and are entertained.

What does the Internet offer you? If you have any business or career orientation at all, it's your ticket for reaching almost anyone, anywhere, and presents you with the opportunity to own a piece of virtual space to represent your own interests, share your thoughts and build communities. You can put up a website, the price of which — both in money and time — keeps coming down. You can put up your own blog in an hour or two. Or post comments and ideas on other people's blogs or posts with a click.

The windows opened by online social media has evolved even more dramatically. Social media provides an array of platforms that lets you target exactly the demographic you want — and precisely measure the results of an initiative. But this landscape keeps changing as new social channels spring up and existing ones develop new features to survive.

From a career perspective, whether you see your future as an employee in a series of jobs or as an entrepreneur, contractor or freelancer, your online life is critical. Even if you view the digital universe as purely a way to explore an interest or passion, connect with new and old friends or expand your thinking, you need to use the tools well.

This chapter and the one that follows focus on helping you create the online presence you want, whatever your goals and whatever your facility with digital media. Good writing is the common ground. All the principles explored in previous chapters apply, but what you write, and how you write it, must adapt to the platforms you choose.

Positioning Yourself Online

When I wrote the first edition of this book in 2013, I observed that the Internet had leveled the playing field for those willing to learn its ways. People could scout for jobs and be discovered by recruiters, reach a VIP with a click or compete with big well-funded businesses armed only with a good idea and a website. Everyone gained the power to be not just an author, but also a reporter, commentator, editor and publisher. No more gatekeepers!

WARNING

All of this and more remains true. But there's a snag: Today almost everyone has landed on that playing field. You're competing not only against professionals in your industry, but also with hordes of talented, well-paid communication specialists. Most companies dedicate in-house or outside resources to manage their websites, blogs and tweets, and to produce videos, create infographics and post cleverly on social media.

TIP

Despite so much digital noise, you can certainly succeed in the virtual universe. Just as when you write an email or résumé or proposal, start with knowing what you want and the people you want it from. The second imperative: Contribute useful information to the people you want to connect with. This is generalized as "content" and can encompass blogs, websites, social media posts, videos, white papers and more. The Internet has a ravenous appetite for good content. Write it and promote it. Tell your audiences about it through your other communication channels, such as email and social platforms and presentations. Plan to be consistent and persistent; there are few overnight sensations online. Establishing yourself usually takes time.

TIP

If you want your messages to support aspirations beyond entertaining your friends or sharing moments of your life, they need to be strategic. Random tweets will produce random responses. Carefully written blogs won't help your cause if they don't tie to your goals. Spontaneous social posts won't build a following that matters if you don't have a plan. Not to mention there are so many options to choose among that you can easily be overwhelmed.

Everything you put on the Internet adds up to a unique social profile that can bring you opportunities, or if you're careless, lose them for you. Therefore, it's better to know what you want to achieve and who you want to reach. This does not mean you need to narrowly focus on "business" all the time. You might blog about rock climbing rather than your insurance agency because you love it. Also, over time, it gives you an extra dimension and helps build relationships.

But what about visually based media: Facebook, Snapchat, Pinterest, Instagram, TikTok and new platforms that are brewing? Why do they require strategic thinking, let alone good writing?

Understanding Visual Platforms

REMEMBER

Visual media start with words. Imagination translates those words into images. Often, the corporate posts you may love do not reflect short bursts of creativity, but are carefully crafted messages created by teams working within a traditional marketing frame. They typically use those most classic tools: writing and storyboarding. What you ultimately see may contain few words or none at all, because the message — or most of it — is carried by imagery.

Exceptions are platforms devoted purely to entertainment, such as videos of people dancing. But companies that advertise on these media put plenty of thought into how to attach their own messages to these videos without violating the site's culture. This is "native advertising," creating commercials that mimic the site's content. And, don't imagine that your favorite social stars find it easy to follow up initial brilliance with a constant supply of equally mesmerizing posts, no matter how well their talents suit the medium. There's a reason why sponsors entice them to keep going as "influencers" with million-dollar contracts, and why even teenage stars are subject to burnout.

TIP

Sometimes a platform's visual orientation is in part illusory. Pinterest, for example, which collects and displays images based on themes, nonetheless delivers plenty of information as infographics. These often involve planning, research, writing and graphic design. Templates make it ever easier to produce them, but an infographic must have something to say!

Choosing Your Platforms

Used well, online channels consume time. They can drain you of energy and creativity, and even shift your focus away from the "real world" to become counterproductive. So be selective about your activity.

I talk about using specific social media platforms in Chapter 12, but it's smart to consider (or periodically reconsider) your options and decide how to budget your energy and resources. Some of the most basic options:

>> **Build a website.** If you're in business of any kind, hunting for a job now or down the line, or spearheading a community or charitable cause, a website is nearly always indispensable. It can be a complicated multipage ecommerce site or a blog — the two have become fairly indistinguishable. You can build a site with all the resources it can take and spend money, or you can put in time and build it yourself with online tools such as Squarespace (Squarespace.com), Web.com (www.web.com), Wix.com (Wix.com) or WordPress (https://wordpress.com). Take into account that an effective website needs to grow and evolve with new content, not be treated as a static brochure.

>> **Start a blog.** Regular blogging helps you establish trust, credibility and authority. You can post blogs on media such as Medium (https://medium.com) or LinkedIn if you prefer not to mount your own blog or want to supplement it. Experts often advise that to establish a following, you need to post new material predictably, but the current outlook favors quality over quantity. Today there are so many blogs (some estimates say 500 million) that they must deliver substantial content. The crowded field makes it hard to build an audience, but a blog is a good backup credential that tells people who check you out that you know your stuff. If it's part of your website or links to it, it's also the best way to keep it fresh and bring readers back.

>> **Become active on LinkedIn.** LinkedIn (www.linkedin.com) is the professional's networker. It's the most important hiring center for many recruiters and employment managers, and therefore, job hunters in many fields. For most consultants, freelancers and professionals, LinkedIn is the essential connector. Those who hire use it to find and check out candidates. Numerous industry-specific sites are also worth investigation, and employment-hub sites like Glassdoor (www.glassdoor.com).

>> **Use "entertainment" social media.** Here the plot thickens, as is sometimes said about films that become complicated. These apps are moving targets. There are always new ones, and the more stable ones constantly change features to maintain and grow fickle audiences. Each platform has its own personality and tools. Take time to familiarize yourself with its content, style and tone before starting to post, and note the most popular posts. Apps such as Instagram, Snapchat, TikTok and YouTube can be important for reaching Generation Z and younger Millennials, but if you can't contribute in line with the platform's spirit, rethink your need for it.

>> **Create a Facebook fan page.** This is useful for a wide range of enterprises, since people of all ages have learned to enjoy this app and its reach is unprecedented — Facebook boasts 2.7 million active monthly users. More than three-quarters of Millennials use it daily. But remember that even

Facebook's business pages are geared for visual entertainment and short news blurbs rather than detailed promotional material. The best post length is considered to be 40 to 80 characters, which isn't much. But Facebook is a great way to build a fan base, launch contests, run events, share interesting and timely happenings and show a company's personality.

» **Participate on Twitter.** This 280-character messaging system has become the world's instant news feed. Government leaders, CEOs and the gurus of every industry depend on it to get word out, voice opinions and keep up with what's happening and what people care about. Many reporters and editors use it as their story source. And it isn't just words anymore; images and video begin to dominate. A strategic Twitter program consumes 5 to 20 tweets per day, and some widely followed users post hourly. It's up to you whether to passively consume Twitter or aim to build a following or participate in a community.

» **Use YouTube.** This platform grows in leaps and bounds and keeps visitors engaged for an amazing 40 minutes on average. People love to be entertained by video, and they also love to learn this way. So, if you have an expertise to share, from how to slice a mango to meditating to exercising a sore back, consider how-to videos that establish you as an authority. Companies and nonprofits can present insider views, interviews, product advice and more. Even individuals can create their own video channels if they can supply a continuing flow of material.

» **Originate a podcast.** Podcasts are proliferating because the medium is attractive, but the landscape has quickly become competitive. To get noticed, build a following and generate income is a daunting prospect, even for well-known people. And it's a lot of work: research, writing, editing, distributing. The technology grows more accommodating, but still, the technical side of producing podcasts is a deterrent for those not grounded in sound recording.

» **Leverage email.** I devote a whole chapter to email (Chapter 6), but I mention it here because it's a marketing tool that interweaves well with online media. Some of the most influential bloggers deliver posts via email or embed a link inside a short curiosity-provoking message. E-newsletters, from Tip of the Week to full-blown mini-magazines, are relatively easy to produce and marketing linchpins for many enterprises. Notice too how sales-funnel strategies on blogs and websites are designed to collect email lists. Don't overlook email power.

TIP

How to begin designing your online program? Some experts advise focusing on a single platform, or a small coordinated set of platforms, and doing them well. Be realistic about how much to expect of yourself. Create a written plan to develop your ideas and make the most of your personal investment. Consider your goal, audience and capabilities — and your skills, time and resources.

The various platforms require different mindsets and talents. Lean toward media that center on what you enjoy doing: Do you like working with words or visuals? Learning a new system or capitalizing on what you already know? Do you prefer working alone or with a team? What persona do you want to develop for yourself: edgy or conservative? Serious or humorous? Creative or analytic?

Social media offer ideal ways to explore your potential strengths. If you're a visual thinker, show that off! You might possess a previously undiscovered gift for humor or creating surprises. Or maybe you simply love spending time on the Internet and finding good things. Curation may be up your alley — share what you have that is of interest to your audience through blogs, Twitter, LinkedIn and e-newsletters (with credit as due).

Social apps give you plenty of room for some trial and error, but aim to choose platforms you can sustain over the longer run that promise to benefit you the most.

Breaking down your goals

I assume here that your central goal is to market a product or service. To brainstorm how the Internet can help you do that, determine your own objectives. Do you want to:

>> Establish your credibility, trustworthiness and likability?

>> Prove your expertise and authority in a field?

>> Interact in real time with customers and contacts?

>> Maintain connection with current and past clients?

>> Connect with new prospects?

>> Humanize your business?

>> Listen in to understand your market and customers better?

>> Generate positive word of mouth?

>> Become an active member of an existing online community or build your own?

Amend and expand this list to suit your own goals. Then think more concretely about platforms and activities that offer the best promise of accomplishing those goals. Review the options described earlier in "Choosing Your Platforms" as well as others appropriate to your line of work.

TIP

The more closely you define your goals, the better you can identify the best communication channels and generate ideas for content. If you want to listen in on your customers, for example, research where they're hanging out and actively plug into that channel. To present a friendly, accessible persona for yourself or your firm, consider using Facebook, Twitter and Instagram to offer "inside" glimpses of your firm's people and what they do, or how your product is created or used.

If you're selling your own expertise and can teach people an aspect of it, or want to educate potential customers, YouTube is a prime candidate as well as short videos on social apps. If you're blogging regularly amplify the impact by promoting posts on Twitter, LinkedIn and industry media. If you feel you merit a connection with an influencer in your field, think about what benefit you can offer that person.

Always keep the long range in mind. No matter how secure your present situation feels, you will benefit from the support of a personal following or a community, and from networking with people in your field. You might at some point want to find collaborators, test the waters for a business idea, showcase your abilities or develop ways to turn a passion into a living. You might want to find a new job or find advice on making a transition.

Finding your audiences

I cover audience analysis in several chapters because it's central to writing successfully in every medium (see Chapter 2 for a basic grounding). But for online platforms, this staple takes some additional twists. Knowing where your audiences are enables you to:

» **Aim directly at your target.** As never before in history, you can reach your audiences without intermediaries. Do you want more customers like the ones you have or prospects from other arenas? Do you want to reach people who share a passionate interest or a specific age group? Analyze where to find your targets and invest in channels that reach them. Each platform offers detailed information on its demographics and ways to find groups. A simple Google search tells you which sites are currently popular with your audiences. *The Internet is all about using easy-to-find information to locate your communities.*

» **Tightly define your audience.** The more closely you know who you want to reach, the better you can draw them to you. Consider the fishing analogy. The ocean teems with fish and each kind has its own food preferences and habitat. Once you're clear on which fish you're after, find out where they spend their time and which food they like. Then you can go where they are and create the right bait. Be specific: If you want to reach "young women," for example, you'll find an over-abundance of possibilities. A 15-year-old cares about very different things than an 18- or 21-year-old, has different interests, and spends time on different platforms. Who do you want to talk to? *The Internet is all about narrowcasting.*

>> **Lead people to your online content.** On the Internet, you need to help interested people track you down quickly through SEO (search engine optimization), which is a process of identifying your content in the ways people are most likely to look for you. You can also drop breadcrumbs in your various platforms to lead people to your website, blog, special offer or Twitter account. *The Internet is all about cross-promotion.*

>> **Expand your audience through shareability.** Delivering content valued by your connections gives you amazing potential to reach others who are like them, and thus, build your following. In every venue people look for material they can share with their own connections by re-tweeting, reposting or incorporating links to your messages or sites. Make it easy for readers to do this. The lucky few succeed in a post that "goes viral," but it's impossible to aim for that. More important, recognize: *For marketing, the Internet is all about generating word of mouth for a product, service or you.*

LEVERAGING THE POWER OF SEO

Search engine optimization (SEO) is critical to online writing because you want to be found when people look for what they need. Search engines such as Google rank content by its degree of value to users. Because searchers rarely look past the first page of the list that comes up, everyone wants to be one of the first ten results.

Search engines continually refine their criteria and algorithms to reflect their perception of highest value. For website and blogs, the perennial values are appealing content that changes often, the number of inbound links (links to your site from other sites), and the effectiveness of your keywords and search terms. Lots of expensive professionals are available to help you optimize your site by adjusting your content and search terms, as well as plenty of books and online articles. Here I give you a brief overview.

To dig into SEO, seriously brainstorm your enterprise to come up with the language your target audiences are most likely to use when searching for your service or product or posts. Try for a pool of at least 30 terms that include your product or service names, location if relevant, and any industry specifications people might think of (for example, portrait photography, Pittsburgh plumbers, ABC certified dieticians). You want to use the most popular search terms — but on the other hand, if everyone in your category is using them, your business may be buried. Many people look for a balance between the obvious and obscure, and cover both ends of the spectrum. Don't overlook the obvious: Identifying your restaurant as The Windover will lose you people who look for diners in Chattanooga, cheap eating in Chattanooga and so on.

Help is available via Google itself. Try entering a search term, then click on "Related searches" to see what competitors are using. Also look into Google Insights (www. google.com/trends) and Google Keyword Planner (https://adwords.google.com/ keyword-planner). Other good learning resources include Moz (https://moz.com) and SEMrush (www.semrush.com).

Once you settle on your search terms, use them liberally! "Frontload" your headlines by putting the keywords at or near the beginning. For example, rather than "the complete guide to men's Christmas gifts," use "Men's Christmas gifts: The complete guide." Sprinkle search words through your website and blog content, and use the most important ones in the first paragraph. Some specialists recommend using three to five per page, but recent algorithms mostly credit those used in the first few paragraphs. Each website page should have its own set of terms to distinguish its content. Keywords are also important to social media bios and posts — savvy people pack even the one-line Twitter bio with keywords as well as hashtags. Fortunately, your groundwork for websites or blogs gives you what you need, adaptable to each platform's guidelines.

The trick to all this is to make what you write feel natural and read well, despite the search terms. Even working in three keywords on a page can undermine your message's impact. If you jam in so many search terms that they interfere with accessibility and enjoyment, you've defeated your purpose.

A few trends to note:

There's a shift toward "long tail" search terms, the more natural way people might look for what they want — closer to the question they would ask. Instead of (or in addition to) "formal bowtie," for example, "tie you wear with a tuxedo." This is in line with the growing use of voice search — as in asking Siri or Alexa to find something for you.

A second big tilt is in favor of mobile communication. If people type in a keyword, it must be short and to the point. On the other hand, if they voice their question, they are apt to use long-tail search terms. Mobility also creates more demanding criteria for your content. The smaller the screen, the tighter, more relevant and fat-free must your writing be. Use this book's strategies to distill your meaning without losing the energy.

Keep in mind that optimization is about content first, then conscious SEO to promote distribution of that content. Keep your material fresh and alive.

Writing for Digital Media

In this section, I offer general guidelines for online writing that apply to relatively stable or "long form" content — traditional channels such as blogs, profiles, newsletters, websites — but the techniques are adaptable to social media as well.

DIGITAL WRITING CHECKLIST

Good online writing gets right to the point, reads fast and reads well out loud. Online audiences are especially impatient. It's hard to keep them engaged with online copy because their natural inclination is to move elsewhere if the material is dense or needs energy to decipher. They know it only takes a few clicks to find more accessible material on the subject — any subject. Aim to include as many of the hallmarks of good writing for digital media as possible:

- Informal, friendly, conversational style

- Warm, personal, upbeat tone

- Ultra-conciseness: no excess words or thoughts

- Lively action-oriented verbs in present tense

- Minimal clutter words (in order to, as a matter of fact, at this point in time)

- Minimal reliance on adjectives (beautiful, magnificent, innovative) and adverbs (very, extremely, totally)

- Short, simple, everyday words (mostly one and two syllables)

- Free of jargon, mystery abbreviations and clichéd business-speak

- Short sentences: 1 to 12 words on average with few clauses (as signaled by commas)

- Short paragraphs: one to three sentences

- Good rhythm that pulls readers along

Support your clear writing with good visuals that are equally simple and draw attention to the most important points. Do not let graphic designers — or yourself if you're wearing that hat — talk you into cutting too many words or sacrificing readability to difficult fonts and visual impact. Graphics should support the message, not draw attention to distracting elements or compete with it. Do respect the need for plenty of white space! Don't jam a lot of copy in; it won't get read.

Does good writing matter online? Absolutely. Those fish I talked about in "Finding your audiences" earlier in this chapter won't snap up your offerings otherwise, no matter how much you know. Moreover, it's indispensable for establishing credibility and trust. People may not consciously evaluate writing excellence, but it's how they automatically decide whether a stranger merits their time and trust. Do you read messages that contain glaring spelling or grammar errors in the first paragraph? Hesitate to buy products that are described in boring or overly hyped or semi-literate language? Do you find badly written arguments persuasive?

The guidelines for print writing presented in Part 1 apply to online writing but more intensively. You need to be more direct, concise, clear and dynamic. Imagine a formal, stiff, academic-style essay — you may have written your share in college — with long, complex sentences, weighty words and a dense look that warns of slow reading ahead. You know the piece may take a few readings to ante up its thought nuggets.

Try to write for online media in exactly the opposite way. First, snag attention. Then make it look like easy reading. Writing that looks and is complex works poorly online because reading anything on-screen is physically harder than reading print material. Our eyes get tired, we blink more, resist scrolling and bypass anything that looks hard to access. As readers, we expect speed and immediacy online — not meandering messages that take work. Strive for simplicity and brevity.

Loosening up

Online writing can ignore many formalities of grammatical correctness. Contractions are fine: for example, *won't* rather than *will not*, *I'll be* rather than *I will be*.

Sentences can begin with words like *and, but* and *or*. Or they can consist of a single word: *Never. Ask. Maybe. Why?* Sentences like these can effectively punctuate copy and make it feel lively.

What your computer's grammar checker identifies as sentence fragments often work well, too:

> *Why web surf? Because it's fun.*
>
> *Too many choices, too few good ones.*
>
> *Better than first-in-class.*
>
> *Hardly ever.*
>
> *Well, you asked.*
>
> *Does it work? You bet.*

But be sure your incomplete sentences are clear in context and read as breezy and conversational, not mistakes.

Keeping language simple and clear

If you're targeting general audiences, stay short and simple by stashing complexities elsewhere. Or keep them in a separate section. Of course, exceptions abound. For example, you may pinpoint an audience that wants technical material or sophisticated thinking. Long-form blogs are generally more widely read and valued than short ones. And if you're trying to establish thought leadership, white papers and opinion pieces must treat their subjects in depth.

WARNING

Aiming for an easy read does not mean you need to simplify complex material so much that it becomes superficial and almost substance-free. It means knowing your material so well that you can present it in clear, concise, direct language. Albert Einstein, who was a prolific writer as well as a scientific genius, said it this way: "If you can't explain it simply, you don't understand it well enough."

TIP

Acknowledge your skimmers and speed-readers by finding ways to present information telegraphically, at-a-glance rather than as narrative. Descriptions and technical specs lend themselves well to this approach. Use introductory phrases to summarize long lists of information and help readers move more quickly through complex material:

> *Product suited to:*
>
> *Kit includes:*
>
> *Caring for your item:*
>
> *How to reserve your place:*

Bulleted lists work well. But don't make those lists too long or present them without context. Start each item with the same grammatical part so that they read consistently.

What about humor? If you can write content with a sense of fun or surprise, good for you. Often such material is hard work that talented teams labor over for weeks, months or years. If you're a writer, of course you want to showcase your skills. But for most websites and other content, good substance presented in a down-to-earth, easy-to-absorb way works just fine.

TIP

If you have a gift for spontaneity and charm, by all means use it. But try your experiments out on your friends before launching them into digital orbit.

Communicating credibility

If you use the Internet to promote yourself or a business, everything you post must convey that you're authoritative, knowledgeable, trustworthy, reliable, responsive, open to input and a nice person, too. Viewers want to know who you are and scout for clues to your credibility. In addition to writing your best and proofing meticulously, convey your trustworthiness with these techniques:

>> Include only verified information and keep links updated.

>> Use technical language sparingly and only as audience-appropriate.

>> Provide clear, easily found contact information.

>> Identify your credentials and highlight any sign that your authority is recognized.

>> Use attributed testimonials to show you've met other people's needs.

>> Invite input in specific ways and respond to it.

WARNING

And never, never, ever:

>> Criticize anyone on a personal level.

>> Conduct personal arguments online.

>> Reveal anything about yourself you don't want the world to know.

>> Reveal anything about someone else they don't want the world to know.

>> Post photos or videos that may embarrass you if your grandmother or a future employer sees them.

>> Use offensive language or an angry tone.

If essential courtesy doesn't prevent you from such lapses of judgment, remind yourself that bad form always rebounds on those who forget to practice good form and communicates that they are not people you want to work with or know.

WARNING

Do not use Internet platforms for blatant self-promotion more than is appropriate to the medium. A website is yours and naturally includes product information and a purchasing pathway. But your pitch must incorporate useful information and answer the questions a visitor might ask. A Facebook page for business is intrinsically commercial but must do that in a soft-sell way. In the case of social media, the message is best supported by creatively interpreting your subject to connect with audience priorities: What might your readers want to learn? What entertains them or makes them laugh? How can they be part of the action? Scout the channel to see how others do this successfully.

Ultimately, you can only reap rewards from Internet platforms if you deliver value in their own terms. For the more purely social platforms this may mean sharing a smile, a bit of inspiration, a behind-the-scenes glimpse, a special moment. On long-form platforms it's giving your readers useful information, teaching them something they want to know or expanding their world.

Whatever the medium, *always share your best.* The Internet is an overwhelming source of information and entertainment. Followers must be earned with authentic contributions. Most successful ecommerce specialists give a great deal away through blogs, videos, webinars and ebooks. This makes sense. As a buyer, why would you send money to a total stranger you'll never meet, who may be thousands of miles away and can't easily be held accountable if you're disappointed? Whatever you want to market, you must prove value and reliability.

Marketers call this chain of events "the customer journey." In the virtual world this means leading prospects from one platform to another to another. An email offering a free newsletter subscription or a discount on a product may lead to your blog. The blog may lead to your website if the customers likes the material. They may then click to a landing page with more specific information and a harder sell. Then they might go to the Internet and search for product ratings and customer reviews. And finally, they may click "buy."

As another example, an e-newsletter might interest prospects in your free online workshop, and if they like that, they might look into engaging you as a consultant. Readers who like your free ebook might order the next freebie and even another, then buy the rest. Other readers may start checking out your books because you spoke at a local library, so don't forget to consider these older marketing routes for your mix.

This marketing process can easily take . . . a long time. A traditional rule of thumb is that establishing trust takes many contact points. Pay attention to the journey you're asking your own customers to take. A slow-loading website, links that don't work, a hard to maneuver "buy" page, bad online reviews and yes, sloppy writing, will lose you a lot. Monitor all points of contact regularly.

Attracting new customers is hard: It can take time, ingenuity and consistency. When you make loyal customers, keep giving them what they need. If you don't know what that is, ask!

Cutting hype, maxing evidence

A century of traditional advertising and public relations may have dulled our sensibilities to highly promotional writing. Although most people claim to hate ads and marketing pieces, they may still skim through blurb-ridden printed material to find kernels of interest. But not on the Internet! Online readers strongly resist the clichéd, overblown and hard to credit. Combined with our limited attention span for on-screen reading, the bottomless supply of good material leaves us with no patience for wordy, overwrought, self-promoting content.

WARNING

Cutting out the dross is even more imperative now that so much reading is done on tiny screens like smartphones, watches and tablets. Skip the flowery language and use your imagination to puzzle out what will deliver your core message and prove your value to the readers you want in the most concise but non-boring way.

REMEMBER

Begin with this simple principle: Make no claims you don't back up. Nobody believes those empty statements like "the most innovative breakthrough in the entire twenty-first-century technology powerhouse" anyway. Tell readers as specifically as you can why and how your whatever-it-is fits their needs exactly.

The Internet demands concrete writing. Try to eliminate nearly all descriptive words that camouflage a lack of substance. Use statistics, facts, testimonials, stories, case histories and visual proof as appropriate. Cite benefits rather than features. Of course, you can include the features or technical specs that readers may want; just place them so they don't distract from the central message and its flow.

Devising nonlinear strategies

I once had an argument with a video producer about a storyline I scripted. The sequence was getting out of order in the editing process. "It's A, B, C, D," I insisted. "No!" he shouted. "Don't you understand that there's no more *linear?* No more beginning-middle-end? That's *over!*"

I've since decided that he was right and he was wrong. In the context of the Internet, everyone has become an information surfer. You may land on any page of a website or in any part of an online conversation, and you don't care about logical development of the entire site or interaction. You don't intend to read it through like a novel.

Material that will probably not be read as a sequence must be modular — presented as pieces that make sense on their own. This applies to the customer journey idea described in the section on communicating credibility: People you want to engage with may enter your sphere from various points, so each element — newsletter, email, landing page — must be self-explanatory while leading to another step.

You must accommodate online reader behavior with matching presentation techniques:

>> "Chunk" information into easily absorbed units so that readers in motion can swoop in and grab what they want.

>> Make sections self-contained so readers aren't required to read other material in order to understand the piece currently in front of them.

>> Repeat some information as necessary so that readers can get what they need.

>> Provide different access points to the material so readers can find and enter the site, or customer journey, from different points.

>> Offer choices: links to other parts of the site with more depth or breadth or different angles on the subject, and links to offsite information sources (remember that doing this risks leading people away permanently).

>> Build in a call to action on every website page and every post: Find out more information here; fill out this form for the giveaway; call me today to talk about your problem.

But don't take modular, nonlinear structure to mean that you can present disjointed bits and pieces that add up to less than the sum of their parts. Every page of a website, for example, must make sense on its own. It must also flow logically through a cohesive plan. A blog post needs a beginning, middle and end. Each channel you use must add something new to your message and align with the others — every one of them. It's confusing and destructive for one communication channel to contradict another. The platforms are all pieces of your personal puzzle. That's what integrated marketing means.

Incorporating interactive strategies

The biggest difference between digital and print media is the power they give you to interact with audiences. People are now so accustomed to responding to what they read with their own ideas, experience and opinions that they expect you to invite input, and respond to it in turn. Today's readers want to be actively involved, not passive bystanders. Interactive tactics are especially critical to communicating with Millennials and younger generations.

The digital world is all about creating relationships. Accomplish this by directly involving readers in every way you can invent.

- » **Blogs:** Invite responses and be specific. What do you think? Has this happened to you? What resulted when you tried it? What would you do? Do you vote yes or no? Did you have a similar experience to share? Do you have a solution to this problem? What blog did you like best? Where have you found the best source of X? What do you think of with the newest Y? What else would you like to explore?

- » **Websites:** Offer tangible things people can request: free information, an e-newsletter, a discount. Invite them to buy something, join something, contribute something or spread the word. Or ask people to rate a product or experience or send a recipe. Make it fun. A site I buy gift chocolates from offers cash toward purchase if you send a selfie of yourself enjoying the candy. The website home page features a wheel for you to spin that reveals a discount on the purchase.

- » **Social media:** Encourage creative interaction. Listening to their audiences is possibly the most important use many organizations make of social platforms. They analyze what participants are talking about to shape their posts and ads. Research that used to require big-time investment can now be done by simply asking questions of platform users: Which logo design do you like? Which dress would you choose? What's your favorite lipstick color? The best meal you had last week? In turn, commercial users offer the latest news and inside views of their brands. They listen and respond to input, especially complaints! They run campaigns and competitions based on what they learn.

REMEMBER

Organizations are enthusiastic about user-generated content for good reason. Today, younger people particularly welcome invitations to send images, selfies and snippets of personal experience. A travel-related company might ask you for the funniest thing you saw on a trip, the most interesting person you met or the best (or worst) food you ate — a universally popular subject. User-created content is the ultimate interactive approach, and because it's virtually free, an alluring way to feed the Internet's endless hunger. Brainstorm ways for users to contribute their stories or images; participate in special promotions or games; write about favorite movies, books or sport experience; and so on, as long as the activity has a connection to your purpose.

Of course, be sure you're equipped to follow through — and do so. Send the freebie, share the results, pay attention to input, respond to comments (definitely including the critical ones), feed the forum and prod it along. Yes, all of this takes time.

Using Social Media Platforms

Becoming ever-newer and glitzier is the hallmark of social platforms. They change their parameters frequently and, in fact, must do so to maintain their user base and grow it. Also, who knows how many developers are out there in garages and computer labs inventing glitzier new options right now? What holds steady is the need to use the platforms strategically and thoughtfully, post by post.

Here's my nutshell advice on how to develop a content marketing strategy for social media, as evergreen as I can make it.

Engaging with social media

First, review the persona you created of your ideal audience member (Chapter 2) or do so now. And the same with your own persona: Review your value proposition or your organization's (Chapter 8) or develop it. These are your touchstones for planning a set of marketing strategies. They give you a firm basis for choosing platforms that accomplish your goals.

Endless information about audience demographics is available from the social apps and online sources. Your marketing demographics should line up with your platform choices. If you want to reach people under 24, for example, consider Snapchat, Instagram, TikTok or newer clones. If you want to reach businesspeople in every industry including those who hire, LinkedIn is a must. If you want to connect your own business to networks of friendly people who are interested in the fun of it, Facebook stands ready.

Know your basic message, and expect to adapt how you deliver it to each channel. A working process:

>> **Invest time in the platform you choose.** Absorb its style, observe the most popular subject matter, identify its conventions and find and follow industry leaders and brands similar to yours. Find communities that relate most closely to your interests. What content do they favor? What do they care about? What excites them?

>> **Explore content streams you can create.** Your content should represent your brand in ways that connect with your selected audiences. What can you share that's entertaining, amusing, surprising, thought-provoking and/or educational in an interesting way? Rather than one-off posts, look for themes you can develop that will themselves suggest a flow of ideas.

>> **Practice the tools of your platform.** Each platform provides some how-to instruction, but scads of helpful directions and hacks are available online. Plan to use social amenities like hashtags, which function across platforms, and embedded links to bring people to your blog, a special offer or something designed to draw in the particular audience.

>> **Think visually.** In addition to creating posts that deliver the message visually for sites like Instagram and Facebook, use imagery of every kind to enliven posts and blogs. Posts with images are far more often opened and read. Translating ideas into visuals can be challenging. Infographics give you a good way to deliver written information on sites that are essentially visual, like Pinterest. Memes (images with captions superimposed) are audience pleasers. Video is the rising star of the digital world and can be mixed with still photos. Even emoji substantially increase your chances of engaging people.

>> **Create posts with substance.** Aim to be relevant, entertaining and interesting, but don't try to collect likes for their own sake. Deliver something real that your fans will value and want to share with friends and avoid obvious brand-promotion that will alienate users. The best advice with all social networks is quality rather than quantity. This doesn't mean every single post must be strategy-driven — entertain when appropriate but don't undermine your overall purpose and credibility.

>> **Write your best!** The words may ultimately be few, but make them well-chosen and correct. Social style is relaxed and breezy, concise and transparent: Get ideas across in simple, instantly accessible ways. You only have five seconds to engage people enough to stick with you even for a short post! If the platform provides space for brief biographies, review how other people write theirs and create one that's appropriate. Include a good photograph when you can. Personalizing your identity is important. Showing some personality and humor helps, too.

>> **Build in as many ways as you can think of for people to actively participate.** Conduct surveys and report on them; ask questions; invite photos and videos, especially if they offer selfie opportunities; encourage fans to offer opinions or share an experience; or ask them to suggest a subject themselves. Keep in mind that they want to be part of the story and invest their own personality and spin.

>> **Respond to comments, questions, input, everything.** Remember, you're joining a community or building one, and either way, you must earn entry and create trust. Look to start conversations and keep them going. Snapchat in particular is geared for fast response because posts disappear after ten seconds, though options for extending this time frame have been introduced.

>> **Consider paid advertising.** Big organizations are investing more and more in advertising on social platforms. If you want to do "native advertising," which means promotional content presented in the platform's style, identify it as advertising or the impact will be negative.

>> **Review results systematically.** Digital media give you unparalleled tracking power. Look at what has worked best for you in terms of responses, number of shares or likes, click-throughs to your other media and whatever else matters to you.

TIP

>> **Think "branding."** You may or may not like thinking of yourself as a "brand" personally, but the concept is helpful. It reminds you that you must always communicate in ways that benefit your reputation and give value to your connections. Social platforms give you good ways to lead people to your blog post, website, LinkedIn profile and so on. Repurposing content for different media is fine, but adapt it to each one's unique personality while maintaining the persona you want for yourself.

Exploring content ideas

It's hard to generate ideas in a vacuum. Instead, spend time with the apps of your choice and see what strategies other people are using that are adaptable to your own purposes. And scan content you created for other uses to mine snippets and images.

TIP

It's also productive to spotlight any social causes you or your organization are involved with. The generations you may want to reach through social media channels especially like organizations that demonstrate ethical practice and community citizenship. If you work with a charity event, an environmental cause or any initiatives that help people, you have prime themes to explore. Angles might include mini-stories and images of people who were helped, benefits organized by your staff, events and so on.

Another resource that keeps giving: the people you work with or collaborate with you on occasion, even if they are few. Social media users enjoy behind-the-scenes glimpses, especially if it's a product they relate to. Show them how ideas are brainstormed, how something is made, how a new product was evaluated, what the staff Halloween party looked like, how individuals spend their spare time, their pets and so on. Give a face to the organization every time you can.

Crowdsourcing is another ideal source of material. Whatever your business, think of photos or video related to it in some way and invite your followers to share with you. Opportunities for people to selfie-themselves at the scene engage their interest. Invite video and photos from an event. Ask people to vote for the best whatever.

Some more content ideas to spur your thinking:

>> Show people using your product, especially in unorthodox ways.

>> Show how to fix a problem related to what you do.

>> Connect to seasonal events and holidays.

>> Demonstrate how to do something, from cutting up an avocado to fixing a tire to executing a yoga pose.

>> Write inspirational quotes on an image.

>> Tell a joke (that won't offend anyone).

>> Present educational tips.

>> Offer advanced tips on a new product or event.

>> Reward followers by showing photos or video of them enjoying your event.

>> Introduce followers to staff members.

>> Curate: Share other posts and snaps generously.

Often you can find a way to connect a popular interest with your own goals. For example, posting mouth-watering food images appeals to almost everyone. Tie that to yourself or a staff member — "Marie's favorite holiday recipe," for example, or "Our SEO expert's search for the city's best taco" gives you great visual potential and a soft-sell connect with your business.

TIP

Working well with each social platform takes a different mindset. Immerse yourself in one and you may be surprised at what you come up with. Remember your strategic plan, but interpret it imaginatively and loosely: You want to communicate that you feel the same sense of fun as do the loyal followers you want.

I can't in these pages cover every platform you choose to use today or tomorrow, but here are some specific ideas for a few of those that are most likely to be relevant to you and are unlikely to disappear soon.

Networking with Twitter

To the shock of many, Twitter has become an essential communication and networking medium despite all the dull "chatter" that still characterizes much of it. Here's why marketers take it seriously: The Twitter community has 330 million monthly users and 140 million daily users. Plus, 500 million people access Twitter every month without logging into an account. The majority are between 35 and

65 with a tilt toward male users. Also, many journalists have verified accounts, and so do 83 percent of the world's leaders. There are a good many reasons to actively participate in this platform or at least, listen in on it.

Creating a Twitter presence that's influential and professionally useful takes commitment. For your tweets to make an impact and build a meaningful following, the social media gurus currently suggest that posting three to five per day is optimal.

And they must be good. If you think writing guidelines don't apply to the 280-character tweet, you're certainly not alone. However, *in a business context*, sloppily written tweets work against you. Hastily written messages make you look like a lightweight. So have a message, and use all the editing tools in Part 1 to drill down to that message succinctly without sacrificing its life. Beyond this, support your post with a good visual whenever possible.

TIP

Treat every tweet as a public statement that's an indelible part of your online profile. You can use @ before a Twitter handle to send a private message, but it remains findable. Assume that when you apply for a job, the hiring manager will review your Twitter account not just to see if you're posting anything blameworthy, but to see how you think. So be sure you are thinking! I know a number of people hired because the employer found and liked their tweets, and also a few — including high-profile cases — where a single thoughtless tweet cost a whole career. Treat Twitter with respect.

REMEMBER

Make each tweet as clear and understandable as you can to the most people. That means editing them for both writing quality as well as content! No abbreviations or mystery acronyms. Second, create tweets to deliver value, not share your favorite snack food. Third, never write anything that could embarrass you or anyone else now or in 20 years. Look up "disgraced politicians" online if you need a reminder of what can happen.

Planning your Twitter program

Random tweeting produces random results. Consciously build a Twitter program that aligns with and complements your website, blog, video, other social media investments and traditional media, too (your print materials and presentations, for example). Unlike formal media such as résumés, Twitter gives you the opportunity to show off your personality and individuality. But don't go freewheeling. Try for carefully spontaneous. Make an active decision about who you want to be and make sure that persona is appropriate to your goals and target audiences.

TIP

What do you want to accomplish via Twitter: Establish yourself as an authority in your field? Build a following? Draw people to your website or blog? Find a job? Market your product or service? Connect with like-minded people — or influencers, those with enormous followings whose opinions are looked to by millions? As for all social, strategize whom you want to reach, best content strands and your degree of investment.

WARNING

Stay upbeat and "nice." Online there's never a good result from demonstrating bad temper, a mean spirit or sarcastic turn of mind — no matter how terrific it feels for ten seconds. If you recognize yourself as someone who's regularly tempted to send out angry or ill-considered tweets, use Twitter's scheduled/delayed posting feature until your better angel has a chance to take back the helm.

Guidelines for tweeting

As with other platforms, keep yourself up to date with trends and features. Twitter has become very "visual" as users find that photos, memes, GIFs (short animated images without sound), infographics and videos exponentially increase the likelihood a message will be read and shared. For most people, being *re-tweeted* is the aim of the game because it's how you grow your audience. Here are a few guidelines for tweeting successfully:

>> **Do a good job on the mini-bio.** Try for a lively description that crystallizes your uniqueness and uses your key words. Twitter's own Bio Generator helps you describe yourself for this medium effectively. Scan through industry leaders and social media experts to find models you like. And, do whatever it takes to provide a good photo of yourself as you want to be seen.

>> **Find people and groups that interest you.** Twitter's own search function enables you to find specific people, brands, customers and clients, jobs, hash-tagged conversations and news. You can also search Twitter to find search terms used in conversations you want to follow.

>> **Listen.** Just as you hesitate to plunge into a party conversation before listening to what's already going on, take time to acquaint yourself with what people of interest to you are saying to each other. Notice the conversation's tone and content. Look for niches with which you're comfortable — questions you can answer, for example, or a subject you can usefully comment upon.

>> **Promote re-tweeting.** Keep tweets briefer than 280 characters to encourage others to re-tweet your messages with their own comments. Use a site such as bitly.com (https://bitly.com) to reduce the space needed to communicate links and URLs. Use hashtags (for example, #businesswriting) to identify your subject matter and relevance. This broadens your audience beyond your

own followers, but don't use so many they interfere with reading the message or dilute its impact. And be a re-tweeter yourself when you like a post, particularly when it mentions you or your business.

>> **Share substance.** Share news, ideas, tips based on your expertise, insights into events, a snippet from a good lecture you heard, an insight from a conference, links to something of interest, re-tweets of other people's messages that you believe others will appreciate and so on. And share discoveries: blogs, articles, books, other people's comments, an image, an inspirational quote.

>> **Repeat yourself judiciously.** Many social media gurus recommend sending the same or somewhat different tweets out several times per day, because different audiences catch up and scout at different times. Use a management tool like Buffer (https://buffer.com) or HootSuite (https://hootsuite.com) to schedule your tweets and other social posts, which will also signal when you receive a response.

WARNING

>> **Don't constantly sell or self-promote.** Yes, you can call attention to your own new blog post, event, workshop, article, book, product or service improvement. It also can pay dividends to let people know where you are — at a conference or when traveling, for example. But resist the temptation to promote yourself or your organization every time you tweet. You'll quickly be discounted as a self-seeker. Some savvy tweeters follow a rule of thumb: Blatantly self-promote one out of four times, max.

You can also use Twitter in ways that big companies find valuable. To accomplish research that would otherwise be very expensive, run surveys and crowdsource. Want to test-run your new website copy? Or a contest idea? Invite your network to visit your website and comment. Need an idea for employee recognition? Or advice on which logo to adopt? Put out the word.

Working with LinkedIn

Online professional networks, such as LinkedIn (www.linkedin.com), XING (www.xing.com) and Ryze (https://ryze.com), are good business connectors for many people and are generally considered the "professional" social media. They are the go-to media for hiring and being hired, establishing a reputation and connecting with whomever you wish to. Don't overlook the potential of local business networking sites such as BARK (www.bark.com) and those that focus on new businesses, such as Gust (https://gust.com) and Startup Nation (https://startupnation.com).

LinkedIn cites a user base of 675 million — 167 million in the United States. About half are active monthly and more than 60 percent are between 25 and 34 years old.

The first imperative of connecting with people you want to know is to create a summary statement about yourself that inspires interest and communicates authority and credibility. The following tips apply to profiles for most other networking sites as well, but check the guidelines for each you use.

TIP

To start, read a batch of LinkedIn summary statements and see what approach you feel works best for you. Check out how your favorite bloggers and industry leaders present themselves. Adopt a style you like and check the platform's guidelines for length limits and tips.

In general, an online profile is a chance to communicate more of your personality than in a résumé. For this reason, write in the first person — "I" — not he, she, they. This automatically gives you a more personal tone and genuine feeling comes across. Write with a sense of where you want to go, not just where you've been and are now. Align your profile with your big goals.

Use the headline to pinpoint what you do so it is instantly obvious to scanners and also appeals to search engines. For example:

Business Writing. Magazine Features. Writing Workshops. Publication Projects.

SHORTCUT

Then create a strong opening statement that instantly tells people what you want them to know about you. Surprise! You can draw this from your core value statement or your story (see Chapter 8 for how to build both). For example, the dentist described there might write:

I remember how I felt the first time I went to the dentist as a little girl. All those shiny instruments, the man in a white coat, the sound of a drill in the next room . . . I was terrified! And the experience didn't make me want to do it again. So when I decided to become a dentist, and all through school, I thought a lot about how to make the experience more positive for children — something they could actually look forward to.

If you're trying for a career transition or new job, take advantage of the chance to say so:

I'm a public relations professional with a great background in the entertainment industry. My special love is hip-hop culture. I'm looking to connect my two passions.

Successful online material doesn't follow a formula. Experiment and adopt elements from the profiles you like, both in and out of your own field. Here are a few more examples I gleaned from scouting LinkedIn for arresting leads:

A recruiter:

I find great people and find them great careers.

A family law practitioner:

Growing up on the playgrounds of Detroit, I advocated against child abuse in the fourth grade when I discovered my friend's mother would extinguish her cigarettes on her daughter's fingers.

Jennifer Lopez:

I'm a mom, partner, actor, singer, film and television producer, fashion designer, bestselling author, entrepreneur, and humanitarian. (Say that 3 times fast!)

Notice that when you're already famous you can be matter-of-fact and laconic (though leavened by her last comment) like Jennifer Lopez. But when you're not yet there, you need to think harder about how to bring yourself to life in writing. The goal: Distill your best self.

If you've developed your personal statement (Chapter 9), you know who you are and your essential value. To express this in your profile review, articulate what you want to achieve with this summary statement. For example, find clients or customers? Connect with an industry? Showcase creative skills? Establish authority? All of the above or "other"?

Some content possibilities for your summary:

>> Share your enthusiasm and passion for what you do: Why do you love it?

>> Tell a story about why you chose your career.

>> Frame your current and past work honestly but to advantage — include the achievements you're most proud of.

>> Identify the problems you solve and for whom.

>> Explain what sets you apart from your competitors.

>> Mention pastimes or hobbies that relate to your work or will surprise people in a good way.

A few don'ts:

>> Skip empty rhetoric and get down to brass tacks; what you actually do and what it means is always more interesting.

>> If you are unemployed, do not say so. You are perhaps a professional interested in finding a new opportunity or making a transition. Or use a generic title that identifies your profession — make one up if you need to.

It's fine to ask for what you want, usually at the end of the summary. If you want people to support your good cause, check out your book or suggest an opportunity, say so. But in a low-key natural manner.

Here are some tips on writing the summary:

>> Write in the first person ("I") but try not to start every sentence that way.

>> Use keywords and search terms so people looking for what you offer can find you.

>> Use conversational style relying on short words, short paragraphs, easy-to-read sentences.

>> Use high-energy verbs: Replace the dull, passive ones by scouting an online thesaurus.

>> Use the say-it-aloud approach to refine your self-definition into natural-sounding language that moves well.

>> Observe the platform's limits, most notably: 120 characters for the headline; 2,000 characters for the summary (which translates to about 300 words, probably two-thirds of a page single-spaced).

>> Use a light touch that shows your personality. Use humor if that's "you" but check it out with a few people who'll give you an honest reaction.

REMEMBER

To use LinkedIn effectively keep your information updated and take advantage of its various features. Join groups that are relevant to your profession or industry. Develop connections with people you know or would like to know — aim for at least 50 if you're just starting to participate. Seek recommendations and endorsements and do a good job when other people ask you to do this for them.

Be sure your writing skills speak for you! It's how we judge people who are new to us. Comment thoughtfully on updates and posts you relate to and do your part to keep the conversation going. Research people in your field and reach out to them, respectfully, via LinkedIn messaging. Respond to all input personally, as when your network members congratulate you on a milestone, for example, and congratulate them when LinkedIn notifies you of events like work anniversaries.

And, LinkedIn is a good platform for your blogs if you prefer not to create and maintain your own blog. It costs nothing to post articles on LinkedIn, and your contributions are potentially exposed to millions of people. Those with an interest in your field can find them. This supports your networking. (For guidance on creating blogs, see Chapter 12.)

Don't forget the visual side of making connections! Use a good photo of yourself and perhaps an inventive banner background. And while LinkedIn remains text-based, images draw attention and engage viewers. Use photographs, memes, video clips, charts, infographics. Post slide decks or presentations.

The site is hospitable to video and encourages video created on the platform or uploaded to it directly rather than linking to YouTube or other locations, in lengths from three seconds to ten minutes. The site states that video posts earn an average of three times the engagement of text-only posts.

Video can be used to conduct an interview, cover a live event, provide testimonials and quick tips, share discussions, take customers behind the scenes, review a book or product, introduce staff members and much more.

In the next chapter I show you how to apply online writing strategies specifically to websites and blogs, and how to use professional-style techniques to create effective video.

Chapter **12**

Creating Content for Your Online Life

This chapter looks at three major tools of communicating for career purposes: the website, the oldest and for many people, the most essential staple of the digital communication repertoire; blogging, an enormously popular platform that may be a good option for you; and video, a medium that is coming to dominate a growing portion of the Internet and is now within just about everyone's capability.

Creating a Website from the Ground Up

For most enterprises, from the corporate to nonprofit to entrepreneur to professor to consultant, a website serves as a marketing and connection hub. If you have been in business for a while, you may already have put your website through several generations. Ideally, treat a website as an evolving entity rather than a stable calling card, ready to respond to everything from world events to shifts in the marketplace and the service it speaks for. So even if your site is well developed, I assume you are open to further discussion.

Think for a moment about how the different iterations of your site were produced. Did the graphic design come first, incorporating some "placeholder" copy, until someone said, "okay, give me some words now to fill the spaces"? That's the trouble with most websites — the graphic component trumps the writing.

REMEMBER

Today you can create a website, or a blog that has many attributes of a website, on your own or with different degrees of professional help. Or you might work for a large organization that devotes a broad team of specialists to the task. At both extremes many people fall into a trap: allowing the design and technology to dominate the production process.

If you do the job on your own, you probably use a template provided by sites like Weebly (www.weebly.com), Wix.com (www.wix.com) or WordPress (https://wordpress.com). Or, a website app dedicated to a specific profession, like insurance agents or churches. Templates are becoming ever more flexible, but adapting your unique enterprise to the format you choose is often a challenge.

On the other hand, if you work with a design professional or a whole team, you may have taken part in a process directed by graphic and technology specialists. Many sites are: How do I know? By reading them. I may find many sites visually captivating, but wonder, where was the writer?

REMEMBER

Research bears out that while visuals entice and entertain, *most site visitors value the words far more than the graphics,* regardless of the industry. Great design is not an end in itself: It should deliver and reinforce the message. The goal of the technology component is to build an infrastructure that enables visitors to easily find what they want and navigate the site intuitively. Properly seen, design and technology serve to make the words work. That's where the message is.

Even more basically, writing is inescapably the engine for planning websites — as it is for all planning. I would not want to rely on conversational exchanges for creating my most important communication tool, any more than I'd have faith in an international peace plan not spelled out in writing.

TIP

Bottom line: A good website must be solidly planned and well written. If your involvement is with a big budget operation, advocate for the writer. Put the writer on the key planning team along with the person in charge of the message. If you are a solo operator or close to it, the good news is that given the excellent, flexible resources for designing and producing your own site, creating an effective one is in your power. Sure, it's great to have a team — ideally including a marketing specialist, a professional writer, a designer and a digital pro. But if you're a do-it-yourself businessperson, maybe with a little help, no problem: You're the all-important client. Who knows your business's goals, audiences and messages better?

Shaping your site to goals and audience

To determine what kind of website you need and to start thinking about content, consider what you want to accomplish. Take a look at Chapter 11 where I discuss breaking down your online goals. Consider also practicalities such as whether you want to sell your product or service on the site; whether you're interested in a local, regional, national or global market; and realistically, how many queries or orders or contracts you can satisfy should you generate interest.

As a medium of communication for entrepreneurs, websites have specific objectives to meet. If you're marketing a product or service, a site needs to:

» Be findable by people looking for a solution to a problem you can solve.

» Keep visitors on the site once attracted.

» Educate visitors about the value of your service or product.

» Communicate that you are an expert who is trustworthy and understands their need.

» Persuade visitors to close the sale or take other action.

» Keep them coming back.

You also want to reach out to them directly in the future, so collecting contact information is high priority.

Choose your website or blog format

The distinctions between blogs and websites are blurry. Online services have become sophisticated and user-friendly enough for you to create either medium on your own. In fact, if you hire a professional designer for the job, they will probably adapt a template from an online web-development platform company such as those mentioned earlier in this chapter. There's an advantage in this: Professional help based on a template is much more affordable than when a site is developed from scratch.

Explore several of these resources to identify one that attunes to your needs technically, according to how much knowledge you bring to it. Find a template you like with a good range of design and color choices and on your own, with some time and patience for the learning curve, you can build a blog that looks like a blog: a page that leads off with a new posting on your subject. Or it can look like and function as a full website: a multipage platform representing your business (or you) that includes a home page and an array of additional pages, perhaps including a blog.

Consider your audience characteristics

Chapter 2 offers an extensive list of audience characteristics that apply differently in every case. Draw relevant characteristics from the list and supplement it with customer factors that relate to your business. For example, if you want to sell a new tech gadget directly to consumers, in addition to the basics — age, gender, occupation, economic status — your list may include the following information about your typical buyers:

>> Degree of technological savvy or interest

>> Purchasing habits (how they shop for such products, where they go for advice)

>> Information preferences (level of detail, type of information, how it is presented)

>> Perception of the problem your product solves and its importance to their lives

TIP

Marketers recommend creating a detailed persona of your ideal customer. To do this, think about your current customers and better yet, talk to them about why they use your product, what led them to buy it and what they like about it. Just as it's easier to write an email by visualizing the person who'll read it, it's more effective to know in detail who your ideal online customers are and understand their needs, points of resistance and the problems your offering solves.

You might also consider secondary audiences for the product, such as stores that sell your tech gadget or people who might buy it as a gift. Defining multiple audiences doesn't mean you must create a website that serves all possible audiences and purposes. If it seems reasonably natural, you may designate different sections of a website for different target audiences. For example, if you want to sell hand-made marbles and cribbage sets, each product can be covered on the home page and occupy their own pages on the same site. But if you're selling marbles and pillowcases, that won't work so well. Separate websites may be in order.

Try This: Bone up on marketing ideas. Mountains of marketing knowledge are available online and in adult education courses, workshops and books. If you're building a website and/or business on your own, but lack marketing know-how, tap a learning resource. When big companies create or revamp websites, they bring whole marketing departments and long experience to bear on the process. Practice thinking like a marketer and your website, and entire venture, will more surely succeed.

Planning a basic website

TIP

Are you creating or rebuilding a website without a business plan or a concrete marketing plan? You may find it either good news or bad news to know that building a good website compels you to develop (or update and refine) both in the process. A good website forces you to center all your business thinking. It's why so many people pay those big bucks to website developers. Sure, the money supports good design and technical quality, but the heart of the process is strategizing the business, and the best professionals help you do that.

Let's assume you originate an idea for a service you believe is marketable. Your first thought is that you need a website. Where to start? Here's a practical process that I demonstrate through an invented service business. The same thinking structure works for selling products or promoting a charitable cause. If you already have a website, I recommend trying out the following process to check if you find room for improvement.

SHORTCUT

Do your own plan in writing! It's the only way to push your thinking where it needs to go. Here's the format:

My business idea/goal: Teach elderly and physically limited people how to use the Internet for entertainment, learning and socializing.

Why: My own grandparents live a thousand miles away and were obviously bored and lonely. I coached them and now they're much happier. They feel their world has opened up.

Goal: Make a business of this and sell in-person coaching services.

Audience: Elderly people like my grandparents and their children or grandchildren, who might want to give my service as gifts.

But that restricts me only to local work with a limited number of individuals. Can I think bigger? Why not . . .

- Use videoconferencing or other online media to coach people anywhere?
- How about senior citizen residences — can I offer group sessions?
- And why not rehab centers for people with disabilities?

I'll need to investigate the practicalities for each new idea, and if they prove out, decide whether to pursue them now or make them part of a future plan.

My core message: People with physical limitations don't have to be bored and lonely. With today's super-easy technology, and me to adapt the equipment and show them how to use it, they can make friends, learn, play games and be entertained. It just takes a little coaching, and I'm especially qualified to do this because . . . . (This is your *value proposition*. Use the process outlined in Chapter 9 to develop this important guiding principle. Think of it as an elevator speech for your business. Whom does it help? Why does that matter? Why *you?* What responses can you anticipate?)

Strategize for audience pain points:

- Physically limited people confined to a small world may be unhappy and bored.
- Loved ones may feel sad or guilty for not being there more, often for geographic or time reasons.
- Group facilities may be challenged to keep seniors cheerful and entertained.

Strategize for audience points of resistance:

The seniors, or their relatives, may think:

- They are incapable of learning.
- The equipment is expensive.
- The training is expensive.
- The elders will fall prey to online scams.
- Online purchase is risky. (Why should they trust me?)

Residences and nursing homes will have many of these pain points and points of resistance plus some of their own.

SHORTCUT

A good way to brainstorm pain points and resistance points is to use the talking points method I explain in Chapter 9. Look at both sets of statements as questions and answer them. How will my service address the pain points? How can I demonstrate my ability to do this? What are my best responses to the points of resistance? This gives you good content guidelines for the whole site.

But you need not do this thinking in a vacuum and should not. You would talk to more seniors, as well as managers at nursing homes and rehab facilities to understand their perspective and gauge their degree of interest. This will help you make decisions on which audience to target and how. Do your online homework too and check out any competition. If your orientation is local, and you find similar services elsewhere, their sites can be helpful resources to support your thinking and refine a niche for yourself.

TIP

To further crystallize your plan, it's wise to consider keywords and search terms at this stage. (See the sidebar on leveraging SEO principles and identifying search terms in Chapter 11.) Assembling a list will help you tell your story more concretely and concisely, and you'll need to incorporate the words on every page. Better to build them in from the start rather than trying to graft them on after the fact.

Once you have your audience, goals and central message in mind, you can move into building a site structure to embody and reflect these considerations.

Creating the site structure

The next step in creating a website is to think about what pages you will include on the site. The candidates:

>> A *Home page* that has a concise magnetic message and supporting visuals to entice visitors to know more

>> An *About Us* page that establishes your trustworthiness, skill and experience, and introduces other team members

>> A *Testimonials* page where happy users of your service relay their experience

>> A *Services* or *Products* page that describes various options

>> A *Landing Page* for each product you want to market, with its own self-contained sales message

>> A *How It Works* page that explains what you do and how

>> A *Case Studies* page that offers evidence of success

>> A *Contact* page that contains full contact information and perhaps a special offer for growing your email list

>> An *Order Page* where users can conveniently make the buy or other commitment

>> A *Blog* to establish expertise, make your business more personal and keep visitors coming back

You might not need all these pages, and you can combine some, like "How It Works" and "Services" or "Case Studies," and the "Contact" and "Order" pages. Testimonials can be scattered around the site rather than self-contained on their own page. You might need additional pages: Q&As and FAQs are popular with readers and search engines. Your type of business may demand a portfolio, and if events and media are part of your mix, you need an online newsroom. A resources page that links to other sites can support site optimization.

If you think I took the long way round to end up with a standard-sounding site plan, you're right! This basic structure has evolved over many years and is commonly used because it works for many enterprises. Of course, you can adapt it to your own needs imaginatively.

But inventing a whole new architecture for a website is rarely a good idea. Audiences come with preset expectations and have no patience for figuring out what you're about or where you put things. Better to focus your originality on what to say within the basic framework, how you support your message with visuals, and how to use video or additional media with impact. Once your general plan is in place, content for the pages starts falling into place — and you will probably find some gaps to fill in your planning.

The clarity-first rule applies to all your navigation buttons, too. Don't go so far astray of the standard identifications (for example, About Us, Testimonials) that visitors don't know what you mean or where to find what they already want.

Assembling and writing a home page

No matter whether you're working on your own or with a team of specialists, the first step for creating a home page is *writing*. If you have a designer on tap, explore your ideas in tandem. The back and forth between writer and designer produces the best communication in most media, definitely including websites. If you have a technology specialist, listen to explanations of what is practical and ask for insights into what else is possible. It's smart to ask both kinds of professionals for choices: different ways to accomplish what you want.

The "classic" components of a website home page are:

>> Your business name, preferably in logo form, or something that looks like a logo

>> A tagline amplifying the nature of your business so it is immediately understood

>> A "positioning statement" that tells your target audiences they are in the right place

>> A call to action — where to go next or something more specific — and contact information (some experts advise putting this on every page)

>> An overview of the whole site, in image or words, and a clear way to access all the inside pages

As appropriate to your business, you might also feature a "news" feature to blurb a new blog post, workshop, newsletter offer and so on. You might also link directly to a video that introduces you as available.

TIP

Once you decide which components your site needs, draw up a simple working plan. Some people like to visualize this as a tree with the home page as the trunk and the other pages branching out from it. This helps you know which pages should connect to which and helps maintain your big-picture grasp of site content.

The stumbling blocks for many people are the tagline and positioning statement. Paying attention to your keywords and search terms can help center you. You'll want to work them into the copy, too.

The tagline needs to identify your business as closely as possible. If your business name is self-explanatory, this is easier. For example, if your name is "Main Street Drop-off Service," you have a lot more explaining to do than if it is "Overnight Apple Repair by Main Street." And remember, you're telling search engines as well as customer prospects who you are. In the case of the vague business name, you'd use the tagline to specify the actual work, such as "overnight repair of Apple products." But if that's already in your name, the tagline can move on to "24-hour turnaround on every laptop, desktop and iPhone problem."

Taglines are worth a lot of thought. But as an old advertising adage puts it, "Don't be clever, be clear." Suppose our theoretical senior coaching business is named "Golden Years Internet." A tagline might read: *"Personal coaching to help seniors and the physically limited connect to the online world."* Or, since the audience is already identified by "golden years," *"Open up the world. Connect. Enjoy."*

TIP

The positioning statement gives you another way to expand on what you do. It's trendy to dispense with this, but ask yourself: Will the visitors I want, who find my site by Googling "nursing home entertainment," for example, or because they were searching for my specific set of services, know immediately they are in the right place?

The positioning statement is a tool for making that match. Unless you're a household name, take advantage of the chance. Actually, even household-name companies take pains to clarify that you're in the right place. They may have numerous and complex websites, so must tell customers they're where they need to be to make payments, find information about a product, file a complaint or whatever.

Our Golden Years Internet positioning statement might say:

In-person in southern Georgia or online anywhere: affordable individual or small group coaching that empowers physically limited people to socialize, learn, explore and be entertained online.

You might incorporate another line elsewhere on the page to address the senior's children (for example, "Give your loved one the greatest gift of all: today's best way to counter boredom and loneliness and connect with the world").

And you could also address your third audience, managers of senior residences: "Entertaining people in their golden years is easy when they know how to use today's inexpensive tools to open up their worlds by Internet."

Another favored home page element is an irresistible offer of some kind — sign up for a free blog, newsletter, ebook, introductory consult or conversation, for example. If you don't now have such materials, will they serve your marketing plan? Can you create them, and do you want to?

TIP

Once you are clear on your message, think about how to translate it into visual form that supports it. Free or affordable resources can provide illustrations, cartoons, symbols and other images, but most often, photographs — also available from these sources — are the answer.

Use photographs that are authentic — not generic stock images of people but real customers and real staff members or as relevant, an actual workshop; a book cover; a product image; you. Another good option is to translate a service — or the impact of a product — into visual form more abstractly (an approach covered in Chapter 8's section, "Translating Words into Visuals.") I don't want to count the number of writers who use some version of the old-fashioned writing quill to denote their profession. Outdated, yes, but more picturesque than a computer mouse.

Video is a valuable way to engage casual visitors and appeal to them on a more emotional level. You can offer links to such videos on the home page or embed them on it. Our Golden Years consultant could demonstrate a learning session or present testimonials from happy customers. Or introduce himself to visitors via video as a warm, caring, responsible, authoritative individual. (Producing video is covered later in this chapter.)

Writing the About Us page

Did you know that after the Home page, About Us is the most frequently visited website page across industries? Often it's the make-or-break part of your site that keeps people with you or leads them to click away.

You want to be your best and most trustworthy self on the About Us page. Therefore:

>> Write in first person: Use "I," or "we," not "they" (the rest of the site can be written in third person or the first person, "we").

>> Center on the problem-solving core of your business.

>> Deliver your value proposition in reader-friendly terms — what your business offers that no one else does.

>> Tell your story: Why you founded the business, why you're passionate about it, what is satisfying to you, what audience success means to you, how you feel about the help you give.

>> Translate your skills or product capabilities into benefits for the customer.

>> If appropriate, say why the opportunity is special or why the timing is wonderful — for example, new technology opens up the Internet to almost everyone, affordably.

>> Include a good photo of yourself, looking friendly but confident: A professional photo is often worth the investment. Video of you in action is a great asset if possible.

WARNING

Cite evidence of your authority, expertise and trustworthiness, but don't lead with it — it's probably boring. No résumé-speak! See credentials as a backup to communicating who you are and how and why you can help. Here is the place to present a vision of how much better life (or something) will be with you in the picture.

A good About Us page prompts the reader to look into the actual product by moving on to your Services or some other page. It's another good place to offer something free and collect email addresses, too: "Click now to schedule a free ten-minute consultation!" "Register for our webinar!" "Ask for my free ebook!" "Subscribe to my free newsletter!" "Follow us on these social media!"

TIP

What if there is no "us"? Then "Meet Jane" or something similar is fine. But it's not a virtual world for nothing: Most consultants and freelancers have allies on call and occasional partners according to the gig. Our Golden Years Internet CEO might realize when writing the About Us page that in fact, he does need to back up his qualifications with other specialists like an occupational therapist and psychologist. Occasional team members should also be introduced on the About Us page.

Writing the inside pages

With your Home Page and About Us drafted, move on to write the rest of the pages your plan calls for. Here are some of the pages most sites need.

>> **Services and How We Work:** Use one or both to get across the concrete options and opportunities you offer and the process involved — what is included and whether you offer a free initial consultation, for example, or a money-back-guarantee. Describe your services in a lively, user-oriented way, and counter any predisposition not to invest in you — the "resistances" list you assembled earlier in this chapter. Our Golden Years Internet entrepreneur might need to explain the technology choices and why they are

affordable and benefit this audience; what can be accommodated; and different service levels, for starters. Try not to over-burden this section, however. Keep descriptions brief and down to earth. Use images as much as you can to shorthand your words.

» **Testimonials:** This is your social proof. People do read them: In fact, some studies say they are the most-read part of websites. Testimonials can be grouped on their own page or scattered everywhere, from the home page on. Some sites do both. In any case, be sure they are real: Never write them yourself, because somehow, they won't be convincing. And you don't know until you ask what clients actually value in working with you (see Chapter 8). Video works very well for first-hand endorsements.

» **Landing page:** This is a page dedicated to a single action, like making a purchase or signing up for a conference. Either as a stand-alone site on its own or part of a website, it's the best place to lead prospects when you've captured their attention with an email, blog, presentation or social post. Often it's the most selling-oriented page and is thus adaptable to a sales page to deliver to prospects who ask for more information via any one of your channels.

A landing page needs a strong headline. Ideally it provokes curiosity and engages people with a vision of a problem solved and a better life in some way: "Can you imagine . . .", "14 ways to . . .", "What would life be like if . . .", "Are you plagued by . . .", "Mark tried everything to . . .", "Here's the secret to . . .". Copywriters still try to match the model created in 1927 as an ad for ready-made music courses: "They Laughed When I Sat Down at the Piano But When I Started to Play!"

Other elements of this page reflect a classic sales formula — identify the problem, elaborate on its awfulness and impact, offer your solution.

TIP

This is a word-of-mouth era for marketing so use testimonials, preferably with photos of the people. We believe people who are like us, not official company statements. Don't overlook this resource.

» **Contact:** Be real here, too! Use at least a first name for email, not an anonymous "info@" address; give a phone number if you can; offer phone, Skype or teleconference appointments; cite your special irresistible offers; and collect contact information from your visitors every way you can.

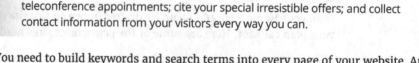

REMEMBER

You need to build keywords and search terms into every page of your website. And keep in mind that websites are global. If you have any interest in an international reach, you have even more reason to create easy-to-read and simple-to-navigate sites.

Content tips for websites

The guidelines detailed Chapter 11 all apply. Use them to create website copy that is genuinely useful to your target audiences. Keep in mind that people look for websites for reasons they are already clear on. They want to buy the best vacuum cleaner for the money, find a consultant to fix their computer, hire a designer for their website, learn something, donate money, solve a problem. Therefore, an effective website is not highly promotional but rather, establishes your authority and trustworthiness by showing that you understand this audience's needs and offer them real information of value.

TIP

Help your audience! Make this your touchstone. Present solid information on your product or service, or what your charitable cause accomplishes, in a low-key non-promotional way. Use your About Us page and How We Work to demonstrate how you relate to their need, testimonials to show how you solved similar problems for other people and what a good experience it was, landing pages to promote the commitment. Incorporate stories (Chapter 8 shows you how to develop stories that connect with audiences). Include articles or blog posts that expand their thinking and provide good advice (blogging is covered later in this chapter).

Writing tips for websites

All the writing advice in Part 1 of this book applies to websites, as well as the online writing guidance in Chapter 11. Writing for this medium demands sustained effort to be engaging, pithy and energetic. Make your website copy as tight and down-to-earth as you can. Use simple, concrete, unpretentious language. Center as many sentences as possible on action verbs. Use short sentences and paragraphing that allow for plenty of white space.

Aim for a friendly, welcoming, conversational tone. The "say-ability" test will support this writing goal. For inside pages that provide information, draw on useful techniques that journalists use. Invest a lot of thought into your headlines and lead sentences or paragraphs. Aim to reassure visitors that they are in exactly the right place. Adopt the "pyramid style" — see the section on blogging for this.

Bottom line: Tell it like it is. Limit your self-promotion sharply — the selling should be intrinsic to what you can accomplish for the visitor.

Graphic tips for websites

Resist the appeal of owning a trendy, glitzy site — unless you're aiming to attract trendy and/or very young users. Since more and more decisions are made using smartphones and watches, be sure your site is optimized for mini-screens. This means distilling your message to its core, building with simple design and providing easy navigation. Remember: Google now ranks websites on the basis of small screen rather than desktop. And when a site fails to open quickly, explorers move on.

A checklist of do's and don'ts when thinking about the visual nature of your site:

» **Go for an audience-centric design.** An elderly audience, for example, generally prefers more neutral colors, clear type, big headlines, and, naturally, pictures of people like themselves. There's plenty of research available on viewer preferences — check it out. Nielsen (www.nielsen.com) and the Nielsen Norman Group (www.nngroup.com) do widely respected research on site usability and media habits.

» **Leave out the flashy introductions and music.** Only include these flourishes if there are obvious opt-out buttons. Recent research tells us that people expect a site to load in three seconds, after which they hit the virtual road! More conservative studies say you have five seconds.

» **Avoid tactics that interfere with easy reading.** For example, tiny type, busy complicated designs, more than two or three main colors, and drop-out type (white type against a black or other dark background).

» **Don't build long, dense text blocks.** If you have more than a few sentences of text, break it up into short paragraphs (one to three sentences each) and add visuals, subheads or bullets. Build in lots of "white space."

» **Limit the need to scroll.** People fade off. Break the material into separate pages as needed. If you believe you need a linear style according to the subject or your audience, be sure to put the most important and captivating part of your message on top, what you most want the visitor to know.

» **Use photos, illustrations and video when appropriate to help keep the words tight and exploit their power to engage and deliver information interestingly.** But never use a visual for its own sake (unless you're an artist or photographer). Viewers resent them. And while it's attractive to use images very large, remember to give them context. A home page with vague words is cryptic. If you use few, be sure they're the right ones so people know what they're looking at and why.

TIP

"Usability research" is a big and expensive deal for large organizations. They want to know how users navigate their sites, identify stumbling blocks and understand negative responses. They want to know what content works best, and even users' tracking patterns when scanning each page. But you can do this research yourself! In fact, the premiere usability researchers, Nielsen Norman Group, recommends the do-it-yourself approach.

To create your own focus group and test drive your finished or in-progress site, assemble one to six people (six is optimal). Friends are fine; you don't need professional specialists. Ask them to use your site and watch carefully to note where they pause, where they stop, where they click. Observe their reactions. Then ask them to talk in detail about their experience. You will emerge with a blueprint for improving your own site, cost-free.

Finally, always look at a website as an evolving work. It's never "finished." To function as you hope, it must be constantly rethought, and you must invest in new fresh content.

Once our Golden Years Internet coach has his basic site ready to roll, he'll think about how to bring his intended audiences to it and ways to expand his platforms. For many business people, creating a blog is one of the first ideas. I look at that next.

Creating a Blog

Whether your goal is to support a business, build a platform to support a book or consultancy, stake a place in the virtual universe, make friends or influence people, the blog may be your medium of choice. However, blogging is a crowded field these days, and gaining attention for a new one can be tough. More modest estimates say that in the United States alone, more than 32 million individuals and organizations post blogs monthly. This crowded field accelerates the move toward focusing energies on video and vlogging, and in some case, podcasting.

If your goal is to earn significant money from the blog itself, whether short or long form, accept it as unlikely. A certain number of bloggers are still able to professionalize their output and generate surprising income — usually by identifying an underserved niche — but that's not a reasonable goal for most people.

The best reason to blog even in such a competitive arena is that it's among the best ways to support your business goals. A blog attached to your website keeps it alive and draws readers back. It bolsters your authority, connects you more personally to your audiences and leads you to deepen your own expertise. Marketing specialists are learning that it's becoming harder to gain attention via Google search, or generate quality traffic via social media. So similar to email, blogging remains basic to marketing for individuals and small businesses as well. It's a medium under your own control.

If you don't want to commit to operating to your own blogging site, you can alternatively post on the LinkedIn Publishing Platform (www.linkedin.com); Medium (https://medium.com), which invites you to "tell your story"; or Quora (www.quora.com), which is a Q&A forum that invites you to answer questions about your field of expertise and potentially build a following. Remember also local or specialized blogs to which you can contribute as a member of an industry, association, community or network. You can also look for opportunities to test the waters as a guest blogger.

REMEMBER

If you opt to blog, unless you're into the joy of self-publishing, it is important to invest your time strategically. Know your objectives: for example, to establish authority, keep your website fresh, promote customer engagement and/or find fans for your service. And of course, know the readers you want. Plan on promoting your blog via email and all your social media, and include it in your email signature and with any articles you write. Track results to see if your investment pays off, but keep in mind that establishing an audience takes time and frequent posting.

TIP

Opinion varies, but general consensus is that a blogger needs to post new material at least weekly. Is it better to blog short or long? Opinions diverge. Make the judgment according to the nature of your material, your audience and personal capabilities. Credible research finds that "long form" blogs, 1,500 to 2,200 words, are better read and valued than short ones (ballpark translation is 500 words per page single-spaced). Some estimates even claim that 2,000- to 7,000-word blogs generate the most interest. One group calculated that longer blogs generate nine times as many leads as short ones.

On the other hand, common sense suggests that we live in a short-bite culture. Many people prefer blogs and tips that require little reading time and work well on their cellphones. Supplying a steady stream of good ideas as "tip of the week," for example, pays off handsomely for many businesses. In other cases, writing relatively few in-depth blogs that your readers will value and even save pays off.

TIP

The current outlook favors higher quality rather than quantity. Regarding short or long, you can have it both ways: Run a content summary or several paragraphs of a long blog in an email message or social post or on your website, with a built-in connection to the full version. Or of course publish both long and short blogs according to how you feel.

The process for writing blogs is similar to writing articles for publication, print or online, so if that's your aspiration this section helps you with that as well. Both formats demand solid substance, but an article is a more "careful" undertaking that needs a more formal structure: beginning, middle and end — a conclusion. A blog can (and should) be more relaxed and spontaneous in tone — more personal. It can focus on one strand of a subject, while articles tend to take a thorough or broad perspective. But these lines are blurring.

Try This: Write a plan for your blog. Or, review your existing one, using one or more of these methods:

>> **Think through your goals and target audiences.** What do the readers you want to reach need? What problems must they solve that you can help with? What interests them? What can you share that they will value?

>> **Analyze your own special knowledge, expertise and interests.** Do you have any special access to interesting sources? Can you tie your expertise into any trends? Are you passionate about something or curious enough about a subject to seriously learn more about it?

>> **Study where your audience already lives.** What are they reading, talking about, participating in? Which blogs are most popular with them and which subjects? Study competitors' blogs to understand your audience better and look for niche areas that aren't being covered, or at least, not as much.

>> **Review the questions people ask** you via your website or in person, and also competitors' sites, forums on your subject or other sites you find in scouting the Internet. This tells you what people want to know and it may not be what you expect. For example, I noticed on Quora that the most frequent question about business writing is "how can I write a letter asking for . . ."

>> **Look to your hobby or a strong interest.** I know a PR professional who blogs about running and a doctor who blogs about opera. This works best for business purposes if you want to communicate "personality" or want mainly to contribute and connect with other enthusiasts. Many people who practice this are sure it connects with business interests over time.

TIP

Before committing yourself to a subject, perform a reality check to see how much similar material is already out there competing for reader attention — and how good it is. Write a short "mission statement" for your blog, a title and a list of 15 to 20 subjects you can initially cover.

Choosing your best subject

During a writing workshop for communication professionals, I asked participants to create a plan for a personal blog and compile a list of ten topics. Some chose a cause, such as eating nutritiously with prepared foods or high-fashion dressing for overweight women. A number wanted to share their opinions about movies, books, television shows or life.

One young man presented a "here's-what-I-think" idea, and I asked him who he imagined would read such a blog, other than a few friends. Can this blog be so entertaining that people who run across it will care about his opinion? And how to build a following for something so amorphous?

A few questions later, it emerged that the young man had pursued a passionate hobby since his early teens that had paid his way through college. He worked as a disc jockey at parties. Could he think of DJ-related topics to write about? He instantly came up with a long list of ideas for sharing professional tools and techniques that can be done at home. More important, his eyes lit up.

REMEMBER

An ideal choice for your blog subject is something you care about because it fascinates you, excites you, prompts your curiosity or just seems important. Like the amateur DJ, you may have real expertise or ideas to share. Great blogs stem from a focused passion of almost any kind, joined with knowledge and a desire to share. Ideally it should relate to the heart of your business purpose, of course, but this can be broadly interpreted.

Will the DJ blog help the PR professional I talked about with his career? I think so because his special expertise makes him unique and with his other credentials, may bring him to PR for the entertainment industry. The blogger who focuses on running is less unusual, but if she provides useful information, rather than just reporting her personal experiences, she can establish a following of people who trust her. She'll be first in mind if a need for her service emerges.

TIP

How-to blogs are endlessly attractive and successful. Ideally, you can provide something new or better, or at least a different angle on the topic, but people also appreciate round-up pieces that gather good ideas and information for them. Acknowledge the source and link to it.

Refrain from giving away all your ideas at once. It's easier to sustain a blog by slivering it into topics to deliver one at a time. This leads you to think more deeply about your work and perhaps research new information.

When you're blogging to support the organization, you work for or your own enterprise, use the same criteria to identify topics. Explore subject possibilities such as:

>> The part of the work or service you care about most.

>> Questions your customers most often ask.

>> Things to which you have special insights or access.

>> Inside tips and behind-the-scenes glimpses into organizations (particularly effective if the business or nonprofit boasts a fan base).

>> Highly specialized information for your field's geeks.

>> Announcement and analysis of new products — yours or a major company's.

>> Reviews of a new book, film, industry trend or initiative in your field.

» Stories and examples of how customers have used or been helped by the product or service.

» Ideas with visual potential, especially video. Many bloggers are embracing video to reach more audiences or to supplement their written blogs — some supply both kind of media at once by linking to video within the blog, or delivering a video and written transcript to recipients so they can choose whether to view or read.

REMEMBER

I shouldn't have to say it but I will: Don't criticize your employer in a blog, even a personal one, if you want to keep your job.

Developing tone and style

Write in a simple, straightforward, conversational way. Easier said than done, I know. Use the techniques explored in Part 1 to write clearly, tightly and transparently. It takes progressive editing to strip the chaff and flowery language that annoy online readers. Graphic language works much better: wording that evokes the senses — primarily sight, sound, touch. Don't be surprised if it also takes careful editing to sound spontaneous, unless you have a natural gift for this. To sound informal but remain authoritative, substitute active, interesting verbs for boring ones and short words for long; and work for a rhythm that alternates long and short sentences and reads well aloud.

TIP

Don't pontificate! Write like you're talking to friends. You may find you have an individual voice. Or you may develop one over time. But don't fret about it. If you're delivering good content in a natural voice, in line with advice throughout this book, you're just fine. Adapt tone to audience: Lawyers and accountants, for example, have not yet noticeably lightened up as a group, so probably require a more formal tone than soccer fans or wannabe DJs.

WARNING

Always be positive and upbeat when blogging — if you're writing critical reviews of a film, book, product or idea aim to sound objective. Be wary of criticizing anything or anyone personally, or be prepared for repercussions. And *never* attack or slur or ridicule anyone personally. Doing so is bad manners and hurts you every time: You lose the respect of valuable people. Plus, you run an increasing risk of being sued or seeing your most thoughtless remarks splashed everywhere when you run for office or compete for your dream job someday.

Drawing from the journalist's toolkit

Useful techniques for blogging, as well as writing articles and other informational material, come from the world of journalism. One core idea is to write in "pyramid style," a formula that's guided reporters for more than a century. Pyramid style is a version of the "bottom line on top" approach covered in Part 1 and fully demonstrated with email in Chapter 6.

Visualize an inverted pyramid — a triangle pointing down. The biggest portion is at the top and the shape gradually draws down to that point. This doesn't suggest putting most of the material on top — rather, it means lead with the most interesting information likely to engage readers. Follow up with information organized roughly by level of importance, in descending order.

The format developed as a practical strategy for editors as well as reporters: It enabled them to quickly cut-to-fit whole sentences or sections from the bottom up, instead of hunting for ways to painstakingly cut through the whole piece. Writing in inverted pyramid-style offers you the same advantage.

Leaving headlines aside for a moment, a strong lead must entice readers into the article with the most significant or relevant information. In a news story this means identifying the facts via the who-what-when-where-why-how imperative. Here's a classic example dating from an 1865 newspaper:

> *This evening at about 9:30 p.m. at Ford's Theatre, the President, while sitting in his private box with Mrs. Lincoln, Mrs. Harris and Major Rathburn, was shot by an assassin, who suddenly entered the box and approached behind the President.*

The body of an article story follows with the salient facts, issues, arguments or examples as suits the subject. The end, or "tail," includes additional content, links or references to related content. The pyramid persists because it gives writers a good structure that works for delivering straight information, and gives readers the option of moving on when they know as much as they want without losing the gist.

Fashion a strong lead

When you're sharing more than just-the-facts, you need to work harder than a news reporter to capture wandering eyes. You need creative leads, such as an interesting quote, an anecdote, a problem that will pull in your chosen readers.

For example, returning to our Golden Age Internet consultant once more, he might start an *article* about how his service transformed the life of an elderly man this way:

> *"I just wish I could chat with my old pals once in a while or maybe play checkers. Or buy a book for myself here and there," 87-year-old Todd Masters told his chief caretaker at the Hobbs Senior Residence in Gilmore, Md. last month. Like most of his fellow-residents, he spends most days dozing in front of a television that's set to loud.*

A *blog* could lead similarly but suggest a more spontaneous, personal tone in the "I" voice: the opposite of the objective tone that characterizes traditional reporting. A blog version:

Last month I visited a residence for the elderly and was introduced to 87-year-old Todd Masters. He was happy to talk with me — his shaky fingers and partial vision limit his activities and give him a lot of empty time. Like most of the other residents, he spends the daytime dozing in front of a loud television set.

How a feature ends, whether article or blog, is also open to more imagination than a straight news story. One way is to circle back to the lead — rather as with an email. But instead of repeating the "ask," return the story to its central message to close it out. As in:

Yesterday I watched Todd open his tablet and order a book from Amazon — The Life of a Flower. "Before I came here, I loved working in my garden every day," he told me. "Now I can find out what happens in Spring!" And for the first time, I saw him smile.

Use a nut graf

More formally known as the *nutshell paragraph*, the "nut graf" is a capsulizing paragraph of one to three sentences that delivers the heart of a story and puts it in a larger perspective. It might summarize previous events relating to the new one, and explain why the subject of the story matters in a broad context. It distills the theme so readers know exactly what's ahead and can decide whether to read on.

If I were writing the Golden Age article, I might follow the lead — the first version in the previous section — with a nut graf like this:

Todd is one of 6,255 nursing home residents in Alberan County who are living out their supposedly golden years in a state of loneliness and boredom. Children live far away or are busy, surviving friends are not mobile enough to visit, there is little scope for feeling independent. But the Internet offers a world of solutions — if Todd and his peers can learn to maneuver it. I know they can.

The nut graf connects the lead with the rest of the content. It's natural to follow with a rundown of how Todd was equipped to join the connected world. Nut grafs work with or without the pyramid pattern and give you a useful technique for a lot of writing tasks.

SHORTCUT

One more journalism approach that will always help you with complicated subjects and large-scale projects, as well as articles and blogs: the single-sentence note to yourself. What is your message about, whatever its projected length and depth? Why should readers care? Figure that out, write it down and keep it in front of you. Or easier, tell it to a friend: "I'm writing this blog about . . . because . . . ."

Creating magnetic headlines

Headlines are critical to getting your post noticed by both readers and search engines. If you're luring people in via email or social media, they must be explicit and a touch exaggerated. Keep them honest — but a little irresistible.

Start your thinking with how the content benefits your readers: Will they find out how to do something faster, better, cheaper? Improve their lives in some way? Observe in your email what captures you to click "open" for a blog. Here are a few that drew me to click and read today:

> *10 save-the-day tips from top chefs*
>
> *How to turn live photos into a video on an iPhone*
>
> *Let's Get You a TedX Talk*
>
> *How Often Should You Wash Your Clothes?*
>
> *How to Recover from a Long Flight According to Flight Attendants*

The first example is the ever-popular "listicle" — text organized around a list of ideas. Listicles appeal by promising specific, useful information in a compact and accessible way. I opened the last example because I'm planning a trip. Timing can be everything — one reason why experienced bloggers recycle material with or without a new angle periodically.

TIP

"How to" blogs are often winners because they are solution oriented. When people search the Internet, most often they have a problem and are looking for a way to deal with it. So, if you offer useful information, and pay attention to your keywords especially in the headline, readers will find your content. Think through the endless variations on the theme: *The Easiest Way to . . ., The Best Way to . . ., The New Way to . . ., The Professional Approach to . . ., 92 Ways to . . .* and so on.

WARNING

Don't use a headline to promise something you don't deliver.

The best ideas come from deeply mining your own subject matter in context of what your desired audiences need. Here's how our friend who runs the Golden Years Internet coaching service might think in planning to blog. A tentative title could be *Internetting in the Golden Years*. Some possible topics:

> *The 6 best equipment choices for Internet explorers over 70*
>
> *10 free online courses perfect for 75+-year-olds*
>
> *Citizen science: How seniors can contribute to today's critical research*
>
> *How to recognize Internet scammers who prey on seniors*

Online games for seniors: Checkers to chess, mahjong to Go

Exercise for seniors — the 8 best online programs

New tablet tools for seniors with limited vision

TIP

If you can't think of 15 to 20 subjects to write about in your area of expertise, consider whether you can find a better niche for yourself.

Organizing with progressive subheads

Dividing your blog text with subheads serves many purposes: It helps organize your ideas, adds white space and keeps people reading. If you use the listicle format, you know in advance how to write your subheads: one for each of the listed points. Subheads every few paragraphs make the material look easy to read. What's not to like? Even a short blog benefits. Alternatively, bold the first phrase or sentence of each item to produce a subhead-like effect.

Writing good subheads is also covered in Chapters 3 and 6, and see more ideas for writing strong leads, also in Chapter 6. And yes, search terms apply and should be front-loaded in your headline and lead.

SHORTCUT

If you need inspiration for potential topics and headlines, here's a fun way to find it. Experiment with an online headline generator. Here are two I like and a few results I received by entering "business writing" as my topic:

HubSpot's Blog Topic Generator (www.hubspot.com/blog-topic-generator)

Will Business Writing Ever Rule the World?

Business Writing Explained in Fewer Than 140 Characters

Portent Content Idea Generator (www.portent.com/tools/title-maker)

11 Things About Business Writing Your Teachers Wouldn't Tell You

How Business Writing Can Keep You Out of Trouble

TIP

Sometimes the silliest ideas prompt really good ones. Copywriters and magazine editors brainstorm that way a lot.

Considering articles for publication

In this discussion of how to blog, you probably noticed I mention writing articles for publication several times and may wonder if there's a market for them. While the print world has shrunk dramatically over the past decade, as newspapers and magazines go out of business and kill journalism jobs, the Internet becomes a hungrier consumer. Most leading magazines and newspapers publish online versions and feed them separately from the print publications.

If you are able to write articles for either online or print use, and don't necessarily need to be paid for it, you may find a niche that benefits your marketing. Unless you already have a national reputation in your field or for some other reason, your best bet is to look locally. Community and regional newspapers continue to thrive in many locations. So do trade, professional and association newsletters and magazines. They are far less besieged by freelancers than the national publications and often more open to a local person with a good idea. The Internet makes the necessary research easier to do than in earlier times.

As you would for a blog, mine your personal expertise for subjects appropriate to the general public or other specialists in your field, according to the media you target. A publication may be open to a personality feature, or one that reflects a national trend on the local level, or shares professional insights with a general readership. What you're doing may be of broad interest — the Golden Age entrepreneur cited earlier in this section might well be able to interest a local newspaper, a technology magazine or one oriented to senior citizens in an article.

Citing published articles remain an excellent credential and widens your reach, so may be worth your time. Think your best idea through well and then translate it into a pitch. See Chapter 14 for tips on approaching the media.

TIP

The advice in this section also applies to creating your own newsletters. Map out your audience and editorial scope. Just as for a blog, come up with a title, a one-sentence description that crystallizes your content and its interest value, type of material to include and lists of specific articles that relate. Plenty of help with formatting and distribution is available from services like AWeber (www.aweber.com) and Constant Contact (www.constantcontact.com). Assuming you aim to develop an e-newsletter, building your address list is critical.

Telling Your Story with Video

Video is in many ways the ultimate storytelling vehicle. Like film, it compels our attention and can leap past our logical minds straight to the emotions by integrating moving images, voice and music. Unlike film, producing it is possible for almost anyone with a device that shoots, records sound and edits — and may even fit into our pocket as a smartphone.

Because the production process has simplified so radically, just like we are all photographers and journalists, today we can all be video producers. And happily, many videos need not be based on sophisticated production values. Authenticity is highly valued in many venues.

Don't for a minute think you need not apply your writing skills to video creation. Even if your final video is purely visual and contains no words at all, you still need them in the thinking stage known as *preproduction*. Video or film that's more than a few seconds long requires planning, and I don't know a way to plan that doesn't require language. Any medium beyond pure entertainment such as singing or dancing that aims to just create a mood or emotion, must first be expressed or imagined in words. Then those ideas are translated into visual form. Completing the circle, the viewer translates it back to language because that's how we ascribe meaning. Further, if you're collaborating with anyone else, you need to write the script so everyone is on the same page and can contribute to the production according to their own viewpoints and expertise.

Between the smartphone video for social media and an expensive marketing video is a wide range of in-between video: the how-to demo for YouTube; your website self-introduction; video blogs, or vlogs; live event coverage; your commercial for an email offering and much more.

How "good" such videos need to be is up to you. But my premise is that knowing how professionals produce video will help you achieve better results when you wear all the hats: director, scriptwriter, cameraperson, sound specialist, on-screen and voiceover talent, editor, art director, animator. Many of the ideas are adaptable to your solo smartphone shooting. If you want higher production quality and can afford a team, these ideas will help you know how to invest your resources.

Using video to accomplish goals

If you're creating mini-videos to share with friends and peers, you may not need to plan much. But it's different when you have a business goal. Then you need to produce a "show" that engages strangers and gives them what they want — usually information of some kind and some degree of entertainment, because we expect that from video. It must also serve your own cause preferably in multiple ways.

Most typically, these ways may include self-introductions for websites and résumés, sales pitches, customer testimonials, demonstrations of how to do or make something and showing your service in action.

Any of these basic ideas can treated as a short-form video (a 15-second customer testimonial) or long-form (a 2- to 15-minute demonstration). And how you use your material is limited only by your imagination. Digital magic allows you to endlessly recycle what you shoot, which often justifies the investment of time and money. Often your video "products" can be used on your website and posted on YouTube or another public venue. A product demonstration can be posted on various platforms and taken along to support in-person or teleconferenced sales calls. You can liven up blogs and just about every social post with video snippets.

To use video strategically, consider some basics about its best use:

» **Know what video can do well and less well.** By integrating picture, sound, voice and perhaps music, film and video have enormous power to grab us emotionally. But they can be less effective as learning tools. Visually based instructional material can demonstrate how to do something, but it isn't well-suited for delivering in-depth detail or abstract information.

» **Regard video as one more tool to integrate into your overall marketing strategy.** Unless you just want to have fun or produce random bits that might find an audience online, think through how what you want to produce fits into everything else you do, how it can be used to carry your core message and how it can amplify the power of that message.

» **Pre-think all possible ways you might repurpose video.** If you are shooting a customer testimonial for your website, brainstorm other potential uses for the material, such as a marketing piece for your website, blog or Facebook page. You can use footage to make GIFs or short looping videos for social media or your site. It's much easier to shoot a little more and cover the extra territory at the same time, especially if you won't have another opportunity. A quality, goal-oriented video demands a lot of time and resources, so plan to leverage that investment.

Scripting your video

Shoot first and ask questions later? No! Script your video first. It's like everything else in life: How can you get what you want if you don't know what that is? Regardless of production values, video improves dramatically when you base it on writing. But remember that every second of spoken word must have correlating visuals, so scripting includes both words and picture.

This multidimensional quality makes scriptwriting a special kind of writing challenge. The picture must be planned right along with the narration or live sound. This becomes obvious the first time you work on a video project that is more than 15 seconds long. During my first experience, I came to the editing room with ten pages of carefully written and recorded voiceover and a few days of on-site shooting. The editor laid down the first two minutes of sound and said, "Okay, what's the picture?" We had only one minute of relevant footage. Out went the script.

REMEMBER

Know what you want to accomplish at the earliest stage and plan based on *simplicity*. It's wise not to get overly ambitious. Pick subjects that support your goals and that you can handle with the equipment and know-how on hand. Be aware of your content options.

According to the nature of your project (and budget), content can include:

» Talking heads (people speaking directly to the camera)

» Live action (such as demonstrations of a process or something happening)

» Cutaways (close-ups of models, charts or details of the scene)

» Secondary footage called B roll, for background and transitions

» Still images, which can be manipulated to give an impression of motion

» On-screen titles, animation and other graphics

» Archival material from your own files, a customer's or a commercial source

Producing video step-by-step

Here's a process to see your video project through. Adapt it to your project, but to emerge with a video you feel proud of, attend to how the work is best sequenced. At each step you reach, you can't go back. When it's editing time, there's generally no way to get the missing picture or comment without insurmountable trouble. The more detailed your script, the better the ultimate results. Here are the stages involved.

Preproduction

Step 1. Define your goal and audience.

Why are you producing this video? Who are you aiming at? What's your basic message? Try crystallizing it Hollywood style, for example: "This video will show that my startup is the most fun place in the world to work and the best programmers want to be here." "Our new gizmo is the perfect gift for people with age-related hearing loss." Know how you envision showing the video, too: At client meetings? On the company website? YouTube? Recruitment fairs? All of the above?

Step 2. Plan production style and content.

Brainstorm how to best tell your story and balance your vision against the practical realities of time, budget, team skills and equipment. Decide on ideal length and components: a mix of live action and interviews, for example. And catalog what you'll need, such as live sound; narration; still images; music; graphics; animation; special effects.

Step 3. Write a Word + Picture script.

Use a scripting app or Microsoft Word's Insert Table tool, which works nicely for creating simple grids within word-processing documents. Or just take a sheet of paper — real or virtual — and divide it vertically down the middle. Label the column on the left "Words" and the one on the right "Picture." This keeps you focused on your video's parallel needs and time frames. It's smart to leave a narrow column on the far left to record time codes (essential to the editing process) and a narrow area on the far right for notes to help you remember things such as "save for opening." Alternatively, use a storyboard approach like many professionals do — a thorough series of sequenced images with notes on the words. There are apps for digital storyboarding (such as www.storyboardthat.com) or just draw it out.

Step 4. Create a shot list.

With script in hand, create a list of exactly the material you need to shoot. For example, Mark demonstrates gizmo; Jane explains features; close-up of gizmo; Jake building gizmo in lab; client Barney says how gizmo helps him. Use your shot list to create shooting schedules for each day and pay close attention to logistics — locations and time. Especially if you're hiring professional cameramen and more, you want as little down time as possible. But setting up lights and other equipment takes considerable time in every new scene, so that needs to be built into your timetable. Consult your specialists on these realities.

Step 5. Prepare for a smooth shoot.

The pros usually scout the location beforehand and check backgrounds and infrastructure like power sources. Prepare people for the action scenes and interviews so they know what's expected in general. Even if you want a documentary-style video, you still need to tell your "talent" what you want them to do, how to dress and what kind of statement you want them to make. But don't tell them so much that they script themselves and lose spontaneity. Bring a prepared list of open-ended questions designed to elicit the answers you want: not "yes" or "no," but full answers that relate to the heart of your subject.

Production

Step 6. Lights, action, camera!

Finally! You've reached the shooting stage. If you're working with specialists, you still need to stage manage actively to be sure you get what you need. Even when you're well-prepared, it's stressful. Carry out your shooting plan and be alert to other opportunities to supplement it. You need to shoot "B roll" — secondary material like pans of the room, close-ups of relevant objects, people walking in and so on. Be sure you have what you want of the most essential material and if possible, shoot it again. If you're working with one camera (or smartphone) it's a good idea to repeat the scene and shoot it from two different angles. Video eats up a lot of footage! And you need variety.

Stay open at all times to unexpected opportunities and recognize that your script keeps evolving as you shoot and edit. Juggling between words and pictures is a continuing process right until the end. But keep your vision of the ultimate product you want in your head — or on a piece of paper — at every step.

Step 7. Interview your subjects.

Ask your questions in the tone you want reflected back: enthusiasm, appreciation, happiness, thoughtfulness, whatever. Tell each person to give you complete answers — not "Because I finally had time for . . .", but "I started my business last year because I finally had time for . . .". Where you strike gold unexpectedly — an answer that lights up your interviewee — follow up. The more you treat the interview as a conversation, the more believable and interesting your result. Help people relax by telling them you'll reshoot if necessary if they're not happy with their answers.

Postproduction

Step 8. Review your video.

Familiarize yourself with the video footage and other materials, too, such as existing material from your files or outside resources and still photos or graphics. You must know what's on hand for the "Picture" side of the ledger. You can never have a blank screen, and you don't want to leave images up so long they bore viewers. More than a few seconds and watchers feel bored! Identify all your best shots, which may be quite different from what you expected. Don't be surprised if you have to adjust the script a lot because you ended up missing some of what you wanted or found good material you didn't plan for. Now you're ready to decide how you can successfully tell your story.

Step 9. Find a good introduction.

Look for something intriguing or interesting about your subject and lead with it if possible. Make sure you have a good visual to carry the words. You may find a natural opening, whatever the subject. For example, start a how-to video with the problem: *"Nothing feels worse than lower-back pain from computer hunch. Have you tried all kinds of meds and they don't help? Or exercises that just make it worse? I'm going to show you how to feel great by investing only six minutes per day."* Or just start with the strong visual. Sometimes a startling fact or statistic or quote works well as an opening graphic, and it can be shown on-screen without spoken words for a pow-erful intro, especially with music. If you shot a strong testimonial, you might start with a short clip of the best bit. Or if there's a good nugget of you explaining your business passion, try that.

Step 10. Match up picture and words.

Work your way through your script section by section, matching up picture and words. Aim to narrate or explain as little as possible and let the picture tell as much as it can. Don't repeat orally what's self-evident visually. At this stage, thanks to your cohesive planning, you often find ways to whittle down the words much further than your original script. But think before eliminating the words altogether, even if the style is documentary. You don't want your viewers to won-der why they're looking at something or try to piece meaning together for you. Use the narration to keep things in perspective, connect, explain or amplify, as necessary.

Step 11. Craft the right words.

For the ultimate narration, aim to distill the essence of the idea or fact into as few words as possible, but don't overlook chances to use graphic, evocative language. Depend on short, easily pronounced words and simple sentences. Break grammar rules freely. Fragments are fine, as are one-word sentences if the result sounds good and meaning is clear. Avoid complicated literary or other deep thoughts. Distill, distill, distill. For example, a how-to on remediating back pain:

> *"Laptop stoop. Pain. Misery. Frustration. It's the twenty-first century's way of saying take a break! Here's how."*

Or more straightforwardly,

> *Hi, I'm Sal Harris and I help athletes fix whatever is hurting them. I noticed that my friends who spend half their day at the computer all have back problems from hunching over it all day. So I came up with an easy five-minute routine you can do twice a day and help your back, your shoulders, your neck feel good. Your wrists, too. Ready to try it?*

TIP

Edit, edit, edit until the narration flows like liquid. Have someone else read it, listen and edit, and rephrase. If you record narration before editing, listen carefully and if your narrator stumbles or sounds awkward, rewrite and rerecord if you have that option. If you're working with professional editors or other specialists, listen to their suggestions, too.

Sharing expertise with video

Most people today go straight to the Internet to learn things: how to fix a computer problem, how to treat a pulled muscle, how to make a quilt, how to delete 60,000 unread Gmail messages. If you're good at something or have specialized knowledge, you probably possess excellent subject matter for how-to videos.

Disseminating such videos can be especially valuable for establishing expertise or authority in your field. Whether you make boots or art glass, teach a distinct brand of yoga or fix carburetors, how-to tips can draw your target audiences. They can also be used to communicate what makes your product unique and perhaps expensive: special materials, a demanding process, years of experience. They are excellent enhancements for your website and blog.

Keep in mind that in addition to your competitors' productions, the Internet offers an astonishing number of videos and blogs that share knowledge purely for the makers' satisfaction in doing so. Think about how to communicate your knowledge or advice as effectively as possible, and do your best with production values. When given a choice, we'll all watch the better-quality video.

TIP

Create your script, as outlined in the previous section, as a step-by-step set of visual-plus-narrative instructions. If you don't have a team of specialists to work with, build one with colleagues who have good ideas and a willingness to experiment. Ingenuity and imagination can go a long way.

If you're basically your own crew, rely on the following production essentials:

- » **Lighting is the big difference between interesting, clear video imagery and indifferent visuals.** It's chancy to rely on natural light or whatever you find at the scene. Invest in a light or two you can position and adjust. Take the time and effort to light yourself or your subject well.

- » **Sound quality counts hugely.** The biggest technical complaint about home-grown video is poor sound. People can forgive not-so-good picture but hate having to strain their ears to catch or interpret the words. Seriously consider investing in a good versatile microphone.

- » **For steady shots, a tripod is necessary.** This especially applies if you're working with a smartphone or small camera. A number of tripods for smartphones are available, or a regular tripod can be adapted to hold a cellphone.

None of these items need be expensive and all are readily available online (as is advice). A good camera shop can be a big help for assembling your kit.

Introducing yourself with video

Video of the company leader is a powerful way to liven up a website or social media page, even if you're a one-person operation. Someone — perhaps you — talking on camera about your business, product, service or career dream is a much more personal introduction than plain old written copy. You and your business become real to viewers and they feel they know you personally.

WARNING

However, not everyone comes across well in living, speaking media. Video is especially high-risk if you plan a talking-head speech with the camera focused fully on you the whole time. You can work out a simple version of a teleprompter, such as cue cards or pages with notes outside the camera's view, rather than reading. Or buy an inexpensive teleprompter. Some are specifically for use with a smartphone, and you can buy some for a few dollars. But using a teleprompter well is a lot more difficult than you might expect. Coming across as warm and natural without some talent or training is difficult.

Try This: Record yourself. Speak directly to a camera for a minute or two and then take a hard look at how you come across on video. Ask colleagues for honest input. If the piece doesn't show you off to advantage, either scrap the idea for now or do a really short version.

TIP

Twenty or 30 seconds of video is usually plenty for an introduction. Think of it as an elevator speech with a camera. Your actual elevator speech, which I discuss in Chapter 9, may give you the core of your video message. Also consider drawing on your personal value statement or your personal story, which I talk about in Chapter 8.

What often works best is to find something about your work that ignites your own genuine enthusiasm or passion. I once reviewed a script for a travel agent that began, "Hello, I'm Viola Smith, and I run a full-service travel agency that takes care of you all over the world." The alternative I suggested: "I'm Viola Smith, and what I love about my work is rescuing people from the travel adventures they didn't expect."

Just like all your communication from email to proposal to blog, the lead is 60 percent of the work. Once it's in place, the rest falls naturally. Viola went on to give a few examples of extreme rescue, like replacing a traveler's stolen documents in time for him to get home for his daughter's birthday. In less than a minute, the video demonstrated Viola's problem-solving skills and above-and-beyond service, which connected well with the common worry about travel disasters. Her core message was a reassuring, "I've got your back and I'll do whatever it takes to rescue you. And I love doing that." Your own core message gives you the backbone of your self-intro.

REMEMBER

You don't need a lot of flash or magical words to introduce yourself. But use your best writing-thinking skills to find the heart of your message, one that you can communicate with great conviction. Emotion is contagious! Be positive and upbeat and enthusiastic on screen.

When you interview other people, ask your questions in the same spirit. If you say "What motivated you to do that?" in a matter of fact tone looking at a piece of paper, your interviewee will say something like, "Oh, I got the idea in high school and I was finally following up," in the same neutral tone. If you look straight at the person expectantly with real interest, they will give you the great answer you want and their passion will shine through.

With the next chapter, I move into the workplace. We all have bosses to report to, whether they are managers, clients, presidents or members of the board. And we all have coworkers, partners and colleagues. Leveraging your writing and media skills to succeed in your work is why you're reading this book, right? So, move along with me.

IS THE VIDEO RÉSUMÉ RIGHT FOR YOU?

With video emerging as a favorite medium for so many purposes, the video résumé may seem like a good option. And it is, for people in creative fields who can best show their skills off visually and do it with . . . well, creativity. It can also work for people in fields such as sales, customer service and employee relations, where personality matters, provided they actually come across as engaging.

Realistically, not everyone can do that. And a video résumé does not preclude the need for a written résumé, which still matters in itself and must align with the script. Sixty to 90 seconds is all you need but your selfie commercial must be well produced: good picture, sound, editing. The best video résumés use graphics and music, too. It's a big plus if you can make the video fun to watch, but make sure your humor works for other people. Sincerity is a good alternative. Here are some pointers specific to a video résumé:

- **Think of this video in terms of delivering a message.** What is your message and how can you best support it? Find a lead that engages the viewer; explain why you'll deliver value, based on career highlights, skills and personality assets as appropriate; close strongly with what you hope for. If you have a story, tell it well.

- **Employ visual variety.** Rather than act as a talking head droning into the camera, aim to use different angles of yourself, perhaps work samples or shots of yourself in action and testimonials to your capabilities by others.

5
Leveraging Your Writing Skills

Learn writing techniques for email, group chat and reporting that help you succeed as a virtual or independent worker.

Understand how to use strategic writing to gain key advantages as a virtual team member or project leader.

Learn how to communicate well as a manager with messages that inspire and motivate, deliver good news and bad, and effectively deliver requests, orders and criticism.

Write strategic messages to higher-ups that gain you respect by considering their perspectives and pressures.

Chart your own communication plan, based on determining your goals and audiences, as an entrepreneur.

Chapter **13**

Writing for the Workplace: Managing Up, Down and Sideways

S uccess depends on how you interact with the people you work with. Do you disagree? Consider that your long-range career prospects, in no particular order, probably include:

» Working inside various organizations for managers and as a manager

» Acting as a consultant, freelancer, professional specialist or other independent

» Creating your own enterprise that may employ others you must lead

In fact, you may at times function in all of these capacities at once. In all roles you may often be part of a team. You regularly depend on collaborators, partners and various specialists to help you accomplish your goals. Decision-makers increasingly recognize this fact and look for people skills in their job candidates and consultants. Good communication is the most tangible people skill, and thus an upfront priority for relating to everyone from investors to voters.

This is why a psychological perspective and relationship-building tactics are built into the whole of this book. It's terrific to own technical skills — if you have them, flaunt them — but it's how you interact and communicate that most often wins the prizes you want. This chapter shows you how to foster positive relationships and use strategic writing to your advantage in workplace interactions.

This entire book is about business writing, of course, but here I focus on the specific challenges of managing up — communicating with supervisors; managing down — communicating when you are in charge of a team, project, department or business; and managing "around" — interacting with peers, coworkers and collaborators. Because you probably need to practice communicating on all these levels over the course of a day, week or month, look for helpful guidance all throughout this chapter.

As I state in earlier chapters, a thoughtful writing process itself helps clarify your goals, reasoning and options. This benefit is especially relevant to writing difficult messages to bosses and subordinates. Of course, I can't predict all the challenges ahead of you, so review the examples as demonstrations of how to use the structured planning for your needs, and especially how to write based on insight into other people's perspectives.

Communicating as a Manager

Most great leaders are admired for their powerful communication skills. Not a surprise: How else can you inspire, motivate and persuade? But alas, most of our direct experience is with managers who are not leaders and who fall short on this skill set. Gallup, the premier polling group, reports that two-thirds of American workers identify themselves as "unengaged." Their yearly report consistently pinpoints poor relationships as the main cause, which often translates as poor manager communication.

A workplace with low morale is an unproductive one. Rampant disengagement generates mistakes, misunderstandings, inefficiencies and high turnover. Why do so many organizations allow this huge inadequacy to persist? It's complicated, of course, but misplaced values, counterproductive reward policies and lack of training all play a part.

If you manage even one other person, or aspire to rise in the ranks, all the techniques for writing and speaking I cover in earlier chapters give you useful tools. Here I focus is on applying those ideas to some typical management writing challenges.

You may think that the higher you ascend the management ladder, the more you can issue orders and the less you need to care about people's feelings. Big mistake! Even if you hit the top, autocratic ways of managing are unpopular and ineffective today.

If you want people to work hard for you, help you perform well, feel enthusiastic about their work and say nice things about you and the company, the word is: You must be more courteous, empathetic and considerate than ever. This outlook should show in both your in-person communication and in what you write.

I do know first-hand that the boss's lot is not an easy one. The messages can be hard: "No, you don't get the assignment or promotion or new office you wanted"; "No, the company won't pay for your MBA"; "Sorry, I can't let you work at home three days a week"; "The company had a bad first quarter so no conference requests this year"; "Everyone's taking a three percent pay cut, well, maybe not everyone." And then there are the routine written performance evaluations and critiques, which are seldom fun.

And those are just messages to subordinates! You must write with great care to your own supervisors and find ways to express your viewpoint when it differs from theirs, even when they don't want to listen. You must represent "your people" and try to protect them from negative impact from higher-ups.

You're expected to feed the chain of command's need for better data or sales figures or donations or productivity so higher-ups can, in many cases, take credit for your team's accomplishments. You must win support for programs and innovations by writing reports and proposals they will only skim. You are probably required to explain and implement directives you don't like. And you may have a host of additional audiences to address: management peers, board members, donors, suppliers, regulators and more.

Where to start on all this? *Tone.* To write strategically — that is, to accomplish your goals with people on different levels — it's especially important to gauge your audiences as individuals, not just as cogs in a corporate machine. You can be most successful by relating to each person above and below you, both within terms of their roles and personal perspectives. If you're really high up the ladder and supervise hundreds of people, it's imperative to relate well to all your department or team heads and delegate a lot of communication to each of them, and ensure that they are willing and able to do this well. Let's look first at communicating with your staff.

Relating to your team members

When you head a department or work unit, you are fully responsible for how the group interacts and operates. This carries some ramifications that all too many managers appear to forget. When you're the boss, you're the role model; don't look for any vacations from that. How you treat people and communicate with them is echoed in how they interact with each other. Remember also:

>> **You're always in the spotlight.** People are intensely aware of any perceived unfairness, inconsistency or favoritism on the boss's part.

>> **You set the standards for level of commitment and respectful behavior.** Hard work, courtesy and consideration are contagious when coming from the top. At the same time, you must hold your team accountable.

>> **You establish value.** People naturally strive to perform in ways they observe the boss to value — if you write well, for example, they typically write more carefully, too.

>> **What you say and what you write may be given far more weight than you credit or intend.** Careless statements can have unintended consequences. Remember all those movies where a VIP said, "If only Smith wasn't around to bug up the works . . ."?

>> **Your communication style affects what your employees choose to share with you and how honest they will be.** It affects to what degree they'll express their true opinions and contribute ideas.

>> **Your tone in communicating has lasting impact.** A badly thought-out or mean-spirited message may negatively affect your whole unit, while positive messages inspire and motivate.

Here's an important corollary of the foregoing principles: *Your responsibility as a manager requires you to control your own feelings and short-sighted reactions.* Professional entertainers are never allowed to have a bad day and neither are you. If you want to be respected, letting negative emotions like anger, frustration, pettiness or bad moods rule will always work against you. The boss is key to the whole spirit of our work environment. We need them to be positive, confident, enthusiastic and cheerful so we can feel secure and supported.

SHORTCUT

Taking account of the ideas you're absorbing in this chapter and others, build a written persona for yourself as a supervisor — the supervisor you want to be. Describe the temperament, personality, management and communication style you aim for. How can you create and maintain trust? Communicate expectations? Improve subordinate performance? Show support and reward good contributions? Think about why the best boss you ever had was effective and about the qualities you didn't like in others. This exercise gives you a vision for yourself to channel into your everyday work life and yes, with a little trial and error it will become real, and reward you nicely.

REMEMBER

Some of the best advice I've heard is that whatever the work, aim to build a team around yourself. Never get so lost in the numbers, pressures or urgencies that you forget this basic commitment or run out of time to handle it. Use everything you write to foster good feelings and commitment.

Set the stage for yourself by looking at your staff members as individuals. Build a profile for each key person with the tools presented in Chapter 2. Take special account of what motivates each person, their strengths and aspirations, and how they relate to the team. Rather than act on assumptions, ask each person about how they prefer to be communicated with and any considerations they feel important to share. In some firms, new employees are asked to cover this in a written document.

TIP

Creating personal profiles of those under your authority gives you a super tool for deploying your forces well and promoting team spirit. Look for strengths and cherish the differences. The better you know your team, the better you can frame your written messages to each person as well as the full group. Let's look at some general guidelines.

Writing to inspire and motivate

The harder your staff works, the more you accomplish, the better you do your job and the more kudos you gain. What's not to like? Many ways of motivating people come down to surprisingly basic ideas. But they are so often ignored that it is easy for you to absorb them and stand out. Here are some ideas to guide the content of your messaging:

>> **Communicate a positive vision.** Every team member should know the goals of the organization, department and unit they work within, and what success looks like and how the team is to achieve it. Knowing how your own work fits into the big picture is motivating and helps everyone do their jobs better.

>> **Share information regularly.** People like and need to know "what's going on." An industry trend? A new edict coming down from on high? Tell your staff as much as you can ASAP, and what it means to them. If people know they can depend on you to share important news, you diminish opportunities for gossip and wild surmise.

>> **Make the most of good news — and don't hide bad news.** If you're recognized for an achievement that took a team, share the glory and celebrate. If there's bad company news, tell it. The news will come out anyway so share it early rather than late to maintain trust.

>> **Stay positive and upbeat in all your communication.** If asked, most people will tell you that having an even-tempered, cheerful boss makes their lives hugely better. Upbeat communication projects that you like your job, know you do it well and expect the best from everyone. Extend trust and most often, people will be trustworthy.

>> **Be clear on what you want and what you expect at every turn.** Each person should understand their role and how it fits into the unit and organization, as well as how they are expected to behave and interact. Hold staff members accountable. Beyond keeping people on track, this helps them feel valued and encourages them to aim high.

>> **Actively encourage your staff to share their own information, ideas and suggestions.** Everyone complains about writing reports, but if your staff includes more than eight people or so, how else will you know what's going on? Respond to helpful reports, and in conversation, listen!

>> **Show appreciation often: for work well done, an over-and-above contribution and good writing!** People repeat and amplify behavior that brings praise, while an unacknowledged good deed may remain a lonely one. Give credit as due rather than appropriating it for yourself. Demonstrate your team is valued by meeting one-on-one with members, regularly if possible.

REMEMBER

Keep in mind that good communication is a two-way street. Technology has changed us: We expect to interact online, not just read, and we want to contribute ideas and opinions and be heard, rather than just listen and follow orders. People want to be part of the action rather than just recipients of information from on high. Practice the old one-way-trickle-down style (colorfully called "cascading") at your own risk. Your most valuable people will not put up with it.

WARNING

Being an active and knowledgeable member of the team is especially important in managing Millennials and Gen Z'ers (Chapter 2). They value "the experience," chances to learn and knowing the why of everything. Such opportunities are more important than money to many young people, and they may quickly disappear themselves if kept on the periphery. So, stay on the lookout for opportunities to encourage active participation. And consider the idea of training programs for your team, and perhaps for individuals to help them develop a useful skill. This benefits your mission and is usually deeply appreciated.

Let's try these concepts out first with messages no one likes to write: bad news.

Delivering bad news

Suppose the head of technology, Hal, has been told that poor company profits for the past quarter mean there will be no raises this year. He's been given a lot of profit-and-loss (P&L) statistics, but not much else to help explain the situation to his department. He knows that top management came close to cutting staff and will no doubt consider doing so should company performance not soon improve. He must break the news to his ten-person team.

First consideration: Should Hal deliver the news in person or in writing? When the news is bad, or you must criticize, always consider face-to-face interaction first. People often feel it's cowardly to hide behind a written message in business — and they're right, just as it's cowardly to break off a personal relationship with a Snapchat post.

TIP

On the other hand, in many negative situations, a written message can be a good opener. It enables you to think through the facts and their meaning, and communicate them in a more controlled way that helps readers digest the information before reacting, or overreacting.

In this case, Hal's *goal* is to deliver the unwelcome news and minimize the bad feelings it will naturally produce. He considers his *audience* and his team members' probable responses. This mental scan suggests that probably at least one person will respond with quick anger that will infect everyone else and set a bad tone for a conversation. Emotions are communicable! He envisions the whole group dwelling on the injustice of it all, making the situation worse.

Hal's decision: Communicate the basic message in writing and follow-up face to face, with a short delay that gives everyone time to absorb the news and come to the meeting with relatively open minds.

Try This: Write the message. Before reading the following version of the memo Hal might write, think about how you would write it. How would you generate a positive outlook without sacrificing honesty? Then read this version:

> Subject: Next year salaries and planning
>
> Dear Ellen, Jerry, Marsh, Quinn, Larry, Jackson, Emery, Jenny, Bob, Sue:
>
> At the Leadership Team meeting yesterday, I learned that the company will award no salary increases for the coming year. This decision was reluctantly made by top management because our Q4 earnings fell 7%, in large part because the Mister Magic launch fell well below expectations.
>
> The decision-makers could alternatively have chosen to make up the deficit with layoffs. While we all feel justifiably disappointed not to receive raises, I for one am grateful that the decision was to maintain full employment. So, none of us is now at risk, and we need not fear for our colleagues, nor worry about extra work burdens falling upon us.
>
> I can also share that this year will see three new product launches. Our decision-makers are hopeful that results will be strong, the P&L picture will rebound, and we'll all reap the rewards down the line. I'm optimistic — but I can't tell you that we should be complacent.

What can our team do at this juncture?

I see a real opportunity for us to prove our value on a broader scale. My idea is that in the coming months, we could push ourselves to move above and beyond our own territory. I would love to see us share our project management know-how with other departments and help them adapt our systems to improve their own productivity. This helps the whole company, of course, and gives us a chance to spread the word on how valuable our work is and how well we do it.

Let's meet on April 10 to brainstorm ideas. At that time, I'll also reserve 10 minutes to talk about the wage freeze and answer any questions to my best knowledge. I'll share the P&L statements if you want to see them.

Meanwhile, please think about my plan and bring your best thoughts to the brainstorming. Let's identify departments that can benefit from our practices and create a preliminary plan of action.

I'm proud of the team we've built together, and I believe we can use our combined skills to contribute more and be valued more. —Hal

Why it works: Hal takes the "us" perspective throughout — we're a team and we're all in this together — but there's no question about who is in charge. He strategizes his content and writing style to accomplish the goal and uses a matter-of-fact, low-key tone. The message acknowledges that readers will feel unhappy, but doesn't dwell on it. He makes the likely assumption that people will not much be interested in the P&L statements, so gives that a light reference that he will supply the material if wanted. He spends the most time framing the bad news in a more positive light by:

>> **Conveying confidence in the company:** He points out that decision-makers could have made a less humane and acceptable choice, firing people, which suggests that the company cares about employees.

>> **Creating a silver lining:** Hal tells his people that though things are not as they would wish, they're okay — and moreover, they can help underwrite their own prospects by pitching in above and beyond now.

>> **Reframing his team's attention from the inevitable "so unfair" complaints into an action possibility:** The idea that as a team, they can work to demonstrate their value is energizing and sets a positive tone for a think-tank session.

In such situations, it's important to create a perspective shift without misleading people or offering false assurances. In many instances, it might seem hard to find a silver lining — but with a little creativity, you may be surprised at how often you do.

SHORTCUT

When people are hit with unwelcome news or a poor result, our tendency is to think "why?" For example, "Why didn't management plan better so the product launch would succeed and we could get our raises?" Or on a personal level, "Why didn't the boss pick me for this great assignment?" "Why" questions have their place in challenging you to think beyond the obvious, but resist letting them generate time-consuming, dead-end analysis.

Switch "why" to "how" and you automatically set your mind to action mode: figuring out practical ways to address the problem. Hal's memo did this for his team members by orienting them to see how they could help remedy the company challenge and improve their own prospects. If you aren't picked for an assignment or job you want, ask yourself *"How* can I show the boss (or recruiter) that I'm ideally qualified next time?" Then map out a plan.

TIP

Notice that Hal's message puts the bad news right up front — bottom line on top applies to bad news just as it does to cheery news. Delivering an unwelcome message in a "sandwich" framework used to be popular. For example, "We have really liked working with you. Unfortunately, we're not renewing your contract. But we had some good times together, right?"

Today's readers don't react well to such tiptoeing. Get the bad news done and then move on to some kind of mitigation, insofar as possible. It must be genuine, or don't do it at all. For example, if you're turning down a job candidate who's jumped through all your hoops, you might end with, "Here is the contact information of someone who I believe might like to know about your skills," or "We'll hire a new set of interns in August and would be glad to review your application again at that time." Such information means infinitely more than, "We had so many great candidates but could only choose one."

What if you have 1,000 applicants to turn down, or just don't have anything helpful to say? Then just close simply but firmly. "Thank you for applying. We very much appreciate your interest in our company."

WARNING

Even worse than the sandwich technique is trying to obscure bad news in a torrent of irrelevant information, or news that's good for people other than the reader. The CEO of a major international corporation made a fool of himself a few years ago by announcing big layoffs in an email that meandered on for seven pages about the company's great future, then got around to announcing that a whole division was eliminated in the interest of this rosy future. Outraged employees immediately hit their share buttons and the whole world jeered.

The CEO overlooked this book's governing principles — know your audience, know your goal and strategize content within that frame. In announcing layoffs or other news that is calamitous to some, those at the top may forget that these messages have multiple audiences each with their own direct self-interest.

If you fire 500 people, whether in writing or in person, what's the message to all the colleagues you hope to retain? Your goal for the laid-off folks should be to minimize their distress and hatred of you as a callous employer. Those slated to remain need to know that the company isn't going under, and there's good reason to stick with it and soldier on. The general public and media are only a click away, so you're inevitably delivering the message to them as well. Therefore, you need to demonstrate that the firm is on solid ground, has made a difficult but valid decision and isn't unfeeling toward those losing their jobs.

Try This: Think the message through. If you've been faced with a challenge like this or can imagine one in the future, use this approach: Combine the goal-plus-audience strategy (Chapter 2) with the talking points technique (Chapter 9). Here's how it might work if you're responsible for telling those 500 people they're out of work:

1. **Define your audiences.**

Your primary audience is the 500 people you're laying off. Your secondary audience is the remaining staff and everyone they might share the message with (the board, the media, the public, stockholders, creditors, competitors).

2. **Define your goals.**

Inform the 500 people that they are unemployed soon as sympathetically as possible. Reassure the remaining staff that the company is in good shape and that their jobs are currently secure and they will not be adversely affected. Reassure the other audiences and in doing so, avoid any suggestion that the company is unfeeling or vulnerable.

3. **Brainstorm to create talking points.**

The talking points for this situation may be:

- Decision was made by the CEO and Executive Leadership Team

- They regret the need for making the cut

- Reason: closing down of unprofitable division that is behind the times technologically

- Remaining staff are secure in jobs but must pull together

- Each laid-off employee will receive a generous severance package reflecting service time

- The company is retaining a career counseling firm to help identify new opportunities for all the laid-off workers and counsel them one on one

Once you've articulated your audiences and clarified what you need to accomplish, the talking points give you good substance to work with. Here's one way to use the points:

> Dear ___:
>
> I am sorry to share that the AeroWing Division will cease operation April 3 of this year, and that all division staff will be laid off. We highly value your nine years of service and regret that we will not be able to continue employing you as of that date.
>
> I made the decision in close consultation with the Executive Leadership Team. We are responding to the division's steady decline over the past five years, primarily because this product has been technologically outpaced by new competitors. We've concluded that unfortunately, the company is unable to support these losses and further invest in this arena at the expense of our other product lines, which continue to grow.
>
> We want to offer you as much support as we can at this time. You will receive a compensation package reflecting your time with Aero that I believe you will find generous. The Talent Management Office will shortly contact you to arrange a personal consultation.
>
> Also, we are retaining a professional firm, BetterNextTime, to provide every member of the AeroWing team with one-on-one counseling. Ten counselors will work on-site for six months to help everyone affected find appropriate opportunities, and their full resources will be available to help you with your next career step.
>
> I hope you will accept my personal good wishes for your every future success, and my appreciation for all your contributions to a division in which we will always feel enormous pride.
>
> Sincerely,
>
> Jack
>
> John C. Berry, CEO

Why it works: The CEO and Executive Leadership Team take responsibility for the decision, and the CEO delivers the message in his own name. This may seem like a small point, but taking ownership matters to people. What is more annoying than bad news delivered in statements such as, "It was decided that . . ."?

The tone is low-key and matter of fact, but also somewhat formal, which is befitting the subject matter. The CEO expresses sympathy to an appropriate degree; going overboard with warm feelings would accomplish little and might be taken as hypocritical. The bottom-line reason for the layoffs is clearly stated in a way that doesn't involve other parts of the company. The primary audience can't argue with the numbers, and few will be interested in more detail.

Secondary audiences, such as the media and stockholders, may well want to see the financials, however, and the company would be wise to have backup material ready. More detailed information should also be tailored for a set of press releases, announcement on the company website and other channels this company uses to communicate with its full range of stakeholders.

TIP

Writing with the structured approach I recommend always helps you think more analytically. In considering "audience" for this sample message, until I wrote the organized list, I overlooked the importance of stockholders, creditors and the company's board of directors. Major clients might also need more tailored messages, as well as strategic partners and government agencies. If the organization is a nonprofit, a major announcement should be directed to supporting foundations, private donors and volunteers. This suggests a broad principle.

WARNING

When you're responsible for communicating with a number of audiences, don't forget them in reporting on an important event. Identify each audience and brainstorm how to customize the message for each: content, level of detail, language, tone. Keep WIIFM in mind — what's-in-it-for-me.

And, know how to reach every audience. Board members may need hand-delivered information packets, different employee groups may prefer social media or email or printed memos, stockholders probably want a letter from the CFO. All too often, organizations unintentionally focus on communicating with a few audiences via their traditional channels and overlook other venues more likely to reach other audience segments. (For a simple way to analyze and categorize your audiences, and cross-match them with the right channels, see Chapter 8.)

TIP

Here's proof that how you write a message matters a lot: Research indicates that effectively handling bad news messages, such as announcing layoffs, makes a difference in how people react and what they remember. Follow-up studies show that departed employees who felt respectfully treated and understood the business situation harbored little or no bad feeling toward the company. Those who feel they were treated carelessly remained angry — and found many ways to share that resentment.

Writing good news messages

Certainly, it's a whole lot nicer to share good tidings, but you may have found that in fact, positive messages are difficult in their own way. But "thank you," "good work," and "congratulations" belong in the good manager's portfolio, and this writing skill should be exercised often.

TIP

Many supervisors dwell on the need to criticize rather than offer messages of appreciation. But in many instances, appreciation is a better way to encourage behavior we want and wean people away from what we don't want. Most employees aim to please their bosses and live up to expectations or exceed them. All too often, the problem is that supervisors fail to adequately communicate what they want! Many employee surveys highlight this destructive gap.

Writing is an ideal tool for making this connection. It feels more official and special when you deliver a written compliment rather than a spoken one, which is fleeting, and may not in the moment be well expressed.

REMEMBER

The key to composing good thank-you and job-well-done notes is specificness. It's easy to orient yourself to be specific if you apply the goal-plus-audience framework. Suppose your subordinate, Allie, has done a good job preparing a slide deck for your client presentation. You know a thank you is in order. Off the top of your head, you might say,

> *Hi Allie, Thanks so much for the slide deck, show went well. —Chuck*

But this is short-sighted. If you more deeply consider your main goal — to encourage future good work — you'd probably see the challenge more concretely:

>> Reinforce Allie's enthusiasm for such assignments.

>> Acknowledge her extra effort — she worked on this over the weekend.

>> Help her feel she's a valued member of the team.

>> Help her feel good about working for me.

Here's one way of meeting these goals:

> *Dear Allie,*
>
> *I presented the show last night, and it went very well! I noticed that Bob, the prospect's division head, smiled all the way through, and 20 minutes of good Q&A about our campaign ideas followed. It's too soon to say if the account is ours, but I'm happy that we gave it our best shot.*
>
> *So, thanks for helping me do that. You pulled the deck together on a tight deadline and translated the packaging ideas into effective visuals. The transitions you came up with tied it all together nicely.*
>
> *Glad to have you on my team. —Chuck*

REMEMBER

Does this message sound like overkill? As always, adapt the ideas to your own style and comfort zone. You don't need to write notes like this every day, of course. But observe what a few minutes of planning accomplishes. In telling Allie exactly what she did well and the results this helped achieve, Chuck shows Allie she is valued as a contributing member of the team; her hard work is appreciated by the person who matters most, her boss; and that boss is a great person to work for. Remember, relationship-building is an underlying goal for *every* message (see Chapter 2).

As Allie basks in feeling appreciated, her motivation can only grow. Will she work even harder to earn further praise? Put in extra time as needed? Come up with more creative ideas? Probably. Well-delivered praise is the best available way that you, as a manager, can promote alignment with staff members and assure that future work is outstanding. But it only works when it's specific and concrete.

Criticizing with kindness

It falls to the manager's lot to coax team members to meet standards and perform better. Many supervisors are uncomfortable with this demand, but it's essential to the role. The good news is that often you can accomplish your goals with a positive approach.

When I began presenting workshops early in my career, I realized that often when someone gives a speech, or reads an assignment to the group, the prospect of feedback terrifies them. Although group input was always meaningful, at times people were unthinkingly (or thinkingly) cruel in their responses. The result was hurtful rather than helpful.

TIP

I stumbled across two techniques that mitigate these harmful interactions. First, invite the spotlighted person to review their own performance with a question such as, "How do you think you did? Anything you'd want to do differently next time?" Next, require that the group deliver only positive comments. When everyone engages in looking for the good, strengths are highlighted, plus opportunities to improve surface naturally without hurt feelings.

If you're reviewing an activity or initiative in a one-on-one meeting, you first might ask, "What did you feel went well with the project?" Or bigger picture, "How would you evaluate yourself (or your experience here) over the past six months?" Follow up with, "What do you think you could have done better?" And perhaps even, "What do you need that would help you do better?"

TIP

Written messages, obviously, lack this back-and-forth potential. But the non-blaming spirit of the idea applies. Suppose Allie had not done a good job on her slide deck assignment. You didn't like all the visuals, the transitions were uneven, the flow was shaky, whatever. You need to hold her accountable, yes, but the overarching goal is for her to improve next time. Delivering all this negativity in writing might crush her initiative and confidence, which is counterproductive to your own interests.

Considering this, you might write:

> *Allie, I appreciate that you got the show done on such short notice. I know that was tough.*
>
> *However, I had some problems with the deck. Some of the visuals were off-target and the transitions were rough in places. Let's talk about this so we're in closer alignment next time. Does Tuesday at 10 a.m. work for you? —Chuck*

REMEMBER

A brief message with not a lot of detail does the job better in this case. Unlike when you deliver compliments, when it comes to criticism, reviewing specifics often is best accomplished in a private conversation rather than in writing. The foregoing memo to Allie prepares her for a thoughtful discussion aimed at helping her improve.

You may need a "nudge" memo that is stronger, according to your judgment of the person and situation. Here's an example:

> *Gwen, you edited the workplan, but you missed a lot. I would have expected you to ask questions if some of the material was unclear to you. Here's my own rewrite — let's discuss.*

An important exception to this less-is-more approach is when you need to create a written record of insufficiencies, such as for legal documentation. Then write in excruciating detail. A lawyer or HR person is probably available to give you these guidelines.

Writing requests and giving orders

The same principles of thoughtful communication apply when you assign work. Routinely see everyday messages as building blocks toward better performance and good relationships. Which request in each of the following memos would you prefer to receive from your boss?

Memo 1:

Jake, here's the material for the Collins report. Due date Wednesday, no fail! Better, get it on my desk Tuesday for review. Thnx.

Memo 2:

Jake:

Here's everything you need for the Collins report. I believe all the sections are covered, but please take a look at the attachments and let me know ASAP if you find anything missing.

This is high priority, and I count on you to get the full draft to me Tuesday. Then I'll do a quick review for delivery to the client on Wednesday. If you run into any problems call me, day or night.

I know this deadline is tight. Thanks for pitching in.

The second message tells Jake *why* he's doing the work on short notice and that it's a contribution to the team. He feels respected and included. Who doesn't want to feel that way? When I talk about this in workshops, often someone says, "But that's my assistant's job! Why do I have to sweet-talk him into doing it?" You don't. But if you want the work done with enthusiasm and resourcefulness, perhaps with unacknowledged overtime, you need to care how the person feels.

TIP

Make it a habit to visualize whom you're writing to (see Chapter 2) so the person is real and individual to you. Decide to use every message to build that team around you. People work harder for a manager who cares about them and tells them why their assignments matter.

I know a successful young department head who frames every request to staff this way: "Would you do me a favor and . . .." "Of course, they have to do it," she explains, "and they always say 'sure.' When I put it like that, it sets a tone that says I appreciate what they contribute. They're happier to 'help me' than if I just said, 'do this.' So, I just give all my orders that way."

Writing to Manage Up

We all report to someone, whether a department or division head, a CEO, the governing board or a set of core clients. We need to communicate gracefully with those above us in the hierarchical chain of command. Fortunately, the guidelines are similar. Like so much of successful living, it's all in the attitude, so that's where I start.

You don't need me to tell you that when you write to a superior, every message should be carefully thought out, well written and scrupulously edited. If your boss sends you cryptic, confusing or non-explanatory messages (such as, "No!" or "Not now!"), do not take that as a reason to write abrupt, careless messages yourself.

REMEMBER

I recommend developing a written profile of your supervisor, drawing on the approach I detail in Chapter 2. You can much more successfully present your requests, suggest ideas and build trust when you take the time to understand the individual, especially regarding communication style and decision-making preferences. Do they want a lot of detail, the big picture or the bottom line? What problems do they want to solve, what keeps them up at night? What's the best time of day to ask for something you want? (Research says that many people are most open and well-disposed after lunch.)

Don't overlook that in many cases you can directly ask many of these questions of a supervisor who's new or new to you. Supplement what you hear with your own observation — or rely on observation should the supervisor not be approachable for such a conversation. And ask for feedback to be sure you're hitting the mark.

See through the boss's eyes and you'll automatically find the right words and persuasive framework. The same process I present in earlier chapters for writing emails, reports and proposals apply when the audience is your manager. When you're presenting an ask to a superior, consider factors such as:

>> What place does the supervisor hold in the hierarchy: Respected? Influential? Has the authority to make the decision you want?

>> What will be the cost to the decider? The benefits of saying yes?

>> Is the individual a negotiator? A risk taker, or not so much?

>> How important to the decider is the subject of your request?

>> What does the person care about: initiative? Their own authority or reputation? Efficiency? The bottom line? Team building? Creativity? Attention to detail?

>> What is the most successful interaction you've had with this supervisor? The least?

>> What clues does this give you?

>> Who does the boss appear most comfortable or friendly with: What does that tell you? Can that person give you tips?

And don't overlook some characteristics that I am 98 percent sure your bosses possess by virtue of position. They all feel:

>> Perennially short of time

>> Faced with conflicting priorities

>> Pressured to show results

And, of course, they report to bosses of their own, with all the challenges you feel and more: The buck-that-stops-here grows bigger at each level. This set of characteristics dictates the need to be concise, and to be aware of what else may be occupying the boss's mind and the relative importance of what you want. Will giving you a yes move a priority forward?

Remember that most supervisors quite naturally do not react well to being brought problems — they feel they have plenty already. Especially if you are raising a new problem, *try to come up with a solution or some options and include them in the message.* You will get a much better reception and present yourself as far more capable.

WARNING

Remember that an email or document sent to your supervisor may work its way up the management line or be included in a report or other material. Even if you enjoy a comfortable relationship with your boss, as a guiding principle, assume all upward-directed messages may have a larger audience and use your best thinking and writing skills.

Most often, with variation based on your profile of your supervisor, your best strategy is to write brief, straightforward emails that stick to one subject. Long detailed emails may be skimmed or not read at all, especially if the subject line and lead don't get to the point right away. In general, any time you're addressing a higher-up, such as board members, donors, executives and government regulators, aim to:

>> **Be direct.** Begin by clearly stating your reason for writing and end with a call to action — what do you want?

>> **Take a positive tone and position.** Better to be perceived as a problem-solver than a problem-bringer or complainer. Stay upbeat and sound objective and in control; provide solutions or alternatives when you can.

>> **Write super-concisely.** Don't include extraneous thoughts or words. Use simple language and short words, sentences and paragraphs.

>> **Write correctly.** Use full sentences, good grammar, correct spelling and punctuation and clear transitions. Be suspicious of abbreviations and beware of emoji!

>> **Create self-contained messages.** Include just enough context so your multitasking reader doesn't have to look up previous material, do research or ask basic questions.

>> **Write with extreme courtesy.** Take time not to sound abrupt or as if you're issuing orders or calling him to account.

>> **Employ good visuals.** Make the information easy to access and grasp. Draw attention to important points with subheads, bold lead-ins and plenty of white space. A plain typeface in the 12-point range is best.

Here's an example of an email that follows these guidelines.

Subject: Hiring consultant by Thursday

Hi, Elaine:

Here are the three best responses to our RFP for a benefits consultant on the Chandler Project, filtered from 39 candidates. If we can announce the decision by Thursday, we can put the paperwork through in time for board approval on June 4.

If you want to talk this through, just let me know. I believe all three candidates are strong and would meet our needs.

If you are able to get back to me by end of Thursday, it will be very helpful in moving forward on schedule.

Thanks! —Sam

Guarding your tone

WARNING

The most frequent complaint upper echelon managers make about employee writing — especially when done by younger people — is that they are "tone deaf." In other words, they address VIPs, including clients and top executives, in the same spirit and language they might use writing or texting to friends. This doesn't come across as respectful. If you feel that respect must be earned, not automatically awarded for reasons of age or relative importance, I won't argue with you. But you can damage your prospects. You'll gain more respect for yourself by communicating in line with the high standards most upper-level people expect or insist on.

SHORTCUT

If you question your ear for tone, especially if writing to VIPs, make a practice of reading your emails aloud and consider: How does it sound — respectful, but like my natural voice? Does it give the impression that I'm annoyed or frustrated or unhappy? That I'm whining? Or don't like the person I'm writing to? Notice when you read messages from other people that you sometimes intuit an emotion without being able to pinpoint what carries it. Try not to betray negative emotions in your own writing!

The impact is even worse than displaying them "live" in work situations. Note your choice of words, and in particular, if the cadence is choppy and staccato — the written equivalent of a stiff-legged stalk when you're angry or offended. If the message carries any negative feeling, put it away for a few hours or overnight as possible and then re-draft. If you can't turn the tone positive, consider whether you need send the message at all. A conversation might be better — or just determine to move on.

WARNING

Should you fake respect or good feelings when they're not genuine? Yes, sometimes. When you communicate in ways that lead others to feel bad, rejected or disrespected, it may never be forgotten or forgiven, especially if you do it in writing. Aim to build relationships, not undermine yourself. And keep in mind that your superiors won't let you near a customer, client or VIP of any sort if they can't trust you to be in control of your own feelings and represent their interests well.

How can you do this when the supervisor (or client or coworker) fails to do their part? Here are some examples of how Matt might handle a delay caused by his boss's failure to get back to him with information. Which do you believe would work best for accomplishing the immediate goal — receiving information — and the long-range one of building a relationship and positive image for himself?

Version 1:

Marge, didn't I already ask you five times to review the draft I spent 23 hours writing and give me your input? Remember? I'm at a standstill! If I don't hear from you by 3:30 tomorrow, I'll assume you have nothing to say and go ahead on my own. —Matt

Version 2:

Marge — I'm still waiting for your input on the draft I sent Tuesday. This is creating problems. Any chance you can get back to me this week? —Matt

Version 3:

Hi, Marge,

I know what a busy time of year this is, but we'll really appreciate your input on the Marshall draft. You may recall we promised to deliver it Monday. Is it possible for you to take a look by the end of the week?

It will be a big help.

Thanks, Matt

Read aloud, Version 1 sounds accusatory, impatient, whiny and childish. If Marge is Matt's boss, she will feel attacked and regard him with suspicion henceforth. If he's a client, Matt may soon be job hunting. If Marge is a coworker, she'll feel angry and uncooperative.

Version 2 is less offensive but still has a negative intonation — I'd call it passive-aggressive. Marge may do as asked, but won't feel warmly toward Matt.

Version 3 is courteous and deferential. If you read it aloud, the tone is neutral and feels respectful. It carefully avoids casting blame. This message has the best odds of achieving its goal, to coax Marge to give the draft a few minutes' attention and also regard Matt as a good assistant.

Avoiding the blame game

Version 3 suggests another good strategy: finding a way to let another person, especially a VIP, save face if they err. No one likes to feel chastised, belittled or implicitly criticized by anyone, let alone someone on a lower level. If the boss or a client ignores your plea for a response, or fails to return a phone call or even stands you up for an appointment, how can you handle it?

TIP

A good general principle is to let that person off the hook without relinquishing what you need. In Version 3, Matt does this by saying that he knows this is a busy time of the year for Marge. It can take a moment's thought to figure out an appropriate mitigating statement for the other person and use it to frame what you want in a more acceptable way. For example:

I know you've been traveling and that catching up is hard . . .

This may have fallen through the cracks when so much is going on . . .

I know everyone's pressing you for figures this week . . .

It looks like we had a miscommunication . . .

A person who feels well-disposed is much more likely to help you out or rectify an oversight than one who is put on the defensive.

REMEMBER

Don't overlook another tool in your strategy kit — the thank-you note. I talk about the value of expressing appreciation to subordinates earlier in this chapter, and the approach is equally effective with supervisors. Executives rarely receive compliments or thanks from people who report to them. Writing to thank them for good advice or a special favor makes you notable. A respectful compliment is also welcome. A message such as, "Tom, thanks for being such a great mentor and helping me grow so much," may be in order once in a while. More immediate compliments may be best delivered in person. For example, "I admire the way you handled the Burke problem and learned a lot from it."

Making it easy to respond

TIP

Here's another idea that gives you better results when you need something from a supervisor, VIP or peer: Make it easy for that person. Recognize that realistically, your messages won't get much attention. Managers spend a lot of energy putting out fires, and the broader their perspectives, the harder it is to keep everything in mind and focus on detail. Here's a theory: In general, the higher up the hierarchy you go with a message, the briefer it needs to be. Or if not brief, the more quickly grasped. Aim to give your superiors just enough to make a good decision, ask important questions or take other action.

See this demand for brevity as a compliment: Busy people trust you to decipher what matters, tell them what they need to know and filter out the rest. Here are some techniques to help you do this:

>> **Be clear and upfront about what the manager needs to do or what you want — upon reading the message.** Make a decision? Take an action? Evaluate something? Stay up-to-date? Figure out what is necessary for that goal and include the right amount of background and detail.

>> **Pay attention to the visuals.** Even an email can use headlines, subheads and bold lead-ins to direct attention to high points and support productive skimming. Dense material is uninviting and a challenge to absorb. Follow the rules for short sentences, paragraphs and words.

>> **Lead with an executive summary.** What, for an email? Yes, if helpful. Your readers may have a particularly short attention span; or you may want to set them up to read the body of the material in a certain light. If this is the case, compose a few sentence mini-version of an executive summary, covered in Chapter 7.

>> **Keep a backup in your pocket.** Have a "stage 2" communication ready should the boss want more detail or context.

TIP

Another way to make it easy for a higher-up is to offer active help. Extending the example in the preceding "Guarding your tone" section, Matt could have improved Version 3 of his memo to Marge this way:

I know what a busy time of year this is, but we'll really appreciate your input on the Marshall draft this week. Would it be easier to talk about this by phone for a few minutes? I could then make the changes for you. If this would be helpful, just give me a call when convenient.

TIP

An ingenious supervisor I know reports to her own short-attention-span supervisor in a government office this way: She sends him an email and also prints it out. She brings the printed copy to the conversation and gives it to him. He reads it in her presence, talks about it as inclined, asks questions and makes notes on the printout. She is thus assured that he read the message thoroughly and is well-equipped for a decision. His annotated printout gives him a secure platform for proceeding.

Writing to Colleagues, Collaborators and Teammates

Most of the guidelines for addressing supervisors and subordinates apply equally to people you work with regularly, or occasionally, and are more or less on your own level. In big and small ways, we constantly need people we have no authority over to cooperate, collaborate, act as resources, respond to questions and give us time and energy. Therefore, practicing all the relationship-building tactics covered in this book helps you build a platform of good will to rely on.

Even when you are comfortable with particular office- or teammates, always remember that the situation is professional. When we write to people we feel are on our wavelength, we tend to write more spontaneous and informal messages. We let down our guard and may become careless.

So, although it's fine to write in friendly ways and assume mutual understanding, maintain your awareness of the impact a thoughtlessly written message can have. Always avoid saying anything negative about other people, or agreeing with someone else's negative remark. Have you not been amazed at how often an email reaches readers you didn't anticipate?

One culprit is the chain email. A friend of mine recently received a thank you for a small charitable donation, atop a series of emails the writer had exchanged with a buddy at the nonprofit they both raised money for. One email referred to the donor as "an old skinflint who could well afford a big donation," and "I'll worm it out of her yet." This didn't benefit the cause. (For a real challenge, try drafting an apology.)

WARNING

The point is, don't depend on other people's judgment about what is worth forwarding and what should remain discrete. Resist sending critiques of the CEO or jokes at someone else's expense. Or inside information or extreme ideas. If you're a CEO someday yourself, the cache of negative emails is bound to surface — erasing them is nearly impossible, as so many politicians seem dumfounded to discover.

Using Backup Memos

When communicating with teammates, as well as subordinates and superiors, it is often smart to confirm mutual understanding in an email or other internal communication format. This can save a great deal of hassle later if those involved emerge with a different memory or interpretation of the matter at hand. Make these memos concise and to the point.

For example, to a supervisor:

Subject: Confirming action on Melody

Dear Luke:

Thanks for taking the time to talk through the Melody account with me this morning. Here is my understanding:

We will recommend two possible courses of action for our client, Gray Builders:

- *Option A is to start the project in June.*
- *Option B is to delay project start until October.*

To flesh these alternatives out, I will:

1. *Ask Terry Thompson in Accounting to crunch both sets of numbers for us.*
2. *Put my staff to work researching the permits from the EPA, municipal authorities, county housing office, etc.*

If any of this doesn't accord with your understanding or needs further thought, please let me know. Otherwise I'll proceed on this basis early next week.

Thanks, Jenny

Take a similar tack when you're asking a coworker to do something, but frame it more graciously. Such a backup memo might read, "Thanks, Ellen, for working out idea X with me yesterday. I appreciate your input very much. I hope you can take a few minutes to look at this rundown of what we agreed to — correct me if I've misstated anything." Then spell out your reader's responsibilities, and your own.

Language for Communicating Sideways

When writing (and speaking) to collaborators and coworkers, aim to invariably be respectful, courteous, tactful and appreciative. Frame requests in language such as:

I would really appreciate your help with . . .

I know how good you are with crunching the numbers, could you give me 20 minutes to. . .

In thinking about the problem we need to solve, I remember how well you handled the glitch with the Blue Project . . .

Draw on the power of *why:* When you ask for help or cooperation, provide the reason:

We need to deliver the proposal by Thursday, so I'm hoping you can help us meet the deadline by . . .

Consider the reasons why giving you what you want may not produce an automatic yes. Is the other person experiencing their own crunch time? Trying to catch up after a vacation? Fielding multiple requests from many directions in addition to your own? Sometimes acknowledging you understand this helps.

I know how many demands are being made on your time right now, so I will be especially grateful if you can process my invoice soon so we can avoid incurring interest charges.

Mitigating the time and energy you need someone to give you can go even further:

I know how tough it is catching up after two weeks away. I'll have my staff do all the preliminary work so I only need 15 minutes of conversation with you.

I realize this is the period where you're busy preparing statements for all the departments. Will it help if we delay the deadline for our report so you can give us some time to solve this immediate problem?

Using Turnaround Techniques

Always, always, we must work with people for whom we don't feel a natural sympathy or who annoy or offend us in some way. Often this happens if our roles bring us into opposition, rather than because the person is actually "toxic" (in which case the only solution is to minimize contact). Or a generational divide can create misunderstanding and resentment. Here are some ways to reset a relationship to make it neutral, if not friendly. Judge in each case whether writing or face-to-face is called for.

>> **Accept that your negative reactions, or assessments of other people, may not always be fair or balanced.** We all have limited perspectives and can misperceive other people's words or actions. Experiment with giving difficult managers and coworkers the benefit of the doubt. Treat others with generosity, even when you don't like them or think they've offended you, and you may find yourself bringing out their better side.

>> **Ask someone to teach you something.** This is a great way to bridge between different skill sets and between generations. If you're a Gen Z, for example, instead of feeling frustrated that the "old folks" you work with are limited in

use of new technology, invite one to help acclimate you to company culture — how things are done and what works at the workplace you share. In turn, you can tactfully offer some grounding or shortcuts in using the new office system.

» **Render a compliment — a sincere one.** Find something you can genuinely admire about the other person or how they handled something.

Your presentations are so effective.

I liked how you fielded the CFO's tough question about X the other day.

I heard from the Y committee that you did a great job on Z.

If the prospect of talking or writing to an "enemy" in these ways sounds unattractive, remind yourself how much you could benefit from a more positive attitude on their part. And that at least some of the bad feelings between you results from the dislike or disrespect you intrinsically project. Enjoy the look of surprise you'll elicit as the person looks at you in a new light. And the satisfaction you'll derive from managing your own emotions to gain an advantage.

» **Write (or talk) to a person you see as "impossible" as if they were the person you'd like them to be.** If this sounds like a highly psychological strategy, it is — the idea was shared with me by a therapist and it's been invaluable. Bosses who are grumpy and bad-tempered may be difficult, but it's counterproductive to respond in kind. So, when writing or talking with them, visualize them as their best selves — fair minded, dedicated to the organization, concerned with quality of work and so on. Address that persona and you may bring out a better angel.

» **Offer help without being asked.**

That's a big job they gave you on short notice. Can I give you an hour of my time to help?

TIP

This is a good tactic to try with anyone with whom you'd like a closer working relationship, as well as non-friends. The best demonstration of it I've seen comes from a new employee in a financial services firm. Gary wasn't getting the assignments he wanted and felt dead-ended and under-worked. He approached a colleague in the office who'd impressed him, Mark, and said, "I have extra time on my hands right now. Can I help you with anything?"

Mark accepted and the teaming arrangement proved very good for both of them. Gary was so delighted that he sent a *well-written* letter to the department head detailing what an excellent member of the staff Mark was, how lucky the firm was to have him, and how much Gary had learned from working with Mark. The letter was circulated on higher levels, Mark was thrilled and appreciative, and soon thereafter, Gary was promoted.

REMEMBER

Smart leaders appreciate generosity of spirit, initiative and of course, good communication skills.

Communicating with a Team of Equals

Many people today find themselves responsible for a project or team without being officially in charge, or part of a team that is given insufficient direction by those who are supposed to lead it. This challenge used to be categorized as exercising "peer influence," but in today's world, it's called "leadership without authority," and is an increasingly common challenge.

Many organizations are "flattening" their management structures and depending on teams to accomplish major goals, especially when operating virtually. Managers like the approach because it breaks down operational silos and they know group thinking can generate unorthodox solutions. Employees like it because collaborating is more fun than just carrying out directives from above.

Unfortunately, few businesses train people to work in teams. They expect natural leaders to emerge — but just as likely, an uneven distribution of work and bad feelings evolve. When you're part of a team without a formal leader, what can you do to steer the team toward its goal, help members work together well and even emerge as the natural leader yourself?

A great deal, by applying the ideas in this book! Scores of other books talk about leadership with and without authority, so I'll focus on the communication aspect. Which, I'm happy to say, everyone agrees is the key to team success.

First, some of the basic strategies that work well for teaming include:

>> **Know your teammates.** Create your written characterizations of each one (see Chapter 2 for how) so you have an idea of their strengths and motivation from the start.

>> **Actively practice empathy during meetings, one-on-one conversations and when you write.** Work at understanding the different points of view, potential contributions and personality factors.

>> **Interact with confidence, a positive can-do spirit and generosity.** Appreciate other people's ideas and abilities and offer help when someone needs it.

Now some practical suggestions.

I assume your team kicks off with an in-person or video conference meeting. If one isn't provided, advocate for it. Seeing each other's faces and hearing each other's voices at the outset promotes success, as do periodic follow-up meetings.

At the early sessions, *ask questions and listen a lot*. Some questions to consider include:

How do we each see the goal? What do we agree on?

What are the roles we need to fill? How shall we allocate them fairly?

How should we plan for checkpoints and what deadlines should we set?

How should we communicate? Hold each other accountable?

What expectations should we set for behavior?

If other people voice the questions, all the better. But prepare yourself in advance with questions that will lead the group to emerge with a common agreed-on project goal, assigned responsibilities, schedule of meetings, deadlines and so on according to the nature of the project.

TIP

Here's a key piece of advice: In addition to any other role you assume, volunteer to take the meeting notes, write up a synopsis and distribute it within a few days.

Taking notes is a hugely underestimated instrument of influence. Your job is to write up what was agreed to, matter-of-factly, concisely and fully, in a neutral just-the-facts tone. But while your summary must be honest, a substantial meeting leaves a lot of room for interpretation.

Use a basic format like for meeting minutes. At the top, list every person who participated in the meeting plus time and place. Then open modestly: For example, *"This is what I heard"* or *"The following describes what we agreed to."*

Then briefly summarize the general interaction as appropriate — what the team is charged with, for example, and what process was used to arrive at decisions. Now you can move into the meat of the event. A good technique is to use the subhead approach explained in Chapter 6. Perhaps:

Project goal

Allocation of responsibilities

Checkpoints and deadlines

Communication systems

Agenda planning

Expectations for cooperative and collegial behavior

Mechanisms for sharing problems

Resources

Next steps

If you and your colleagues have done a good job addressing these topics during the discussion, the report should be easy to write. When you discover significant gaps in the joint thinking, either:

>> Put "Remaining questions to answer" in the Next Steps section and specify them.

>> Fill in the gaps based on your own judgment of how things should be done but clearly state you are doing so.

You might include a blanket statement in the introduction to the document noting that highlighted sections indicate that a conclusion was not explicit, and you have made a logical assumption, subject to group review. For example, you might explain that *"In describing our plan for future meetings, I noticed that we didn't give time to sharing any personal news or problems with our assignments. I've jotted that in for consideration."*

End your minutes in an open-minded way:

Please get back to me by Friday with your input and let me know if I've overlooked anything. I will make any corrections needed and send the new version to you for review and signature.

Make adjustments as called for by the feedback. I think you will be surprised at how little input is provided. If you receive a change request you don't agree with, query the group and come to a conclusion. After some give and take, you have in hand a written blueprint for the whole project with agreed-to responsibilities and deadlines. If someone fails to deliver, misses a checkpoint or deadline or behaves counterproductively, there will be no question of what is owed to the team.

Every meeting should be fully reported in this way. Continue being notetaker/reporter and you may well become the de facto team leader.

As I note in the beginning of this book, today's career paths tend to zig and zag, rather than following a straight line. You may be an employee now, but also tomorrow's entrepreneur, consultant or freelancer. Or you may become a full- or part-time remote worker. These scenarios bring their own set of communication challenges. The next chapter focuses on the tools and techniques for working well independently.

Chapter **14**

Writing for Entrepreneurs and Virtual Workers

oday, three major trends in the U.S. economy converge to transform how business is practiced, and business communication hustles to catch up. One trend is the growing number of people working as freelancers. In 2019, this group already accounted for 35 percent of the U.S. workforce with 53 percent of Gen Z workers engaged in freelance and gig work. Fueled by new technology that makes independent work practical, this trend reflected the situation *before* the coronavirus pandemic in 2020 upended the job market and accelerated the need to earn a living in nontraditional ways.

The second trend is toward a remote workforce. Those who work for an employer but carry out their jobs from a home base full-time comprised 18 percent of the workforce in 2019, and another 34 percent based from home part-time. Those figures also represent the pre-pandemic situation, and now we see the trend accelerate at a dizzying pace. The health catastrophe showed many enterprises that they can function well or in some cases, better, with a fully remote or partially remote workforce and more short-term workers.

The third trend is a growing reliance on teaming. As business hierarchies flatten in line with newer ideas about leadership, a project orientation flourishes and team performance becomes a prime concern. A growing proportion of work is assigned to in-house teams as well as outside teams, with many projects mixing the two groups together.

These trends together are pushing all varieties of enterprises to recast their business models and reimagine their workforces. Leaders have learned that remote workers lighten the need for expensive real estate, business travel and in-person meetings. For their part, many employees like the flexibility of working at home, at least part-time. A growing number embrace the independent lifestyles of freelancing and entrepreneurship. Most people like working in teams.

So, everybody wins, right? Well, not exactly. Competition for those on all sides of the equation is more fierce than ever. For industry, nonprofits, professionals and even education, "agility" is the new watchword — the ability to sense how winds are blowing and quickly reset the sails. For remote and freelance workers, the corresponding imperatives are "flexibility," "creativity" and "resourcefulness." And there is more focus than ever on communication skills, the subject of this chapter.

Communicating as a Virtual Worker

TIP

Everyone agrees: In today's economy, effective communication powers success for the one-person operation, small business, remote worker and big enterprise alike. In fact, it's emerging that to work successfully in remote, freelance or team mode, *communication is key.*

This makes sense. How else can you inspire, organize and manage people you never see at a distance? Or win the jobs, function as a team member and demonstrate your value? New needs demand smart use of classic and relatively traditional tools — emails, letters, marketing materials, social media, blogs, newsletters. It's also necessary to adapt other platforms to new needs, like presentations and chat media, as well as media that may be new to you such as videoconferencing. But few of us are trained to function well in a virtual environment.

This section focuses on using written communication, as well as oral communication that depends on writing, in this "new normal" perspective. Think of it this way: Today, we are all in business. If you have any need at all to make yourself known, connect with other people, build relationships, find work, create trust, collaborate and promote your own causes, it's time to polish your communication skills.

In general, if you work from a home or office base apart from those to whom you're responsible, it's a good idea to *over-communicate* — especially in writing — more often than you may be used to or is required. Keep the boss at headquarters, your client or your team members updated on what you're accomplishing, significant insights you're developing and what you need to do your job well.

Document as much as you can for sharing and record-keeping because depending on casual conversation and updates won't work. Also, when the team is scattered in different time zones all over the country or world, communication is asynchronous. This makes it more important to make information and decisions easily accessed by everyone at times convenient for them.

Organizations that are experienced in remote operations ask employees to not only submit frequent reports, but also write about what they do and how so a central repository explaining company practices — information that often resides in people's heads — is universally available.

Writing can give you more "presence" for supervisors, collaborators and colleagues, so use it to advantage rather than just chiming in at established checkpoints or when asked.

Teaming Techniques and Practices

Communication technology opens up new possibilities and ever-easier ways to collaborate virtually. But they come with a learning curve. Based on groundwork laid by teamwork's early adopters, guidelines for what distinguishes successful teaming are emerging. Virtual teaming adds to the challenge.

Except for occasions when we see our virtual coworkers on screen, as with teleconferencing, interaction is generally by written messages and perhaps occasional phone calls. This brings a host of drawbacks. You must collaborate without being able to read people's facial expression, body language and perhaps, intonation because people don't behave naturally on screen. Therefore, it can take much longer to understand people's perspective, establish trust and know what to expect from each other, essentials of working together smoothly. If you participate in short-term projects with new teams every time, developing a set of good practices is especially important.

If your role is as project leader, your responsibilities are broader than with in-person teaming. You must devise ways to help team members who work independently connect more personally than may readily happen. This can take the form of an ice-breaking activity at the start of each meeting or a coffee break together or an ongoing set of virtual get-togethers during the project course. Using teleconferencing breakout features is a good option to promote understanding via smaller groups.

TIP

If you have a choice, try to kick off your collaboration in person. Meeting face to face at least once pays many dividends. Second choice is to use a virtual channel with visuals, such as videoconferencing, Skype or even Facetime for getting-to-know-you sessions. And don't forget the plain old telephone: Hearing someone's voice is important, and once it's in your head, you can communicate more effectively with the individual, written messages included.

The initial work meeting should fully clarify the team goals and objectives; establish guidelines and milestones; assign individual roles and responsibilities; set timelines and meeting dates and consider each person's availability, taking locations and time zones into account, as well as working preferences (for example, are folks reachable at night? On weekends?). Include a checklist to keep track of progress and preferably, a system for holding team members accountable.

And far from least, establish communication processes, channels and tools for sharing, such as Google Drive, Google Docs and Dropbox. All these factors should be covered in a written document distributed to everyone involved.

If possible, plan for periodic meetings by videoconference if not in person to maintain momentum, coordinate tasks and solve the inevitable roadblocks — all are handled much better face to face or as close as you can get.

TIP

It's important to know who's in charge of a team. If there's a designated project leader, that person's role should be fully specified. If "everyone is equal" and no one is centrally responsible, it's a good idea for the group to agree that a specific person will coordinate, keep everyone on track and keep team members accountable. (See Chapter 13 for ideas about leading without authority.)

A notetaker or communicator-in-chief should for designated for meetings. If this unpopular task is up for grabs, volunteer! In notetaking lies power. You'll know more: Everyone shares information with you. And when you're the reporter, you create the perspective.

Here are some ways to be a good virtual collaborator and a good team member, whether or not you lead:

>> **Communicate always in a positive, upbeat way that promotes relationship building.** Avoid a negative tone, which more easily arises when people are physically distant from each other. Express appreciation for other people's good work or contributions — written notes are especially valued, especially when the recognition is shared with the group.

» **Be sensitive to the language of other specialists and take trouble to understand it.** At the same time, be aware of your own field's jargon and its use. Don't assume your team members have the same knowledge base — part of the challenge is to educate each other. When participants literally don't speak the same language, work through some basic meanings.

» **Listen, listen, listen.** Actively absorb information and ideas voiced by teammates but practice asking good questions to clarify the interchange for everyone.

» **Learn to use the chosen communication channels well.** Write clear and concise messages and respect good-practice demands of media like Slack and Zoom, covered later in this chapter. Many organizations find that training in these media, and a set of guidelines, is useful.

And if you are team leader:

» **Think about incentives.** They are less clear for good work as a team member, especially if it's functioning virtually. It's worthwhile to come up with tangible ways to inspire or recognize strong performance in line with what's possible for the organization. Don't forget how writing can help: Send personal notes when someone beats a deadline, contributes an idea, helps a team member or goes above and beyond in any way.

» **Hold everyone clearly accountable.** At meetings, call on everyone to speak. Make it clear that there's no room for sitting back. Virtual meetings make invisibility impossible, so use this to advantage. Be sure that responsibilities are handled fairly. Nothing undermines team spirit so much as needing to shoulder the burden for slackers, and rather than blow the whistle, most people will suffer in silence. The work stands to suffer substantially.

» **Introduce a written repeat-it-back technique to confirm everyone is on the same page.** Doing so prevents misinterpretations, especially if there is a shift in direction. For example, confirm your own actions with notes such as, "To follow up on our conversation Tuesday, I plan the following . . . ."

» **Routinely ask for written feedback on each meeting.** Solicit ideas for accomplishing the agenda more efficiently and productively.

» **Build in one-on-one or subgroup meetings to promote efficiency, more personal collaboration and camaraderie.** It's wise to regularly meet "privately" with team members in order to show appreciation, field personality problems, discover roadblocks and find solutions early on.

Using Everyday Communication Tools: Email and Group Chat

For everyday sharing, reports, project-hunting, client correspondence and more, you need email. For the ongoing back-and-forth between team members, you may depend on Slack or another instant messaging channel that is restricted to a group. The difference in how we use email and work chat today is that we need to help counter what is lost through the growing absence of in-person contact.

Making email more personal

As you depend on email to help bridge the gap between yourself and the rest of the world, consider thinking about more conscious, strategic use. One appropriate adaptation, in line with the more isolating lives many people now lead, is in *the tone of your messages*. An upbeat, positive tone is always more than welcome and supports relationship-building. A few specifics:

>> Avoid giving your message a negative vibe with statements like these: "This is not what we agreed on"; "It worries me that . . ."; "I don't really like . . ."; "You seem to have forgotten that . . . ."

>> Frame even a critical message in a positive spirit: "I appreciate how quickly you provided the report"; "I have some ideas for clarifying the data next time around"; "You make a lot of good points. It led me to think about how we might improve . . . ."

TIP

>> Use positive sentences that lead people to feel good — it costs you nothing! "I appreciate that . . ."; "What a great job on . . ."; "I really liked what you said about . . ."; "I enjoyed working with you on . . . ." And always and perennially, "Thank you for . . . ."

TIP

>> Humanize your messages. Use people's names in the salutation ("Dear Sarah") and/or the body of the message. ("Thank you, Sarah, for crunching the data so quickly.") Use a conversational and somewhat personal tone to make yourself real to people, rather than coming across as an efficient, narrowly focused work machine.

>> Take space to connect emotionally: Show empathy, or interest, in the other person on an appropriate level. Rather than

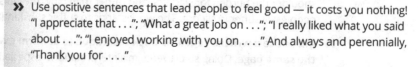

Dear Al: To follow up on the plan to print flyers . . .

try

Dear Al: I hope this finds you and your family well. Are the west coast forest fires affecting you much in Nevada? It's sad to read about what's happening in California.

I'm writing to see if this is a good time to follow up on the plan for the flyers . . .

Even if you spend just a sentence on the weather or sharing how you spent the holiday, you can warm up a virtual relationship incrementally over time.

» Use writing deliberately to stay connected with clients, collaborators, prospects and more. Develop a list of people important to you and check in on them via email — and/or consider whether to increase your social media and blogging activity or use teleconferencing and other channels, such as an e-newsletter.

Using team chat to your advantage

There are numerous instant messaging apps to facilitate collaboration on a company-wide or team scale, including Slack, Google Chat, Skype and Microsoft Teams. They are at the top of the informality scale for business communication, so I won't advise on writing style, except to remind you that clear and concise is always in season. Issues with chat media for business revolve more about protocols. If the organization does not provide guidelines, set your own with group discussion, and consider these:

Don't:

» Deluge coworkers with a steady shower of messages and notifications that are irrelevant to them.

» Write messages that are rude or inconsiderate in tone or substance, air grievances or criticize people, especially in an all-staff channel.

» Tell jokes or include any humorous material that could offend anyone.

» Attend to chat so much that you are distracted from the project or goal — team chat is not a social media tool.

» Use chat to communicate about complicated matters that demand nuanced conversation.

» Use chat as the constant default channel. When you need an immediate response or need to discuss something personal or sensitive, pick up the phone!

Note that you can create channels or rooms to accommodate specific teams and projects. Separate public channels can be set up for non-work interactions, so social life is supported separately from work needs and people can elect whether to participate and to what degree. Some groups see this as a water cooler stand-in; other groups dedicate channels to recipes, personal news and so on according to group interest.

If you're not team leader, suggest a conversation about setting such rules at a meeting or via teleconferencing — my next subject.

Using teleconferencing effectively

TIP

At first blush you might think, why would this book cover a visual communication tool that doesn't involve writing? Think again: Videoconferencing tools like Zoom, Microsoft Teams and Skype are not a simple substitute for live events. They impose different demands. Meeting by video takes more planning to succeed, and this depends on solid written preparation and less improvisation to be productive. Far more than in-person meetings, videoconferencing depends on good written agendas, plenty of informational materials and thorough documentation.

Beyond serving as the new meeting rooms for groups and teams, videoconferencing has become indispensable for interviewing job candidates and interacting with clients. In these situations, too, writing is prime. When you compete for a job or contract virtually, your written credentials need to do a lot more speaking for you, and you need to be extremely well-prepared to make your case.

Therefore, to use videoconferencing tools to your advantage, call on the tools of good writing covered throughout this book, from analyzing your goals and audience to writing clear and concise emails; developing résumés, elevator speeches and presentations; creating stories and using talking points to field questions and challenges. Here I focus on some particularities of teleconferencing that require rethinking the usual approaches.

Recognizing videoconferencing limits

When a group of people gathers for a purpose in person, the experience is three-dimensional. We see each other and interact subtly through body language, facial expression and reactive glances. Side comments arise. A comment can tip the conversation in a more creative direction. A group spirit develops — enthusiastic and goal-driven if the meeting is well planned and managed. But these elements don't naturally happen with a video meeting.

REMEMBER

Videoconference-style conversation is linear: We speak one at a time to many, which has a different effect than addressing one person. We learn not to interrupt a speaker and may even be asked to raise our hands to speak. We avoid making even a sound of approval or interest. Body language is basically absent, since we typically can't see anyone's hand gestures, and subtle facial expressions are hard to discern.

There is little small talk or interplay, and the natural bouncing off each other that good meetings generate is typically absent. It is hard to promote a conversation or debate that leads to a creative solution. The experience is more akin to watching a series of speeches and giving our own, rather than participating in an interactive meeting of minds.

On a personal level, people are self-conscious and less forthcoming when they talk into a computer screen rather than a live situation, especially since it's hard not to fixate on our own face or how visible we are to everyone else. Small talk is minimal and generating trust is difficult. In short, the impersonality of the video-conference experience does not easily lend itself to camaraderie, flights of imagi-nation or creative brainstorming. To counter the agreeableness that meetings tend to fall into, some companies deliberately foster conflict. They present a goal or idea — for example, what should we change about X — and channel people to take sides.

More commonly, many organizations react to videoconferencing shortfalls by making meetings briefer and more structured, tightly focused and efficient.

Structuring meetings with agendas

If it's up to you to plan and run a meeting, remember that many people feel "Zoom fatigue." Acknowledge this by scheduling meetings only when you need to accom-plish something specific, rather than hold them for the sake of it or because you always meet on Monday mornings. For many enterprises, experience with video-conferencing is leading them to backtrack on how they approach in-person meet-ings as well. The new-normal agenda is the key.

TIP

A central principle: Build each agenda around a concrete and clearly expressed objective. That objective — which may be to generate ideas, decide on an action or solve a problem — can often be framed as a question, such as: "How should we counter online criticism of our customer service?" "How can we trim $X from the department budget so we can support more training?" Once an objective and the outcomes you want are clarified — which isn't always easy — you can deter-mine the process needed to achieve the outcomes specified. This too should be spelled out: who will speak on specified topics and which components are to be involved — brainstorming, SWAT analysis and so on.

In "earlier times," an agenda might include a whole series of decision-oriented items or just list topic areas or people's names ("John Smith, update on HR"). But given our shorter patience with teleconferenced events, savvy organizations are finding it better to hold short, more closely focused meetings with a single purpose.

TIP

To make the most of group time, create and distribute all relevant informational materials and written input from team members in advance of the meeting. When everyone prepares for the session by reviewing everything before they meet, they need not sit bored through a tiresome on-the-spot grounding. When they think through their own part of the discussion in more depth, they come up with ideas, commit them to writing and are prepared for a more useful discussion. This enables the group to accomplish the goal in a tight time frame.

If your organization dictates a format for agendas, which might require following *Robert's Rules* or a company protocol, you may need to cover a range of items such as approval of minutes and categorize topics under labels like "new business" and "old business." Then just fit your objective, process and outcome into the format.

Don't be surprised if a good agenda — one that engages everyone in addressing a specific situation or problem — takes time to create. It forces you to think the challenge through much more thoroughly.

WARNING

Do not depend on open-ended brainstorming, where everyone is asked to throw in bright ideas on a subject, on the spot. This can occupy a lot of time and yield little concrete results. It's better to have team members brainstorm their own ideas and commit them to paper before the meeting.

TIP

Should you start meetings with a touch-base or socializing time? Research shows, as you probably know from your own experience, that the most successful teams are characterized by mutual trust. Ideally this is achieved through some light-hearted activities or personal sharing, which deepens over time. Teleconferencing, however, does not offer a warm atmosphere that invites personal confidences — participating feels more often like being a deer caught in the headlights.

An intermediate approach is to make an opening exchange less personal: For example, go around the table asking each person to remark on the best and worst of their week. Better if possible is to devote a session to getting acquainted before launching the collaboration. In general, stay aware of realities and show some flexibility: A work-at-home parent may have children at home and an occasional guest appearance may be hard to avoid. If a home is small, it's hard to silence the sound of a barking dog. Technical glitches happen.

REMEMBER

Take advantage of the breakout room feature of some teleconferencing apps and build that into your plan, or use it impromptu. The larger your online group, the harder it is to focus on specifics. Breakout rooms offer a good way to assemble people in smaller groups to work out an aspect of the shared challenge.

Reporting on meetings

These are often called "minutes," which understates their value and influence. I recommend calling them "reports" and assigning this role to someone with good judgment who thinks fast enough to take good notes and also writes well. The report's format can vary as long as it's clear, concise and complete to the right degree. Distribute to all — these reports are indispensable documentation. Without them, team members will have entirely different memories of what occurred and what needs to be done. Trust me on this.

An agenda gives the notetaker a healthy head start on creating the report efficiently. It can follow the same structure, and most include discussions and approval of proposed actions and follow-up. It should always detail responsibilities, deadlines and a next-meeting alert if called for.

How thorough should a report be? In most cases, as complete a record as possible will provide a good resource for the immediate future and beyond. It's also an official record that belongs to the organization. The questions that arise usually center on how much of an open discussion to report. Minutes may need to be publicly posted, and in controversial or sensitive situations, a discussion can be specified without necessarily including details.

Writing as an Entrepreneur

If you own your own business, consult or freelance, you're an entrepreneur. My first recommendation is to define your own "value proposition" — your unique selling points. Chapter 8 shows you how to do this. If your enterprise is new or you want to build it further, you then need to explore your audiences and how you connect with them.

Communication technology opens up a wealth of possibilities. How do you know which communication channels to deploy when time can only be stretched so much? Here's a practical way to chart out your priorities and clarify your goals, audiences and best communication channels. It can help you customize your messaging to different groups, too.

Charting your communication plan

This marketing analysis starts with simple lists. It may not immediately sound like a shortcut, but in the long run it saves you a load of costly trial and error. It also gives you a good jump toward a business plan, a necessity.

As an example, consider Jed, the arts technology specialist I talk about in Chapter 10. He's just left a job and plans to freelance. Here's how Jed described himself on his last résumé, when he was job hunting:

Arts Administrator, Art Historian, Practicing Artist
Experience and advanced training in archiving, preservation and photography. Special expertise in designing computer systems to perform administrative work more efficiently and economically. Adept at training people to use new technologies cheerfully. On every job, recognized as the go-to person when computer glitches happen.

Who might hire him for short-term projects? He brainstorms a list:

Museum directors	Preservationists
Historical sites	Art collectors
Historical associations	Art galleries
Museum associations	Museum consultants
Museum curators	Book publishers
Museum IT officers	Art bloggers
Archivists	

This list is just a start — for almost every group on it, subcategories should include national, state, regional and local levels, because Jed might want to connect with them in different ways. Jed might add the International level should he want to travel. Once he fills this list out in more detail, it becomes obvious that he has to identify a much narrower niche and make decisions about geographic aspirations and priority audiences. A sensible choice is to start locally, because it's easiest to connect with nearby places and people. Moving up each level geographically demands a more impressive track record.

Next, he thinks about how to deliver his message to his priority groups. Channels might include:

Website

New brochure

Email

Letters

Blogging

Associations in his own and adjacent counties

Museum directors within 50 miles

Publication articles for historical associations

Publicity in local publications

Speaking at regional conferences

How-to videos on YouTube

Social media groups: Facebook, LinkedIn, Twitter, Pinterest

Now Jed knows where he must start: with a strong website, which every contact is likely to check out if their interest is sparked. A blog could be excellent for establishing credentials, too, but will need its own campaign to find readers. A print or virtual brochure? Maybe.

On the other hand, some ideas are clearly long range. Securing conference speaking engagements and publishing articles in industry magazines can easily take a year at best, since they are typically planned far in advance. Other options are more controllable: an email campaign, for example, and posting video about an aspect of his work that's relevant to photographers. Jed must calculate time against probable value in each case.

With tentative choices determined, Jed can turn his two lists into a chart by writing the target audiences as a vertical column on the left, and the media options horizontally across the top. Doing such a chart — or just the lists — will accomplish several interesting things for you:

>> Push you to choose your audiences so you can aim for realistic targets

>> Show you which channels could reach more of your target audiences

>> Discourage you from over-focusing on any one audience or channel, and from concentrating marketing efforts on channels less likely to create value

>> Help you evaluate the relative merits of potential channels and the resources each will take, enabling you to better assess the practicalities

>> Enable you to better customize your messaging to your chosen audiences

>> Help you sequence and integrate your marketing efforts so they are more productive

TIP

By the way, if you are more advanced than Jed and are already an active marketer, try charting out the communications channels you use against who you need to reach. It is always enlightening. When businesses and nonprofits alike analyze their effectiveness this way, they invariably find major gaps, such as over-focusing on some audiences and entirely disregarding others of great importance.

Pitching the media for free publicity

Coverage in print or online media is an attractive proposition for most businesses. It gives you free exposure, right? The catch is that everyone knows this, so gaining media space is competitive. On the other hand, more outlets materialize every day, especially online, demanding a steady flow of new content. Finding opportunities takes some time and energy.

Keep in mind that today's magical Internet enables you to publish and distribute your own news. You can post it on your own website, distribute it by email or use a service that reaches journalists such as PR Newswire (www.prnewswire.com), 24-7 Press Release (www.24-7pressrelease.com) and eReleases (www.ereleases.com). You can also subscribe to a site called HARO (Help a Reporter Out, www.helpareporter.com), which works in the opposite way: Journalists from everywhere look for sources by posting requests for experts to contact them.

TIP

If you want to have your product or service publicized a print or online outlet, know that the bigger its audience, the more it is flooded with professionally crafted media pitches. Even mid-sized organizations maintain in-house PR departments or hire agencies to do this work.

If you run a small business, or a one-person operation, generally assume that:

>> **Your best target is local media.** Local editors see their role as giving people in the community opportunity to shine and, of course, share news of interest to their readers. Community and city newspapers, regional business publications and local magazines flourish in many locations. Most publish online versions as well.

>> **Your best strategy is to pitch by email.** Or possibly by telephone, depending on the editor. If you study the media in which you're interested, you can easily learn what the organization looks for and figure out how to relate to those needs. Watch for perennial interests such as stories that relate to the seasons and holidays, ideas that help readers with common problems and material that speak to the heart.

Informal releases that don't adhere to the traditional format can be fine, but many of your targets prefer the familiar approach. In any case, knowing how to write a traditional release sharpens your thinking.

Writing traditional "press releases"

REMEMBER

This formal press release format works best when you have "real news" to share — meaning something of interest to a publication's audience is happening. For example, it's of local interest if you're holding a benefit concert and a well-known performer will appear; you're being presented with a significant award; or your business is opening a new office. Such events are good fodder for a community newspaper or regional business publication.

If you're fishing for coverage of your event, bear in mind that a static meeting, speech or presentation is rarely worth a journalist's time. But you can provide an after-the-fact account yourself. If you handle this as a reporter would by writing in the publication's style and supplying a good photograph, and if the editor has space to fill in that issue, your event may earn some of it.

TIP

You can make even a static event interesting with specifics. If a notable CEO gave an interesting speech, for example, reporting what he said is much more appealing than simply stating he was there. If a high school student was presented with an award, exactly what earned the recognition? What did the student say at the ceremony? What are their future plans?

A media release is traditionally structured as follows. Let's assume your subject is an event:

>> Date and full contact information — a specific person reachable day, night, weekends!

>> A compelling action-oriented headline.

>> Subhead with supporting information.

>> Lead focused on most interesting or relevant information *for the editor's audience.* Important: Is the public invited? Is the editor or a reporter?

>> A few paragraphs with essential information. The guideline is to cover who, what, when, where and why. An interesting quote can be included and any specific photo ops.

>> How the editor should follow up. Can you supply a schedule of events?

>> "Boilerplate" statement describing your business in a few lines.

Writing email pitches

A good alternative to writing a traditional press release is the email pitch, and in fact, many editors prefer it. But it must be carefully thought through. *Know your story.* Here, too, you need a compelling headline that will be your subject line.

Then construct a few tight paragraphs that make your happening interesting, important and relevant, and also answer the who–what–when–where–why questions. For example:

> Subject: Clever Computers Help Disabled Nursing Home Residents Explore the Internet
>
> Dear Mike:
>
> Nursing home life is a lonely enterprise for many of our community's elderly. The busier family members get, the less they are able to visit, and many residents have few chances to leave the limiting premises.
>
> My colleagues and I at Clever Computers have been teaching nursing home residents how to socialize with family and friends on the Internet, and pursue their personal interests through online resources and online courses. But we discovered that a number of these seniors cannot handle the keyboard well enough.
>
> On Monday, July 24, we'll show ten residents of the Maple Tree Home who are unable to type how to access the Internet's wonders through voice control alone.
>
> We invite you, or a member of your staff, to join us and witness first-hand how these senior citizens experience their power to open up the world for the first time.
>
> Clever Computers (www.clevcomp@bgs.net) is a 10-year-old community-based company serving the business community with computer troubleshooting, networking systems and training.
>
> *[Event time, place, date, directions go here]*
>
> Call me any time for more details. A photographer is most welcome. We expect the best time to catch a heartfelt moment is 10:45 a.m.
>
> Sharon Fisher, CEO

An alternative approach is to invite coverage with a Media Alert, delivered at least a week before your happening:

> **MEDIA ALERT!**
>
> From:
>
> Contact:
>
> Event: (Headline)
>
> Event date:
>
> Event time, including best photo op:

Place:

Description of what will happen and its significance, who the organizer is (up to three short paragraphs)

More information about organizer (with website address)

Direct invitation to attend

A local newspaper, magazine or business publication is likely to respond to either form of pitch. They are increasingly short-handed and able to show up only at high-priority events. Therefore, the editor may invite you to send a write-up after the fact, or a high-resolution photo and caption. Then, the better you do the reporter's work and deliver well-written, ready-to-use material, the better your chances of gaining some media space.

If you want to contribute a full-fledged article, or columns based on your special expertise, it's wise to pitch the idea in the same manner before writing. If interested, editors will provide guidelines to help you produce what they need. My advice on writing blogs in Chapter 12 can help.

Check out whether your community has an online news channel, always starved for news. And consider local television. But to draw a video crew to the scene requires a promise of strong visuals. You might be able to produce acceptable footage of the event yourself and submit it. Or hire a local videographer.

Finding ideas for the media

TIP

You may have thought in reading this section that your enterprise doesn't offer attractive activities like teaching nursing home folks to use the Internet, or running a charity concert or opening a new office. Companies and nonprofits identify good ideas in two basic ways: First, they constantly keep eye and ear open to notice what the organization and every member of it is engaged in that is shareworthy. Second, they create activities that merit publicity.

Clever Computers, for example, might have decided to initiate its nursing-home program because someone recognized the need. Or they might have thought about what they could contribute to the community that would be of value and justify media attention. The desire for publicity is a motivating force behind many wonderful programs. Every enterprise today wants to be known as a good community member and looks actively for ways to connect through good causes.

TIP

If you are doing something wonderful or truly innovative in your industry, look to the wider range of possibilities. Trade and professional publications need material, too, and if you have something to offer, their doors may open. Pitch editors as I outline in the foregoing sections, taking account of your suggestion's value to the audience.

News venues also thrive on relationships. Do your homework and become familiar with your local outlets: what interests them, their presentation style, their scope. Professional freelance writers always study at least several issues of a publication before making a pitch to analyze how the editors see their market and distinguish their product from all the others. You advantage as a businessperson is being able to write for free, since money from writing is (I assume) not your motivation.

Find out how to reach editors and reporters. Find opportunities to talk to them locally. If you're interested in the national or regional level, note that most major publications today scout for ideas and accept pitches through social media. Follow them on social channels to understand their orientation.

If you want to connect with online communities and bloggers in your field, the same approach works. Follow a blogger who's interested in what you offer and rather than just hitting them with a request, familiarize yourself with their blog and comment on it frequently. Think about how they aim to serve their audience and how you can help them with that: Contribute items of mutual interest? Give them a free sample of your product to award to a follower? Cover an event? Interview a celebrity in the field you share? Exchange guest blogs?

Creativity scores.

Writing Challenges for the Entrepreneur

Many of the communication channels are covered in other chapters of this book, but of course I can't cover them all. But you'll never go wrong if you use the basic strategic thinking explained in Chapter 2. Your messages, major and minor, succeed when they're based on your own deep thinking about what you want to accomplish and the specific people you want to connect with. My goal is to equip you with a thinking structure, not formulas.

To demonstrate how to use this structure, here are some examples of how to handle difficult messages that challenge many entrepreneurs.

Introducing yourself in writing

When you open a new business, assume a new role in your company or join or take over a professional practice, consider introducing yourself to your significant by letter. It's an important step toward building relationships and sounding the right note.

Suppose you're an accountant and you're taking over as head of a firm specializing in corporate tax counseling, or head of that department in a large practice. Your primary *audience* is the firm's existing clients and your *goal* is to retain and start building relationships with them.

TIP

Asking "What's in it for them?" — *the audience* — grounds your content decisions. It's good to think through your particular audience's characteristics as explained in Chapter 2. But the ultimate question is, what can you say that will help this audience feel comfortable and well-disposed toward dealing with you, someone they know in a different capacity or not at all?

SHORTCUT

When people need to introduce themselves, they often make the mistake of thinking in terms of "what I want them to know." Instead, consider "what do *they* want to know." Put yourself in their shoes and brainstorm what points to make, remembering that people center on their own interests. They want to know how a change affects them. For example:

>> Will I receive the same level of service?

>> How do I know the new person will do a good job?

>> Will I be inconvenienced in any way?

>> Is this a nice person, someone I'll like?

The accountant can then translate this set of needs into a content list:

>> Demonstrate my respect for the former business owner (whom clients presumably liked) and mention why they're gone (but never cite a negative reason).

>> Assure clients that service to them continues with absolutely no inconvenience.

>> Tell clients about myself:

- Where I'm coming from, plus my most impressive affiliation and clients

- My specialized expertise or experience (early work for the IRS and certification in relevant subject area)

- Honors I've received that prove I am an expert

>> Mention my plans for improving client service (plan to implement new technology to make records more accessible).

>> Share my contributions as an active member of the community (to show I'm a nice person).

>> Explain why I love my work and/or want to know my new clients personally.

>> Offer to meet all or most important clients one-on-one.

TIP

Notice how few items on the list speak to professional credentials. Contrary to many examples I see, an introductory letter is usually *not* best viewed as an opportunity to detail your accomplishments and qualifications at length. Most people overestimate others people's interest in credentials. Unless you're hiring someone for a staff position, it's often enough to provide just enough to establish your suitability. People tend to take for granted that you are qualified. Supply a highlights version of your professional history and spend the rest of the space communicating how life will be better when the client works with you. And show how nice you are.

Once you've outlined your substance, the letter nearly writes itself. Most often aim for a friendly but somewhat formal tone. Fashion your lead: a down-to-earth simple opener that explains why you're writing is fine. It may help to visualize your favorite client (see Chapter 2). One version:

> Dear Ms. Wish:
>
> I'm happy to introduce myself as the new Managing Partner of Donnybrook Tax Accountants, Inc. As you may know, my good friend and colleague Tom Marx retired in June. I want to assure you that my goal is to give you the same level of personal service and counsel you're accustomed to, in every way.
>
> I have been an enthusiastic tax consultant for 22 years . . .
>
> I discovered my passion for this work when . . .
>
> Most recently, I managed tax services for . . .
>
> I had the privilege of serving . . .
>
> I am especially proud to contribute to our mutual community, which was recognized by . . .
>
> I am working on additional ways to make your tax experience pleasant and productive with new technology that . . .
>
> I would very much enjoy meeting you in person soon if that is possible. If you would prefer a phone conversation or videoconference, just let me know and I'll arrange my schedule to accommodate yours.
>
> Sincerely,
>
> Len
>
> Leonard March

Len can email the letter or send a "real" one via the post office. If he evaluates his readers as older and probably conservative, he'll choose the post office and sign every letter. In blue.

TIP

An introductory letter need not be reserved for taking over a business. If you were promoted into a role that brings you new contacts, it's wise to write a similar letter. If you're a freelancer in new territory — geographically, or because you're undertaking a new line of work — introduce yourself to the community and potential customers. If you join a consulting firm, an introductory letter is a good way to tell clients and prospects how your presence expands the firm's capabilities. If you work for a nonprofit, use letters to announce your new role to grant-giving organizations, major donors, relevant government offices and other stakeholders.

A well-written letter is easily adapted for secondary audiences. If the tax specialist hopes to bring clients over from his former situation, they can slant the content to them (providing they have the legal right to solicit them). They can also quickly adapt it to reach new prospects. It's also easy to adopt the information to a press release or profile on the company website.

Sometimes a bad example can make the point clearer. One I received myself was from a dermatologist taking over the practice of a doctor I'd gone to for years. After a standard lead sentence stating his reason for writing, he supplied three long, dense paragraphs naming every disease that he customarily treats; every stage of his education; and all his professional affiliations and journal articles.

My reader reaction: I did not look forward to becoming his patient. Citing all the dreadful diseases he was familiar with was more horrifying than impressive. The mistake was basic: He mistook his audience. Rather than communicating that he cared about people and would provide a comfortable, knowledgeable experience, he wrote as if to peers from whom he wanted referrals.

WARNING

If you're part of an organization or representing one, make sure introductory letters are in line with your organization's culture and that the contents won't surprise your higher-ups.

REMEMBER

Our digital environment does not preclude the usefulness of a traditional letter, direct mail, local marketing initiative or print media. In fact, the digital world itself enables personalization: curated and tailored content, individualized messages, micro-segmented target audiences, strategies to generate active participation and word of mouth. In addition to being sent as a letter, a written introduction can take the form of an advertisement, a conference exhibit, an online profile, your website "About Us," or be used for many other purposes.

Writing to pitch your services

If you're a solopreneur or partner in a small business or a salesperson, you may regularly need to write pitch letters or deliver cold-call messages. Typically, your goal is to bring you, or your product or service, to someone's attention and obtain an in-person or teleconference meeting.

Such letters are important for professional specialists of many kinds. One approach is covered in the proposal section of Chapter 7. Here is another oriented to a specialized consultant, a historian.

Sarah knew that a county preservation office would soon need someone to organize an application to obtain landmark status for a local building. Aiming for an appointment to present herself, Sarah drafted a letter.

Dear Mr. Johnson:

I had the pleasure of meeting you last July when I accompanied Jane Maxwell of the city preservation office and architect Roger Brown on a site visit to Marigold House. At that time, Jane and Jeremy were working on the city's new Local Landmark designation for properties of historic and cultural importance outside the Big City Historic District . . .

The Pritchard Building was officially approved by the City Council on November 28 . . . . I served as the consulting historian, preparing a historical title search and the land use, cultural, and biographical information necessary to establish the significance of the health center.

The nineteenth-century Marigold House has more than 300 years of stories to tell and a number of them are nearly unknown. For example, the eighteenth-century correspondence of Margaret Green and Eleanor March . . .

I would like to research the title and history of Marigold House and prepare the significance portion of its application for Landmark designation in conjunction with Lisa and Roberta and the city preservation office. Can we schedule some time to talk about this?

Sincerely, Sarah Jones

Did you have trouble getting through this version, even in its abbreviated form?

Try This: Outline a new version. How would you improve this message? Compare your ideas with my version.

Dear Mr. Johnson:

We met at Marigold House last July when I accompanied Jane Maxwell of the City Preservation Office and architect Robert Brown on a site visit. I'm taking the liberty of writing now because as a professional historian, I would very much like to work with

Jane and your office to research the property's title and history for its application as a designated landmark.

This eighteenth-century house has more than 300 years of wonderful stories to tell. For example:

- *The correspondence of . . .*
- *Mary Jennings' 1810 book of poems . . .*
- *The first-hand account of the slave Emelia who escaped . . .*

All these stories contribute to Marigold House's historical and cultural significance, but only a few of them are now part of the official registries.

I would like to prepare the significant portion of the application and include these stories and many more.

I've previously worked with Jane to develop the city's new Local Landmark designation regulations and I served as the consulting historian to establish the significance of Margaret Field . . .

I am the former resident historian for . . .

Can we schedule some time to talk? I will welcome the opportunity to explain my qualifications to research Marigold House and support its application for Landmark status.

Sincerely, Sarah Jones

Based on comparing the original and revised letter, here are some useful guidelines that apply to many pitch letters:

>> **Say what you want ASAP so the person knows why you're writing.** When you have a personal connection, begin with that because it positions you, establishes trust and builds instant connection.

>> **Format the letter to be quickly read and easily understood.** In the revised letter, the short, bulleted list breaks up the copy and gets the examples across more effectively. Shorter paragraphs and sentences encourage reading.

>> **Make the most of what's interesting, relevant and/or close to the reader's heart.** The "wonderful story" examples are highlighted in Version 2 rather than buried, which enlivens the whole letter and also speaks to Sarah's knowledgeability better than listing credentials.

>> **Use a writing style that relates to the audience and your goal.** In this case, the writer is addressing someone with an academic orientation similar to her own, so a slightly formal tone feels right.

>> **Include credentials, but not necessarily up front.** They are often not your best sales points, as I explain in the previous section, "Introducing yourself in writing." People respond more to your understanding of their challenges and what you can do for them, rather than what you've done in the past. This isn't really counterintuitive: *Knowing how to bridge your expertise to solve other people's problems is a hallmark of professionalism.*

TIP

If you came up with a different version you like better, that's great. Editing and writing are far from scientific. It might be nice to think you can follow formulas or use templates, but "canned" approaches come across as overly general and boring. Practice thinking each challenge through with a goal-plus-audience framework in mind, address head and heart, and you'll get results.

Creating letters that get you in

Writing "cold call" letters to sell a product is a work staple for professional copywriters, and for good reason. So many pitches compete for attention today that people are automatically skeptical, impatient and bored with the piles of "buy me" messages from direct mail to emails, videos and social media. While today's online environment offers amazing opportunities to create and deliver a marketing message, don't expect to do so easily. It takes work. Here are some ideas to draw on:

>> **Aim for incremental steps toward your goals.** Don't expect someone to respond to a single communication by putting a check in the mail. More realistically, aim to pique reader interest, begin to establish trust, and entice them to the next step. An initial message need say just enough to interest your reader in going further. Adopt the "customer journey" outlook.

>> **Know both the organization and important individual.** If you're selling, it's your job to understand the business's challenges and explain how you can help. Think also about the particular person you're writing to — their goals, pressures and role, which I talk about how to do in Chapter 2. Treat everything you write as an opportunity to advance a relationship.

>> **Make a connection.** People trust people who appear to be from their own worlds. This isn't prejudicial; it's just hard to trust strangers. When you have a connection, cite it: "We met at the such-and-such event" is good. More possibilities:

- We have a friend or professional connection in common.

- I talked to your company rep at a trade show or conference.

- We work with a client you know.

- We won an award for achievement in our mutual industry.

Or perhaps you read a blog the person wrote, heard them speak or read about them in the business journal. Dig as you must.

>> **Start strong.** Try to combine both a personal connection and your problem-solving capability in a single opening sentence, such as:

Chuck Smith suggested I contact you to explain how I solved his most pressing problem, one I'm sure you share with him: reducing government audits of overseas investments.

Alternatively, lead with a story, a hot button, an unusual benefit or offer, a surprising fact or statistic. It's nice to be catchy, but don't go crazy trying to be clever or funny. Better not to tell a joke than one that falls flat or could be misinterpreted. Knowing your value and how you can benefit the other party puts you on sure ground toward making the match.

>> **Remember "the ask."** If you want the reader to check out your website, request a free ebook, sign up for your blog or ask a question, say so. If you want an appointment, say so. It's smart to set a time frame: Offering to establish your value in ten minutes, for example, is more attractive than requesting an open-ended commitment and suggests you're focused and won't waste the person's time.

>> **Prepare to be checked out.** Keep in mind that if you piqued their interest, readers will likely look you and your organization up on the Internet. Your website and LinkedIn profiles, among other platforms, should be in good shape to support your marketing message. And if you can find any embarrassing posts related to your personal life, rest assured a sales prospect or decision-maker will, too. Clean up your act — and screen yourself in the future to avoid losing valuable opportunities.

Never take existing clients or customers for granted: New ones are hard to get, even for big corporations, and they are expensive to replace.

Here are some ideas for using your writing skills to both protect your own interests and handle problems proactively while minimizing the risk of relationship damage.

Spelling out services performed

If you're self-employed or operate a small business, balancing your desire to retain a client with your need to communicate something uncomfortable can be hard. You must sometimes balance the need to protect your interests against the risk of relationship damage.

Prevention is always the best cure. Clients can have short memories, so use your writing skills to make problems less likely. One way is to routinely communicate the specifics of the work involved in each project both at the agreement stage and when invoicing.

TIP

For example, if I write a marketing publication for a project fee, I don't say:

> For writing service: Marshall & White overview brochure — $X

My invoice reads more like this (the agreement would be similar but a little more general, specifying deadlines rather than dates):

> For Marshall & White overview brochure: 16 pages, 4-color glossy to serve as linchpin for major marketing campaign:
>
> - Meetings with Executive Team (June 1, June 8, June 22, July 7)
> - Ongoing telephone consultation
> - Presentation with PowerPoint to Board, June 14
> - Concept development: delivered three creative strategy ideas
> - Full treatment of chosen concept: 16 pp. mockup
> - Content recommendations: CEO "ideas" letter, employee spotlights, infographic of 10-year advances
> - Informational interviews with 9 staff members, 7 clients
> - Overseeing photo shoot, July 10
> - Coordination with graphic design

And more. Notice that the list doesn't yet include copywriting.

REMEMBER

Even well-intentioned clients only see the tip of your work iceberg. They observe a product, like a finished brochure or a workshop or situation analysis, and because the work is distant from their own expertise, have little idea of what went into it. They also may overlook that preparing for and attending meetings consumes a lot of time (not fully paid workdays like in their own case), and that creative work involves a lot of thought that doesn't tangibly show and doesn't stop at 5 p.m. It's a rare client that likes to pay a consultant for thinking, even though that's often the crux of the service.

TIP

Anticipate the tasks a project demands and specify them in the agreement. Keep track of them as accomplished with dates, which forestalls many arguments, and put them right into the invoice. And if what you provide is intangible — like consulting — spell out as many tangibles as you can: creating the survey instrument, the 32-page report, the PowerPoint, the graphs for the website and so on. If you can cite early evidence of the project's success, work that in, too.

Collecting on your invoices

No matter how carefully invoices and contracts are written, every consultant, freelancer and entrepreneur has trouble collecting money at times. How to maintain a good relationship while pressing for payment?

REMEMBER

Ideally, head this problem off from the beginning by requiring a retainer on signing, no matter how much you trust the person you're dealing with and how steady a client the firm has been. People are known to leave jobs and those who replace them may prefer suppliers of their own, or bring the work in-house. Companies have gone out of business without warning. You may also encounter disputes about whether, in the buyer's opinion, you delivered to the standard expected.

No one with honest intentions will ever fault you for acting in businesslike ways. And don't lay the groundwork for cheating yourself if the nature of the work means you'll do a major portion in the beginning, like coming up with ideas or creating the blueprint. Set up the payment schedule to cover this aspect of the job should the agreement dissolve, and specify the number of re-do's included in the fee.

When payment is running a little late, minimize resentment by saying as little as possible in a perfectly neutral, blame-free, impersonal tone. Make the person you're writing to a partner in the collection effort:

> *Subject: Can you help?*
>
> *Dear Tardee,*
>
> *My payment for the Tyler project hasn't come through yet, though the work was finished two months ago. Is it possible for you to nudge the machinery a bit on my behalf?*
>
> *I'll appreciate it very much. —Marty*

Or:

> *Subject: Friendly reminder*
>
> *Dear Tardee,*
>
> *I'm wondering if it's possible to speed up the processing of my second check for the Curio Design work. In line with our agreement it was due September 4 but has not arrived.*
>
> *I'll appreciate your help with this.*
>
> *Thanks, Marty*

TIP

There's never a reason to plead poverty. Don't say you need the money to pay your bills. Late payment messages, unlike most I talk about in this book, work better when they are impersonal. The same minimalist approach is useful when you bear some responsibility. A friend was embarrassed to discover that she had neglected to deposit a check and it was too old for the bank to accept. She wrote to the client:

> Dear Mr. Black:
>
> In tracking invoices and payments for tax purposes, bookkeeping has brought to our attention that your check #9174 written on January 12 of this year was rejected by ABC Bank due to endorsement requirements.
>
> Our records indicate that the check was not redeposited.
>
> Attached is a copy of the check that was not credited to the Marketing Pro account.
>
> Would you kindly issue a new check to replace the one that was originally provided?
>
> We apologize for any inconvenience this may have caused.
>
> Thank you,
>
> Marcia White

Assuming the editorial or kingly "we" along with the formal tone depersonalizes the request and presents it as a glitch between bureaucracies, though the writer runs a very small company from a virtual office.

Sometimes, however, a true "letter of record" is called for to document an event or problem or present your claim more formally. This kind of letter may have legal implications that involve lawyers. That's beyond my scope, but I can share a strategy to keep in your back pocket for severely late payments and other confrontational situations: a chronological accounting. Here, it's all about the facts.

TIP

Marshal all the relevant bits and arrange them in a timeline. Then create a letter that simply marches down each item on your list in a dispassionate, matter-of-fact way: no frills, no flowery adjectives, no emotion. Start each item with the date.

Suppose you're an independent graphic designer and a client hasn't paid your last bill, which was due six months ago. He now hints that the work wasn't done to his satisfaction and won't take your phone calls. You don't want to go to court, but you do want your money.

Your letter can go this way:

> Dear Mel:
>
> On July 6 of this year, you contacted my firm, Morning Glory Design, to inquire about website services for your firm, Thompson, Ltd.

On July 8, we met at your office for two hours to discuss Thompson's needs and goals.

On July 15, I sent you a summary of our conversation with our suggestions for a website to meet your specifications. You called and said "I like the approach very much, go ahead."

On July 22, I sent you an agreement specifying that Morning Glory would provide the services outlined (see attached contract pages 1 and 2) at a proposed fee (see attached contract page 3) and a schedule of payments.

On July 22, we both signed the contract. You remitted the one-third payment due.

On August 10, I presented the preliminary design. You said "with some revision it would be exactly what I want" and that you'd mail the second payment at week's end.

On August 19, I presented the revised version based on your input. You said, "It looks fantastic, let me take a more careful look with my staff, and I'll check about the payment you didn't receive."

And so on. Further entries might include the dates the invoices were sent, when the new web design went live and every other relevant detail — the more, the better. The close:

In sum, I have met every obligation of our contract in a timely manner and with your full approval. The site is online exactly as I designed it. But six months later, you have not paid two-thirds of the fee to which you agreed in writing. Kindly remit the balance owed immediately.

Very truly yours, Natasha James

TIP

This may be the only place in this book that I recommend a stilted, formal language with an archaic tone. Such a letter sounds as if a lawyer is advising you. Or at the least, your reader will recognize that you have a good case and are prepared to seek legal redress. If Mel doesn't come through and you decide to take the legal route, your letter becomes part of that process and serves you well.

The approach works just as nicely when you're on the other side of the fence, presented with charges you believe to be unmerited. Moreover, if you don't want to pay an unfair bill and clearly *state that you have no intention of paying*, the other party's recourse may be limited, depending on the state you live in.

TIP

Underscore your letter's legal undertones by mailing it — or better yet, certify it and require a signature to prove receipt.

Raising your fee structure

Most freelancers I know hate talking about money. Often, writing is a good way to do it. You can marshal your thinking points and articulate them more effectively without the person present, and give them breathing space to consider your request as well. Clients typically don't enjoy these conversations any more than you do and may blurt out a negative response that's hard to reconsider.

TIP

Many successful consultants sidestep cost questions before presenting a written proposal because they're not ready to specify all the work involved (similar to the invoice structure I suggest in the "Spelling out services performed" section). Writing also enables them to analyze and define the larger value of the proposed work to the company. This sets the stage for a better conversation.

One challenging need is a request for a fee increase. Most people who hire independent workers are content to continue in the same groove forever. I can't recall hearing of any instances where a freelancer was offered a raise. Ask you must, whether your business and living costs are going up like everyone else's, or because you've experienced "scope creep" — that is, you find yourself investing more time than your fee structure covers fairly.

The approach for collecting on invoices also works for this problem. List your possible content points. You will have specifics according to the situation, but here are some fairly universal points to make in framing the message:

>> I'm raising my rate 5 percent.

>> I haven't increased my fees for three years.

>> My overhead and operating expenses go up inevitably.

>> My work is valuable to you, as proven by . . .

>> My service this coming year will be even better because . . .

TIP

The last point is optional, but if you can think of something that doesn't really cost you anything — like a staff expansion or new capability you planned on anyway, an offer to meet more often, or a way to repurpose your work for additional uses — you provide a mitigating factor that inclines the client to agree more easily. They're spending more, but getting more.

WARNING

Remember that a message like this will probably be passed up the managerial chain and reviewed by financial people, so supply your connections with information to help them win approval on your behalf. And use an impersonal but still friendly writing style.

When you spell out your basic points first, with a list like the one a few paragraphs ago, you spare yourself a lot of agonizing. Just follow the trail!

Dear Anne,

I'm writing to alert you, as a client of many years, that Marsh Sisters will raise our project fee rate by 5 percent this coming year.

I know you'll understand that just like Tailor Enterprises, our operating expenses steadily increase. We have not raised our rates for three years, and did so only once in the seven years we've worked together.

Of course, we want to continue providing Tailor with the best possible service. We were very proud to earn the March Association Award of Merit for the Chancellor Project this past year, and even happier to know our work played a part in helping Tailor increase its Blue Division revenue this past quarter.

We have plans to support you in meeting your business goals even more effectively. We're implementing a new software system right now that will give you more detailed reports, with even faster turnaround.

All of us at Marsh look forward to working with you this year and together, know we will achieve new heights.

Sincerely,

Maggie

In writing difficult letters as an entrepreneur, always check yourself out with the ultimate criteria: If I got this message, would I say yes?

And don't overlook all the material relevant to your needs in the rest of this book: Building your writing and editing skills in Part 1; writing emails, letters and business materials in Part 2; principles of persuasion, creating presentations and hunting for jobs or gigs in Part 3; writing for digital media and creating your online presence in Part 4; and the chapter preceding this one, on workplace writing challenges.

And this, dear reader, is where I leave you.

But don't go away quite yet: The following "Part of Tens" chapters give you two sets of quick helpful insights about using your writing skills to advantage.

I hope you will take the foundation this book gives you to enjoy writing, practice it in your daily work life and keep learning. I know this investment will always reward you — often in unanticipated ways.

6 The Part of Tens

Learn how to use writing to solve problems creatively, sharpen your thinking skills, take charge of your emotions and prepare for on-the-spot situations.

Discover how writing out a career plan can help you reach your long-range business and personal goals.

Decide whether writing a book is for you and understand your choices: ebook or print, commercial or self-publishing, solo or with outside resources.

Walk through the steps of writing your own book from creating a proposal to organizing and drafting the copy to marketing the finished product.

Chapter 15

Ten (or So) Ways to Grow Your Personal Power with Writing

Writing well is always its own reward: Effective messages achieve what you want much more often. But writing can also be put to use in personal ways — to catalyze your thinking and problem-solving skills, understand important people in your work life and strategize how to advance toward where you want to be. This chapter gives you ten ways to build your personal power. Refer to the writing techniques covered throughout this book to carry out these ideas.

Use Writing to Problem-Solve

Psychologists say we humans have lazy brains. Deep thinking consumes so much energy that we only undertake it when forced. One result is that when faced with a difficult problem, we try to solve it by instinct, which doesn't always end well, or we endlessly circle and recircle around the same ground without finding a way out. Writing enables you to break out of this morass.

TIP

Try defining the problem as thoroughly as possible in writing. Sometimes just working through the details clarifies your view of what the trouble is and how it developed. This often paves the way for a solution. Also look to shift your perspective by changing what you say to yourself. Suppose you defined the bottom line of the problem as "the boss doesn't give me the best opportunities so I'm not learning or moving ahead." Reword this as: "How can I show the boss I'm worthy of better opportunities?"

This simple shift channels you to deal with the challenge creatively and moves you away from dwelling on the "why" — as in "why doesn't the boss appreciate me?" — to practical ways to achieve what matters to you.

Write a "Pro" and "Con" List

When faced with a tough decision like whether to accept a new job or stay with the one you have, take a piece of paper and split it into two columns vertically. Write "pro" at the top of one column, and "con" at the top of the other. Now list all the factors you can think of that would lead you to say "yes" to the new job, and those that prompt a "no," filling out each column until you run out of thoughts.

Look at the length of each column: Is one longer than the other? More important, does one column include factors that matter more to you than the others? For example, maybe the new job would bring you to a place you'd like to live, or give you more flexibility in allocating your time, or let you work for a cause you believe in. This simple pro-con strategy gives you perspective and helps clarify which route is best for you.

Handwrite to Spark Creativity

Neurological studies show that the mechanical nature of handwriting taps into wholly different parts of the brain than typing or using your voice to dictate messages. Writers of fiction and poetry have always known this, and even today, most creative writers draft their new work by hand. Professional writers who use keyboards often rely on handwriting at critical points such as planning out content, beginning a new work or finding a direction when stalled.

TIP

Try writing by hand when you have to create a difficult message of any kind, solve a knotty problem or prepare for a challenging situation.

Not coincidentally, making handwritten notes also works best when you're learning something new. In deciding what to make note of, you process the information. When you keyboard or record the audio, in contrast, your brain does not filter the information or give it perspective. Taking notes by hand amplifies understanding and recall exponentially. Research proves this, too!

Write to Take Charge of Your Emotions

The essential message of this book is to plan everything you write in context of your goals and your audience and the content that best connects these two basics. This thinking process will help you analyze tough situations and make decisions even when writing is not involved.

REMEMBER

Especially when interacting with other people, rather than giving in to a spontaneous emotion like anger, pause to think: What's my real goal? What do I really want? Vent my feelings? Get even? Hurt the person who hurt me? If you'd rather fix a glitch in the relationship, ask yourself, what is the better way to address the issue?

Unfortunately, in work situations, losing your temper (or crying) marks you as unprofessional. Another way to prevent yourself from succumbing to a damaging emotion is to write about the emotional event in detail, perhaps in the form of a letter to the person who provoked the feelings. This clears your mind and is safe venting — provided you take care not to send the message.

Remind yourself that practicing controlled, strategic behavior empowers you to keep your cool and equips you to achieve good outcomes and respect.

Take Notes about Your Work

Some of the most efficient managers I've known keep a notebook ready at hand to record decisions, requests and work events as they happen. Their ability to leaf back and cite specifics is confounding to everyone else, since our human tendency is to forget or reinterpret a deadline, decision or plan, given a little time, and particularly when forgetting makes life easier. And of course, this record-keeping enables you to refresh your own memory upon need.

TIP

Keep a notebook in your desk and jot down outcomes and loose ends during or after meetings, conversations, decision-making and so on. This technique is equally useful for entrepreneurs and independent workers, among others.

Take the Meeting Notes

A little-recognized fact: Acting as the notetaker at business and office meetings is not a lowly occupation — it spells *power*. The person who records what happens and writes it up creates the official recap that becomes group memory and guide to action. Some amount of every discussion is open to interpretation, and it's the notetaker who makes those judgment calls.

Rather than this being a secretarial task, it's an opportunity to create a perspective on what happened. I've rarely seen this questioned — people reviewing the "minutes" typically focus on spelling errors. A bonus: You make yourself the information hub because participants feed you follow-up data, new input, clarifications and more. You become the person who knows more about everything. And you know what they say about knowledge.

Take Notes of Your Anytime Ideas

Personal journaling — devoting a certain amount of time every day to writing about what's happening and what you're thinking — is a nourishing activity for many creatives. If you're building a business or a career that profits from inventiveness, try it.

TIP

Another easy-to-practice tactic is to carry a mini-notebook for jotting down your ideas and inspirations in real time. Why do our best thoughts materialize when there's nothing to write with, and/or it's not convenient to record what we want to remember? Be prepared. The fun way is to use reporter's notebooks: handy little 4 x 6-inch notepads that fit into a purse or pocket and make you feel like a professional journalist when you whip them out.

Prepare for Confrontation

Equip yourself for situations where you're put on the spot just like the politicians do. Whether it's a job interview, a questions and answers session with your CEO, or a meeting with your boss to ask for a raise or discuss your performance, prepare by developing *talking points*.

Brainstorm all the points you can make in your favor. Think each one through but capsulize it in a line or two, just enough to trigger your memory. Work with the list until you completely assimilate the points and are ready to speak to each as the conversation allows.

TIP

Go a step further: Imagine every question you might be asked, especially the ones that keep you up at night. Prepare good answers and you might even link these up with your talking points. Enlist a friend or colleague to make the process more fun and ensure you don't gloss over the worrisome areas.

Write a Long-Range Career Plan

Applying an analytic frame of mind to your long-range career goals always pays handsomely. In writing, explain where you want to be in six months, a year, two years, five years, ten years or more — you choose the time frames — and what you want to achieve in each one. Then review each period of time against the one furthest from the present: Are you taking the steps you need to move from one period to the next and to your ultimate goal? Do you see a clear progression, step by step, or do you see gaps in preparing for each forward leap?

This process enables you to see if what you're doing now, puts you on the right track and illuminates how you can move toward your goal. Do you need a certain kind of experience or training? Do you need to connect with certain people or groups, take on particular assignments or find intermediary roles?

Major bonus: You're better able to recognize opportunities you might otherwise overlook, make better decisions and avoid straying too far off the path. Of course, stay open to adjusting the plan according to a shift in the realities or yourself.

Create Profiles of Your VIPs

Write in-depth descriptions of your boss, CEO, difficult coworker, collaborator or all of the above. These people are your most significant audiences, and just as you can create a persona for groups you want to engage with, you can thoughtfully analyze the people who most impact your work life.

Scan the characteristics presented in Chapter 2 and create a list of relevant factors, including the person's management style, communication preferences and approach to decision-making. Is this person partial to ideas, statistics, their impact on people or their own ambitions? Also note their hot buttons, enthusiasms, vulnerabilities, positioning in the organization and biggest worries.

Draw from your notes to write a cohesive portrait. Magically, you will find it easier to assume the person's perspective. You know how to ask for what you want, score opportunities to shine and improve — even turn around — relationships. You'll take giant steps toward practicing empathy, a quality that is increasingly valued in the workplace.

Write Gratefully

You have probably come across the idea of sending sincere, well-thought-out thank-you letters to people in your present or past life. It's good advice, especially because the busier and more pressured we feel, the less time we take to express appreciation to people who deserve it. A note of gratitude not only makes the chosen person's day, but also is treasured forever as proof of value. Such notes stand out because so few are received.

Even more effective is to keep a "gratitude journal," or add this element to your journal writing if you already keep one. This is the place to write — daily if possible — about things you are thankful for: a favor rendered, an opportunity gained, a special person in your life. Or how beautiful the sunny sky outside your window looks, how wonderful it is to have a friend who is there for you, an inspiring memory or whatever gives you laughter, solace and support. Psychologists say that writing in a gratitude journal counterbalances the negativity that often overshadows the good things around us. So, writing can make you happier! It's great practice in developing your skills, too.

Chapter **16**

Ten Steps to Writing Your Own Book

For many people and for many reasons, writing a book feels like a paramount achievement. It's an "end product" of our knowledge, experience and professionalism. There's something exciting about the idea of holding your book in your hands, giving it to people, even signing copies or seeing it in a bookstore — though this is no longer where most books are sold. A book feels like the ultimate way of sharing, branding and making a mark.

TIP

If producing a book is a dream or a practical business tactic for you, there's never been a better time to do it. Publishing traditionally is more competitive than ever, but self-publishing has come a long way from being called the "vanity press." You can write and produce your own print books, ebooks or both, without endorsement by gatekeepers. You can handle the whole process yourself, or access a growing range of services and support systems to help. You can market your books directly to your selected buyers and sell them yourself.

Books are attractive propositions because they can produce "passive income" — money that accumulates over time and requires little effort once it's published. There are two big "buts" to this idea. First of all, very few books make money.

Commercial publishers support their constant stream of new books with the proceeds of a few blockbusters. Second, books don't sell themselves. Authors learn that even a traditionally published book demands active marketing, and self-published writers find that this can be a full-time job.

Bottom line: Don't plan on your book being profitable. It does happen but not often. It helps to be famous or have a subject that hits a universal nerve; have access to something or someone special; or have a ready-made "platform" — an audience presumably eager to buy your book because you have a social fan base, a popular blog, media coverage, an impressive reputation or rare skill. Otherwise write your book because it will give your "real" career a nice boost or will just make you feel very good.

TIP

The guidelines I give you here assume you want to write a how-to book of some kind. But most of the ideas apply with some interpretation to most types of books — and also to developing other large-scale and intensive writing projects.

Envision Your Finished Book

How do you see your final product: as a self-published print or ebook? Or a commercially published book? This decision affects your choices from the outset.

REMEMBER

If you aspire to traditional publishing, almost always you need to land a literary agent — a feat in itself — and create a solid proposal that includes a promising platform. The publisher customarily covers editing, design, production and distribution and in theory, marketing. You only get 10 to 20 percent of the royalties on sales. But a traditional book still carries the most cachet in the business world, especially for consultants.

If you choose self-publishing, an ebook is a good option. You sidestep expensive printing costs and the headaches of storing all those heavy books. You can earn 70 percent or more on sales and keep the copyright. Amazon's Kindle division facilitates many of the production tasks, and many other services offer supplementary resource packages. Or, hire freelancers as needed. Otherwise you are responsible for all the functions like editing, graphic design for the cover at least, and perhaps help with formatting (converting Word to digital), as well as marketing.

TIP

A nice option that many new authors use is print-on-demand. You can publish an ebook and also order small batches of physical copies rather than a huge number of physical books at once.

In making decisions, take into account how much material is called for. A traditional hard-cover book requires 60,000 to 80,000 words, at least 250 pages. The publishing process is slow: It easily takes a year or two. Ebooks can be any length, and a number of authors produce steady income by slivering their subject into a series that readers lap up if they like the first one or two.

Create an Elevator Speech for Your Book

A book is a message that's definitely on a much grander scale than an email, but the planning is not that different. Create a good base for what may be a long-range commitment by writing down your goal as specifically as possible. Write a detailed portrait of the book's audience. Think through what your intended readers will gain. Then write a crystallizing statement of your intention. For example, here is the one I used for this book:

> Business Writing For Dummies *will help readers on many different skill levels improve their writing by using professional techniques across media, so they can be more successful in their own field — whether business, government, nonprofit, freelance or consulting.*

This gave me a practical mission statement that kept me on target and steadily aware of my intended audiences.

Also, write down your own purpose in undertaking the book. You're committing yourself to an extended period of hard work — no two ways about that — and need to keep your motivation strong. How effectively will your book support your consulting business? Establish your authority? Give you something on your desk to smile at? Remind yourself!

Think about Marketing — Early

It's never too soon to think about how to publicize and market your book, and if you're aiming for a commercial publisher, you need an almost full-fledged plan to sell it.

A website is essential for selling directly if you choose to do so, and for publicizing. You might create a site solely for the book, or attach it to your business website and give it a landing page and promotion on the home page.

Review your existing platform: Do you blog? Are you active on certain social sites and have built up followings? Do you give workshops or speeches that bring you into contact with likely buyers? Might you go to conferences where you can talk the book up? Many good tactics take time to put in place so the advance work, done incrementally, makes a big difference.

REMEMBER

Savvy authors start putting the pieces into place right at the beginning, maybe even before starting to write. You might plan to up your blogging schedule or refocus it . . . dig deeper into a social platform that will support marketing . . . develop speaking engagements . . . make useful contact with bloggers in your field, and other influencers. You may want to join relevant associations.

Experienced authors use their existing channels to generate excitement during the writing process, and may report on progress to their connections. Some bring their fans into the process and ask for input, or offer an advance chapter to read and comment on.

It's inspiring and useful to plan your book launch early, too, whether as a party of friends or at a bookstore, library, clubhouse or even via videoconferencing. Many bookstores actively support local authors. Offer to speak about your subject and sell books.

Break the Writing into Pieces

Brainstorm a simple master list of all the components you plan to cover. This will make the work far less formidable and enable you to organize it from the beginning. For example, if I want to write a book on "Entrepreneurship for Gen Z," I'd think about what this cohort wants to know and what my experience suggests they should know. Ideally, I'd supplement this with a reality check — in this case, I'd talk to a bunch of Gen Z'ers and successful entrepreneurs who are one generation older: Millennials.

Think about where your readers are now in relationship to the subject so you know how basic you must be, at least in part. Consider also demographic factors such as age, which may suggest factors like attention span. This might affect your presentation style.

For starters, my list for the entrepreneurship book would include the pros and cons of starting a business, evaluating ideas for a business, choosing and understanding your customers, researching the competition, using outside resources, and marketing, publicity, financing and legal issues. Perhaps also success stories, tips on presenting an idea, how to organize time and so on.

Create a Folder System

Whatever the time frame a publisher gives you or you give yourself, take advantage of the chance to build the material incrementally. Equip yourself with a large file and start throwing into it all the relevant material that crosses your desk or dining room table in the normal course of your days, from newspaper and magazine clippings to conference handouts, and your own notes from your notepad and paper napkins. Make up a virtual file as well for storing all the related blogs, articles, websites and other useful information.

The magic of focusing on a topic is that suddenly, everything becomes relevant. Your file will fill up quickly. Before it becomes unwieldy, scan through it and sort everything into subtopics from your master list, plus additional ones that your research-and-thinking period prompted. Make up a physical folder and a virtual one for each subtopic. Keep the virtual ones in the cloud so you can access them on any of your devices. I like Dropbox for this (www.dropbox.com).

Now, whenever an idea occurs to you or you see something worth saving, or feel inspired to write a few paragraphs, toss the material in either the actual or virtual file for that subtopic. You develop a stockpile of information and ideas you can't possibly duplicate by sitting down to write "cold." Add to your files as you go about the rest of your life. Continue doing this even after you start drafting.

Check in periodically with what's collecting. If a necessary file is looking thin, work on amplifying it with research, consulting associates or whatever it takes.

The payoff of this folder strategy: In addition to an already-organized system, you end up with a working outline of your chapters!

Assess the Practicalities

Recheck how much time you have to complete the project, or want to give it. This may suggest trimming down your ambitions to what you can reasonably accomplish in the time frame and your chosen format — whether a physical book or an ebook.

Also assess your capabilities. Will what you have in mind require help with the design and layout? Cover? Editing? If it's an ebook and you're self-publishing, what must you know about that process so you write to suit it?

Do you have a platform or can put one in the works now — a ready-made means of marketing via a successful blog or circle of influencers, for example? Figure out where you will need help and what it can cost. One essential is a professional editor, or at least, someone with a good eye for language who can save you from careless mistakes.

Don't let the answers to your check-in necessarily discourage you: Just take realities into account to determine your project scope and scale. Visualize the finished project as you'd like it to be, all over again.

Write a Proposal

Whether your book is planned for traditional or digital publication, write a proposal — even if no one else but you will ever see it. Pulling a proposal together sharpens your thinking and focus like nothing else. Is it a lot of trouble? Yes, but it sets you up for the whole project so you invest your time more productively and never find yourself floundering. Well, not as often.

REMEMBER

Researching the competition is especially important. You need to know what's out there and why your book will be better or different. Don't despair if you do find books on your subject. On one hand, publishers like knowing about existing books because it tells them there's a market for that subject. On the other hand, they'll check the sales figures for each one and want to know why yours will sell. If the competition looks strong, consider whether you can find a narrower niche for yourself. The Gen Z entrepreneur author might decide to narrow the focus to creative service business or video game start-ups.

Use facts and statistics when possible to make your case. For example, a quick Google check unearths that a Nielsen study, as quoted by *Forbes*, documented that 54 percent of the Gen Z cohort want to start their own businesses. But does this group read books? Studies also show that they do in fact search out books of interest, and the proposal can include that as well.

A typical proposal that might gain you entree to an agent's services, and eventually a publisher, generally runs 25 pages or more. If you don't plan to send it anywhere, you're on the honor system — do enough to nourish your project. It saves time later. Trust me. The components:

>> **Title and a tagline:** Long ones that suggest the book's unique content are in fashion.

>> **Nutshell description:** Like an elevator speech for your book, as pithy and zingy as you can craft it.

- **Audience description and their need for this book:** Who will buy it, with figures on potential audience size; why they'll want it and what it will do for them; how it differs from available sources.

- **Rundown of the competition:** Typically describe six to ten of the closest books and mention their pros and cons relative to your idea.

- **Chapter outline:** A paragraph or more describing each chapter's content.

- **Your credentials for writing this book:** All the relevant qualifications you can come up with; any evidence that you are capable of delivering.

- **Your platform for marketing the book:** Include useful connections, memberships, activities, followers, reputation, email list, networks, newsletter, media coverage and more.

- **Sample chapters:** If you're submitting to a publisher — preferably via an agent — you may need to also supply three written chapters including the first one so they can evaluate your ability to write and follow through.

Draft the Copy

Follow your roadmap! Start at the beginning to set the context and tone you want. The first chapter usually needs to explain to the reader (and yourself) why you're writing this book, what it will give this reader and how to use it. A short ebook might require only a page or two for this. You will probably revise this opening piece later.

Depending on how you work best, proceed chapter by chapter or start with those you feel most prepared for. You need not necessarily proceed sequentially, but it works best to finish a chapter, or at least a section, before moving elsewhere.

Review all the material you collected for the chapter. It will probably need further organizing into subtopics. Assign new folders for each. These folders may serve nicely as subject heads and subheads for the full chapter. Try that, and tweak as needed so the material flows well.

TIP

Develop each section piece by piece. When you hit parts that you don't feel ready to write, skip them until you feel like doing some research or analyzing the issue in more depth.

All of this book's advice for writing and editing comes to your aid. Some authors like to imagine they are sharing their ideas with a friend. This helps make their writing:

>> Conversational

>> Fast to read

>> Simple, clear, direct

>> Easy to understand and follow

>> Expressed in concrete rather than abstract terms

>> Relatively free of modifiers (adjectives and adverbs)

>> Logically organized

A how-to book's tone should be down to earth and "business casual," like most everyday communication channels. It must be scrupulously correct in spelling and grammar — notice if you scan online book reviews, how often people dismiss a book scornfully because it's full of errors (though there may actually be only a couple).

A self-help book can be told in first person ("I") rather than the more impersonal third person. This also works well when stories are an important component. Keep words and sentences short, maintain a pull-along rhythm by alternating short and long sentences, use active present- and past-tense verbs and cut the fat.

Liven Up Your Content

REMEMBER

Stories, anecdotes and examples liven up every subject and highlight your first-hand experience. How-to books benefit from some entertainment value, too, helping adults to learn better and stick with the experience. Case histories also work beautifully. So does your own story.

Another option is to incorporate "view from the field" mini-features by people who are expert in a particular angle of your subject, such as a financial advisor, an investor, a copywriter and a professional marketer for the Gen Z book. Ask contributors to write a short piece themselves (which you edit) or write it yourself based on talking with them. This carries a bonus: You can ask them to help promote "our book" and may gain some enthusiastic marketing partners.

Check Out Self-Publishing Options

Every aspect of self-publishing has a raft of consultants and services to support authors, reflecting the popular appeal of writing books. Check them out to see which best suits your needs.

The main retailer is Amazon's Kindle Direct Publishing (https://kdp.amazon.com), which publishes and distributes books for their Kindle device. Because this service dominates 75 to 80 percent of the ebook market and makes it easy to create a book, don't overlook it, though you may have to give them exclusive selling rights. Amazon also operates CreateSpace, which prints physical books on demand.

Apple Books (https://authors.apple.com) is Apple's ebook publisher and retailer and offers the advantage of wide international distribution. Kobo (www.kobo.com) is a Canadian company with international reach and some distribution services in the United States.

Other platforms to know about for print books and e-versions include Book Baby (www.bookbaby.com), IngramSpark (www.ingramspark.com), Lulu (www.lulu.com) and Smashwords (www.smashwords.com). They offer various production and marketing services, as well as distribution.

You can of course hire freelance help, essential for editing and cover design. Fees are all over the place depending on professional credentials. Know the difference, reflected in fees, between a developmental editor (helps shape the content), line editor (helps improve language), copy editor (does light rewriting and addresses inconsistencies) and proofreader (fixes spelling and grammar errors). Know what level of help you need and request project fees.

Many authors claim good experience with Fiverr (www.fiverr.com), a resource of hungry editors and designers offering creative services at rock-bottom prices.

Index

About the Author

Natalie Canavor is a business writer, communications consultant and workshop leader. She has also been a national magazine editor-in-chief responsible for four start-ups, and an award-winning journalist. As communications director for a major educational agency, she built and managed a 12-person creative department.

Natalie has also worked in public relations, sales promotion and nonprofit communication. Her byline has appeared frequently on feature articles for the *New York Times, Newsday* and publications for businesspeople. Her column, "Women@Work" ran for five years in a regional business newspaper, and she was also a long-term columnist on better writing techniques for the International Association of Business Communicators.

At each stage in her career, Natalie has created workshops and courses to teach adults practical techniques for writing more powerfully and strategically. Ultimately, she taught advanced writing seminars for NYU's Master's Program in Professional Communications, and now helps colleges improve their business writing programs.

In addition to this book, she is the author of *Business Writing Today* (Sage Publications); a college textbook currently in its third edition; *The Truth about the New Rules of Business Writing* (FT Press), coauthored with Claire Meirowitz; and *Workplace Genie: An Unorthodox Toolkit to Help Transform Your Work Relationships and Get the Most from Your Career* (Skyhorse Publishing), coauthored with hypnotherapist Susan Dowell.

Natalie lives in New York City and Annapolis, Maryland. She welcomes conversation about how to improve practical writing. Reach her at: ncanavor@gmail.com.

Author's Acknowledgments

I am happy to acknowledge how much better this book is because of my enthusiastic Wiley editor, Lindsay Lefevere, and my sharp-eyed (but sensitive) project editor, Katharine Dvorak. Who said editing isn't fun? Thank you, Katie.

Publisher's Acknowledgments

Acquisitions Editor: Lindsay Lefevere
Managing Editor: Michelle Hacker
Project Editor: Katharine Dvorak
Technical Editor: Cassa Niedringhaus

Proofreader: Debbye Butler
Production Editor: Siddique Shaik
Cover Image: © AntonioGuillem/Getty Images